Good Morning, Mr Mandela

Good Morning, Mr Mandela

ZELDA LA GRANGE

ALLEN LANE
an imprint of
PENGUIN BOOKS

ALLEN LANE

Published by the Penguin Group
Penguin Books Ltd, 80 Strand, London WC2R ORL, England
Penguin Group (USA) Inc., 375 Hudson Street, New York, New York 10014, USA
Penguin Group (Canada), 90 Eglinton Avenue East, Suite 700, Toronto, Ontario, Canada M4P 2Y3
(a division of Pearson Penguin Canada Inc.)
Penguin Ireland, 25 St Stephen's Green, Dublin 2, Ireland (a division of Penguin Books Ltd)
Penguin Group (Australia), 707 Collins Street, Melbourne, Victoria 3008, Australia
(a division of Pearson Australia Group Pty Ltd)
Penguin Books India Pvt Ltd, 11 Community Centre, Panchsheel Park, New Delhi – 110 017, India
Penguin Group (NZ), 67 Apollo Drive, Rosedale, Auckland 0632, New Zealand
(a division of Pearson New Zealand Ltd)
Penguin Books (South Africa) (Pty) Ltd, Block D, Rosebank Office Park,
181 Jan Smuts Avenue, Parktown North, Gauteng 2193, South Africa

Penguin Books Ltd, Registered Offices: 80 Strand, London WC2R ORL, England

www.penguin.com

First published 2014
001

Set in 12/14.75 pt Dante MT Std
Typeset by Jouve (UK), Milton Keynes
Printed and bound by CTP Printers, Cape Town

Hardback ISBN: 978-0-241-00401-2
Trade paperback ISBN: 978-0-241-01494-3

Contents

Contents

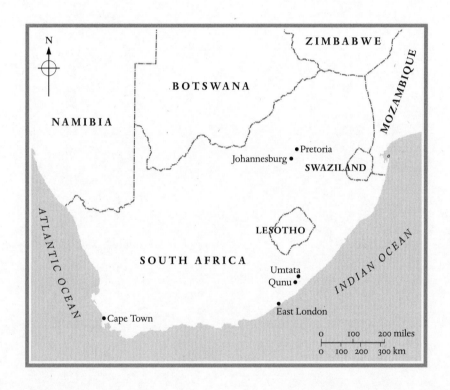

Author's Note

In June 2013 the son of the ANC stalwart Oliver Tambo, Dali Tambo, conducted an interview with President Robert Mugabe of Zimbabwe. Mugabe said: Nelson Mandela is too much of a saint. He has been too good to white people at the expense of blacks in his own country. Some agreed while others protested. To some extent I think the man had a point. It could well have been perceived that way. And yet, in a conversation with Richard Stengel, quoted in *Conversations With Myself*, Madiba himself said a long time ago, 'People will feel I see too much good in people. So it's a criticism I have to put up with and I've tried to adjust to, because whether it is so or not, it is something which I think is profitable. It's a good thing to assume, to act on the basis that . . . others are men of integrity and honour . . . because you tend to attract integrity and honour if that is how you regard those with whom you work.'

Somehow in the Mugabe interview I felt responsible for this perception that he has been too good to white people. Indeed he has been too good to me, but I want to believe that he felt proud of how he changed this insignificant life. He often said that if you change one person for the better, you have done your duty. He has not only changed my life but millions of others. He has done way beyond what is expected of a single human being and perhaps for that he deserves to be hailed as a saint after all.

In another conversation with Richard Stengel, Madiba said, 'Your duty is to work with human beings as human beings, not because you think they are angels. And, therefore, once you know that this man has got this virtue and he has got this weakness you work with them and you accommodate that weakness and you try and help him to overcome that weakness. I don't want to be frightened by the fact that a person has made certain mistakes and he has got human frailties. I can't allow myself to be influenced by that. And that is why many people criticize me.'

I try not to think 'Why me?', to understand why Nelson Mandela chose me. If I do, I think of these quotes above. In the nineteen years we spent together he learned my weaknesses, he learned my strengths, and he invested in my strengths to make me the person I am today.

I served him for almost twenty years and was his PA until he left us on 5 December 2013. In 2009 I decided to start writing this book to pay tribute to him. I mostly wanted to record my experiences in the hope that others would be changed and influenced by my story too. My book is therefore a tribute to Khulu, as I knew him.

This is not his story. This is my story, and I am content with it. But the reader may be disappointed if they expect me to wash too much dirty laundry in public. I would not disrespect the trust Nelson Mandela had invested in me. That is the biggest honour he could have bestowed on me – to trust me – and I intend to cherish that for the rest of my life. What I decided to write about and what I decided to omit as far as he is concerned is based on that trust. It is therefore not a tell-all book.

It is also not a book of great political insights or a thematic dissection of his life. It's a simple story of my experiences with him. One of the most important lessons I have learned from this great man over the years, reaffirmed by his wife Graça Machel to me later in life, is that you only have one person to account to and that is yourself. You have to go to bed at night with your own thoughts and conscience, and after writing this book I need to feel the comfort of a pillow of a clear conscience. I need to make him proud because as much as it feels that our lives were overshadowed by negativity and turmoil over the last couple of years, there is a beautiful story to be told, and I need to admit that I am part of that story and that it is my duty to tell that story. Above all, I need to know in my heart that if he had to read this book he would be happy with what I told and he would agree with the detail, and spending sixteen of the last nineteen years with him, day in, day out, I know what he would be comfortable with in the public domain and what he would not, and that is what is mine to protect.

The book is therefore a collection of anecdotes, sometimes at my own expense, of a road well travelled. No regrets and only lessons to be learned. I am an emotional billionaire, and if nothing extraordinary happens to me for the rest of my life I will still be content with my memories until the day I die. I have had a rich life. Most people will not experience what I have been witness to, and my story is therefore one of change, of slow metamorphoses of the mind and a belief system to where I am today. The reader has to decide if there is any part he or she can identify with or lessons they can learn from my story. It is not for me to decide.

It would also be incorrect to assume that I was the only one, or a special one, around Madiba. I played a particular role in his life, mostly concerned with his public life. But there are many others, household staff, office staff, security and medical personnel, who played equally important roles in his life and who he was totally dependent upon. Some of them are included in my story but I simply couldn't pay tribute to each and every one of them.

I have tried my best without exception and that is the best I have to give. I hope to contribute to Nelson Mandela's legacy in a small way by sharing the privileges and experiences I have had to anyone open to receiving them. If I change one life by touching another with my story, I have done my duty.

I remain grateful and indebted for ever . . .

Prologue: Zeldina

It was early 2000s. I was in my thirties. I stood outside our office door in Johannesburg, as usual, awaiting the arrival of Nelson Mandela to receive him, escort him into his office and brief him on events for the day. Whenever his car appeared around the corner, my face lit up, no matter how much pressure I was under. The smile that painted my face was one loaded with love and admiration, like one would have when you see your dearest grandparents. His car came to a standstill and the bodyguards emerged. We greeted and briefly exchanged pleasantries before they opened the heavily armed car door for Madiba to step out of the car. Madiba is Nelson Mandela's clan name in South Africa. It is also the term with which people endearingly refer to him. Some call him *Tata*, which means 'Father', but most people refer to him and address him as Madiba. I called him Khulu, an abbreviated version of *Tata um'khulu* which means 'Grandfather'.

While getting out of the car, our eyes met. I exclaimed, 'Good morning Khulu.' He called me Zeldina. He was handed his walking stick to support himself to get out of the car. The stick was made from ivory, a gift from his good friend Douw Steyn. He didn't care much for material things but his walking stick was one of the few items he valued and protected with his life.

'Good morning Zeldina,' he said as he emerged from the car. His face lit up with his usual smile although I detected some reserve. Once the bodyguards had him steady on his feet, they handed him to me. He would support himself on his walking stick and hold onto my arm with his left hand.

'How are you this morning Khulu?' I asked.

'I'm fine Zeldina,' he said but he didn't continue as he usually did, asking after my well-being. That was another sign that something bothered him. As we walked into his office I thought of giving him a few moments to gather his thoughts before I started overloading him with information about the day. Once his office door was closed he opened up:

'You know Zeldina, I had a dream last night.'

I responded with a 'Yes?'

'I dreamt that you left me, that you deserted me . . .' he said.

I was dumbstruck. Me? Zelda la Grange? Abandoning Nelson Mandela? How could he ever conceive me doing something like that? At the time I had been in his service for almost ten years. What would cause him to feel that I would abandon him? To the contrary, because of my early childhood I was the one who feared abandonment. I had to set his mind at ease. I put my left hand on his left hand which was holding onto my right arm and said, 'Khulu, I would never ever do something like that and you should please never think about that ever again. I can give you my assurance that I will never abandon you.' And then added on a lighter note, 'In any event I think you are going to abandon me or chase me away before I can abandon you.'

He looked at me, laughed half heartedly, lifted his eyebrows and then responded: 'I will never do that.'

That was the warmth of our relationship. We needed affirmation from each other. We looked after each other. I have grown to love this man who was once my people's enemy. He resembled fear in our eyes. Growing up in apartheid South Africa as a white Afrikaner, we had spent our lives oppressing the same people that Nelson Mandela represented. He was the voice of the oppressed and the liberation struggle. Less than fifteen years after his release from prison, here I was trying to explain and defend my commitment to the man we once despised.

Apartheid was the system introduced by the white government in South Africa in the 1940s. It advocated for white supremacy and black oppression and was a clear set of legislation providing for the separation and segregation of white and black in South Africa. The laws of apartheid were upheld in churches and schools, on beaches and in restaurants, and any areas where the white minority could feel intimidated by the presence of black people.

Yet I walked next to Nelson Mandela for most of my adult professional life – each of us holding onto the other. I was a young Afrikaner girl whose views and mindset were changed by the greatest statesman of our time. Yet to me, he was more than my moral conscience. I had learned to care for him, because he cared for me. He shaped and changed my thinking because for him to employ a white Afrikaans-speaking young woman as his Personal Assistant was not only unprecedented, it was unheard of.

PART ONE

'If it isn't good, let it die'

1970–1994

I

Childhood

On 29 October 1970 in Boksburg to the east of Johannesburg, South Africa, I was born and not left to die but to make it good, like most babies that are brought into this world.

On the same day, Nelson Mandela was already beginning his ninth year in prison. In prison since 1962, and then convicted for treason after the Rivonia Trial in 1964, he was sentenced to life imprisonment. He and other political prisoners were incarcerated on Robben Island, a desolate island off the coast of Cape Town, for opposing apartheid.

At the time my father worked at a construction company and my mother was a teacher. They were very poor. My only sibling, my brother Anton, was three years old when I was born. Because our parents were white, we were born to legal privilege. That was the way it was in South Africa in 1970. Even though my parents' families shared the same holiday destination every December, my parents only met in Boksburg once my mother was studying to become a teacher and my father was working in the postal service.

My grandfather's family originated from French Huguenots who fled the south of France during the 1680s to escape the persecution of Protestants by the Catholic authorities. The La Grange family originated from a small town called Cabrières in the region of Avignon; a place I discovered and visited twice in the decades after my birth as a result of working for Nelson Mandela.

My father was one of two siblings. Their parents lived in Mosselbay, a coastal town along the picturesque Garden Route in the Cape Province. My grandmother's sister was the first qualified female pharmacist in South Africa and up to this day the Scholtz family own and run a reputable pharmacy in the town of Willow-more in the Eastern Cape. She was therefore quite an impressive woman and someone we automatically looked up to as a result of her unique achievement.

I was also very fond of my dad's father. His name was Anthony Michael but we just called him 'Oupa Mike' (Grandpa Mike). He used to visit us a few times a year and then stay with us for a few weeks. He smoked a pipe and the smell of smoke irritated us. He would sit on one particular chair and constantly wipe his hand on the arm rest. His skin was old and cracked and the tobacco from stuffing his pipe stuck in those cracks. When he left our home the armrest was black, much to my mother's irritation, but nobody ever said he couldn't smoke in the house.

My mother was the eldest of three siblings from the Strydom family. The only famous family with that surname was that of J. G. Strijdom (also sometimes spelt Strydom), the sixth Prime Minister of South Africa who served between 1954 and 1958. He was succeeded by the 'Father of Apartheid', H. F. Verwoerd. When I learned as a child about a Strijdom being Prime Minister, I convinced myself that we were somehow related even though no real connection exists.

My mother's father died in a motorcycle accident when my mother was only twelve years of age. I often asked my mother whether she recalled the night they received the news about her father's death. She has mostly avoided talking about it, but has said that she recalled been woken up by someone knocking on their front door and then hearing my grandmother crying hysterically.

My grandmother had few options about the upbringing of her children. She had a clerical job at the South African Railways and it was financially impossible for her to raise three small children by herself.

She decided to send my mother, being the eldest, to an orphan-age. The children's home was in Cape Town, which is why my mother still detests the city. For her, it stinks of abandonment.

Ma only saw her siblings and my grandmother once a year during the December holidays. Both the La Grange and Strydom families camped in the same area close to Mosselbay, called Hartenbos, during the December holidays, but they never knew about the other's existence.

My mother's childhood memories are limited to suffering, neglect, sadness. The world was suffering the consequences of the Second World War, slowly recovering from the economic recession, and my mother, even as an Afrikaans child in the 1940s in South Africa, felt those consequences through poverty. I greatly admire her for not holding a grudge against my grandmother, whatever the circumstances.

Grandma Tilly, my mother's mother, was part of our everyday life, even though she had given up my mother as a child. She lived close to us and I would often visit her on my way from primary school, as she conveniently lived halfway between our house and the school. Before she moved closer to us, Grandma Tilly lived opposite the Union Buildings. Sitting on the hill overlooking the city of Pretoria, the administrative capital of South Africa, the Union Buildings were built by Herbert Baker and were the seat of the apartheid government. Imposing, monumental and beautiful – for my family, it was like living across from the White House.

On Sundays the La Granges and the Strydoms, my uncle's family, would all visit my gran in her apartment for lunch and then go for a walk on the manicured lawns of the Union Buildings. The Union Buildings represented ultimate authority and we walked up the steps with great respect. My cousins, brother and I would play on the grounds, rolling down the sloping lawn, laughing all the time. We were happy children growing up in apartheid South Africa.

Ours was a typical privileged white family, benefiting from apartheid through good education, access to basic services and a sense of entitlement to the land and its resources. Apartheid was our regime's political solution to enforce segregation and the separation of races, classes and cultures.

Instituted by the Afrikaner leaders in the late 1950s, the then Prime Minister, Hendrik Verwoerd, called it 'policy'. 'Our policy is one of good neighbourliness', implying that the Afrikaner cared for all racial groups in South Africa. But the reality was that apartheid was a way of ensuring that Afrikaners benefited from the economy, opportunities and wealth of the country's natural resources, at the expense of others.

By the mid 1970s the apartheid government had created a racist state based on decisions taken in the Union Buildings. Black and white people were separated, not allowed to marry, befriend, have sex together or to live in the same cities. These were the so-called Group Areas Act provisions in South Africa, an attempt to prevent people from freely moving around and living lives within the same boundaries. Black people couldn't ride in the same buses or swim in the same sea as whites. Due to its apartheid policies, South Africa was suspended from participating in the business of the United Nations in 1974, and followed by a resolution passed in 1977 a mandatory arms embargo was imposed against us. However, the United States, Britain and France opposed the expulsion of South Africa from the UN despite several resolutions calling for it.

Even though my country was an international pariah, we kept on playing and laughing at the seat of government. This was because my people were protected. Protected from men like Nelson Mandela. It was people like him – black and determined to overthrow the government, challenging white superiority – who we feared.

Neither of my parents were politicians or worked for the government. But we supported the regime. We were, I suppose, racists. We epitomized the typical Afrikaner middle-class family at the time: law-abiding citizens, cheerleaders for whatever the church and government dictated. Our respect for authority and the ties to the Dutch Reformed Church superseded common sense. Like any other Afrikaans family, we attended church services on Sunday morning without fail and participated in all related activities to exhibit our model citizenry.

So apartheid was in our home. We lived by segregation. It was all acceptable and unquestionable, not only because the Nationalist Party government in power dictated it but also because our church endorsed it.

Black people were anyone who wasn't white. Coloured and Indian people were black in our eyes too. 'Coloured people', now referred to as 'brown' people, originated from different groups, just like the Afrikaners, but some of their forefathers were Qash-skinned. Therefore they were regarded as 'black' in South Africa.

The white Afrikaner has a mixed genealogy that includes Dutch, French, German and British blood. Although unthinkable at the time, it has emerged in modern history and studies that almost all white Afrikaner people have DNA that can be traced to black and brown ancestry in South Africa – facts not all white Afrikaners easily accept.

At the time of apartheid you didn't even contemplate anything but simply did it. I knew that all black people were required to carry a pass book and they had to show their pass books randomly to police that stopped them. I didn't know that they were only allowed to move in areas that their passes allowed them to move in, and if they didn't have a pass for a specific area they would be arrested for transgression of the pass act and thrown into jail, before being deported to their own area. If you had a pass for Johannesburg, you couldn't move in Pretoria – two cities barely thirty miles apart. It was the government's way of controlling black people's movements.

According to our church, we were right. We did the 'right' thing. And yes it was right, as in direction to the right. The utmost conservatism.

Like most white families we had a black live-in domestic worker. Her name was Jogabeth. Reminiscing about those days one cannot help but come to the realization that most white children of my age were brought up by black people. They were not only domestic workers but surrogate mothers. As a child Jogabeth was part of our family to a certain extent, and within limits – apartheid limits. She stayed in a back room. She had a toilet but no bath or shower. She had a separate cup and cutlery and was not allowed to use 'ours'. I cannot recall that my parents ever told her she was not allowed to use anything of ours but she knew and we knew. It was unspoken. Yet, Jogabeth was my lifeline.

Touching a black person was taboo. Apart from the fact that white people were considered superior to black people, we were brought up to believe that they were not as clean as we were, they apparently smelled different and the texture of their hair was different to ours. You would never dream of touching a black person's hair or face. It was just unthinkable. Yet Jogabeth carried me on her back when I was a toddler. Although I never would have touched her hair, her hands, arms and her bosom comforted me whenever I needed it. Because she brought us children up, in our eyes she wasn't as black as other blacks. She posed no threat to us and she served us and therefore she was more acceptable to us than other black people.

I remember on many occasions being bullied by my brother and how Jogabeth had to comfort me after losing the battle. She was my safe house and I knew that, as long as I was in her care, I was protected from my big brother's bullying. And then during such times, I found comfort in her arms, close to her chest.

When I was twelve years old and my father was employed by the South African Breweries, eventually working his way up to become logistics manager, political unrest against apartheid played a role in my life for the first time. The head offices of the SAB were situated in the Poyntons Building in Church Street, Pretoria. On Friday, 20 May 1983 my dad was scheduled to fly to Cape Town to attend to business there. Just before 4 p.m. a bomb blast shook the entire city of Pretoria in its core. The story broke on the news immediately and it was reported that the car bomb exploded right in front of the Poyntons Building.

When news was received my mother called my dad's office, but there was no response. She called the airport to check whether he was on the flight at around 6 p.m. but the airport authorities refused to release information on passengers, as they always do. We couldn't find anyone that could confirm whether my dad was still in the building at the time of the explosion, whether he had safely left by the time of the explosion or whether he possibly walked past or drove out of the parking garage at the time of the explosion. He often attended business luncheons at restaurants in the surrounding areas of his head office and we feared for the worst. It was only at about 9 p.m. that night, when he arrived at his hotel in Cape Town, that he called to inform us that he was safe. It was the longest five hours of my life. We were relieved that he was unharmed. I didn't ask why resistance to apartheid would be so strong, or take such violent forms. The violence only served to strengthen my belief in apartheid, the inherent difference between black and white.

Umkhonto we Sizwe (MK), the opposition African National Congress's military wing, accepted responsibility for the bomb in which 19 people were killed – 8 black people and 11 white people – and more than 217 were injured. The Church Street bomb exploded at the height of rush hour. The two men involved in planning and executing the bombing were also killed, as the bomb was detonated by accident too soon.

Umkhonto we Sizwe, 'Spear of the Nation', was established in 1961 after Nelson Mandela and other founding members of MK decided that violence in South Africa was becoming the only way to respond to the violence exercised by the apartheid government. Since the government resorted to violent means in fighting the ANC and keeping black people oppressed under apartheid laws, MK was the ANC's response to such violence. In Nelson Mandela's speech during the closing moments of the Rivonia Trial in 1964, when he was charged with acts of terrorism and after which he and others were sentenced to life imprisonment, he noted about MK: 'It would be unrealistic and wrong for African leaders to continue preaching peace and non-violence at a time when the government met our peaceful demands with force.'

Having gone to Ethiopia and Morocco in 1962 to receive military training and to secure support for MK, Mr Mandela was prepared to resort to violence. However, I am not sure whether he knew while he was imprisoned what ANC cadres were doing outside and whether those imprisoned were consulted about such acts of violence. In 1983 Oliver Tambo was President of the ANC; Nelson

Mandela was already sixty-five years of age, spending his twentieth year imprisoned, and communication was difficult with prisoners. I subsequently asked him whether he was aware of the Church Street bombing and he said that they had been briefed after the incident.

The ANC knew it needed to force the hand of the racist regime. To do that they would have to turn to violence. The government was not prepared to abolish apartheid or improve the living conditions of black people and they would rather fight the black force with violence. The ANC's response was violence. They did that by targeting strategic installations, crucial to the state. The Poytons Building was strategic because the South African Air Force Headquarters was situated in the same building.

I was generally oblivious to what was happening in the country, the poverty of blacks and the violence, but I knew that we lived in separate cocoons and that we were fighting one another in a bitter battle because we were not able to co-exist. It was pressed upon us instinctively, because of the way we lived, that when approached by a black person, you turned and walked the other way. You didn't make conversation and you feared them. They were not our friends. I was quite happy with my life as it was and knew that we were locking doors and windows from an early age out of fear that black people might attack us at night. It never crossed my mind that we could be harmed by white people too. It was always 'black' people. I didn't ask why they might attack us, or who they were, or what their lives were like. I only knew that they were dangerous.

On Sundays we solemnly prayed in church for the men defending our borders. It was the right thing to do because everybody else did it. Well, all the other whites in my community. I didn't know which border but I knew they were fighting black people. My knowledge was limited to whites protecting the border from infiltration by more black people. How strange that then one didn't ask the question, which black people? Were we protecting our borders from infiltration by more black people or were we protecting our borders from other military forces in the region infiltrating South Africa to support the ANC? You were told just this: we are fighting black communist people. I was brought up to believe that all black people were communists and atheists. Yet on Sundays black people gathered in small groups in open spaces, holding church services. I disregarded seeing that and cannot remember that the contradiction to what I was brought up to believe ever bothered me. As a child it is easy to follow when you grow up in an environment that is safe. Perhaps if I had been oppressed, didn't have access to a decent school, a proper house, electricity and water, I would have asked different questions, and my brain would have developed into being more inquisitive about injustice at an early age. In any case it didn't.

Today I also realize that the community you are brought up in chooses to live in a particular way. The people around you, grown-up adult people, decide what is socially acceptable and what is not. You live that life not realizing that there is a life beyond: issues, policies, world events and tendencies that influence your world. When you live in comfort you don't ask questions, and there was no need for me to question what was happening beyond the walls of our house. No person is born a racist. You become a racist by influences around you. And I had become a racist by the time I was thirteen years old. By that calculation I should never have become Nelson Mandela's longest-serving assistant. But I did.

2

Change

Perhaps something in my childhood suited me to Nelson Mandela.

When I was growing up, my mother often had severe spells of depression where she would simply cry for days or stay in bed and be depressed. We were never neglected but I do remember her sadness. One felt disempowered to do anything about it, not understanding what it was.

My mother is to this day one of the most decent, softly spoken, ladylike people I know. She has never sworn or used foul language in my presence. She has never spoken in a degrading manner to or about anyone, not even people that made her angry or people that harmed her in any way. She has calmness about her and reserves her extreme emotions for her inner self. I also never recall her being overly happy or excited about anything and she is moderate by nature. Her time spent in the orphanage while she was growing up obviously taught her to hide her emotions. It altered her. I recognized that burying of one's self in my years with Nelson Mandela later in life. He too had to suppress his emotions to survive prison.

My dad often got frustrated with Mom's depression and they would end up arguing about it and fighting because my mom would be so passive. My dad is a social person, the more the merrier, while my mother likes her own space and not socializing too much. I inherited that anti-social tendency from my mother. None of us realized just how troubled my mom really was.

One Friday afternoon, after playing at a friend's house, I returned home to an empty house. When I opened the kitchen door I heard mom's car in the garage. I didn't open the door to the garage but merely slipped into the house, lounging around. After a while,

I heard that the car was still in the garage, idling, but I didn't hear her opening the garage door to leave. I decided to go and look what was happening. When I opened the door between the house and the garage I vividly remember my mother resting her head against the window of the car, the car idling; she seemed asleep. I rushed to the car door and tried to open it. It was locked. I then noticed a pipe from the window and traced it to the car's exhaust. Only then did reality hit home. She was trying to commit suicide. I screamed and cried all at once and tried to force the door open.

I was twelve years of age and had little strength to make an impact. I slammed against the window but she didn't react and the rest of the events I cannot remember. I know that I called my grandmother and my gran arrived quickly because she lived around the corner. I don't know how my mom got out of the car to her bedroom, I don't know at what time Anton, my brother, came home or when the doctor arrived or my mom's best friend came. I don't remember if and who called my dad, who was travelling on business again. I don't remember where he was and I don't remember how they got hold of him – cellphones were not yet invented at the time. I do remember that this was the last day I smelled anything in my life. And that smell was gas. Doctors say that from the shock my body's ability to smell was shut off, a psychosomatic reaction to trauma.

My mom was admitted to a clinic for people suffering from depression, and stabilized. I was left constantly wondering why she would decide to leave me, just as she had been by her mom; wasn't I good enough? Did she love me enough to live? Was it me and my brother's endless fighting as siblings that drove her to do that? I was never angry at my mother, perhaps rather sad, and I felt abandoned.

Those events in the gas-filled garage in 1982 determined my relationships for ever. I am constantly terrified I will be abandoned. Left alone. So I overcompensate. I sacrifice myself to please people, hoping and trying to avoid a situation in which I find myself abandoned. And with the fear of abandonment comes the constant need for affirmation. It is not an ideal recipe for relationships of a romantic kind but it is ideal when you dedicate your life to your job and the world's most iconic statesman. In a strange twist, Nelson Mandela needed someone to devote themselves to him. To help him. He needed someone who was always there. Available to support him and to be depended upon. We complemented each other in a slightly co-dependent way. My need to please fitted with his need for absolute loyalty.

But this was still to come. In 1988 I turned eighteen and completed school. The news was dominated by reports of killings of either policemen or 'cadres', as liberation fighters were referred to. Not a month passed without a bomb blast somewhere in the country. It became such a common occurrence that one later doesn't pay attention to numbers. There was death everywhere. South Africa was on the brink of a civil war. Violence erupted more often than not, and for the middle-class white Afrikaans people perhaps going to war against black people seemed like the only solution.

For me, though, life continued as before. My father had asked me: 'What do you want to study?' I had no idea, but since I was always engaged in cultural activities at school I opted to study acting. He gave me a definite 'No' and said that unless you are Sandra Prinsloo – one of South Africa's most successful and admired actresses – you had no chance at succeeding in the performing arts. It was my life's dream to become an actress. From childhood I remembered role-playing to be a secretary whenever I accompanied my dad to his office at weekends. My father convinced me, like most Afrikaner parents would have done at the time, to opt for a career in which job security took priority over following your passion, and I decided to enrol for a three-year National Diploma as Executive Secretary at the Technikon (now the Tshwane University of Technology) in Pretoria.

In September 1989, almost a year after my eighteenth birthday – the age at which South African citizens become legitimate voters – a general election was held. It excluded black people. No coloured, Indian or black people were allowed to vote under the apartheid laws. In South Africa's last national race-based elections the National Party lost ground and only managed to secure 48 per cent of the vote. The National Party had ruled since 1948. Its policies were based on apartheid, segregation and the promotion of the Afrikaner. People who supported them were known as Nats. Being a stern conservative, even more conservative than the Nats, I voted for the Conservative Party in 1989.

The Nats were beginning to talk about reform: allowing black people to vote, bringing an end to the Group Areas Act and discrimination against people based on the colour of their skin. The Conservative Party opposed any change to apartheid laws and that year they became the official opposition, securing 31 per cent of the white vote. Though the total population at the time was estimated to be in the region of 30 million (there are no official figures available because black people were not counted as citizens), only about 3.1 million voters (all white) were registered, of which just over 1 million voted for the National Party's reform policies.

Unbeknown to anyone, Nelson Mandela had had his first meeting with the then President, P. W. Botha, on 4 July 1989. Mr Botha was known to oppose black majority rule, yet his willingness to meet with Mr Mandela set the tone of concessions to be made. At this point Nelson Mandela was spending his twenty-sixth year in prison. He had become the figurehead of the oppressed in South Africa even though very few people really knew him apart from his cadres. He was becoming the symbol of freedom for the masses in South Africa, even though the pictures that appeared of him were from the 1960s or were sketches of what people imagined he looked like at the time. No one was allowed access to the prison to ever take photographs of the ageing Nelson Mandela.

P. W. Botha abruptly resigned as President in August 1989, a month before the elections, after he felt that the then Minister of Education, F. W. de Klerk, had not consulted with him after a meeting he had with President Kenneth Kaunda from Zambia. Mr Botha felt undermined and resigned; Mr de Klerk was appointed Acting President for the month prior to the elections.

At this time, Nelson Mandela had been moved to Victor Verster Prison in the Paarl, close to Cape Town. He regularly met with President de Klerk and Mr de Klerk announced the release of the first long-serving political prisoners barely a month after becoming President. This was a landmark in South Africa's history: change became inevitable. I knew nothing about the prisoners being released and I can hardly remember that I paid attention to the announcement. These prisoners included Walter Sisulu, Andrew Mlangeni, Raymond Mhlaba and Ahmed Kathrada among others, some of Nelson Mandela's closest friends and colleagues. Who could have imagined that I would later adore some of these prisoners.

On 2 February 1990 President de Klerk announced the unconditional release of Nelson Mandela after being imprisoned for twenty-seven years. February in the north of Pretoria where my family lived is one of the hottest months in our summer. I was swimming in our pool when my father came outside and the fact that someone was watching me distracted my attention. I could see that he had something on his mind. 'Yes Dad . . . ?' I said. He just looked at me and after a few moments of silence he replied, 'Now we are in trouble. The terrorist has been released.' My response was: 'Who's that?' and he replied: 'Nelson Mandela.' I had no idea who it was or what this meant to us. I could sense that he was worried but I continued swimming and left him to ponder about his announcement.

It was only much later after I had joined the Presidency that Mr Mandela told me that Mr de Klerk visited him a few days before the announcement of his release. He unceremoniously told Mr Mandela that he was free to go. Mr Mandela indicated that he couldn't leave immediately and that he needed to afford his people time to allow them to prepare for his release. He asked for an extra few days to allow people on the outside to prepare. If someone told me 'You are free to leave' after twenty-seven years I would ignore courtesy and run out, yet Mr Mandela wanted to stay to allow his people time to prepare. I often asked him whether he wasn't scared that the government could change its mind in those extra days. He looked at me, surprised that I would mistrust people in that way, laughed and then said 'No.'

It was of course only much later that I could comprehend what actually happened in South Africa at that time. Little did I know that Nelson Mandela was already aged seventy-one when he was released. Little did I know that he lost his mother and his son during his incarceration and that he was not allowed to attend their respective funerals at the time. The fact that he was a human being, a person with emotions, didn't cross my mind. All I knew was that we were in trouble, because my dad said so.

By 1992 the white National government called a referendum to decide on the future of apartheid. But, of course, whites only were allowed to vote in the referendum. The apartheid system that had been implemented in 1948 was withering. The white population was asked to express themselves in support or against the reform policies started by President de Klerk. Very few people shared the notion that reform would go further than they anticipated, but it was clear that apartheid was losing its few remaining supporters in the international community.

A total of 2.8 million whites voted in the referendum; 1.9 million were in favour of reform and an election in which non-white South Africans could vote; 875,000 of my compatriots voted against the abolishment of apartheid. I voted 'NO' too. And I was proud of it. This was my contribution, I thought, to ensuring that the country remained governable. There was always this white Afrikaans fear that if the country was run by blacks it would become ungovernable and that they would run the whites into the ocean, take revenge for what whites denied them of for centuries.

Really it was all over by 1990, when Mr Mandela was released. It marked the end of apartheid and the beginning of a country where 'one man one vote' would apply, irrespective of the colour of your skin. But it all kind of passed me by as I was enjoying the life of being a student – the partying and late night studying to catch up on work that fell behind as a result of such partying. I had no involvement or even thought about politics or where South Africa was heading, even though I knew that apartheid had ended and that black people were free to move as they please. At social gatherings we sometimes referred briefly to what was unfolding in South Africa but never with informed detail and all playing on each other's white Afrikaner fears that, indeed, 'we were in trouble'. That was the totality of my understanding of the political situation and I wasn't bothered much.

I do recall driving to my uncle's farm in Ellisras in the north over Easter in April 1993 when we heard the news on the radio that Communist Party leader and chief of staff of the military wing of the ANC, the charismatic Chris Hani, had been killed. For whites in South Africa the communists held the real threat to our safety, security and financial future. Somehow Nelson Mandela was also considered a communist. Because South Africa, or our white world, was dominated by religion and what the church dictated, it was unthinkable that the Communist Party would ever occupy a legitimate space in South Africa. We were a capitalist state in which the whites owned and controlled all the resources.

When I asked my parents later about Chris Hani, I was told that it was a big mistake by whoever initiated his killing because even though Hani was a communist, surely he was a better deal for the white people than the so-called terrorist Mandela. I was confused by my parents' pronouncements because to me anything communist posed a serious threat, and even though Nelson Mandela had not been officially named a member of the Communist Party, surely Chris Hani was more dangerous, being the leader of that party? According to my parents, Chris Hani had exhibited some tolerance towards white people, probably because he hadn't been imprisoned on Robben Island like Nelson Mandela, and therefore they obviously assumed that he didn't have the hatred Mr Mandela supposedly had.

Little did we know, or care, that Mr Mandela had no bitterness.

He had secretly been talking about negotiations with the government from prison, determined to bring about a peaceful transition.
As Ahmed Kathrada, one of Madiba's closest friends and a fellow
prisoner, said, 'Forgiveness is a choice.' One inherently always
expects the worst and we expected Nelson Mandela to live up to our
expectations.

It was during these riveting and dangerous political times that I
fell in love and got engaged. My aspirations were limited to getting
married and having children, like most young Afrikaans women my
age. I was only twenty-two years of age but it didn't matter. I had
also graduated and I started my first job at the Department of State
Expenditure in 1992 as a secretary. A few months into the job I
became bored and asked for a more challenging position. I was
transferred to the Human Resources division within the same
department as an administrative clerk, working in mid-town
Pretoria.

Apartheid had ended but life continued unchanged. We didn't
feel the end of apartheid in our everyday lives. We still 'lived' apartheid even though politically changes started to emerge prior to the
1994 elections. Violence and unrest continued in far off communities, and we were continuously confronted with the pictures of
dead people in rural areas. The violence was no longer only black
against white but now also due to tensions between the ANC and
Inkatha Freedom Party. The IFP was the ANC's biggest rival at the
time.

Then my engagement ended. I was distraught and lost. What I
usually do when relationships fail is that I throw myself into my
work, completely and utterly, as a way of dealing with pain.

On 10 May 1994 South Africa's first democratically elected black
President was inaugurated. I was twenty-three years of age and
putting in every extra hour of overtime to build my career in the
Human Resources department of the Department of State Expenditure. Even though the day of his swearing in was a public holiday, I
was on my way to work to put in extra time. There was hardly any
traffic and people avoided the streets out of fear for the outbreak of

violence following the inauguration of the ANC government, which was seen as the enemy to all white people, even those whites who voted in favour of reform and for apartheid to end. An ANC government in power meant that the majority of our leadership would change to black people, and that seriously challenged white supremacy. It was pay-back time and we expected black people to settle scores with us whites for centuries of oppression. Military vehicles were visible everywhere in the suburbs and police cars ready to respond on instructions. Still, this didn't affect my life and I found myself safe in the comfort of my office during the inauguration. As long as the police, still from the previous regime, were visible in the streets, surely we were safe. I do recall driving home seeing black people along the street and people smiling, looking happy, cheering and dancing. My thoughts were simple: Yes, you can now do as you please but please don't kill us tonight because we are white.

Prior to the elections some white people collected tinned food and perishables out of fear of civil war, violence and disruption. We expected black people to take over the country and now deprive us of basic services, that they would raid shops and create absolute chaos, sabotaging water and power supply to white suburbs. People stocked up and gathered bottled water, candles, tinned food and whatever would last them and be needed in an emergency. We expected revenge.

But that night nothing happened and we all woke up the next morning, went back to work and to our normal way of life, untouched by the previous day's events and whoever was leading this country. Life continued in a strangely unaffected way. We still had our house, we were still alive and water still came from the tap. Nothing was there to indicate that soon the very foundations of my life, my ignorance, my beliefs, my values were to be shaken up and tested. Little did I know that I would emerge from that paranoid, white cocoon of fear and denial and that the man who would lead me out of that – gently holding my hand – would be Nelson Mandela.

PART TWO

Start of a New Dawn

1994–1999

3

Meeting Mr Mandela

Soon after the elections in 1994 the incoming government needed to recruit new people. My department was tasked to help with the huge project of making the former apartheid government more 'representative', in other words we had to hire more black people. It was the beginning of transformation. South Africa was to be governed for all. It would represent all its people.

Thousands and thousands of people applied. It took us weeks to come up with short-lists for posts advertised. It was clear that there was a great shortage of skilled people but that indeed people in South Africa were desperate for work. A lot of applications couldn't be processed as a result of illiteracy, applicants having been denied a decent education during apartheid. I worked very hard to process these applications. There was no incentive to do so but my nature is such that if given a task I have to complete it in the shortest possible time. I am one of those people who like to clear things off their mental notes and I often work unnecessarily at a pace that is not required. I was looking for a new job, I wanted a new start, away from my broken engagement, but in the meantime I focused all my attention on processing applications.

Then a colleague told me about a typist's job being advertised in an administrative department attached to the newly established President's office. The position would mean being based six months of the year in Pretoria and six months in Cape Town. Whenever Parliament was in session, politicians, their families and support staff lived and worked from Cape Town as our Parliament is housed in Cape Town. Whenever Parliament went in recess, politicians and their families and staff would move back to Pretoria, the administrative capital. It is something I had always dreamt of doing and the fact that the job was on a lower rank than the one I currently occupied didn't matter. What I also found attractive was that the position was advertised for the Minister without Portfolio and I thought that surely someone without a portfolio didn't have a lot of work and it therefore couldn't be too hard to work for him. Later of course I learned that 'without portfolio' simply meant that the minister could be tasked with ad hoc issues and therefore had no fixed portfolio or agenda to attend to.

I soon started discussions within my own department to inform my seniors that I would apply for the job, providing that I could be transferred on the same salary scale if I was successful in the application. They agreed.

The job interview was at the Union Buildings. Not only was I no longer rolling around on the lawn, but a black man was now the most powerful man in South Africa. And he was making sure people like me, conservative Afrikaans white folk, were included in this new government. People were friendly and relaxed and I noticed that there were still a lot of white faces around despite the new ANC government being in power.

During the interview, a black lady entered. She appeared cheerful and flamboyant. Dressed in a colourful satin outfit it was a picture I was not used to – that of a black lady dressed in such style and clearly in something that was more expensive than my mother's most prized outfit. We were rudely interrupted by her during the interview but she exclaimed to my interviewers: 'I need a typist and I don't care if she's black or white but I need her right now.' I smiled and thought: I'm your person. I had no idea what her position was. She briefly exchanged a few words with my two interviewers and then left. My interviewers telephoned me hours after the interview to ask whether I would be interested in a typist position in the actual President's office itself, and it was explained that it would involve working in his personal office. I only had Cape Town in mind, and since they assured me that the job would be on the same terms as the advertised post, I said I was interested.

They told me that the lady that had entered the interview before was the President's private secretary. My understanding was that I was going to work for her, Mary Mxadana, and she looked fairly pleasant. While still working at the Department of State Expenditure I had been tasked to train two junior black officials who had joined our department after the transformation process kicked in. They appeared friendly and I ended up working well with them. Slowly but surely I was starting to see black people a little differently. I was no longer inherently scared of all black people. I was starting to converse with them in normal language, without thinking that they could only understand broken Afrikaans or English. Mary was friendly and she made me feel at ease even though I had my doubts.

I realized that I was going to work in an office that was closer to the political centre of the beliefs I still opposed but I thought it was just a job and I wouldn't have much to do with real politics. I was willing to compromise and by then toyed with the idea that I actually liked the President of the Inkatha Freedom Party, Dr Mangosuthu Buthelezi, the opposition to the ANC. I liked him from seeing him on TV during the election campaign and I thought that since I had changed my mind about him, Nelson Mandela couldn't be that bad either. I was willing to give it a try but was very realistic about the fact that if I didn't like working there, nothing would stop me from leaving.

I can't remember feeling anything except relief when I was called and offered the position. Two weeks after the interview I assumed duty in the President's office as senior ministerial typist.

On 12 October 1994 I walked into the Union Buildings for the first time as an employee of President Mandela's personal office. I had seen pictures of him but knew nothing about him apart from the fact that he spent a long time in prison on Robben Island and that my family regarded him a terrorist. I didn't expect to have any interactions with him or ever see him.

I was well on time and received in reception by another staffer who took me through several glass doors and through security checks to reach what was known as the President's suite. It constituted a few offices along a corridor. She showed me a desk and computer in what looked like a 'pool' office, even though the only other desk was hers. She was an administrator answering the President's private office switchboard and assisting with ad hoc administration.

She explained that the President's personal office consisted of only Mary, herself and Elize Wessels. Elize was from the de Klerk government and used to work for the former First Lady, Marike de Klerk.

I sensed there was a tense atmosphere between the 'old' or white staff and the 'new' or black staff and that people were still marking territory and claiming positions in the new government. It was also clear that the 'old' guard were there to slowly ease the new leadership into power, guiding and teaching them, willing or unwillingly.

It was only much later that Mary arrived at the office. She had a presence about her that could be felt even without noticing her at first. She carried authority and dressed colourfully, which added to her vibrant personality. She entered the office like a whirlwind and hugged me to welcome me to the office. She was extremely friendly and made me feel at ease. Not having worked for a black person before, I was reluctant to let my defences go too soon. There was a superficial trust between black and white people. We still didn't know what to expect of one another. I was prepared to work for her but I held on to my political beliefs, thinking that my practical and financial situation had forced me to be in this office.

It is not necessarily a trait of all Afrikaners but generally speaking we have respect for people of authority or elderly people; whether we agree with their policies or not we were always courteous. If your principles did not allow you to respect a person you would simply ignore that person. I found I respected Mary. She told me about the liberation struggle. I started to be intrigued by the history of my own country. It felt like I had lived on another planet and I was completely unaware of anything she was telling me. Perhaps it was precisely that innocence and ignorance that made her feel at ease with me. She was very warm and friendly towards me and we shared a passion for music. She told me about her choir and brought me a CD to listen to. Her husband was the conductor of the choir and she was one of the founding members. They sang like angels.

Over the next two weeks I was orientated more about the operations around the President. He was nowhere to be seen or heard and I started assuming that I would possibly see him at a distance 'one day', but I did meet a number of people, from Parks Mankahlana, whom I was told spoke on the President's behalf, to Tony Trew, whom I was told helped write all the President's speeches, to the head of our office, referred to as the Director General of the Presidency, Professor Jakes Gerwel. It took me some time to figure out who did what and to remember names.

My main task was to type for Mary and to update the President's programme regularly. She soon taught me how to distribute the programme to the President's security and I was told to ensure that I sent it to both the white and the black commanders of his security team simultaneously. The South African Police Service was going through a transformation process like all government departments and amalgamating the ANC's old military wing, Umkhonto we Sizwe, and Apla from the Pan Africanist Congress (PAC), another of the old liberation struggle parties, into the old white-dominated police force. Not everything made sense immediately and I would have to send the same fax twice to the same number but mark it for different people's attention. It was clearly a cosmetic merger in the police force and the two sides were very much operating independently, still trying to establish trust. But I'm a person who lives by the book. If instructions are issued, I follow them to the letter, and I did so without questioning or arguing about practicalities.

About two weeks into my time at the Presidency the President was scheduled to be in the office for the first time. By this time Mary had told me a little about the President, what type of person he was and that he was kind but disciplined. Afrikaners grow up with a sense of respect for any authority and before having met him, I had respect for him, purely because he was the President of the country.

He hadn't done anything publicly to prove the contrary and I therefore had no reason to disrespect him.

From my early arrival at the office that morning I could sense an unusual tension within the building but at the same time a kind of excitement. The police guarding our private office were alert and their uniforms neatly pressed, and soon a team of men in dark suits arrived presenting themselves as the advance team of the President's bodyguards. It was then time for the President to arrive and I closed the door leading to my office so as not to disturb anything that might be happening in the corridors. From passing footsteps and ructions I gathered that the President had arrived and he went past my office down the corridor into his office. Guests arrived to see him and were taken to his office without delay. They were all punctual and everything flowed with military precision. I sat quietly in my chair, awaiting instructions from anyone. I had noticed that the bodyguards were all armed and I was tense and cautious not to make any sudden move that could be misinterpreted. It was my first encounter with armed people in close proximity, and it made me nervous.

A few hours later Mary asked me to type something and bring it to her office once I was ready. So I did. I was looking at the piece of paper in front of me when I nearly bumped into President Nelson Mandela as he was exiting Mary's office into the corridor surrounded by bodyguards. He extended his hand first to shake mine; I was confused and not sure whether it was proper for me to greet him. I said, 'Good morning, Mr Mandela.' One doesn't really know what to do at that point except cry. Which I did. It was all too much. I was sobbing. He then spoke to me but I didn't understand him and was completely in shock. I had to say 'Excuse me Mr President' for him to repeat what he had just said to me, and after gathering my thoughts or guts – I'm not sure which – I realized that he addressed me in Afrikaans. My home language.

He was visibly old and appeared kind. I focused on the wrinkles on his face and his warm, sincere smile. He spoke with a caring voice and in a kind manner and asked me my name. I was ready to pull back my hand after shaking his but he held on. I could feel the texture of his hand on mine and I started perspiring. I wasn't sure if I was supposed to hold this black man's hand. I wanted him to let go but he didn't and he asked where I came from and where I worked. I wasn't sure whether to answer in Afrikaans or English and cannot remember which I chose, but we conversed in a mixture of Afrikaans and English. I was completely overtaken by emotion and couldn't continue. I then had a feeling of guilt that swept over me. I felt guilty that this kindly spoken man with gentle eyes and generosity of spirit spoke to me in my own language after 'my people' had sent him to jail for so many years. I instantly regretted voting 'No' in the referendum. How do you correct all of that prejudice in five minutes? Suddenly, I wanted to apologize. I hadn't given any thought to what twenty-seven years of imprisonment would be like, but I knew I was not even twenty-seven years of age. I was a mere twenty-three, about to turn twenty-four and I couldn't comprehend an entire lifetime in prison.

Mr Mandela noticed that I was unable to continue our conversation and still held onto my hand as he put his left hand on my shoulder and tapped it while he said, 'It's OK, calm down, I think you are overreacting.' I was firstly not used to someone being so direct to me to tell me that I'm overreacting and, secondly, I was embarrassed that it was a President telling me this. I calmed down and he was obviously in a hurry so we parted. His last words were 'I am happy to meet you and hope to see you again.' As we parted I thought: Ye, right. How can I be important to a President? After all, it's my people that put him through all that suffering.

I was in shock for the entire day and went home, telling my parents that I met the President today, and what a nice man he appeared to be. He spoke to me in Afrikaans. My parents didn't ask any questions and continued doing whatever they were busy with at the time, unaffected by my announcement. Probably used to me exaggerating a bit, I got the impression that they thought I was lying. I went to sleep puzzled by our encounter, not knowing where my thoughts or feelings were about this gentleman, perceived by my family and community to be a terrorist.

The next day I interrogated Mary about the fact that the President was so fluent in Afrikaans. She explained that he had learned Afrikaans in prison and he did so purposefully to communicate with his warders. It only struck me later that he obviously also charmed the apartheid leaders with his Afrikaans whenever he met them during negotiations. It is quite an amusing experience when events override what your brain expects. The last thing any Afrikaner would expect from Nelson Mandela was that he spoke to you in Afrikaans. It all became clear when he told me much later that, 'When you speak to a man you speak to his head but when you speak to him in his language you speak to his heart.' And that is exactly what he did. I came to understand that by learning the language of the warders he could almost seduce them. Afrikaans, being the language of the oppressor, was a much-hated language at the time and synonymous with the apartheid regime. I later also learned that Afrikaans was imposed as the main language for black education in 1974. This resulted in the Soweto uprising in 1976 in which about 20,000 black students took part, and although official figures estimated that the uprising resulted in 176 deaths it is widely believed that up to 700 students died during the protest. Black people were not accounted for in South Africa in those years and therefore official figures and estimates never correlated as there was no existing official register.

In the weeks that followed I saw the President at a distance on a few occasions as he passed in and out of the office. I concentrated on my typing and supporting Mary and never bothered to be around or be seen when he was in the office. Instead, I befriended the bodyguards, black and white. Some of them were very caring about me and inquisitive about my background. I was never sure whether they were checking on me or not, asking questions out of pure interest or whether it was as part of their job to establish any threat I may pose to the President.

Every time the President passed my office, I ensured that my door was closed so as to avoid having another emotional interaction with him. I literally hid away when I heard him approaching and only saw his back as he was passing the office. I was happy with his presence in the office though, as it brought about some excitement and a list of interesting visitors. I was more intrigued by him than by the visitors and hardly took notice of them, apart from knowing that some of them had names I recognized from the media or magazines.

I do recall the newly crowned Miss South Africa visiting, Basetsana Makgalamela. I had some practice before she arrived in pronouncing her surname and managed by the time she arrived. She met with the President and we were called by Mary after the meeting to meet Miss South Africa.

Mary announced one afternoon that the President wished to see all his personal staff for lunch at his official residence the next day. Soon after his inauguration he renamed the Presidential house Mahlamba Ndlopfu, meaning 'start of a new dawn'. I thought that was quite appropriate. I was extremely nervous and definitely not ready to eat with any President. I had no idea what cutlery to use first, and one of my colleagues told me to simply watch her and follow her example, which put me at ease. I had also asked my mother the night before what to do about a selection of cutlery and she grabbed her Emsie Schoeman book – a South African lady who was considered the authority on etiquette – and I got a crash-course in table manners.

Arriving at Mahlamba Ndlopfu we were escorted to a sitting room. The President was still in a meeting but our arrival was announced to him. He ended his meeting and joined us in the lounge. He greeted us each by shaking hands and in a relaxing way conversing with us as a group, walking us to the dining room. By now I managed to control myself and I didn't cry. It was a kind gesture from his side to invite his staff to lunch, and looking at my colleagues it crossed my mind that the seven of us at that point were almost representative of all races in South Africa: Mary Mxadana, his private secretary, was black; Morris Chabalala, one of the assistant private secretaries, also black; Elize Wessels, the other

assistant private secretary, white; Alan Pillay, the administrative officer, Indian; Lenois Coetzee, the receptionist, white; Olga Tsoko, the
other receptionist, black; and then me, the most junior in age and
rank, white.

I was told that shortly after his inauguration the President called
all the staff from the old Presidency, people who had served the previous regime, to a meeting, allaying their fears of being fired or
made redundant without discussion or them having a choice in the
matter. He asked people to stay and help build the new government
of national unity but also gave them the option of leaving if they
wished to move on. Staff greatly appreciated the President giving
them a choice. The President's office was now a mixture of black
and white people representing the 'Rainbow nation' he often
referred to in speeches.

I'd noticed, too, that in Tuynhuys, the President's office in Cape
Town situated next to Parliament, the pictures of the old Presidents
and Prime Ministers continued to hang on the walls. Again I'd found
it strange that he wouldn't erase the past, seeing as how these people
had spearheaded the oppression of his people and imprisoned him.
But I was told that President Mandela insisted that those not be
removed. That they were part of South Africa's history, no matter
how unpleasant the memories were.

At the lunch, a round table was set and I quickly chose a chair far
from his to avoid any uncomfortable conversation or difficult questions from him, and I didn't want to take a chair of someone that
wanted to sit next to him. It was 1 p.m. and instead of lunch, one of
the housekeepers entered the room with a small FM black box-type
radio. It looked like an antique and something that was not seen
often being used any longer. It was time for the news and the radio
was switched on and put on the window shelf. While the news was
being read on radio we all looked at one another uncomfortably.
The President listened with concentration, clearly taking seriously
what was being read. I vaguely recall mention about South Africa
acting as a peace-keeping force in Africa, the *Achille Lauro* sinking
off the coast of Somalia and Cindy Crawford and Richard Gere

announcing their separation. I was trying to concentrate on the news but my thoughts wandered about the President, what he felt and thought at that time and, most importantly, how he felt about the three white Afrikaners at his lunch table.

Following the news lunch was served. To the contrary of what I expected, lunch was simple. It consisted of a starter, main course, dessert and coffee. The food was home-cooked, without fanciness, and you knew exactly what you were eating. The President had a glass of wine and even though we were all offered wine I settled for water. During lunch he started to tell us some stories about his years in prison and I had to press my fingernails into the palm of my hand to prevent me from crying again. By the time dessert was served I couldn't control myself any longer and my eyes were filled with tears. I felt *so* sorry for him. He told us about his precious tomato garden in prison and how he cherished his crop. He also explained how they worked in the limestone quarry, and how the reflection of the white rock damaged his eyes, and with his exceptional ability of story-telling he transported our imaginations to South Africa's Alcatraz and his prison cell on Robben Island. I tried to comprehend season upon season in a prison cell, cold cement floors, sharing a bathroom with other inmates, never having privacy, eating at specific times and limited tasteless food for twenty-seven years. It was still too much to comprehend. What struck me was that while he was telling these stories he didn't appear to be sad. To me it sounded like tragedy, yet he recited the stories in a colourful way as opposed to my grim imagination.

Lunch was soon over and back at the office we shared our experience with each other and I was free to express my sympathy. Clearly the President didn't want sympathy. It was something he considered to have been part of history and not to determine the rest of his life. I soon found a quote that expressed it so well: 'It's not important in life what happens to you, but how you handle what happens to you.'

I read later that he had written that it was easier to change others than to change himself, and to this day I often wonder about the struggle within himself as far as it concerned forgiveness and reconciliation, trying to imagine to what extent one has to really work with oneself to change your thinking and your beliefs: to take that decision to forgive, as Ahmed Kathrada told me. But as Madiba said, by deciding to forgive you do not only free the oppressed but you also free the oppressor.

Later that year, a prominent and progressive South African, Dr Johan Heyns, was assassinated and the President called all the generals in charge of the security forces in South Africa to a meeting in his office. Dr Heyns was one of the senior leaders of the Dutch Reformed Church in South Africa. The church was prominent during the apartheid era, justifying it through religion and Dr Heyns was one of the few Afrikaner leaders who criticized apartheid at a time when it was not fashionable to do so. Now it was suspected that a third force was at play, trying to destabilize the country and create tension between black and white at a time when South Africa was still vulnerable. As someone who had walked the Damascus road and showed eagerness to work with the new government, it was believed that Dr Heyns was assassinated by white Afrikaner extremists, the same kind of conservative people I once religiously supported. The conservative Afrikaners did not welcome such gestures of reform. I had slowly started to think about my own beliefs and although I was still a little confused, I had softened up and realized at least that resisting change was neither logical nor justifiable.

As the generals marched past my office to the President's office I couldn't help but feel a sense of pride when I saw them in their uniforms. We Afrikaners are proud people, especially of our generals and people who hold such positions – inherently so, but also because we trust them unconditionally and without prejudice. I felt proud of their presence even though there was tension in the office.

The President also called on General Constand Viljoen, who was the leader of the right-wing party called the Freedom Front and opposed to Mr Mandela on matters ranging from power sharing to land reform. I was extremely proud to meet General Viljoen as he was a pure Boer in every sense of the word (*boer* is Afrikaans for 'farmer'). He was also happy to find a girl in the President's office looking like and epitomizing a real Afrikaner. I imagined it made him feel comfortable seeing someone with the same culture and background in the President's office. The President didn't want to speak to him in his office, probably out of fear for listening devices, and met with him on a couch at the entrance of the ladies' bathroom in our offices across from my office door. When they sat down, the President called me. I was introduced to General Viljoen in Afrikaans and the President smiled warmly as he told General Viljoen that I was a real Afrikaner.

What did President Mandela mean when he said I was a 'real Afrikaner' or *boere-meisie* (farm girl)? Was it because I spoke Afrikaans? Did he sense I came from a conservative family? Or did I simply look like an Afrikaner? Only later I thought that perhaps my weight also played a part in epitomizing a real Afrikaner, something about which I was quite sensitive at the time. The Afrikaners are generally largely built people with a bigger bone structure. Most of them, my family not excluded, love to eat, particularly bread and meat. Did Nelson Mandela think I was really the image of an Afrikaner farm girl?

I went home that night with the same pride to tell my parents that I had met General Viljoen. I still had no interest in politics and only knew that he was there to discuss the death of Dr Johan Heyns. My parents were visibly more impressed by this announcement as General Viljoen was seen to represent the conservative Afrikaners at the time. An intelligence report on the death of Dr Heyns later crossed my desk but I had no interest in reading it, much to my regret in later years.

As the year passed, I started to feel more at home in my new environment, keeping Mary up to date on security, briefing the airforce on the President's movements, working with his staff at the ANC. On Mondays the President spent the entire day at Shell House, as it was known, the ANC head office in Johannesburg (later the party moved its head office to Luthuli House, named after the founding president of the ANC, Albert Luthuli). We were not allowed to interfere with Mondays and in five years, unless we were on travels abroad, the President didn't miss one Monday going to the ANC head offices. We never knew what he did there or who he interacted with, and his party political work was separated from his official duties as President. But he was part and parcel of the ANC, never to be divorced from the party that shaped his life and entire political career and in the execution of his daily tasks as President he honoured the ANC's policies and framework.

Then one day I received a call from Mary to say that the President wanted me to drive to his private house in Houghton, Johannesburg, to help him with some Afrikaans. He was having trouble with his eye following an operation on it and we were told that he would be at home recovering for a few days.

Upon arrival at his Houghton house, I found a few security vehicles parked outside. The President himself was seated in a comfortable chair outside in the garden under a tree. He was wearing sunglasses with his two feet raised on a foot rest. He was wearing sunglasses obviously to protect his recovering eye. We shook hands and greeted warmly. He asked me to take a seat next to him and handed me the *Beeld* newspaper (the Afrikaans daily newspaper in our area). He then instructed me to start reading to him. Panic struck, I think I thought for a moment that I had forgotten how to read.

I struggled until he stopped me and told me to relax. There was humour in his voice and he told me to start from the top and read at a slower pace. It was easier. I then came across the surname Mamoepa in the article. Ronnie Mamoepa was the spokesperson for the ANC at the time. Reading across the surname I pronounced it exactly as it is spelt. The President interrupted me. He corrected my pronunciation to Mamo-epa. I thanked him and continued reading. Coming across the next mention of Ronnie's surname I tried to pass it as quickly as possible but the President interrupted me again and corrected me patiently, prompting me to repeat after him. The third time I realized I had to pay attention and that he was not going to be amused by my lack of trying, so I did and when I crossed the name for the fourth time he congratulated me on my good pronunciation. I felt like I had won an Olympic Gold medal and was almost embarrassed by the fuss he made. I relaxed a little but was still very tense. I also read too fast and he told me a few times to slow down. It was pure tension. He then asked me to explain a term he didn't understand and I read the sentence again and explained the context. After reading a few more articles I was dismissed to return to Pretoria. I remember perspiring like a marathon runner from pure nerves and was happy to be back at home, recovering from another shock interaction.

We returned to business as usual and the next time the President was in the office it was easier to face him. I didn't have any business dealing with him directly but now and then I would walk into him in the corridors or see him passing my office. I was no longer hiding or feeling shy and accepted the fact that if he wanted to get rid of me because I was a white Afrikaner, I would just deal with it when it happened. For the time being it appeared as if I was not going to become a victim of such actions, and although still somewhat sceptical about his feelings towards whites, I took comfort in the fact that he had only shown warmth so far.

I was trying to get an understanding of the political world around me. It wasn't easy and I literally had to do a crash-course in South African history. One of the bodyguards offered to take me and my two best friends, Pieter Moolman and Andries Ellis, to Soweto on a tour. Soweto is a formerly black township on the outskirts of Johannesburg, where the black people were grouped together and restricted to live in, during apartheid. We were nervous and scared but also curious to see what it looked like.

The bodyguard took us to President Mandela's first house in Vilakazi Street, showed us where Archbishop Tutu stayed – in the same street – and the Hector Pieterson museum, and related the stories of the student uprising in 1976. Hector was a child of thirteen years of age participating in the uprising in 1976 when thousands of students marched against Afrikaans being made compulsory as the medium of education for black people. The march was intended to be a peaceful demonstration but turned violent when the police arrived and shot at students to disperse the crowds. Hector was shot, and an iconic image taken of another student carrying him and running from the scene while Hector was dying in his arms became the image the world saw of South Africa under apartheid law. Hector was a hero.

The police officer taking us on the tour showed us some spots that were used as hideouts in Soweto by the ANC and its military wing when they were operating underground, and we were excited to learn but nervous at the same time for being in Soweto. White people didn't easily go into Soweto at the time but I was at ease as he was armed and I knew he would be in trouble if while in the care of a bodyguard of the President something had happened to us in Soweto. We drove around for a while and saw that Soweto was not the township of squatter camps like slums I had imagined it to be. People were building proper houses, some of them mansions, and there was nothing visibly to be afraid of. I later learned that the gentleman who took us on the tour was closely linked to National Intelligence, and I often thought that he was probably only eager to take us on the tour to enable him to dig a little into our lives and assess us on a threat level, as my presence so close to the President warranted.

At the end of 1994 the President went on holiday to Saudi Arabia. I couldn't imagine why anyone would want to go to Saudi Arabia on holiday. I was told the President visited a hospital while he was there, meeting with some South African nurses, and that he had friends there too, but I couldn't comprehend how one has a holiday in a desert like Saudi Arabia.

On the day of the President's return from Saudi, Mary invited me to accompany her to the airport to go and meet him. I was so excited and jumped at the opportunity. By now my attitude towards him had changed. His interactions with me were always pleasant and he was very friendly and warm whenever he spoke to me. I was therefore looking forward to any opportunity to see him. Mary said I had to bring my telephone book in case he wanted to make any calls from the airport, which he then did. By then I had armed myself with a telephone book and any numbers that Mary or the President could need. It was not something she told me to do but I assumed to be effective one had to have certain information at hand at all times, so I started compiling a telephone book with the important numbers Mary frequently used.

Arriving at the airport the President appeared happy to see me and he said that he'd thought about me. Again I thought: Ye right. I'm sure a President has more important things to think about than a typist in his office. Later I realized that he had already probably started working on his strategy to use me as the perfect example of including an Afrikaner in his office and how minorities would react to him doing so. It didn't cross my mind at the time though and although what he said flattered me I did not really believe it.

A huge media contingent awaited the President's arrival at Waterkloof airforce base where the Presidential plane touched down. Just after he greeted me someone took a photo of him and Mary walking towards the VIP arrivals hall at Waterkloof. The photo appeared in the *Sunday Times* newspaper the next day and my dad telephoned the newspaper to have a copy of the original photo sent to him. To my surprise they also took a photo while I greeted the President. It was my most precious possession ever when I received the photo and by now I was noticing some pride in my father, regardless of the fact that he had not met President Mandela but was merely creating an opinion based on the stories I told at home about our few interactions. Nelson Mandela was changing South Africans' views one by one. My dad included.

4

Working for a President

We received the strangest calls and requests sometimes in the President's office. On one occasion a gentleman called to say that he had a parrot that could imitate the President and whether he could please bring the parrot to the office for the President to hear it. I was the lucky person to take the call and I obviously said, 'No Sir, I don't think so.' One day I received a call from an Afrikaans gentleman who said, 'Good morning lady, please give me your pints.' I responded by saying, 'Excuse me Sir.' He said again: 'Your pints, I need your pints please.' I said, 'Sir, I think you have the incorrect number as I don't have a clue what you are talking about.' He then explained that he was calling from a dairy farm and dialled the wrong number: he was looking for the pints of milk our dairy produced for the day. I replied, 'Sir, even if I had the pints I wouldn't know how much a pint is.'

A South African serial killer on the run, Collen Chauke, also called our switchboard and wanted to speak to the President, and the President only, to hand himself over to the police. He wanted the President to help him, probably because he was scared that he might be shot when he handed himself over to the police. Olga was on the switchboard that day and acted swiftly to alert the police from another telephone line. The police arrested Chauke a few hours later and he didn't get to speak to the President. We therefore sometimes dealt with serious matters and on other days you had to keep your sanity in check because of the ludicrous things people would suggest or call about.

Things happened at an enormously fast pace. Especially when the President was around. In his presence things were calm but behind the scenes it was running and organizing at speed. There would be very little time for anything else than work. Somehow Elize based in Cape Town managed much better than us. She had a more balanced life but in Pretoria we raced against time to get through the day. As I have mentioned, Elize had served the former First Lady, Marike de Klerk, and was one of the staff members from the old regime who remained in the dispensation. The rest of us really had no knowledge or skill of having been in a President's office before and a lot was done on trial and error.

The Presidency was focused on implementing the interim constitution and setting up structures to enhance the functioning of the constitution, which was signed into law in 1996. The President himself was very focused on reconciliation and nurturing both black and white people's emotions that were bruised as a result of apartheid.

Apart from typing up the President's schedule and distributing it daily to security, households, airforce and concerned parties, Mary tasked me with a few other mundane things. She would occasionally ask me to bring tea to the President or his guests or even drive her car to be filled with fuel and fetch her dry cleaning. I didn't mind doing anything and whatever was asked. I often dropped off documents at the President's house in Pretoria, received visitors and learned how to deal with any enquiries that came to the President's personal staff. We started operating in a more structured way, where work was divided between the three private secretaries and Alan and I had to deal with most of the administration. Although operating within the larger office as the Department of the Office of the President, the President's personal staff dealt with more of his private matters and day-to-day appointments and movements as well as requests directly related to him or requiring his personal attention, while the Department dealt with policy, cabinet and political issues.

I now knew Professor Jakes Gerwel, the head of the President's office, a little better. Professor Gerwel – or Prof. as we called him – was an academic and anti-apartheid activist since his early life, and was a brown man originating from the Eastern Cape. He was head-hunted from the University of the Western Cape to become the Chief of Staff at the President's office and the Secretary of Cabinet in the first democratically elected government. He was my first introduction to a real intellectual and when I met him for the first time I was a little surprised that a brown man could have so many academic qualifications. Most of his qualifications he obtained *cum laude* and all of them in literature and language. In my ignorant view only white people could be that learned. I was told about all his qualifications before I met him. He was a very likeable person who clearly respected people without prejudice – I had expected to be looked down upon by a person with so many qualifications. Even though it didn't sound right, I was told that he was an Afrikaner too. Again my own prejudices made it difficult to believe that anyone who wasn't white could be an Afrikaner. Prof.'s smile and his hair were his trademarks. His hair was very disorderly and in an afro-type style. It reminded me of Albert Einstein's. Whenever the President was in the office, Prof. Gerwel would frequently pass our offices on his way to see him and always stopped to enquire about our well-being. The president relied heavily on Prof. Gerwel for advice on every detail of his presidency. They had a very close relationship and the President had a lot of admiration for Prof.'s calm and calculated approach not only to matters of national importance but even in dealing with issues in his personal environment.

It was February 1995 and we were all preparing to move to Cape Town for Parliament's first session of the year.

In Cape Town all Parliamentarians lived in a village exclusively built for them called Acacia Park. According to rank and years of service you got allocated either an apartment or a small house, also depending on the size of your family. For us single girls, bachelor apartments with a small kitchen and a bathroom were adequate. I loved the independence and soon made friends with some of my colleagues. Maretha Slabbert was one such person; she worked in the Cabinet Secretariat at the Presidency at the time. Seventeen years later Maretha and I still worked together and she was single-handedly the most important support in my life to date, both professionally and personally.

Come July, Parliament would go into recess and we would all pack up and move back to Pretoria for the rest of the year. It was not something I looked forward to and I was hoping to avoid going back to anything that deprived me of my independence, like living at my parents' home and having to report to anyone. Yet, I looked forward to seeing my friends and sharing my experiences with them, and then of course to certain home comforts such as having your clothes washed and ironed automatically in the course of everyday life and not having to worry about those things. Often at parties my friends would tease me, telling people that I now worked for the 'enemy'. I took it as a joke but as we grew older and more mature we eventually started debating history and politics more seriously. I felt more informed and at least able to converse in an intelligent manner on something I thought I was gathering knowledge about. These debates often ended in heated argument because my perspective on events in South Africa was slowly changing, due to my interaction with the President and the knowledge I had acquired from some of my colleagues.

Mary also spent more time with me and told me about the President's private life; his failed marriage to Winnie Madikizela and about their daughters, Zindzi and Zenani. Apart from official events where the President needed a companion and he would ask Zindzi or Zenani to join him, I rarely saw them, and judging from his diary one realized that the President didn't have much time for a private life. I was also told that he had two surviving children from his first marriage but we never saw them or had any dealings with them.

I had noticed, now, that whenever the President had Afrikaners visiting him, he would call me to deliver documents or ask me to serve tea in his office. I didn't mind as it posed another opportunity to see him. He was removing my defences day by day, chiselling away my prejudices and the layers of apartheid that had grown on me in the same way he chiselled the limestone while he was imprisoned on Robben Island. He would ask with real interest how I was, about my parents, about my well-being. Every time he saw me he would ask something different. Any person that takes an interest in you automatically becomes likeable, no matter what your preconceived ideas about him or her. And then it was done with sincerity in this case so I enjoyed the attention. I had never imagined that I would be of significance for a President to enquire about my well-being.

On one such occasion a documentary was being filmed around the President's day-to-day life. I was instructed to serve tea in his office that day during a meeting attended by Jay Naidoo, Minister without Portfolio in the Presidency, and the man I would have worked for if fate hadn't brought Mary into my interview. I wasn't prepared and didn't feel properly dressed to serve tea in his office that day. I nevertheless served the tea and the President introduced me to Minister Naidoo in Afrikaans. The Minister smiled unconvincingly. I found it hard to be sure whether all former anti-apartheid activists had joined Mr Mandela in the decision to forgive.

When the documentary aired, my parents were taken aback by reports that some friends of theirs had decided to cut ties with them because I served tea to a black man. The entire Afrikaans community was not adapting well to the changes in South Africa. Their interaction and relationships with black people remained on the same level as during apartheid – that of master and servant. Life for most whites continued unchanged, in the same bubble of their materialist comfort as before, and not all white people were actually making a concerted effort to change the country into a non-racial society. Sadly many remain in that bubble even today.

My parents found themselves in an awkward situation. They had no reason to suspect that I wasn't happy at work. They could see that I worked hard and I liked what I was doing, yet it was clear that the community wasn't going to support my endeavours. (Years later the same people wanted to talk to me about having books signed by then retired President Mandela and I took pleasure in arranging this. Whether their views had changed only towards the President, I don't know.)

*

That autumn I got a call from Rochelle, the President's niece who looked after him at home in Johannesburg, to say that he wanted me to accompany him to a United World Colleges event in the Carlton Hotel that night. After the President left his then wife, Winnie Madikizela Mandela, in 1992, his first permanent residence was in a suburb called Houghton and Rochelle moved in with him to look after him, organizing his house and workers but also providing him with some personal support at home. I was in Pretoria at the time of the call and panic struck. I asked my mother what to wear and we selected a simple black skirt and jacket. I was expected to be at the President's house at a certain time and Rochelle said that he wanted me to drive with him. That made me even more nervous. What was I supposed to say or do in the car sitting next to a President? No one prepares you for these things.

I arrived at his house and asked Rochelle what was expected of me. She said I should just go along and when he is supposed to speak I should put the speech where he is supposed to speak from, as well as his reading glasses, make sure he had water to drink, and security would take care of the rest. I was anxious to hear from Rochelle that the President called Mary to inform her that he wanted me to go with him. It made me somewhat uncomfortable that she was not the one instructing me to go with him. That was the totality of Rochelle's briefing.

The President came downstairs and he greeted friendly and invited me to get into the car. The security opened the heavily armoured door and I could barely move it. I didn't want to intrude in the President's space so kept to my corner of the car and sat as close to the door as possible. Tense. On our way to the Carlton Hotel in mid-Johannesburg the President said that I would now meet Queen Noor, the wife of the King of Jordan. I asked him how I was supposed to address her and he smilingly explained, 'No, you see, you call her Your Majesty' because she was a Queen. The President always started his sentences with a 'No' whether the answer was yes or no, and it usually was followed with 'you see'. I paid so much attention to his every word that I couldn't help but notice it.

He had a way of addressing people with the utmost respect, no matter who you were, and even his choice of words conveyed that respect. Starting every sentence with 'No' didn't have any negative connotation. It was just habit and a gentler way of starting off with any sentence.

Arriving at the event people quickly started crowding around the President and the security found it difficult to keep people away from him while at the same time trying to allow him to walk towards the door of the event. At the door he was met by Her Majesty. The President introduced me by saying, 'Your Majesty, this is my secretary Zelda la Grange': a) I wasn't his secretary, and b) I really didn't think she cared. But to my surprise she took interest in me and asked how long I had been working for the President. My answer: almost a year. The fact that I didn't have a long history with him clearly didn't discourage her to show interest in me. She was one of the most beautiful ladies I've ever met and she had the stature of a Queen. She moved with grace and I had to pinch myself not to stare. I had met a Queen!

Little did I know that a greater surprise awaited me inside. The security led us to the main table. I had never experienced such chaos in a crowd before and was trying my best to stay as close as possible to the President. I felt bewildered as people pushed against us, preventing us from moving freely, in addition to the security forming a tight circle around us. Everyone wanted to touch the President or see him close to. As soon as he and the Queen stood behind their chairs in the hall people quietened down and got ready to take their seats. I turned around and asked the security: 'Where am I supposed to go?' I was relying on them to guide me and teach me what to do. They showed me my seat, right next to the Queen. I blushed and felt blood and my heart pumping in every muscle of my body. There was no way, none, zero, absolutely no chance that I had to sit next to a Queen. What would I say? What do I do? I couldn't even remember from my crash course on etiquette what cutlery to use first. Somewhere in the back of my mind I remember overhearing my mom saying 'start from the outside'. OK, that deals with that then.

But still this cannot be happening. I told the security that it was a mistake. In the meantime the President and Queen took their seats and I was confused, nervously trying to get away, at this point being the only one in the room still standing around.

The President looked at me in a way that exclaimed 'Zelda, take your seat.' I looked into his eyes, mine filled with panic as if to say, 'Rescue me; tell me to go away.' But he nodded his head instead to signal sit down. So I sat. The Queen and the President exchanged pleasantries and I had no idea who sat to my other side. The person could have been naked or dead. I wouldn't have noticed. I followed the pattern on the table cloth with my eyes and later put my hand on the table to draw the lines of the pattern with my finger. I was hoping to appear to be relaxed but I was dying inside of tension and nervousness. I knew I was supposed to keep my elbows off the table but I could no longer disguise my ineptness and I thought placing my elbow on the table would ground me a little more. Surely seating me next to a Queen was completely against protocol. Even I knew that.

The Queen turned to me and started talking to me. I smiled and looked past her to the President again with a look in my eyes that said: 'OK Sir, you are supposed to help me here.' I was a bit upset with him as he didn't come to my rescue but only smiled, clearly not noticing my anxiety. The Queen started asking me about the political situation in the country, where I grew up, etc. I cannot remember what I responded but I knew I had to sound like the eternal optimist because I assumed if I was with the President it was expected of one to be positive about the future of South Africa. I didn't really know what I was talking about and I wasn't sure what to think yet: whether I really saw a future for South Africa and where we were heading. My opinion of the new South Africa had not really evolved beyond the fact that I now kind of liked the President.

And then, I was saved by the bell. Proceedings started and after the Queen's speech the President was asked to speak. He was speaking from his seat and a microphone was handed to him. I handed him his speech and glasses and he put his glasses back on the table and started reading his speech. I thought: Why would he need his glasses if he doesn't use them? After completing his speech he handed it back to me and said out loud: 'Thank you darling.' His words were filled with consideration and gratefulness. I wasn't used to anyone calling me 'darling'. Later I realized that it was just an affectionate term he used for many women from time to time. If a woman or a stranger calls me 'darling' I have always felt that there is a derogatory connotation to it. But surely you don't mind Nelson Mandela calling you 'darling'? Blood rushed to my head and I was shy with shock – almost the same feeling as when your mother used to kiss you in public as teenager, somewhat shy over the association and affection. I thought I had done my duty however, and was ready to relax and start eating.

We sat waiting for food for about five minutes and then the President said, 'Zelda, I think it is time for us to leave.' The master of ceremonies announced his departure and off we went. As years passed I also realized that he wasn't fond of eating anywhere. He simply adored his home-cooked food prepared by one of his long-serving Xhosa chefs, Xoliswa or Gloria, and therefore he hardly ever ate at public events.

On the way to the car someone approached with a copy of the President's autobiography, *Long Walk to Freedom*. Security turned him away but the man insisted, reaching the President himself, who couldn't really say no. After he signed the book, he handed it to a security officer and moved to the car. When I looked round the security man had ripped the page with the President's signature out of the book, telling the man that he should not have disobeyed instructions. I went into complete shock. Little did I know that I would become one of the people who had to try and maintain order no matter what it took, although I luckily stopped short of tearing pages out of books.

On the way home, I told the President that I thought it was inappropriate that I sat next to the Queen. He smiled and said, 'Don't worry, it was OK.' That made me even more nervous. The

President wasn't fazed by it at all. At home he invited me in for cof-fee but I was eager to head back to Pretoria. This was too much to handle. He insisted that security drive with me 'to my house' he said, but outside I convinced them that it wasn't necessary. They were tired and I was definitely not going to have anyone follow me home. When I later accompanied him more regularly he would insist on the security driving with me and we learned to agree only to break our agreement as soon as we left the door.

In the winter of 1995 the President was invited to a town in the Western Cape, Swellendam, a small village-like Afrikaans town along the Garden Route in South Africa, to receive the Freedom of the Town. It was an act of unity for a town that was dominated still by white Afrikaners to offer the President such an honour, and he agreed to accept it. Again, a few days prior to the event, he announced that he wanted me to go with him. He called me to Genadendal the day before, his official residence in Cape Town, and upon arrival asked me to sit down. Genadendal is the name of a small brown Afrikaans community in the rural Western Cape. He adopted the name for his official residence in Cape Town to pay homage to the community of Genadendal, which means some-thing like 'valley of gratitude' when translated directly.

He announced that he wanted to practise his Afrikaans and I had to help him with pronunciation as his entire speech was in Afri-kaans. He fired away and unceremoniously started reading. At first I didn't have the heart to correct him but then he would look up every now and again to seek approval. I nodded like a real teacher and hated myself for appearing to be such a supremacist. Although I had been asked to help him, the situation presented was so typical of the apartheid era of a white overseeing what the black man was doing and the black man seeking approval from the white. I also couldn't really understand what he was reading and I had to adjust my concentration level. Then he wanted to re-read the speech for a second time. So I agreed – who wouldn't? – but this time I gathered some courage to add a few corrections. He was becoming more nervous to read and would peek at me over his reading glasses, this time seeking less approval but more affirmation. I nevertheless nodded.

It was my first helicopter ride ever. I was nervous but I watched the President's face and saw that he was at ease in the big military Oryx helicopter. I relaxed. It was being flown by white military pilots and I wondered whether he trusted them. By 1995 very few black pilots had been trained and qualified to be absorbed into the transformed military forces. On our way I thought about his speech and wondered whether he was going to remember the words we'd practised the previous day. I was nervous for him while he appeared relaxed, as if he was on his way to a social gathering of some sort.

Arriving in Swellendam he was received with open arms and insisted on first walking among the ordinary people, and when a little girl came to greet him on stage his face and body language opened up completely. He spoke to her in Afrikaans too and she responded although she was shy. He enjoyed that interaction and I could see that he had a special connection to the child. He delivered his speech and remembered the words I had helped him with. It was perfect. By delivering his entire speech in Afrikaans he reached out to the community's heart and people adored him for that.

Back in the office in Pretoria it was on one of the occasions that I served tea in his office, although he was by himself this time, that he requested me to take a seat at the other side of his desk. I nervously did, not knowing what to expect. The President didn't easily tell you to sit down at his desk. I thought I was in some kind of trouble and tried to remember what stories I told to whom in the last couple of weeks, trying to assess why I was in trouble. He then said, 'No . . . you see, I want you to come to Japan with me.' My first thoughts were: Would that not be considered inappropriate to travel abroad together? and then I thought: Oh no, I'm convinced this is similar to my experience of my first encounter with him; I simply don't under-stand what he is saying. I think I replied with 'Excuse me Sir?' and he repeated the question while I needed time to process what he was saying. 'I want you to come to Japan with me,' he repeated.

And all I could think of to say was, 'Thank you very much Mr President but I don't have money to go to Japan right now.' He burst out laughing, probably not knowing how to respond to such stupidity.

He saw the surprise on my face to his laughter and he quickly composed himself to repeat the question, this time with a bit of essential detail: 'I want you to travel to Japan as part of my delegation on our state visit.' I had a vague idea that this was work but he continued to say that I should go to the Director General, the Chief of Staff of the Presidency, Prof. Gerwel, who would explain everything to me. I thanked him and left his office. I didn't say a word to Mary and I cannot recall if she was in her office as I passed through to my own office. I returned to my desk to digest what had just happened. I didn't know what to do with the information in my head and who to contact next. The President made it sound so easy to speak to Prof. Gerwel but he was, after all, the head of our office and it was not as simple as walking through his door and demanding answers. So I decided to leave it there and not speak to anyone about this again and forget that it had ever happened. I was convinced it was just a mistake.

A few days later Prof. Gerwel passed our office on his way to the President and greeted us as usual. He approached me at my desk and told me that he had spoken to the President and that he had mentioned to him that I should be included in the delegation. I was nervous. He pointed me to the Department of Foreign Affairs to have a passport issued and told me who to speak to, to make arrangements. He also told me that we would be joined by another young lady from the Western Cape. Her name was Melissa Brink. The President encountered a debate with her in the Western Cape at a public meeting with the brown community, during which he was impressed by her inquisitiveness and the way she challenged the ANC to provide her with the education that her parents believed would be provided if they voted the ANC into power. In her view, progress was too slow and she had the courage to challenge the President when she had the opportunity. He liked the fact that such a youngster was so serious about her education to have the guts to question the President over it.

I had no idea why I was invited to go on this trip and no one else knew either. What I really thought was a bonus was that I wasn't expected to pay for anything but rather received an extra allowance for travelling abroad. When I heard the amount I would be paid I was alarmed as it sounded like a danger pay of some sort. I think I drove the officials at Foreign Affairs crazy with all my questions – clearly a sign of my inexperience. I also had a sense of guilt towards Mary. I didn't know whose duty it was to inform her that I would be accompanying the delegation on this trip or what my role would be and I felt uncomfortable being in a space where she was uncertain about my role too; after all, I was working more for her than for the President.

The day arrived for me to depart with the advance team for Japan. I don't think I've ever been so excited in my entire life. Armed with my diplomatic passport, newly sewn clothes and manners recited from my mother, I departed on my first ever trip abroad. Before that day, I had never left the borders of South Africa and my first trip overseas being to Japan was almost like a fantasy.

Upon arrival in Tokyo we were met by officials from the Embassy and driven to the Osaka Palace Hotel. I could sense that all the officials were as puzzled with my presence as I was. Mary arrived a day later and things were tense between us. People were careful not to offend me because they knew my presence was the result of a direct instruction from the President. I was trying to figure out who did what on a state visit but it was not easy. We were surrounded by security and protocol officials and I soon took a liking to a gentleman by the name of Johan Nieman from Foreign Affairs. Johan guided me and explained things in great detail. He was also the first person to say: 'So how did you get to be put on the trip and what is your role?' I explained that I was merely the typist and I had no idea what my role was, but he comforted me with the fact that the President personally invited Melissa and I and therefore we should not be intimidated by anything or anyone. That made me feel a little better.

In my conversations with colleagues on the trip I got a sense of why we were there: for the South African government to strengthen its economic ties with Japan. We were accompanied by a few ministers and it became apparent what is expected of such office bearers during state visits. I was slowly developing a sense of politics.

President Mandela was to meet the Japanese Emperor. Upon arrival at the Emperor's palace we were told to stand in a receiving line. The most senior officials, the ministers, closest to the President and then in order of seniority down the line to the most junior. Of course Melissa and I were right at the end.

It was the first time it dawned on me why Melissa and I indeed accompanied the delegation on the trip. Melissa was introduced as a coloured, mixed-race young lady and I was introduced as an Afrikaner. I looked at my colleagues and realized that our delegation was completely 'representative', and I was happy to be part of that. The President wanted all the races represented in his team. He was determined to show the world that just as he preached reconciliation to the South African public, it was something he felt so strongly about that he wanted to apply that methodological thinking also in his own office, and commit to bringing about unity in South Africa even in his closest environment.

When the President got to me he introduced me to the Emperor by saying, 'This is Zelda la Grange, she is my secretary and a real Afrikaner *boere-meisie*.' I wasn't sure the Emperor knew what an 'Afrikaner *boere-meisie*' was and he appeared puzzled, but courteously smiled while he shook my hand.

I also soon discovered that I could speak to the President in Afrikaans whenever I didn't know what to do and that he would calmly direct me on the right protocol. He was being briefed by protocol officials and whenever he saw me hesitating, he would speak to me in Afrikaans and direct me. When the President had rest periods we didn't move from the guest house. Other delegates went out shopping and sightseeing but I was too scared to move. What if the President called me and I wasn't there? It was inconceivable. At the state banquet I sat at a good distance from the President but I could see and watch his every move.

*

Life for ordinary South Africans still hadn't changed much since President Mandela's inauguration in 1994, although there was a sense of optimism. What one saw of the President on TV was that he always greeted people respectfully and without prejudice. The public liked that. Our economy stabilized and investors started having confidence in the new South Africa. However, a watershed moment in President Mandela's Presidency approached in 1995 and an opportunity to show the world that South Africa would survive; that we were healthy and well.

The Rugby World Cup was being played in South Africa. Rugby was still very much considered a white man's sport in South Africa, even though I later discovered that black people, especially in the Eastern Cape, had played rugby for decades, but because of apartheid they were never allowed to participate in the sport publicly, or to be active spectators. Rugby is something most white Afrikaner people religiously follow and support, but the teams and attendance of public matches during apartheid were restricted for whites only. Prior to the World Cup the selectors included a brown Afrikaans-speaking young man in the national team (the Springboks) by name of Chester Williams.

The President met the Springboks before the start of the tournament at their training camp in the Western Cape, and on the day of the opening match in Newlands he was there to cheer them. When Chester (or Chessie as I later fondly addressed him) entered the field the crowd went crazy cheering him along. Chester was scoring points during matches and for that, white people started supporting his selection.

I never knew that the President even knew the rules of rugby but apparently he did – probably understanding more about the game than I did. He sat next to the Managing Director of SA Rugby, Dr Louis Luyt, as well as the Prime Minister of Australia, as the Springboks were playing the Australian team, the Wallabies, in this opening match. The President was in good spirits and took a bet with the Prime Minister that whoever won that day would win the tournament, and the loser would send the other a case of wine as both countries had reputable industries. South Africa won the match and we went right through to the historic day of the final in Johannesburg. (After our victory, the wine arrived from Australia and it was donated to a charity for fundraising purposes.)

I heard Mary calling around a few days before the final asking for a Springbok jersey, but didn't know why or for who. Then the day before the match, when we said our goodbyes at the office, she told me that the President would enter the field on the day of the final wearing a Springbok jersey. I thought that was quite original but didn't make more of it.

Mary gave me two tickets to the final match and I invited my dad to accompany me. We were well on time at the stadium and the crowd was excited and the vibe explosive. Shortly before kick-off the announcement came: 'Ladies and Gentlemen, please welcome the President of the Republic of South Africa, Mr Nelson Mandela' and he entered surrounded by bodyguards and rugby officials. The crowd cheered but when they caught sight of him in his green and gold jersey people started chiming 'Nelson Nelson Nelson'. At first I thought it was disrespectful to call him by first name but then when I looked around me people didn't seem to think about that but like one man they stood up and started screaming, whistling and shouting with excitement to see the black President in a Springbok jersey and cap. People felt a sense of pride irrespective of their political convictions. He greeted both teams and the National Anthems were sung.

It was a tense match and my dad and I jumped up and down with excitement like old buddies. Then in the extra time Joel Stransky kicked a drop goal which led South Africa to victory. The crowd exploded. People were hugging and kissing strangers, some even crying with joy. For a few hours our past didn't matter; we went colour blind and people embraced the opportunity to celebrate as South Africans. South Africa was excluded from the first two Rugby World Cups in 1987 and 1991 because of apartheid and was only allowed to participate in the international sporting arena after our first democratic elections. It was our first participation and we won the tournament.

It remains one of the best strategic moves of Nelson Mandela's Presidency in uniting the country to wear that jersey that day. The world saw South Africa as a united nation. He embraced what was considered the 'white man's sport' and by taking that leap into their most emotional territory he reached way beyond the borders of race and touched the people's hearts. He was proud of the Springboks but he was also proud of every citizen in the country, for them and with them. He would often refer to that day when saying that sport had the ability to unite people way beyond borders of division, and in a humble way I think he underplayed his own genius on that day.

The President soon invited the Springbok team for lunch after their victory and from there his close association with rugby started. He was fond of Francois Pienaar who captained the Springboks, but as proud of all the other players that led us to be not only a victorious team but a victorious nation. For years to follow the President would be very supportive of rugby until he got criticized for supporting it too much and not paying enough attention to other sports. There was always a juggling act to maintain. As much as he had to nurture the rugby players in the beginning he then had to learn to create a healthy distance.

Later, in 1998, the former President of the South African Rugby Union, Dr Louis Luyt, took President Mandela to court to contest a Commission of Inquiry that the President had established into the affairs of South African rugby. Luyt contested the President's constitutional right to appoint such a body to investigate rugby for alleged racism and nepotism, the SA Rugby Union being an independent private body. Luyt was described in the *Sunday Times* of 16 August 1998 as 'the nearest thing to a rugby war lord and the man fans loved to hate'. The now late Steve Tshwete was the Minister of Sport and Recreation at the time and he was concerned about the President's insistence to defend himself in court. The President's lawyers and advisors offered to represent him but he refused.

Judge William de Villiers was presiding over the case and on 19 March 1998, when the President walked into court, he walked to the applicant's lawyers first and shook hands with each and every one of them, including Dr Luyt. He then greeted his own team and took his seat. I was angry on the first day at him and thought that if these people had the audacity to question the President, why should he give them any attention or even be friendly with them? When I raised the incident with the President during tea time he taught me a lesson I would never forget: 'Remember, the way you approach a person will determine how that person reacts to you.' If you start off by disarming your enemy the battle is halfway won. The prose-cutors were indeed caught off guard by this gesture but they quickly recovered when they launched their attack. The other thing he said was never to allow your enemy to determine the grounds for battle. If they wanted the courtroom to be the battlefield, we had to neu-tralize them by showing them that it was not a personal matter, but by being friendly we have moved the battle to a psychological advan-tage. I heard and believed what he had said but to me it was very personal and ugly.

They eventually called him to the stand and he insisted on stand-ing while being questioned, regardless of the Judge inviting him to sit down. The advocate would ask him questions in different ways and then the President would answer by saying, 'My Lord, I believe Mr Maritz has already asked that question and I responded.' The Judge would ask the prosecutor to continue and again the President would respond by saying he had already answered the question and that he felt his intelligence was being undermined if the prosecutor put the same question three times in a row in a different manner. It was tense in the courtroom as the President was getting angry. The trained lawyer within the President bloomed. He was shining in court even though I felt they were being unreasonable.

During lunch we would let his food be brought from Mahlamba

Ndlopfu and he would sit quietly in a chamber eating. He was thinking and reflecting and strategizing for the next session. In the afternoon he was back on the stand. I had to pinch myself several times to keep quiet as I was disgusted by Luyt's lawyers. On more than one occasion I wanted to offer my remarks too. I gasped a few times at the way they tried to ridicule the President. How times had changed! Dr Luyt was a pure Afrikaner. Now I was siding with the President. Not because I worked for him but because I believed in what he stood for and his right as President to ask for this inquiry to be established. After proceedings had closed I made no secret of my feelings and told the President. He was calm and collected as ever, tired but not emotionally affected by proceedings like I was.

The government and therefore President Mandela lost the case but then appealed. The outcome was overturned much later by the Appeals Court but by that time the Commission of Inquiry had lost its relevance and never resumed its work.

While still recovering from the bruises of our defeat in court, we were preparing for the state visit of President Jacques Chirac of France to South Africa. A massive state banquet was being planned in Johannesburg. The President called me and told me to ensure through our Protocol department that Dr Luyt as well as his legal team be invited to the banquet. I agreed but when I put down the phone I thought: Over my dead body. I will deliberately just forget about it. Why would we invite people who belittled the President the way they did? He had not an ounce of bitterness in him towards white people despite apartheid, yet they wanted to so badly prove him wrong, not in private but in public. How could I be party to inviting them to enjoy a banquet which clearly every person in South Africa wanted to attend? So I neglected my task and I didn't tell the Protocol section about the President's request. The next day he specifically called me to ask: 'Did you invite Dr Luyt and his legal team?' And I said, 'No Khulu, not yet.' I also didn't reveal my plan to conveniently, deliberately forget about it. But the next day and the day after he reminded me again. And I realized he was not going to forget and that if he looked for them at the dinner, which he then did, I was going to be in an enormous amount of trouble if we hadn't invited them. He wanted to greet them and I was shocked. Despite all that had happened, he was his charming self and greeted them like old friends. My ego's most expensive lesson: that is how you deal with the enemy.

5

Travelling with a President

In 1996 the President asked me to accompany him again, this time on his state visit to France. I was excited having the opportunity to visit France, obviously, because of my ancestral history. The only difference this time was that I was the only secretary to accompany him and it was therefore my first fully fledged working state visit. In Paris a lady visited him and I was suspicious about her presence. She arrived at the guest house with our Ambassador to France, Barbara Masekela. Barbara escorted her straight to the President's suite in the guest house. The President's suite had a dining room, its own lounge and ample space befitting for a President. But Barbara soon left, without the visitor, and the door to the President's suite was closed. I knew that was never allowed – that a door be closed when he was alone with a female. I rushed up to Parks Mankahlana, the Presidential spokesperson, and with panic in my voice announced that the door was closed and the lady was still inside. Parks told me it was Mrs Graça Machel, the widow of the late President Samora Machel from Mozambique. What crossed my mind first was: Oh hell, I don't know all this history, and then: Well, they've closed the door and I may be in trouble about it.

It was one of the very few occasions that Parks was irritated with me and told me 'leave it'. So I did.

Before we left for a public reception, the President called me and formally introduced me to Mrs Machel. And he said something I remembered and tried to adhere to for years to follow: 'This is Aunt Graça Machel. She is my friend. We are going to this event now and I want you to stay with her at all times. You are not allowed to lose sight of her at any time and I need you to take care of her.' That made me nervous because I didn't know how I was supposed to look after both of them at this event. Somehow I managed.

After we returned to South Africa it was leaked to the media that Mrs Machel and the President were in a relationship. I was shocked at first when I saw it in the Sunday papers, fearing that someone might think that I leaked it to the media, but Parks later told me it was deliberately leaked.

On Wednesday, 12 February 1997 a debate followed in Parliament after the President's State of the Nation address a few days before. The debate was about racism and minority groups accusing the government of the aforementioned. The President said during his debate:

> May I challenge each and every one of those honourable members to come out with me now, not to fight [laughter] but to show them evidence which will disprove all their propaganda. However before I refer to that, I was asked the same question that has been raised by my friend here, F. W. de Klerk: 'Why are you applying racism in reverse and letting our people down, punishing the Afrikaners?'
>
> I said, 'Very well. Can you give me some statistics? How many Afrikaners have been dismissed? When? Who replaced them?' He said: 'I do not have the facts with me.' I said: 'I am very surprised that a professor should put a question like that to the President of the country without facts.' I said I would give him time and asked how long he needed before he could supply me with that evidence. That was the last time I saw him [laughter].
>
> I want to say that whilst we are empowering those who have been discriminated against, we are acting sensitively to the people who were there before we took over. Just outside this Chamber is Superintendent Riaan Smuts, who comes from the apartheid regime. I have retained him. I have two white secretaries from the old regime, typical *boeremeisies* [laughter]. They are Elize Wessels from Kakamas and Zelda la Grange from George. Those honourable members can go through my staff.

I laughed when I heard of this. Elize was never from Kakamas and well, I've never been from George, although for years later Madiba still believed I was from George. My grandparents and father were from that region and because I told him that we often go there he accepted that I was from George, which is a well-known sizeable town in that area. It worked for him so I left it at that. Years later Mrs Machel corrected him one day and then the story disappeared. He appeared disappointed in his own story.

After this debate I was approached by a journalist from an Afrikaans women's magazine in South Africa called *Rooi Rose* (Red Roses). They wanted to do a feature about a white female bodyguard and wanted to include me as one of the white ladies around the President. At first I said no, but it came to the President's attention that I had been asked and did not want to participate, and he called me into his office and instructed me to do it. He told me he wanted me to participate when asked. I was part of his Government of National Unity, and he would not succeed if he preached to the world something he was not operating in his close environment. By now I understood what the President wanted with me. It was becoming more than a job for me. I was becoming dependent emotionally on him, while he afforded me the opportunities of a lifetime. I was not skilled for everything he asked me to do, but he wanted to ensure that a white, young Afrikaner, who epitomized the community, remained close to him.

I looked forward to every opportunity to spend time with the President. He was kind and always interested about my well-being. That made me even more committed to support his efforts and I made an effort to ensure that I was diligent in every possible way. But the fact that he would contact me directly and involve me in his affairs caused some tension in the office. I tried to remain in Cape Town as much as possible, even during the recess in Parliament, for the sake of peace, though I was promoted to acting assistant private secretary in March 1997.

My parents were intrigued by my commitment and change of heart towards the President. They sensed that I adored my new boss and when I spoke of him it was with fondness. My dad appeared sceptical but my mother embraced and encouraged the loyalty I was expressing. I didn't discuss work much at home but they saw that I was completely focused and dedicated to my job. They hardly ever saw me and when they did, I slept most of the time. Whenever I wasn't at work, or with the President, I slept. I no longer went out with friends and I alienated myself from the social scene, for reasons both intentional and unintentional. I wanted to avoid being constantly quizzed about my job. Having very little free time I wanted to isolate myself in that short space of time to digest whatever was happening at work, to internalize and process and plan, but also to provide myself with the space to accommodate the changes that were happening within me. When I now look back over those nineteen years the days are all faded into one large chunk of life. It was at such a pace that I find it difficult to remember individual or isolated incidents. There was little time to ever digest and even though I was proud, grateful and totally committed, my work absorbed my entire life.

I was embracing the new South Africa through serving the President. I was changing from within and in general felt more tolerant and respectful towards people despite the differences of the colour of our skin, our cultural or political beliefs and the texture of our hair. It was something my friends and some family found difficult to comprehend because they had not been exposed to the same diversities that I had been exposed to. We were not accustomed to interracial relationships in South Africa, whether platonic, romantic or professional of nature. We still operated and lived separated in our clusters of comfort. It was starting to be problematic having conversations with friends and family as I was growing to accept and embrace the diversity of people. I often walked away from conversations with friends thinking that some of the black and brown people I worked with were much more intelligent than most people we as white friends knew, yet some of my friends maintained their position of superiority over anyone who was not white. I had grown intolerant of people who didn't open themselves for change, but at the same time I realized I was privileged because of my closeness to the President and exposure to non-racialism.

People often ask me: 'Did you keep notes of your experiences?' And I think to myself: With what time and energy was I suppose to do that? They say: 'You must have been to the most spectacular places', and I think: Can't remember. Then they say: 'You don't have kids and aren't married', and to this day I calmly smile and respond appropriately but think: Where and when could you imagine that could have happened in the last nineteen years? Your being becomes consumed by the job and you wake up worrying and stressing about what lies ahead, not contemplating anything else that would resemble 'normality.'

It was around this time that my relationship with the President took a step forward. Even though I was in Cape Town most of the time, I knew that he was negotiating with Laurent Kabila and the incumbent President of what was then known as Zaire, now known as the Democratic Republic of the Congo. In addition to attending to the duties of a President that included dealing with domestic affairs, keeping opposition politicians at bay, debating changes of legislation and so on, the President would fly off to Zaire in the morning, be back at night and the next day have an incoming state visit to attend to. He did his duties without ever cancelling or failing his obligations, yet he was determined too that it was not only South Africa that had to benefit from our democracy. Africa had to succeed as a continent too and he was devoted to bringing about a regeneration of the continent at the same time.

The DRC is a country rich in resources on the west coast of Africa. But the country and its people were impoverished as a result of greed – that of the ruler and dictator for more than twenty years, President Mobutu Sese Seko – and an ongoing civil war in the region. The President's intention was to get Laurent Kabila and Mobutu to meet on neutral ground and for them to start negotiations to enable Mobutu to step down in a dignified manner and hand over power to Kabila to effectively run the country on new terms to benefit its people, hoping that a free, fair and democratic election would follow. Kabila was threatening to overthrow the government and take over by violent means, and to ensure stability in the region it was in the best interest of all concerned that a peaceful transition be negotiated. President Mobutu, who was sixty-six at the time and suffering from prostate cancer, said he would never bow to Kabila, but international pressure was increasing.

To prepare for this meeting a South African navy ship, the SAS *Outeniqua*, was sent to anchor in international waters off the coast of Zaire to provide that neutral ground for the affected parties to meet. For days the media was dominated by reports that Mobutu refused to meet Kabila on the ship. Once they had both agreed to meet, the President flew off to Pointe Noire in Zaire with the Presidential plane, the Falcon 900, to attend and facilitate the meeting. He was scheduled to return late the same night.

My duties at that stage included the tasking of the Presidential plane: to provide airforce staff with details of departure and arrival times, passengers on board, food to be consumed during return flights and return times. Meticulous detail. In turn, they would provide me with flight times and from there an arrival time at each side could be determined and the programme for the day could be negotiated. The President specifically didn't take a secretary with him on that particular trip due to the sensitivities of the talks and the fact that there were only men on board the SAS *Outeniqua*. He probably also had a premonition that things would not go according to plan. They arrived in Pointe Noire and were taken by helicopter to the vessel. And there he started preparing himself for the meeting.

I was usually in constant contact with the pilots of the plane so as to establish what time they departed and to enable me then to provide an expected arrival time back in South Africa to all parties concerned.

On that night it didn't happen. No one contacted me and I contacted our pilots to enquire about their plans. They informed me that they were still waiting for word from the President but that it was already 9 p.m. and they didn't have hope of him returning that night. Then luckily the President called me and told me that neither Kabila nor Mobutu had arrived for the negotiations, but he'd sent word to them through our embassy that he was waiting. The President had a way of instructing his peers to do things in which they felt obliged to adhere to. And he was waiting for the two to respond. He told me that he was going to spend the night on the vessel and wait for them to arrive the following day, but if they didn't arrive the next day he was going to return. I remember asking him whether I should not help to call them from this side and he laughed but said it wasn't necessary.

He then asked me to inform Mrs Machel, which I did. I called the Director General of our office, Prof. Gerwel, every time I received an update, and then also the Minister of Foreign Affairs and the Minister of the Defence Force. To me, they all had to be informed that our President was stuck out on one of the navy's ships on the open seas. It was just common sense. I had no training in dealing with matters of this gravity but did what I thought would be expected of me. The President also asked me to call him back and give Mrs Machel's response. I called back and said that she sends all her love and hopes that he is OK and sleeps well. When I called to the only satellite phone in the vessel, a young man answered and I had to try to convince him why it was necessary for this Afrikaans woman to speak to the President. They found it suspicious.

The pilots were accommodated in either a hotel or they slept in the plane, I don't know, but they were informed that there was no flight back that night. The next morning I called again. This time to inform the President that the plane crew didn't take personal items to stay overnight and they had to return to South Africa to go and regroup or to send up a relief crew. They were also working against time as aviation regulations didn't make provision for them to be on standby for that long and soon they would not be allowed to fly, and there would be no relief crew to return the President home.

I called again, and again the young man answered the phone and we started being acquainted. I then asked him to call the President, which he did, and the President came down the stairs to take the call. 'Yes darling?' he responded. By then I had started calling the President 'Khulu', the abbreviated version of the Xhosa word for Grandpa. It was only in formal situations where protocol was required where we would call him Mr President. Everyone else called him either Madiba, or 'Tata' (Father) or President Mandela. I had asked Parks for a word that would help me be at ease with him a bit more and he suggested 'Khulu'.

I explained the situation but then said something stupid, again. 'Can we send you some toiletries and clothes at least?' His response was, 'That would be very thoughtful of you but also send me newspapers.' Always newspapers. He used to read all five daily newspapers in his region every day, including those in Afrikaans. He often said that the Afrikaans papers reported in a much more accurate way than the English papers and I guess he meant it is because Afrikaans is such a descriptive and expressive language.

We sent his toiletries and newspapers back with the plane that returned almost immediately after it dropped off its crew, refuelled, and took on fresh crew and food for the return flight. The fresh crew knew somehow that it may still be a day or two before they returned so they took their own personal items too.

The President never carried telephone numbers with him, but by now he knew my number by heart from constantly calling me (which is also why the cellphone company Vodacom always allocated me some simple numbers to make it easy for the President to remember the number whenever I had to change it). So while he was on the ship he kept calling me to call people, ask questions and then to call him back with responses. Two days later Mobutu arrived. It appeared that he and Kabila were willing to negotiate a peaceful settlement, but a fortnight later the Zairean army informed Mobutu that they could no longer protect him. He fled the country and Kabila declared himself head of state and suspended the country's constitution.

Upon his return to Cape Town, the President made a point of calling me into his office to commend me for the support while he was on the SAS *Outeniqua*. I felt proud of keeping things going during that time, of course with his guidance. Though I was puzzled he could think it would have been any different. It was thoughtful of him though. It was the moment, perhaps, that it was clear that he relied on me, and clear that I would always be there.

One day Mary sent me to fetch dry cleaning for her. I'm not the type of person who minds doing anything for anyone as long as it remains within the law. It is probably as a result of my Calvinistic upbringing: we serve, we obey, and we are humble to anyone in a more senior position than us. We basically do what we get told.

I was on my way out of the office when the President was on his way in, and our paths crossed. By now we had established a good working relationship and we were comfortable with one another. He asked me where I was heading and I told him that I was running an errand for Mary. He was furious. 'How can you do that?' I responded that I didn't mind at all. He insisted that it wasn't proper and I ended up begging him to let it go, like one would do with your father to save a sibling from being disciplined, and realized that I shouldn't have told him. I was really surprised that this angered him. The President liked strong women but Mary was perhaps too strong. He never liked people telling him what to do. I discovered he wanted to be given input but in a consultative manner rather than being prescribed, which one can understand of a person that had been imprisoned for twenty-seven years, following the authorities' schedule of when to eat, sleep, exercise and put the lights out – it was his way of winning back the little freedom he had, by at least feeling in control of his own life.

He called me to his house shortly after this and by now I was driving to Houghton myself – as long as I didn't have to go anywhere else in Johannesburg, I was fine to drive between Pretoria and Houghton, not being familiar with Johannesburg and its surroundings. This time when I arrived, he handed me some letters to prepare for him but then asked me to sit in his lounge and told me one of the most valuable things ever: 'There is no room for cowards here. If you are going to be a coward you are not going to last here for very long. I cannot always defend you so you need to defend yourself by doing what is right.' It was only when I drove home that I realized he was referring to the incident in the office that week and that he expected me not to simply take instructions but to question them. These words will remain with me for the rest of my life, and in later years, when he was indeed no longer able to defend me, they gave me strength in whatever battles I was facing.

And so on the President's insistence I had to be considered too when it came to international travel. Since the secretaries took turns to accompany him I now had to be added for consideration. Soon I was tasked to accompany him to India and Bangladesh, and then to England in the summer of 1997.

The President went to Oxford and I was overwhelmed by the beauty of the town and the real English countryside. Prince Charles attended the event at Jesus College at Oxford. This was after his divorce from Princess Diana had been announced and we were all a bit wary. The President however was his charming self and despite all the bad press about the Royals he was extremely courteous and respectful towards Prince Charles. The President didn't judge people.

Earlier that year Princess Diana paid a visit to Angola and South Africa. The President was hugely impressed by her gesture of visiting HIV/AIDS-infected patients in Angola and sitting on their beds while conversing with them. She was helping to destroy the stigma attached to people suffering from AIDS and he said, 'For a Princess to sit on AIDS patients' beds goes to show that people have nothing to fear but that we have to care for people with AIDS.' On the day that Princess Diana visited him at Genadendal, the official residence in Cape Town, the President arrived in his lounge with his slippers on. He had forgotten to put on his shoes and humbly apologized to Princess Diana once the entire room realized he had asked for his shoes to be brought from his room. The Princess wasn't fazed at all.

The President had no trouble laughing at himself and sharing such small embarrassing moments with others.

I was increasingly struggling to marry my past and the present. I was a daughter of apartheid, yet I was supporting and serving the same man my Afrikaner compatriots warned me against. I was guided and taught so much by Parks Mankahlana, the Presidential spokesperson, and Tony Trew, the director of communications in our office, and one day I had the courage to go and tell them that I needed to speak to someone to try and come to peace with myself about the way we lived when I grew up under apartheid laws, and the fact that I was so ignorant. They suggested I go and speak to the Reverend Beyers Naudé. I also met Ronnie Kasrils, who served in President Mandela's Cabinet and who had been an early leader in MK, the group that was responsible for the Church Street bombing in 1983, when we couldn't trace my father for some hours. I had these struggles within myself, not knowing what was right and wrong. Rev. Naudé started his career as a Dutch Reformed priest but later left the church when he spoke out against apartheid and was put under house arrest for several years as a result. Yet he had no bitterness. I knew a bit about him but it was limited to that he was seen as a 'sell-out' by many white people. Parks and Tony arranged for me to have tea with 'Oom Bey' (Uncle Bey) as he was fondly known.

I drove nervously on my own to Johannesburg to go and see him. I was met by his wife upon arrival and joined him in his sitting room. It felt similar to being received by my own grandparents – with love and hospitality, even though the Naudés had never met me and didn't know much about me. I told him my story and we conversed for about two hours about life in general and religion, and he emphasized to me that I should not put so much pressure on myself by wanting to take responsibility for everyone around me and what apartheid did, and that I should come to peace with the fact that this journey is probably part of my own awakening. We prayed before I left and I felt emotional. I was so grateful to God for the enormous opportunities in my life and all my blessings, yet it was the same God in my eyes that allowed apartheid to happen and Nelson Mandela to be locked up in a prison cell for twenty-seven years. My journey of discovery included questions about the role of organized religion, coming to the conclusion that my relationship with God is a personal issue for which only I can account within myself and to Him one day. Indeed, this journey has led me to some strange beliefs and I would argue with my mother about the creation of institutions by man but then claimed as if God created these.

Sometimes Mrs Machel accompanied us on visits abroad and sometimes she simply was too busy with her own work. By now she was becoming a prominent part of the President's life and the President often boasted about the important work she was doing. She would often attend official functions but also spend time with him in private. I knew it made the President happy when she was around so I was fiercely protective over their private space and moments too.

Mrs Machel and I had a cautious relationship at first. The President had many duties to fulfil and targets he wanted to achieve, and in addition the world wanted him to be everywhere at the same time. His objectives were mainly focused on reconciliation and education but also bringing about stability in South Africa in a unified manner to ensure a favourable climate for the country to grow economically. I was often caught in the middle of having to ensure that he was satisfied with the pace at which he was working but then also setting enough time aside to be a husband.

I had to work many years to establish a solid working relationship with Mrs Machel. I didn't expect her to like me. It was my government and my people that brought down the plane in which her husband, Samora Machel, was killed in 1986. In later years, when we became much closer, I would often ask her and her children to recite the details around the events of his death. It was very hurtful but by arguing the events I think she also perhaps saw that I had a certain understanding for their pain and loss, something they

71

appreciated. (Following Madiba's passing I also had the opportunity to see Samora Jnr's two boys, Samora III and Malick, for the first time in about ten years, and the resemblance to their grandfather was striking.)

The Machels are warm, hospitable, caring people and despite challenges we faced in the beginning we are close now. I have always been close to Mrs Machel's children. They say life takes a little time and a lot of relationship and indeed it took Mrs Machel and I a long time to build the relationship we have today, but we did with effort from both sides and I cannot imagine my life without her influence and the stability she brings about in my small world. I also admit that any two people work on a relationship and I had as much blame to take for the more difficult times as I wanted to give her.

At first I thought Mrs Machel was just asserting her position as wife in the President's life and it felt as if her expectations of us were too high. But then one noticed how she made the President smile. She awakened his senses again. She allowed him to live. She made him dance and see the beauty in flowers, appreciate good music and see the wonder in every sunset and every sunrise. On many of our travels she insisted that we all watch the sunset together, something he missed for so many years, being locked in a cell before sunset. She brought about a different appreciation of life for him again and made him love life more than I thought he was capable of. If you truly love someone, like I loved Nelson Mandela, you want what is best for him and you want him to be happy. And when he was with her and he lived again, despite the confines of their schedules and the pressure of their work, he was truly happy. Slowly I came to the realization that she was not there to assert her space; she was there to make him happy and we had an even better boss because of her. There was no single bigger gift to Nelson Mandela's life than what Graça Machel brought about with her presence.

This is in stark contrast to the presence of Winnie Mandela in my life – I didn't meet her until much later and never saw her during Madiba's Presidency. She seemed to have little presence in the President's life after they separated. He never spoke about her and I didn't ask. No one tells you but you assume it's not something you ever raise. As time passed he spoke more openly in confidence about these events in his life. However, sometimes he seemed sad and I often wondered about the silent pain he was going through.

When I came to the President's house I often found him sitting alone at the breakfast or dinner table. He usually had lunch at his official residences whether in Cape Town or Pretoria. One couldn't help but feel the loneliness whenever you entered his Houghton home while he was having a meal by himself. It was only when Mrs Machel became part of his life that this changed. It was as if light entered the sombre household, the curtains were opened and the entire house was filled with life.

When one sat down with him, he started telling his stories. Stories about prison and the years that he grew up in the Transkei. Meals were times for him to 'reflect' and relax. I loved listening to his story-telling as I've always loved my own imagination and it was easy for me to picture what he was telling me and virtually be transported to the scene he was describing. He often told me about Justice, the boy he grew up with and who was his best friend. Justice was more than a friend, he was the 'brother' Madiba never had. They ran away together when they both suddenly found out they were being set up for arranged marriages by the Regent who brought Madiba up, like people usually do in the countryside and in accordance to their tradition at the time. Madiba and Justice fled the Transkei to Johannesburg where his life was shaped into politics. He spoke fondly of Justice but sadly Justice passed away while Madiba was still imprisoned. As a result of too much drinking, Madiba said.

I often thought about Justice. If there is one person I wished to be alive to be part of our lives it was Justice. I wanted him to know what happened to his friend and I wanted him to know what one could become despite their humble beginnings. I wanted to turn back time and warn him to stop drinking, to tell him that he would be reunited with his friend some day, and I wanted him to witness and share in the life of his best friend. I knew he would have been invited to the Inauguration if he was alive at the time and

I imagined his joy and excitement over his best friend taking the oath. I think, however, once Madiba was imprisoned Justice perhaps gave up hope of ever breaking the cycle of poverty in his family and resorted to drinking.

His wistful remembrances of his boyhood in Qunu and his adolescence in Mqekezweni with Justice seemed to take up a lot of Madiba's quiet time. It was like he travelled there – to those old, simple days – to get peace, to get a sense of himself. Over and over again, I would find him remembering his childhood. Those experiences seemed not only to shape him as a man and define his values, I think his memories of his childhood became an escape – it was also a survival mechanism he probably used in prison. Those experiences – of herding cattle, of stick fighting, of roaming the hills of the Eastern Cape, listening to village elders, of stealing out of beehives and finding gooseberries – became like movies in his head that he could access when the realities of prison or being President just got too much. He replayed those images, those pastoral scenes, in his head and retold the stories so often that many of us who heard his whispered remembrances can recite them word for word. But those are not my stories, they are his.

When Madiba left prison, everyone had grown up and grown away. It seemed it was difficult for him to open up emotionally. Prison had taught him how to hide his feelings. I saw him try with his grandchildren but he was a reserved disciplinarian, which often did not go down well with the young ones. He yearned for his children while imprisoned and he wanted to have a part of such pleasures. But it wasn't easy.

I would often go to the President's house in Johannesburg as he hardly ever slept at the official residence in Pretoria, Mahlamba Ndlopfu. Four of his grandchildren were living with him at the time. They were the four sons of Makgatho, the President's only living son at the time from his marriage to his first wife, Evelyn. Mandla, the eldest grandchild, was in the last years of high school; Ndaba, the second born, was a teenager and then the two younger boys, Mbuso and Andile, were still small toddlers. They were adorable and loving.

Their father lived somewhere in Soweto but the President enjoyed having them around. They were effectively raised by the house-keeper, Xoliswa – who they referred to as Mama – and then Rochelle, the President's niece, until she left. At the time they provided liveli-ness to the house in Houghton and some sense of family.

In the early years I often found myself alone, other staff being in Pretoria, in the President's office in Cape Town. I was handling the President's personal office switchboard when I was called by recep-tion one day at the entrance of the building. The police on duty at the entrance informed me that I had visitors who wanted access to the President's office. This warranted me to get up and go to reception myself as no one was allowed access to the President's office. Upon arriving I was introduced to someone from NI (National Intelligence, even though I didn't make the connection immediately). I found it strange that two men randomly showed up at reception and told me that they needed to 'sweep' the President's office. I had no idea what they were referring to and told them, completely innocently, that we had cleaners in the office who swept the office daily, thank you very much.

I remained speechless in reception until the police working at the entrance told me that they were National Intelligence officers and that they used the term 'sweep' to mean looking for listening devices that could have been planted in the office by other parties. I felt extremely embarrassed and allowed them access. For years to come security would tease me over this. I took it in my stride. It was all part of this new world opening up to me, totally foreign to my past.

That summer I was also asked to accompany the President on a two-day rest to Bali, followed by a state visit to Indonesia and Thai-land on which Mrs Machel accompanied us. It was now generally accepted that even though I was still the senior ministerial typist, I would accompany the Presidential party on visits abroad and perform the duties of secretary. In those years I was too scared to enjoy anything and I didn't enjoy the waters of the swimming pool or the sea. I was determined to stay in my room for whenever the

President may call on me. And he did. He got used to the fact that I was always there and I started sleeping when he did, eating when he did and following his routine to ensure that I was always available in my room whenever he called.

Part of our duties included making sure that he got served food at the right time, his clothes were unpacked and packed whenever Mrs Machel was not around, and things around him were the way he preferred them to be. In his programme we also had to find time for him to have massages every second day, and press clippings had to be sent from South Africa every day in the absence of news- papers. I made sure those arrived before breakfast and took every effort to ensure that things were exactly the way he wanted them. No matter which time zone we were in, the poor staff at the office had to work shifts to prepare news clippings and send them in time. Even after computers and the internet dominated our lives, he insisted that the clippings be exactly that – newspapers cut out, photocopied and faxed to us no matter where we were. I tried my best to introduce alternatives, also to lighten the burden on the staff back in South Africa, but he wouldn't have anything but the originals as they appeared in the particular font in the newspapers.

The President was always very uncomfortable if left alone with massage therapists. Either security or I had to be in the room with him at all times when these therapists were around. It was extremely frustrating to me as I am not a person that can sit still for an hour. It was way before we had BlackBerries or smart phones and there was literally nothing to do to pass the time. On several occasions I tried to get security to take my place but he would then usually call me back when he noticed I wasn't there or called upon me and I didn't answer. I did it probably more than a hundred times and he called me back more than a hundred times over the years, until I explained to him one day that I really cannot sit still for that long and he accepted the fact that one of his security people would be with him, which also made a little more sense practically. An hour to me meant falling behind on work or things to be arranged. In any event I thought, how was I ever going to be of any use in an emergency?

It was better for a bodyguard to be there from a security point of view. It also gave me at least an hour to do some other things, email the office, go through programmes or return phone calls.

The President had this enormous ability to break things down to the simplest method of reason and argument. He always told us that Oliver Tambo, another liberation struggle hero and former President of the ANC, never wanted to have massages and he was convinced that if Oliver had done, he would still be alive. What he meant was that he thought that Uncle Oliver, who died of a stroke, would have dealt better with the stress and pressure if he had learned to relax by ensuring that he took care of his physical well-being through massage or physiotherapy. The President had a unique way of relating stories and he would use the exact same words and phrases whenever he repeated a story. They were precious. And the conviction with which he conveyed this started worrying me so much that I also later imagined that it was necessary for me to have massages when I became too stressed.

From Bali we went to Indonesia, to the capital Jakarta on a state visit. I didn't see much of Jakarta and all we experienced was heat and humidity, but while he was there the President had a special meeting. It was done secretly. He only agreed to pay a state visit to Indonesia if he would be offered the opportunity to meet with Xanama Gusmão. The Indonesians delayed, probably thinking that the President wouldn't insist, but he did. One night Gusmão, the leader of the resistance movement of East Timor, was snuck in via the emergency staircase of the Presidential guest house. Gusmão was considered the equivalent of the political prisoner Madiba represented while imprisoned. His hands were cuffed. I found the visit exciting and wondered how Madiba dealt with it. After all it was only seven years before that he had been that very same prisoner.

Gusmão looked well under the circumstances and was friendly. He was alone with the President and Prof. Gerwel and others for a while before he was taken back to prison. It was agreed that he would be allowed to visit South Africa a few weeks later where he would feel free to talk. President Suharto agreed and a few weeks later we received him in South Africa. It was less exciting as he now no longer had handcuffs or seemed like a prisoner in normal clothes. Years later he visited the retired Madiba in Johannesburg to thank him for the negotiations and only then was I reminded about events of that night. He was by then freed and the legitimate President of an independent East Timor. It is believed that Madiba's intervention put Suharto under pressure to release Gusmão.

Wherever there was conflict around the world, people would ask for the President's intervention to negotiate a peaceful settlement. He often declined to intervene in the domestic affairs of other countries because he said we did not have enough knowledge about the intricacies of the problems they faced. Yet the political will to help where it was possible or where he thought we had a chance to succeed made him do otherwise.

From Indonesia we went to Bangkok. We stayed in a lavish hotel and I came to the realization that I was becoming an expert on hotels worldwide. However, even though I could recite their room service menus I didn't see much of any cities. My experiences were limited to the extent of the President's sightseeing experiences. We were not there on holiday but to work. The President only asked to do sightseeing on a few occasions but usually limited it to the main tourist attractions and if there was anything he had read about before that could be of interest to him. Generally there was no time for sightseeing as his schedule was packed with meetings and then time blocked off for much needed rest. He was seventy-nine years of age and he needed rest at any given opportunity.

Despite spending every waking hour helping to make the President's day faultless, I was unfortunately not a paragon of diplomacy. In Thailand, we were sitting at an official lunch hosted by Prime Minister Chuan Leekpai and by now advance protocol teams doing planning knew that the President liked to have eye contact with his secretaries at the table so that when he called for them or needed them, he could just look at us and we would know. Seats were therefore arranged accordingly. I could see his face but it luckily wasn't too close for him to witness what happened next.

I had a long-sleeved blouse on and the sleeves were wide. The first course was served and breadrolls were served on our side plates. I reached out for the butter on the table in front of me and I didn't realize that my sleeve caught the breadroll on my plate, and as I picked up the container of butter to bring it closer to my plate the breadroll touched my elbow, where it had now rolled down my sleeve. Not realizing what had happened I reacted with shock and thought something had crawled into my sleeve. I was already nervous from not knowing what I was eating and this didn't help. I quickly jerked my arm back to get whatever was crawling up my sleeve out, and the breadroll flew over the table to the middle, where it landed. Silence followed in my immediate surroundings. Luckily the Thai people are extremely friendly and hospitable. They laughed it off and the gentleman next to me said it meant good luck. My first thought was that it seemed everything in this country meant good luck no matter how unfortunate it appeared to us foreigners. I took his best wishes and quietly reached for another breadroll, swallowing my own embarrassment with each piece of bread.

The President was travelling non-stop and working relentlessly. When he was at home, he would take time to address union organizations like the National Union of Mineworkers, the National Union of Metal Workers of South Africa and the National Education, Health and Allied Workers' Union. He was always balancing, always ensuring that he was not seen to discriminate in any way and applying his fair mind to every situation possible. He was driven to lay the foundation for a prosperous future for South Africa but back in July 1996 he announced publicly that he would only serve as President for one term of five years. He honestly believed that younger people could achieve more than him, and by announcing that he would only serve one term he had hoped that other heads of state would follow suit and not be tempted to become hungry for power and serve for endless terms, becoming dictators.

At every public event he called upon the police on duty afterwards to greet them, or if there was a choir that performed he wanted to shake hands with each and every one of its members. He would also always spot children in a crowd and call upon them to come to the front so he could greet them. In the beginning I thought it was just something he occasionally felt up to, but then when I realized that he did so without fail at every event, I would start making plans for this to happen at all events once I got there. It was his way of acknowledging the small people.

However, he could become harsh with people who he didn't feel were loyal to him. He would give, give and give and then if there was the slightest indication that he felt someone was not behind him 120 per cent then he would abruptly cut ties. He inspired loyalty but then he expected you to be faithful. This happened with Mary Mxadana. The working relationship between Mary and the President was increasingly tense. Mary was friendly with the President's ex-wife, Winnie Madikizela Mandela, and that unsettled him. He asked for her to be transferred to a diplomatic position in the Department of Foreign Affairs. Mary left gracefully. Very sadly a few years later she passed away after a hernia operation. I was really sad when I saw her in hospital and I will always be grateful for the role she played in my life.

The President would spend his Christmas holiday with his grandsons in Qunu, the village where he grew up. It is in the Province of the Eastern Cape of South Africa and about 30 km south-west of a town called Mthatha in what was formerly known as the Transkei. By then, his niece Rochelle, who had looked after him, had left the house to further her studies in America, and the President relied on me to take care of some issues Rochelle had done before. One of them was organizing a Christmas party on his farm in Qunu on Christmas Day for the children of the village. Well, that is what it was supposed to be.

He made a list of a few people to be called and asked them all for donations of sweets, toys and other simple Christmas treats. The first year I was involved it was 2,000 of everything. I took responsibility for orchestrating the collection of the goods and making sure that they arrived in Qunu a few days before Christmas. I realized we needed bags, so bags were bought, and I involved the children from the community, and even our security, to help pack parcels for the 2,000 children expected to come to the President's house on Christmas Day. I set up a proper production line in one of the facilities around his house and we packed parcels for days ahead of Christmas, sometimes losing encouragement when so overwhelmed by 2,000 of everything. One only knows what 2,000 constitutes when you've packed and handled 2,000 parcels. When the President told me that for many children from the region this was the only day they had a proper meal or received something for Christmas, I didn't believe him at first. But when Christmas arrived, truth was put to the President's words. Thousands of children descended on Qunu.

The majority of black people in South Africa lived and still live in severe poverty. It was going to take a very long time for economic transformation to be implemented and to affect the lives of rural communities in a beneficial way. Things have somewhat changed now but not nearly as fast as we had hoped for, and people in rural South Africa are angry and disappointed for not having benefited from democracy yet. And as the crowd descended on Qunu I realized that the people in these communities had not tasted the fruits of our newly achieved freedom. When I asked where they came from the President said that some of them started walking the previous night to be in time. When I arrived on the farm from town on Christmas Day at around 7 a.m., which I thought was a reasonable time, children had already lined up along the fence of his farm all the way up the hill – about a kilometre. I couldn't believe what I saw. We prepared to hand out parcels and the children would then be taken to the yard at the back of the house where they were fed. The very friendly Mr Bread, a bakery in Qunu, would take care of preparing food for the elders and VIPs from the region, together with Madiba's eldest grandson, Mandla.

Soon the children started streaming through the gates. The President sat outside for most of the day, greeting children as they moved along and got handed their parcels before they went to eat. Shaking hands with each and every one of them, one by one, and conversing with them briefly. Being the disciplined, organized person that the President was, he appreciated my military precision for order in the way things were handled. Children filed past in single line and got handed a bag of surprises from the helpers, after which they were guided to the lunch area. I made sure we didn't overlook anyone and they all had the opportunity to shake hands with him for the time he was seated outside.

Since many of them had never been accustomed to the belief of Father Christmas because of the remote areas in which they lived, this was their fantasy and what their entire worlds revolved around – seeing President Mandela and receiving gifts from him. When a company donated frizbees for all the parcels you would soon see thousands of frizbees flying around and people dodging them everywhere. The next time there might be balls, and balls would be heading for targets such as your head. We assume all children know what a ball or a frizbee is, until you see how children in rural South Africa live and you understand that they do not recognize something we take for granted. One year someone wanted to donate plastic play guns and we had to decline as we didn't want to promote violence with our message of goodwill. The children were not entirely sure whether they were happier about the parcel or shaking hands with the President. It was precious to see. And then the evidence of the President's comments about their only meal. The proof was there. I saw children infected with diseases without names. Underfed, deformed, mistreated, neglected. I could finally relate to what he described. Somehow when you see the innocence and gratitude in their eyes you manage to look past appearance.

Some of them had never seen white people before, and one child rubbed my arm to see whether the 'white' of my skin gives off in some way. I adored picking up the little ones, although the white of my skin sometimes scared them. It was so ironic – years earlier I had conformed to the racist approach that it was inappropriate to touch a black person because we inherently feared them. Some of the children were scared of me and the few other white bodyguards. We must have been aliens to them. On more than one occasion I had a child 'bound by my hip' for the entire day . . . probably encouraged by curiosity to see whether I returned to a different planet afterwards.

When you spend a day like Christmas in such a poverty-stricken area one is truly and honourably thankful for your own privileges, and an event like this brings a different meaning to Christmas. It was the first Christmas I celebrated without my parents, without presents and the focus on 'what I'm receiving for Christmas'; the focus changed to what can I give and do and that in itself brings so much more fulfilment and meaning to Christmas. We had lunch with Madiba following the children's party and some of his grandchildren and elders from the area visited.

The following year we realized that preparing for 2,000 children was not going to be sufficient. We increased to asking for donations for 5,000. This time around the President left everything to me. I consulted him about decisions and asked advice on certain matters but by now people knew about his initiative and it wasn't difficult to find sponsorship. Again in December we prepared a few days before Christmas but this time for 5,000. We still didn't have enough gifts and food. The following year we increased to 10,000 until we ended with 20,000. Again, packing 20,000 parcels is no joke. Yet the children of the area and some of the grandchildren participated in the preparations and somehow we managed. The last year of our private party we ended up packing for two weeks around the clock prior to Christmas. And all I repeated to encourage people helping was 'remember, for some children this is the only opportunity during the year to get a decent meal and a gift bag . . . this is the *only* gift they get for Christmas', reciting the President's exact words. Not that the children in the village were used to much more but it made the bodyguards participate in my task at hand.

In the last year, Oprah Winfrey asked to participate following our visit to Chicago and the President telling her what we did in Qunu over Christmas. I think they prepared for 25,000 children in

Qunu and she also distributed around another 25,000 to other rural schools across South Africa. But she did it properly. Children received clothes and school stationery in addition to sweets and a very nutritious meal. We underestimated the size of the crowd and how widely it was advertised that both Oprah and the President would be there and we ended up avoiding a stampede. Some mothers travelled with children from as far as the Free State, hundreds of kilometres. Buses of children were offloaded and security was insufficient. It was then decided that, after closely escaping tragedy, the Christmas party would be taken over by the Nelson Mandela Children's Fund and decentralized to regions.

At the time he initiated the annual Christmas parties in Qunu, the President then also initiated visits, close to the end of the year, to pre-primary schools in both Johannesburg and Cape Town. He loved interacting with children. Again the first year he instructed his niece to handle matters, and when she left for the USA I inherited the job. The President was teaching me valuable lessons on how to ask for donations and support for people in desperate need of resources when you yourself cannot afford to buy them something. In return for sponsors donating sweets and goods for him to hand out during his visit, they would get to spend an entire day with him while he was handing these out, as well as exposure on television and in newspapers. The plan was simple but worked like a bomb. We would then invite a media contingent to follow us on the day when we visited the crèches, and the media representatives got to spend a day with their beloved President too, while giving the sponsors the exposure that the President promised. At the end of the day the media and sponsors were invited to a lunch at our offices or a nearby hotel where the President thanked them for their support. News spread and people were eager to help in the years to follow.

On a few occasions politicians tried to hijack or interfere with his arrangements, upon which he made it clear that the initiative should not be limited to any one political party but that the parents and teachers of these children should be respected for their political views too. I always had to make sure that the selection of schools was

100 per cent representative. If we visited five schools it had to be two black, one Indian, one brown and one white school. As schools got more integrated after transformation in South Africa it became quite a challenge and we had to visit the schools in advance to make sure that we had the correct denomination of each race group covered. We also had to be careful not to visit a predominantly Xhosa school – Xhosa being the ethnic group to which the President belongs. He was extremely sensitive about matters of this nature and it became a blueprint in my mind that if we did something for one group, we had to do something for another. He never wanted to be seen to be prejudiced or accused of favouritism, and it was as if he was determined to remain the figurehead of nation-building, regardless of efforts from people to tag him to a specific group, race, religion, class, whatever.

I have no idea why I ended up carrying the responsibility of the Christmas parties or pre-primary school visits and why he didn't hand it to his Children's Fund that he had established even before I joined him. Although I benefited emotionally from taking on this task, being introduced to a new meaning of Christmas, I had more than enough work pressure and challenges to deal with. I was happy when it was decentralized to the Children's Fund.

At the same time the President initiated his schools and clinics building project. He managed to persuade business, both locally and internationally, to build schools and clinics in the most remote countryside in South Africa. More than a hundred schools were erected through this initiative and more than fifty clinics. President Mandela was never the greatest administrator but his intentions and strategy were faultless.

At first government didn't pay much attention to these new structures being erected. The process was simple. The President would speak to a particular chief, the person from the traditional leadership in a particular rural area in charge of his community. The chief would plead for a school. The President would read of excellent financial results of companies in newspapers and then task me to start looking for the CEO or managing director or owner of the company. He would then invite them to have breakfast or lunch with him. Who would say no to being invited by the President? Towards the end of the project business people teased among one another that if the President invited you for breakfast, it could be the most expensive breakfast of your life. Only on two occasions did people promise to build structures that they never fulfilled. It was impossible for government to provide services at the pace at which the public expected them to, and the President did what he could to speed up the process by involving the private sector to support these efforts, education and health care being his priorities. He always said that education is the only weapon with which one can fight poverty.

First we would arrange for the business representatives to fly with us to these rural areas to be shown where the school or clinic had to be built and to be introduced to the community leaders who had to oversee the project. We spent hours and hours travelling to remote areas. Once the project was completed, we would return with the businessmen to the area and the President would personally open the school or clinic.

In the advanced stages of the project, and by the change of government in 1999, it was discovered that many of these structures were left abandoned. Government was not providing the teachers, equipment, nurses or facilities and infrastructure to support the initiative. While one can appreciate their challenges it was a pity that there was no co-ordination in time for them to be able to provide the backup to ensure the efficient running of these institutions. The President was also sometimes to blame as he too gave in to requests from traditional leaders too easily, without any proper investigation into whether a school or clinic was really planned in the right area. In later years the Nelson Mandela Institute for Education and Rural Development partnered with the University of Fort Hare in the Eastern Cape to support some of these schools the President initiated.

Sadly the education system in South Africa, and specifically in the rural areas, tends to fail its learners. To date, this is one of the biggest challenges South Africa faces, the education of our children.

The teaching profession is one of the worst paid professions in South Africa and as a result it has stopped attracting people with a passion for the job. Teachers can simply no longer afford to support their own families and in rural areas the infrastructure fails in supporting teachers in terms of providing them with the right tools and textbooks. Because of the remoteness of the location of some of these schools they hardly receive support from the national education department and it is at the same time difficult for the department to exercise discipline.

On each visit where a rural school or clinic was built, the media was invited to accompany the President as well. The exposure for any company associated with this project on prime-time news, with the President, was worth the money they had to fork out. Many of them still continue to support some of the schools and clinics they erected originally and shared in his passion about education for our youth.

In 1998 President Bill Clinton faced the biggest challenge of his political career. The scandal over the relationship with Monica Lewinsky threatened his political career and was making world headlines. In the middle of the fallout he was scheduled to be in South Africa on a state visit. When in trouble, one cannot ask for a better friend than Nelson Mandela. The President was never going to condone what had happened, but he had a way to put things in perspective of one's humanity. You would still feel guilty, but he made you feel safe and in a gentle way persuaded you to take responsibility without feeling humiliated. Observing this over time I realized how my thinking had changed and how I assessed things I would feel very opinionated about before. President Mandela was never scared to admit his own mistakes and then almost jump at the opportunity of apologizing and then to move on. He consistently told people whenever they wanted to sing his praises that 'a saint is a sinner who keeps on trying'.

That doesn't imply that he ever justified something that was without integrity or honesty but he inherently believed that people always had the best intentions and that they stumbled occasionally, as all human beings do. What was important to him, and became clear to me, was that those who faltered, sinned or stumbled didn't feel alienated because they made mistakes. He was honest about their mistakes but assured them in a way that he acknowledged their humaneness while making it clear that honesty to admit one's mistakes was far more important to the event in forgiving yourself and moving on. President Mandela welcomed President Clinton with open arms, admitted the personal difficulties he was facing with regard to the Lewinsky saga, but reassured President Clinton that he still respected him and had faith in his ability to lead.

On 27 March 1998 a banquet was hosted in honour of President Clinton's visit to South Africa. By now the secretaries were all taking equal turns in attending events and supporting the President. I was surprised to be asked to work during the state banquet held at Vergelegen, a wine farm in the prestigious wine lands close to Cape Town. It was a rare historical event and everybody wanted to work that night. Vergelegen is a forty-five minute drive from Genadendal, the President's official residence, so to avoid traffic and save time security decided it would be better for us to take a helicopter to Vergelegen.

I was never good (and still am not) at dressing up. I am most comfortable in my favourite jeans, flip flops and a shirt or t-shirt. However, I realized for this banquet I had to really make an effort. This was, after all, the state event for what was considered the most powerful nation in the world. I had a black long dress made for the event, nothing extravagant, and decided on shoes with a bit of a heel, not too high though, as we are usually on our feet all night.

Our military helicopters were rough and soldier-like. I could always imagine us being on our way to combat whenever we were in the helicopter. The Oryx is a solid military machine, considered one of the best helicopters manufactured in the world, with space for sixteen passengers in full armour. By now I loved flying in our helicopters. I loved the sound of them and especially when the pilots manoeuvred it a bit; always being fond of a bit of adventure.

We landed at Vergelegen and the steel steps to disembark were put in place as soon as the rotorblades stopped. According to protocol, the President always enters a plane last and disembarks first. Then if Mrs Machel accompanied us or he had an official partner, that person would follow, and then whoever could manage to get to the door first. The security detail usually jumped out of the helicopter as it was low. The President disembarked and Mrs Machel followed. As the President started climbing down the stairs he started talking to me and asked me a question as he reached the ground. The question probably dealt with something about the programme or President Clinton's arrival time. He was about to turn round to make eye contact and get my response when I came flying down the stairs and landed on both my knees behind him. It turned out that my long dress got stuck over the railing of the steel steps and prevented me from stepping down further. Everyone around me started laughing, except the President and Mrs Machel. It must have been the funniest sight people ever saw. It's one thing falling, then another dressed in evening wear, but it surely is a sight when doing all of that out of a helicopter. The President was still trying to make eye contact with me on his level but found me on the ground behind him. He commanded 'Help her up, help her up' and was very concerned about my well-being. 'Did you spoil your dress?' he asked and I did a quick check, but all seemed to be OK.

People had great difficulty composing themselves. As President Clinton was also expected to arrive by helicopter, the entire area was filled with secret service agents. They were hiding in bushes everywhere and it looked like a sudden wind blew through the estate as the people in bushes started laughing at my entrance. The President was the only one that seemed troubled by my tumbling down and the rest of the people all laughed and had great difficulty to get themselves to be serious again. I composed myself and we moved to the house where we were going to await President Clinton's arrival.

President Mandela was given a seat in the house adjacent to the marquee where the banquet was to be hosted, to await the arrival of President Clinton so they would enter the banquet simultaneously. I remained outside to try and gather information about his expected arrival time to enable me to give feedback to the President. Vergelegen is a private wine farm and the house beautifully decorated in Cape Dutch style. While waiting outside I met one of South Africa's best comedians, Pieter-Dirk Uys. He was getting ready for his performance at the banquet and I was distracted from earlier events. The President loved his satirical performances and he usually didn't spare anyone in his comic interpretations of South Africa's politicians. Upon stepping back into the house where the President was waiting I didn't see a brick placed in front of a door to keep it from being blown closed by the wind and tripped over it as I entered the building. This time I didn't fall but rather found myself much faster in front of the President than expected. He just said: 'Oh no darling, rather get a chair and come and sit down.' I was very embarrassed and obviously more nervous than ever when I handed the President his speech at the podium when he was expected to speak later that night. I prayed as I walked up the stairs to the podium that another disaster wouldn't strike. It didn't and the rest of the evening was uneventful.

I was now often looked to by both the President and Mrs Machel. We were having great difficulties marrying their diaries. We had to find time for them to be together but it was not easy. Mrs Machel continued her work in Mozambique and across the world, mainly advocating for children's rights, and she was travelling a lot. I was often in trouble for not finding time for her and the President to spend together, but it was a nearly impossible task. They both worked at a pace, almost racing against time. The President would want a hundred things done in a week and when we managed to fit in everything, Mrs Machel's schedule was packed. Often the President would agree to arrangements and then the day before the entire diary would change, not because of Mrs Machel but he would also have pressing priorities or simply change his mind about something. We were running out of excuses why we had to cancel arrangements at short notice and we always feared that people might suspect health problems being the cause.

In those days, if the President had as much as a common cold South Africa's currency, the rand, would plummet at the news of any rumours about the President's health – the world fearing that South Africans would be dumped in chaos and burn the country to the ground. The President was the symbol of stability to all South Africans, black and white, and the world knew it. Using his health or 'not feeling well' as an excuse was therefore never even contemplated unless it was the absolute truth. He was almost becoming a super-being in the public's eyes. If he wanted to take a rest, public speculation about his health would start.

Early in 1998 the President was scheduled to do a fundraiser for the Nelson Mandela Children's Fund. The Children's Fund was established by him in 1995 to help children, especially orphans affected by the AIDS crisis. In addition to donating his prize money from the Nobel Peace Prize to establish the fund, he also annually donated a third of his salary towards the fund and set out on a fundraising drive for it when time allowed. On this particular occasion he was scheduled to host some top international celebrities and models and they would then embark on a trip to launch the newly refurbished Blue Train – South Africa's luxury passenger train – after which he would do a trip on the QE2. People could pay thousands of dollars to join him and Mrs Machel, proceeds that would obviously benefit the Children's Fund and so the journey was sold out.

It was also during these events when the much-disputed diamonds were given to Naomi Campbell by then President Charles Taylor of Liberia. Naomi was a supporter of the Children's Fund right from its inception and was one of the first international donors to the fund.

During the trial of Charles Taylor at the International Criminal Court that recalled events of the fundraiser, I was interested in the order of events. No one asked any of the South African security officials at the time who the bodyguards were that knocked on

Naomi's door in the Presidential guest house and handed her the 'bag of stones'. If they were South African bodyguards, they would have opened the bag before handing it to her. No one, not even a President, got to deliver a gift on official premises without the gift being opened and searched. If anyone asked security they could well have verified how many stones were inside and it would be on record whoever entered the house that night. A South African police officer is required to keep what they refer to as a pocket book. In there they write every day whatever they do and they account for every minute, precisely, for in the event of court procedures they could refer back to the pocket books. I doubt the South African police would have allowed two Liberian bodyguards unaccompanied into the Presidential guest house, and the answers are therefore somewhere on record in South Africa. We knew nothing of the gift, but Naomi said that she handed the bag of diamonds to the CEO of the Children's Fund, although he was later found not guilty of possessing uncut diamonds.

We embarked on the *QE2*. It was a lovely experience although the vessel was clearly equipped for elderly people. It was grand and old-school. People dressed up to go and have dinner every night but to me it looked like they were going to church. There were no parties for young people but rather ballroom dancing. It was sweet though to see elderly people dancing and still so in love. The President and Mrs Machel didn't go dancing though, but enjoyed being on the *QE2*. They attended only an introduction and a dinner on the ship and the rest of the time they finally had some privacy and quality time together away from the pressures on the 'mainland'.

After the *QE2* trip I fell ill, for the second time in four years. I just couldn't maintain the pace. The President was driven by many factors, one being that his retirement from public office was less than a year away and he wanted to capitalize on being in a position to fast-track the changes he had hoped for, for his Presidency. The doctors said it was a repeat of a myocarditis infection I had sustained after our state visit to Japan in 1995 and that I was just exhausted. I was put on sick leave at home for four weeks and after about a week

I got a call from the bodyguards to tell me that the President wanted to visit me at my little house in the government village, Acacia Park. I didn't think it was appropriate for a President to come to my little simple one-bedroom house, and I called him to try and persuade him that I was fine and would report back for work soon and that it wasn't necessary to visit me. He insisted and soon arrived with the most beautiful basket of flowers I have ever received.

While visiting and encouraging me to regain strength he also very innocently said, 'You know only weak people get sick.' I thought he was going to show a bit more sympathy. He had believed all his life that you are very much in control of your own body, and in the process of healing your mind had to be stronger than the medicines applied. You also had to have the determination to get better.

No matter how difficult things became, how much pressure we were under or how tired I was, seeing his face and his smile lighting up the room was a highlight every day of my life. I later couldn't help but smile whenever I saw him. When you work closely with someone you inevitably start reading the other person's emotions and moods. Yet still in the most difficult times the smile was never far from my face, sometimes just reserved to my heart.

So I continued to work at a relentless pace, though the stress and fatigue were overwhelming at times. Once Madiba read me an article that appeared in a newspaper about a study on people who carried more weight around the hips and buttocks and that it was found that they deal with stress better. The first time he read it I took the point and said: 'You see Khulu, that's why I still deal with all the stress, because my hips and my bum are big.' He laughed out loud and then read the article to me for a second time. I didn't find it funny. He was teasing but I was able to stop him.

He was always very attentive to people's weight and health. He would often ask a lady whether she was pregnant even if she had just picked up a few kilograms around the waist. Sometimes he would request a private discussion with a visitor and then lecture them on their weight. I have lost count of the number of times he would point out someone's big tummy and then tell them, 'You have to reduce.' Some people find it offensive to have their weight discussed but it is extremely embarrassing when Nelson Mandela tells you 'you have to reduce', implying you have to reduce your food intake or reduce your weight. We tried to avoid these discussions at all costs and whenever he said he wanted to have a 'private discussion' with people we would try and tell him that he shouldn't do it and it was not appropriate. He would laugh and find it very funny that we would try to spare people from having to go through that with him. And then sometimes people insisted that they have their private discussion with him because they thought he was going to reveal confidential secrets and they would insist on having the private time with him, only to leave a few minutes later feeling not so fulfilled.

On one occasion I was waiting for his arrival at a public event; when he disembarked from the car he asked whether I had been there for long waiting for him. I said, 'Yes indeed.' And his response out loud was: 'I can see because you look hungry.' I wasn't. Always concerned about my security and always concerned about whether I had eaten or not.

One time I was on a diet and I declined to eat the food that was offered at the table prepared for him but rather stuck to my salad, and he questioned me and said I wasn't eating enough. I spoke to him openly and said that I was trying to lose weight. He then said that my weight didn't matter because I moved quickly. What he meant was that even though I was overweight it didn't affect the pace at which I walked or moved. He had such a funny way with food and body weight. When you didn't eat he encouraged you to eat more, but when you took a second serving he would watch your plate with disapproval. I've always been sensitive about my weight but somehow not with him. When I complained about my weight he just said, sweetly, 'But you are dignified.'

That June the President had lunch at Mahlamba Ndlopfu with Wolfie Kodesh. The President told me that he had stayed with Mr Kodesh before he was incarcerated and I was very impressed when I learned that Mr Kodesh had actually hidden Madiba for a while in his apartment in Johannesburg in 1961. The President used to exercise early in the morning and he would jog on the spot in Mr Kodesh's apartment for ten or twenty minutes a day. Despite the warm friendship that I witnessed between the two when they were reunited, I couldn't help but imagine the annoyance of having a person jogging on the spot in your flat at 5 in the morning. Altogether their tolerance of one another, these liberation fighters, distinguished them to be a special breed. I admired their patience and tenacity.

I had once seen the seriousness with which the President exercised early in the morning in a hotel room. I had to control myself not to yell, 'Khulu, you are going to injure yourself' as he did his exercises. He was tall and trim but you underestimated his strength unless you saw him exercising. He resembled a boxer training and did every movement with conviction and determination. Whenever one asked him what exercise he was doing, he would freely offer advice, and on more than one occasion while we travelled abroad I had to find a medicine ball for him to roll on. He said I should try it as it makes your stomach flat. At times, his exercise routine would be frenzied. So much so that Rory Steyn, his bodyguard, and I would find it hysterically funny. We would have to hide our giggles while Madiba exercised manically in some luxury hotel somewhere. I may not have been to all the touristy things in cities across the world but I can advise anyone on the hotels with the best room service menus, and where to find a medicine ball.

By now Virginia Engel was the head secretary of our office, after Mary had left. The President still knew my cellphone number by heart and simply kept on calling me for each and every thing, which sometimes put me in great difficulty having to report all his calls to Virginia. He would call me at night and tell me what medicine he wanted to be delivered the following day, or sometimes he would call me to remind him of something the following day. It is never a nice feeling to feel undermined by anyone and although I was really committed to my job, and adored the President, I am sure it was difficult for anyone not to feel undermined by these events.

During those years I tried to keep away from him as much as possible. I believed that the closer you get to the fire, the easier it is to get burned. I didn't want to impose myself upon him and tried to create a healthy distance and to avoid a situation where he ever felt cramped by my presence. In later years it became more difficult as he would become uncertain whenever I wasn't close in a professional situation. He knew I knew exactly what he wanted and how he wanted things to pan out around him so that he could comfortably deal with them. He wanted to know exactly what to expect from each moment or meeting and he trusted completely that I would ensure that order prevailed around him and that his needs would be my most important focus. Because they were. But officially at this point, I was simply one of the President's assistant private secretaries.

Another of my colleagues was Morris Chabalala. Morris was one of the sweetest people I ever met. He was softly spoken and had a very kind and humble demeanor. In a certain way the President was very old-school, not easily accepting the fact that a man could be his secretary too. It was not that Morris did anything wrong, but the President just felt different about women in particular positions. The President never discriminated but would simply move focus to the women. It was the same situation with pilots. As soon as female pilots were trained in the airforce they started flying his plane or helicopter, and even though he never expressed reservations he was a bit more alert knowing there was a woman behind the wheel. We would always tease him about being discriminatory but he admitted that it was just something one had to get used to. He was very conscious of these stereotypes and he never showed his reservation publicly, but if you knew him you could sense his uneasiness. As much as he was for equality he admitted that he had to work harder at changing his own perceptions first.

Once Morris had to deal with a particular diplomatic incident. It involved the Spanish and Portuguese embassies. Morris was supposed to hand-deliver a letter to the Spanish Embassy that contained information that South Africa would in future recognize the Western Sahara as an independent country. Unfortunately he mistakenly and totally unintentionally delivered the letter to the Portuguese Embassy and not the Spanish. The Ambassador didn't report the incorrect delivery but opened and sat on the note for days before the President discovered that the letter he had sent to the Spanish Embassy had never been received. Morris figured it out himself that he had delivered it to the wrong embassy and called Professor Gerwel, who reported it to the President. The Spanish were livid.

The mistake caused a diplomatic incident and the President expelled the Portuguese Ambassador instantaneously from South Africa, for holding on to the note and not reporting its delivery. It was unethical to sit on information of national importance without alerting the government and could have potentially resulted in a very serious international diplomatic crisis. The President then felt he had to take action within his office as well, to demonstrate both the seriousness and fairness in dealing with the issue, and Morris got transferred, ironically as it may seem, to the Foreign Affairs Department. I pleaded with Prof. Gerwel and the President to give Morris another chance but the President was adamant that he had to take action, and once the President decided something not even something the scale of a military invasion could change his mind. I checked on Morris on a few occasions and he seemed to be happy in his new job, despite the turmoil and hurt his departure caused.

This incident, no matter how upsetting we found it, was a very clear indication of how President Mandela performed as a diplomat. Even though there may be nothing diplomatic about it. In a matter of days, the public had forgotten about the incident. He was swift with a response, both publicly and in private, took decisive action and the matter was resolved. Recently in South Africa, by way of contrast, it was found that friends of our current President, Jacob Zuma, were allowed to land at the military airforce base in Pretoria without proper authorization. The family that landed there had planned a lavish family wedding at the Sun City resort outside Pretoria. Despite the availability of commercial international and private airports in the region they landed at the military base and were escorted to the wedding venue in official police vehicles. Politically very little was done about this case.

As the year progressed, so did the President's travels. He was working hard to show the world that South Africa was a healthy country. So we travelled to Burkina Faso. It was an African Union meeting attended by all heads of state. In the first few years it was interesting to watch and be part of these large gatherings of heads of state around the world but it becomes your worst nightmare because of all the time wasted waiting around while protocol is being observed.

Accommodation was newly built in Burkino Faso, but apart from providing for food for the heads of state we were very much left to our own devices to find something to eat even though we were housed in these newly built guest houses. It was usually chaos at meetings of this sort and everything took hours. Other heads of state all argued for private audiences with President Mandela. Sometimes he agreed and sometimes he wanted to avoid too many individual meetings. Presidents were expected to arrive at the plenary in alphabetical order, either by name or the name of their country, as seniority was always a point of dispute – some heads of state had been in power for ever, originally by election but then by means of dictatorship. For some reason my father gave me a huge consignment of biltong (beef jerky) to take along on the trip and that became our staple food, together with fresh bread that we went to buy along the road from an informal stall. A former French colony, the French influence remained in Burkino Faso and we bought hot baguettes off the street stall, filled them with biltong and for two and a half days the security guards and I lived off that shipment of dried meat.

In comparison to other delegations, ours was always the smallest. It usually consisted of a secretary, a doctor, two close protection bodyguards and then between three and five bodyguards who arrived in advance, plus at most two people from Protocol: one from the Presidency and one from Foreign Affairs. Ministers got added when they were required for certain bilateral talks but we never exceeded fifteen to twenty people in our entire delegation on our biggest visits, and that was only by exception and to countries with which South Africa had very close trade relations. Other heads of state travelled with delegations of twenty plus people and the Americans were the biggest with delegations of over two hundred, but they also had the money for it. Our President showed through his actions that we had other priorities and wastage was not going to be tolerated. While one appreciated that it also mounted the pressure on us as individuals to multitask.

Because of the President's advanced age – he was seventy-nine by now – he also liked continuity and he didn't like too many unfamiliar faces around him. Whenever there was a new member of staff on the delegation he would ask behind closed doors: 'Who is that person? What does he/she do?' And you would know that he spent time thinking about costs and productivity too. He often asked about costs involved, whether we were travelling locally or abroad. 'How much does the hotel cost where you are staying? Who is paying for it?' Regardless of your answer one knew that he was concerned about expenditure.

Following the visit to Burkino Faso we went to the United Kingdom and stayed at a house in the countryside belonging to the Roode family. They had a very large food company in South Africa. It was my first time in the English countryside and I loved it. After a few days' official visit in London, we went to Wales.

We paid a courtesy call on the Queen in Buckingham Palace and I was struck by the warm friendship forged between the President and the Queen. 'Oh Elizabeth' he would say when he greeted her and she would respond 'Hello Nelson'. Being a dog lover myself, I was intrigued to find the corgis' food bowls at the side entrance we used to Buckingham Palace.

After Wales we went to Italy for a state visit. We also paid a state visit to the Vatican. The President had a private conversation with the Pope, after which they called our delegation inside. The

President always insisted on introducing his entire delegation to the head of state and it was the same with the Pope. We each got introduced and the Pope, already frail at the time, shook hands, blessed us and gave us a rosary. I had no idea what a rosary was and thought it was some sort of Catholic necklace. I called my mother that night and told her I thought the Pope could see the sins in my eyes when he looked at me. Although some of my colleagues felt the same experience my mother laughed it off.

While at an official state lunch in Italy, one of the ministers choked on a prawn. He started by coughing and then suddenly silence descended on the table as he dropped off his chair. Luckily for President Mandela his doctor was at the official ceremony. Because we travelled with such a small delegation he always insisted that all his staff be included. Our doctor was able to literally save the minister's life at the table.

Later he also insisted on inviting the Presidential plane's aircrew to banquets even if it meant he had to request the head of state / government himself to allow them to attend. He never treated any of his staff as just the hired help.

It was also on this trip that I was introduced to Yusuf Surtee, whose father used to be the President's tailor before he went to jail. Their family business continued supplying the President with suits and his famous patterned shirts. Yusuf brought a famous Italian gentleman, Stefano Ricci, representing the famous Brioni brand, to greet the President. As much as I resembled the typical *boere-meisie* Stefano was the typical Italian: jovial, lively and generous. He would always send the President the most beautiful clothing and one could always feel the love and care that went into the selection of clothes. Whenever Stefano sent clothes via Yusuf, Yusuf's shops would adjust whatever needed to be changed if needs be. Both Yusuf and Stefano had exceptionally good taste.

The President's eightieth birthday approached. A massive party was being planned by the ANC, the Mandela family together with Suzanne Weil, a business partner of the Mandela daughters, for the night of the President's actual birthday, 18 July. The President's entire personal staff were invited to the glamorous event at Gallagher estate in Johannesburg, together with the cream of the crop of the South African social scene as well as people like Naomi Campbell, Michael Jackson, Quincy Jones and Stevie Wonder, to name but a few.

Earlier in the week speculation started doing the rounds that the President and Mrs Machel were going to get married on the 18th. I thought about it and decided that it was not true. Nothing out of the ordinary happened in our environment for me to believe that there was any truth to the speculation. Parks Mankahlana, the spokesperson for the President, was repeatedly asked: 'Are they getting married?' And Parks would at first say he wasn't sure, then he vaguely denied it, and finally he said that there was definitely no marriage. I called Josina (Mrs Machel's daughter) earlier in the week to ask if she knew anything. She didn't and we just laughed it off. Josina stayed with the President at his official residence in Cape Town during his Presidency while she was studying at university there. We therefore spent a lot of time together and became close friends. I said to her: 'Zina, if you are lying to me you know I am going to have to kill you.' Jokingly. We were excited about the birthday but we really didn't know. On Saturday 18 July I woke up to newspaper headlines that read: THEY ARE GETTING MARRIED. I just smiled. I was, among a few others, asked to go and work at the Houghton residence later that day. I thought they were probably expecting family for the birthday celebrations and therefore needed extra hands.

The President and I were used to speaking on the phone. He would give me tasks or I would call him with messages or questions. We were on the phone all the time, much to the irritation of many people. He got to know my voice and could easily hear me, whereas with others he had difficulty hearing them clearly over the phone. So on his eightieth birthday I decided to call him in the morning to wish him happiness for his birthday. I would never call or disturb him if I didn't have a very good reason to discuss business, but on this day I thought that it was such a special birthday that I had to call, despite knowing that I would see him later in the afternoon at his residence.

The President and Mrs Machel spent the Friday night at Mahlamba Ndlopfu, the President's official residence in Pretoria, something which didn't often happen as they preferred to stay in Johannesburg. The household staff transferred me to him and I said: 'Good morning Khulu' and started singing 'Happy Birthday' to him. After the last note I said: 'I hope this day, today, is the most beautiful day of your entire life.' I could hear his amusement and he knew that I was fishing for information. He just said: 'Thank you darling, it definitely will be,' and then I knew, *they were getting married*. I felt like a jack in the box. I couldn't contain my excitement but I didn't want to say a word to anyone. I spent the entire day trying to figure out where/when/how. I then recalled the President asking me to call on a jeweller to see him at Mahlamba Ndlopfu a few weeks before; when the jeweller arrived they went outside and sat under a tree for their discussion. I thought it was someone the President knew from before and didn't pay attention. I felt that they were surely going to get married at the official banquet since they would have all their friends and family there but I was too scared to speculate.

They had a lunch at the Presidential guest house where the family was gathered. Staff were not invited. We proceeded to the Houghton house and arriving there it was clear that the media was not going to let go of the story. There were media everywhere, some trying to jump the walls and some climbing into trees from the adjacent plots. The security people had their hands full. We went inside and things were somewhat sombre and quiet. We stayed in the back and started putting out cups and whatever was needed for a tea later on. Soon the President and Mrs Machel arrived, followed by a few other guests. Again I didn't want to intrude and stayed as far away from them as possible. Then, like a veldt fire, news spread through the house: 'There is a wedding here in a few minutes.'

Things were simple and beautiful. Only a few people attended and really people closest to them: Archbishop Desmond Tutu, Thabo and Zanele Mbeki, Prince Bandar bin Sultan of Saudi Arabia, Yusuf Surtee, George Bizos, Ahmed Kathrada and the Sisulus, to name a few. And in true Madiba style there was complete representation of all the religious denominations in South Africa. Although they were married by the Methodist Bishop Mvume Dandala, all other religions had some role to play. It was very respectful and stylish. We saw Mrs Machel coming down the stairs by herself, gracefully, almost like her name says: Graça. Most of us couldn't control our emotions, and peeking from an adjacent room we couldn't help but wipe our tears. It was so beautiful and the President deserved to be happy at last.

That evening was every bit of the celebration it should have been. When Madiba finally took to the stage to say a few words on his birthday, his first words were to roaring applause when he said: 'My wife and I . . .' The country was celebrating with and for them.

It was a great evening and wonderful celebrations. I continuously had to check myself as if to pinch myself. Was all this real? I had never dreamt that I would ever be at the eightieth birthday and wedding celebrations of Nelson Mandela. The short journey with him at the time had already changed me so much. Luckily we were too busy and under too much pressure for me to ever sit and become complacent or conceited about where I found myself at any given point.

On 10–12 September 1998, a SADC (Southern African Development Community) meeting was held in Mauritius. Member states included countries from Southern Africa and the meeting was chaired by South Africa at this particular time (heads of state assumed the chairmanship on a rotating basis). When the President and Mrs Machel arrived in Mauritius a few days before the meeting, there was already word that Lesotho, a tiny kingdom surrounded by South Africa, was on the brink of a coup. We were regularly in contact with Prime Minister Mosisili and King Letsie III of Lesotho and even though I didn't understand why, I knew that they were facing difficulties. Both the President and Deputy President Mbeki were out of the country at the time and Minister Mangosuthu Buthelezi was Acting President of South Africa.

After President Mandela's inauguration, the National Party had joined the newly elected ANC government and that tenure of co-operative rule was known as the Government of National Unity. But by this time the Government of National Unity had been dissolved following the National Party's departure from the government. The Inkatha Freedom Party (IFP) was therefore the biggest opposition party in Parliament and appointing the leader of the IFP, Minister Buthelezi, as Acting President while both the President and his Deputy were abroad was a gesture of trust on the ANC's side.

I remember the President being bitterly tired and upset with events back home in which around 134 people were reportedly killed as a result of South Africa's invasion of Lesotho, in what is referred to today as the biggest mistake during Mr Mandela's Presidency. The President was literally on the phone throughout the night consulting with Minister Buthelezi and the Lesotho government.

It was no fun being in Mauritius for the first time. Instead of swimming in the beautiful waters of the Indian Ocean we attended to official engagements from banquets and meetings to a visit to the Botanical Gardens. I wanted to swim rather than stare at a rare flower that only bloomed once every seventy-five years. We were also tired and disturbed by events back at home.

The following day the SADC meeting convened. The meeting was scheduled to start at 10 a.m. but President Mugabe from Zimbabwe entered the room more than an hour late. President Mandela didn't like chairing meetings and would usually open a meeting and then hand over to someone else to ensure the rules were observed. No one ever questioned this peculiar arrangement, and he would only occasionally comment on proceedings or nod to add his approval to process. While President Mugabe entered another head of state was busy addressing the meeting. President Mandela interrupted him and asked him to stop his address. This was unusual for him and the atmosphere grew tense as silence descended in the big hall; it was one of the few occasions that President Mandela interrupted someone while he was speaking.

President Mandela waited for President Mugabe to be seated and then launched into an off-the-cuff speech of about twenty minutes about being disrespectful and wasting other people's time, and that 'some heads of state' considered themselves more important and therefore thought it was acceptable to arrive late. He didn't mention President Mugabe's name once, but we all knew. He subsequently used words that never left me: 'Because you hold a particular position, doesn't mean that you are more important than anyone else. Your time is not more valuable than anybody else's time. If you are late you show that you have no respect for another person's time and therefore no respect for other people because you consider yourself to be more important than others.'

After President Mandela finished his speech President Mugabe allowed proceedings to continue for a while and then quietly left as unnoticed as he could. That was the last time I ever saw any kind of interaction between them and there was no contact again that I am aware of, except exchanging courtesies whenever they shared a stage at an all-Africa event.

President Mandela often related the story that before South Africa's democracy Zimbabwe was considered the star of the continent, but then when South Africa became a democracy they said the sun came out and the star disappeared. I was of the opinion that was one of the reasons why President Mugabe felt bitterness towards South Africa's efforts on the continent. More recently in an interview, President Mugabe paid back by commenting on President Mandela being too much of a saint and pleasing white people at the expense of black people. President Mandela was no longer able to defend himself due to his age at that point, and I thought that Mugabe had waited for a very long time to seek revenge through public humiliation. His comment clearly lacked understanding of the South African situation and that had it not been for the focus on reconciliation at the time, our country would have gone up in flames, ending up much like the state in which Zimbabwe is today.

The President was scheduled to pay a state visit to Saudi Arabia and I was asked to accompany him. John Reinders, the Chief of Protocol in the Presidency and I, together with some security members, set off to Riyadh a few days in advance. I had received correspondence from the South African Embassy in Saudi and staff offered to 'rent' an *abaya* for me – the 'cloak' Muslim women wear to cover themselves. Since I didn't know what they were talking about, I agreed to that.

Upon arrival in Riyadh it was clear that this country, culture and religion was very different to any place I had imagined. I was handed my *abaya* at the airport and told to cover up immediately and every time I appeared in public. On our way to the Presidential guest house I was given a crash-course in the Islamic faith and Muslim culture. I was stunned to learn of all the rules that applied mainly to women only. I didn't take most of it seriously until I spoke to some of the officials later that night, who told me that they still had public executions in Riyadh for people committing 'religious crimes'. Being a bit of a deliberate rebel I decided to test the boundaries of this belief system on me as a 'Westerner'.

First we went out to a night market. As I jumped into the first available limo with an open door I heard a lot of people starting to argue around the car in Arabic. Apparently the argument was over who was allowed to travel with me and who not. As an unmarried woman, one is not allowed to travel in the car with any man who is not a relative. Especially and definitely *not* a married man. So I drove by myself.

The custom is that shops only open around 10 a.m. and at noon every day everything closes as they all go to the mosques to pray. At 1 p.m. they open again and around the hour some shops close for people to go and pray again. You could find yourself in the front of a queue to pay for something in a store and be chased out of the shop when the sirens for prayer time start. It was therefore better to go to a night market where things would be open until late and praying wouldn't interrupt shopping as much as it did during the day.

In my briefing I was also told to watch out for the Mattawa, the religious military police. They were there to police people observing the Muslim culture. They walk around, dressed in uniforms similar to that of the ordinary police but they carry sticks with them dipped in red paint, I was told. If they catch someone not observing the culture they hit you with the stick on your ankles and the red paint sticks. If you are caught a second time, they arrest you. And who knows what then. I was once reprimanded in the market with a 'cover up, cover up' but quickly ran away before they could mark me with the paint and didn't see the paint myself. There were so many beautiful carpets to see and things to buy that it distracts you from focusing on the things around you, and I appreciated with what ease we lived back in South Africa. I nevertheless enjoyed the experience, so different from what was familiar to me. One was not allowed to visit Saudi as a tourist at the time and the visa process was thoroughly controlled and checked by the Saudi authorities. I therefore considered it a privilege and unique experience to be able to visit Saudi.

We had our first meeting scheduled with the chief of protocol the night before President Mandela's arrival in the country. It is definitely not one of the easiest countries to work in, particularly being a female. We waited for days to confirm a time with their chief of protocol to discuss a programme of some sort. The only response one would get is: 'wait'. So you wait. You can't go anywhere and you sit around for hours waiting for word from the officials.

The meeting was scheduled in the Presidential Palace where President Mandela was going to stay. At first the gentleman dressed in his traditional Arab garb seemed friendly. I avoided eye contact as I had been told. The Saudi chief of protocol started the meeting with the usual exchange of courtesies and how honoured they were to receive President Mandela, etc. We felt honoured. But I wanted him to stop and get to details of the programme. It was late and I was tired. By midnight, however, we were no closer to any details on the programme. By that time President Mandela's plane had already left South Africa.

John Reinders would put a question to the chief of protocol and he would pick up the phone and converse in Arabic with someone on the other end. He would end the call and move to the next question. After two hours of this I had enough. John decided to go outside for a smoke break and I followed. We discussed what was happening inside and I told him that when we returned to the office I think I had to take over. Which I did. John was completely capable of negotiating by himself but we had run out of options in our approach, trying to get answers. I completely disregarded custom and looked the man straight in the eyes. I said: 'Sir, President Mandela is on his way here right now. In a plane. It is the first time in my life that I've heard of a state visit without a programme while the head of state is already on his way. The President expects us to know what will happen to him when he arrives but at this stage you are not helping us.'

The chief tried to avoid eye contact and picked up the phone again. He then excused himself and John and I started laughing. It was really ridiculous. When he returned thirty minutes later I lost it. It was well after 1 a.m. I slammed my fist on the table and said: 'Sir, if you do not give us any details now, right now, we will instruct the President's plane to turn around as we cannot expect our President to arrive in a foreign country without a programme for his visit.' I felt that he undermined our responsibilities to the President and he was simply not willing to share information. The man was clearly disgusted by me. Women just don't talk to men like that in that country. 'Madam,' he said to me, 'please calm down.' That is the second worst thing you can say to me. I said, 'I will not calm down unless you give us details now.'

He picked up the phone and clearly, without me having to understand a word, told the person on the other line to rush to the office. John calmly said to me in Afrikaans: 'I think they got the point.' Not long after two other gentlemen arrived and we moved to a bigger meeting room. A programme was laid out, and although times were not completely confirmed at least there was an indication of what was expected of the President.

The next morning I noticed that none of the staff in the palace spoke to me any longer. I assumed it was because of my behaviour the previous night. I didn't give a damn. About three hours prior to the President's arrival and an hour before we left to go to the airport, the entire palace came to standstill by the announcement of a prince arriving. Everyone rushed to the front door and formed a receiving line. We didn't know who to expect and I was told it could be one of 2,000 princes. Much to my surprise it was Prince Bandar, President Mandela's close friend, who was serving as Saudi Ambassador in the United States at the time. Clearly he was respected by everyone in the Palace.

When he entered he greeted by nodding his head and walked right up to me and kissed me. 'Oh hello Zelda.' I noticed from the corner of my eye how people's faces around me dropped. I was the only woman in their company, unmarried, and here a prince kisses me. 'How are you Zelda? Welcome,' he said and we exchanged some pleasantries. He walked me to a sitting room where he asked me about the President's arrival, programme etc. When he left, I was treated like a princess.

The Saudis are extremely hospitable people. They don't spare any trouble to ensure that one feels comfortable – that is, once you behave. They are generally friendly as long as you observe their culture and respect their beliefs. Madiba was accompanied by a few female ministers but we learned that even they were not allowed to attend the state banquet or meeting with the King. All the women subsequently went to a private dinner at a businessman's house. The state banquet that the President and his fellow men attended only started at midnight and they were only back at the Presidential guest house after 2 a.m. The next morning we were all tired, but despite our exhaustion the President had his breakfast at exactly 7 a.m. as usual. He was an eighty-year-old at that stage yet his enthusiasm and spirit was that of a young man.

When we departed the next day I was fed up with the rules and regulations and I wanted to be home in my own environment. As we checked in at the airport to board our commercial flights back home, the security men got stopped and their luggage was searched. They usually carried firearms with proper licences they obtained from the hosting government and security equipment like radios and their own metal detectors that they needed to perform their duties. Yet they got stopped, searched, and had to take every little piece of equipment apart. I made no secret of my disgust at Saudi bureaucracy. For goodness' sake, we were leaving the country not entering it! Why did it matter to them what we took back home!

Strangely, in the years to follow I became fond of Riyadh. We returned on a few occasions. Once you know a place and you know what to expect and what not to resist it becomes easier. I liked the food and I knew then how to approach things . . . with calmness and a *lot* of patience. I guess one also matures and becomes more patient with age. In all the Arab countries we visited I learned that their governments rarely provided a lot of detail in advance. It was a question of hurry up and wait . . .

6

Running to Keep Up

The President visited a schools and clinic project in the Northern Cape on 19 February 1999. It was a Friday afternoon and I was working in Cape Town at the time. Virginia accompanied the President on his visit on that particular day. As I had befriended the commander of the Presidential Protection Unit in Cape Town, Hein Bezuidenhout, we decided to have a drink in their canteen to end the week and avoid peak-hour traffic when going home. These were the days before news spread as fast as it does now; not everyone had a cellphone and people were not connected on the internet to get news updates continuously.

As I prepared to join Hein in the canteen I received a call from former President P. W. Botha on my mobile; he wanted to speak to the President to tell him that Schalk Visagie had been shot. 'Lady, I want to talk to Mr Mandela right now.' He spoke to me in Afrikaans but he was obviously angry and irritated. He never called him President Mandela, but always Mr Mandela. It was as if he couldn't make the leap to having complete unconditional respect for Mr Mandela as a President. I told him that the *President* was in mid-air and I could hear that he didn't quite believe me. He ended the conversation without saying goodbye. Schalk was Mr Botha's son-in-law. He was a policeman and the President liked him as he was progressive in his thinking and clearly had some influence over his wife, Rozanne. Rozanne was very conservative and earlier the President had tried to get them to persuade her father to appear in front of the Truth and Reconciliation Commission, established in 1995.

On 11 February 1998, eight years after the President's release from jail, he invited Rozanne and Schalk Visagie, Rozanne's sister Elsa and her husband to join him for dinner. The President asked me to arrange the dinner and I was somewhat uncomfortable calling on Rozanne Botha, knowing very well how the family felt about Nelson Mandela. It took me some hours to respond to the President's request. A request by the President for someone to have a meal with him was usually greatly appreciated and welcomed by those invited. I knew in this instance it might be different. It was clearly not a great deal for Rozanne to be invited by the President to have dinner, but I realized that they were still filled with anger and regret because their father was driven until his back was against the wall to surrender power at the end of apartheid and to hand over to President F. W. de Klerk, who would later call the first democratic elections in South Africa.

The President met with them over dinner to try and lobby them to persuade their father to appear in front of the Truth and Reconciliation Commission, a body set up by President Mandela's administration to allow people the opportunity to apply for amnesty for deeds they may have committed during the apartheid years. If perpetrators came clean and presented the truth on injustices they may have been party to, they could apply for amnesty. This was to give people on both sides of apartheid the opportunity to first of all make peace with themselves, but also for families who lost loved ones and who still had unanswered questions to get closure. People wanted answers and thousands of people in South Africa wanted closure surrounding the deaths or mysterious disappearances of loved ones. It was not a matter that needed closure by any one side only. South Africa needed to heal as a nation and it was only going to be possible if all parties decided to participate in the TRC hearings. The Botha family couldn't agree unanimously on the matter – Rozanne was especially fiercely opposed to it out of fear that her father could be prosecuted or humiliated – and former President Botha went to his grave years later with many answers that could have provided solace to many people.

I knew that the President would be concerned for Schalk so I tried to reach him, but was told that they had just taken off from the venue they had visited. They were en route back to Pretoria. News quickly broke of the incident and I could sense tension in the air. I thought therefore that I had to inform the President as on many occasions I'd learned something like this could snowball into a much bigger political issue if one procrastinated. I called the control tower of the South African airforce in Pretoria to contact the pilots and ask them to inform the President that Schalk Visagie had been shot. My idea was to tell him once he landed in Pretoria that Mr Botha was livid and insisted on speaking to him.

Hein and I had our first drink. I told him what had happened and he called some of his colleagues in the police force to try and get more information. Schalk was previously part of a gang-related investigation unit in the police and from the information the police had at the time they suspected that it was possibly an act of revenge from a gang after he brought some of its members to book.

Then I received a call from the airforce to inform me that the President decided to turn his plane around mid-air and proceed to Cape Town. He'd instructed them to let me know and said that I would know what to do. Hein and I got into action. It was like gears falling into position as everyone started calling whoever had to be informed of the President's expected arrival in Cape Town. We decided to proceed to the airport ourselves. It was Friday afternoon and the traffic was moving at snail speed. Hein managed to organize half a convoy and an advance team to go to the hospital, which was not far from the airport. We were both very tense. We took our jobs extremely seriously and this was one of those occasions where that mattered. The President landed and while we drove to the hospital I briefed him.

Upon arrival at the hospital Rozanne appeared, obviously still in shock. Schalk was still in theatre being stabilized and the President called Rozanne and other family members into a private meeting room. Mr P. W. Botha wasn't there as he lived in a town called 'Wilderness' at the time, about five hours' travel from Cape Town. The President expressed his sympathy and offered support to the family in a genuinely sympathetic way. We called Mr Botha too and the President expressed his sympathy and sadness over the matter. Mr Botha was brief but told the President that he had warned him that crime in the country was getting out of hand and that the President had to really step up and take this to task. I couldn't hear the entire conversation but the President seemed calm while I could hear Mr Botha raising his voice on the other side. Then as we left, Rozanne accompanied us to the exit and told the President, waving her finger at him as her father was known for doing: 'Mandela, if something happens to Schalk tonight it will be on your conscience. It will haunt you for the rest of your life.' She was obviously in shock and I cannot imagine her fear at that point, but I thought she was completely out of line and disrespectful.

I was always very offended when someone didn't call him Mr or President but just addressed him using his first name or surname. In a way it was derogatory. And it was an Afrikaner thing to address people with respect (or then with the lack thereof if you didn't have respect for them). I turned to her and said: 'That's enough, Rozanne. We have to leave . . .' and we left. As we walked outside the President took my hand but he was quiet. I was visibly upset, and thinking back to that day I realize how much the world had changed for me by then. Here was the black President holding my hand to comfort me while we were leaving behind my people in distress. He was genuinely concerned for Schalk but I think he didn't take easy to all the emotions being flung around. Schalk did survive and we didn't hear from him again.

Like the country, I had moved a long way from the time of P. W. Botha and apartheid. Many people in South Africa, especially the black youth, feel that Madiba's attempts to reconcile and unify our country were over-credited. They are of the opinion that the moments when South Africa was unified were limited to sporting events when the country briefly appeared to be in celebration mode. According to them, those were superficial moments that did not last. I understand how they feel, although such thinking in my opinion is also prejudice. We have not made the progress in economic transformation which we had hoped for and generally people are frustrated and angry. Some young people even go as far as saying that Madiba sold out to the whites, because he did not force transformation fast enough. Yet, what South Africa needed at the time was healing and to present a consolidated front to the world to gain the confidence of international investors. Madiba was like true north on a compass: we all know where we are supposed to go but he knew that we had to take a slightly different approach to achieve stability first.

Some angry young people feel that things have not changed, but the advantage of my age is that I can attest to the change I have seen and experienced. I am a product of that change.

The end of an era was approaching. In May 1999 the second democratic elections were planned in South Africa. President Mandela repeatedly indicated throughout his term that he would only stay for one term of office, after which he would hand over the reins. He did so mainly hoping that others would follow suit but also because I think he was eager to have a bit of freedom himself. In 1997 Deputy President Mbeki was elected President of the ANC and voted their Presidential candidate for the elections in 1999. President Mandela symbolically handed over power to the Deputy President two years into his term. He was adamant that Deputy President Mbeki was at the helm and that his own role was purely ceremonial. It wasn't that easy though. While the day-to-day running of the country was largely left to Deputy President Mbeki, President Mandela was still lawfully the executive head of state and there were certain obligations he couldn't give up.

We hardly had anything personally to do with Deputy President Mbeki and very seldom saw him in the buildings we shared. President Mandela would often call him to report events to him or even to ask for his advice. Being the considerate human being that he was, he never wanted to be seen to make anyone feel inferior to him. On the occasions that we did see the Deputy President their interactions were limited to formal exchanges, and I personally got the idea that the Deputy President felt that the President didn't always do the right thing. That was my personal impression from a distance. I also learned that Deputy President Mbeki's father, who was imprisoned with President Mandela, wanted a more senior role in government after his release but only became a Member of Parliament and that was apparently the cause of uneasiness. I never dwelled on it though. Mrs Zanele Mbeki was always friendly and stately but quiet.

I was literally surviving day by day. The President was depending on me even more than before, and even though a new private secretary had been appointed it still didn't prevent the President from calling me day and night. He would sometimes call me at 2 a.m. and ask me to remind him to do something the following morning. It was not that he was more considerate for those with families but he knew that I didn't mind him calling on me.

It is widely documented that there were differences within the ANC about who would succeed President Mandela. Cyril Ramaphosa and Thabo Mbeki were the contestants. Senior ANC members were divided on the matter. From the first time I met Mr Ramaphosa I liked him. Mr Mbeki was distant and appeared dismissive towards me. Regardless of my lack of knowledge about the ANC I was always trying to uphold the ANC's good intentions in public. I often wondered whether the President regretted supporting Mr Mbeki's nomination as President of the ANC or his successor at a time after his retirement when the government really treated him badly, but soon learned that the President considered regret as the most useless emotion and there was no use in asking 'what if'.

President Mandela was always forthright in that he didn't run the country but that the Deputy President did most of the work. President Mandela's role was that of nation-builder and he passed with distinction. To this day I think history has provided us with the right leader at the right time, or South Africa could have easily gone up in flames. I often compare our democracy with the growing process of a child. Up to the age of five you simply have to feed the child, care for it and love it. That is what President Mandela did best. From five to fifteen years you have to start educating the child and shape it into a personality, and that is exactly what President Mbeki did. With distinction. Now we are in the teenager phase and we experience the growing problems in our country similar to that of any adolescent. And as with an adolescent we can no longer blame our youth and we have to start acting responsibly.

In the first few months of 1999 the President worked at a pace that would see any younger head of state crawling on all fours. He was campaigning for the ANC, building schools and clinics, attending to official obligations and in between finding time and insisting on fetching and dropping his wife at the airport, attending to his children's and grandchildren's issues and then also embarking on saying 'goodbye' or taking leave of structures, people, business, institutions and even foreign countries before his retirement. Or should I say from the outset, his first attempt at retirement? The President's private secretary, Virginia Engel, had a health condition and she was off sick for an extended period of time, so most of the travelling and work load came down on me. But I was ready to take on whatever was needed to see the President through the last couple of months of his term. Change is inevitable and I was ready to drive myself past the finish line, probably for the first time in my life at full speed. I often sat in planes and helicopters trying to comprehend what had happened to me. A certain sadness would then fill my heart. I hadn't fully experienced what had happened because I was so obsessed with doing more than what was expected of me, always over-delivering, that I probably missed some valuable opportunities to get a deeper understanding of what was historically happening around me.

On 1 April 1999 the President took representatives of McDonald's, Datatec and Nokia to the Eastern Cape, visiting three different areas where he wanted these respective companies to build schools and clinics in the communities of Bizana, Mbongweni and Baziya, very remote communities in the rural Transkei. The President never had a McDonald's hamburger. He just never ate fast food and he didn't know what a hamburger was. It is not something he was brought up with and his distance from society also meant that he missed out on many things that evolved around us. We take it that everybody should know what a hamburger is. During his speech in the community where he introduced McDonald's the name slipped his mind and he referred to them as 'the people who make these sandwiches'. I thoroughly enjoyed that reference and so did the representatives from McDonald's. It also provided much laughter to the community. There were these moments, some of them which seem so distant to me now, when you completely forgot that this was Nelson Mandela.

The President had no problem calling together competitors to work together. In his schools and clinics project he would easily call together rivals, like the two cellular phone operators at the time or both BMW and Mercedes-Benz. When I once asked him about it he said that when people are competing to do good, it inspires them to do even better. It made perfect sense although I thought it was only Nelson Mandela that could get some rivals to sit together sometimes. It was entertaining to watch how companies would almost compete to showcase what they were able or willing to do.

President Mandela made sure he left not necessarily the best but the biggest for last. His last state visit was scheduled for April 1999 and would include Russia, Hungary, Pakistan and then China. He was hoping to strengthen ties with these countries prior to his departure from public office and to pave the way for a solid relationship to trade on in future. He also wanted to thank both Russia and China for their support during the apartheid years by honouring them with a state visit.

On 28 April 1999 we arrived in Moscow with all the fanfare, bells and whistles one could expect. President Boris Yeltsin was our host. We stayed in the Kremlin and I still consider it one of my most awkward experiences. I always felt like I was being watched, even alone in my room, although I was probably just imagining so. Passages were as wide as highways and people behaved like machine-like robots. Emotions were rarely expressed and everything appeared to have been rehearsed a thousand times. It all unnerved me but, being a disciplinarian myself, I kind of liked it. Language was a big problem. It was difficult asking for food to the President's liking and then when it came to our own food it was even worse. Rich food and vodka for breakfast. The only way I could get an egg for breakfast was to imitate a chicken several times. Saying 'cluck cluck' in the Kremlin while flapping your imaginary wings is never very graceful.

We visited the burial sites of J. B. Marks and Moses Kotane, former ANC leaders and communists who were instrumental in shaping the President's life. We laid a wreath and spent a few minutes of silence around their grave sites.

Next we visited the mausoleum on the Red Square where Lenin's body was exhibited. One of the little pleasures of travelling with the President was that they would close down the mausoleum for our visit so we could do so in private without interference from the tourists around the site. On the few occasions that we actually did sight-seeing we avoided having to stand in queues to buy tickets or get access to places. Protocol officers briefed us before descending into the grave site: No talking, no eating or drinking and under any circumstances, no photographs. We quietly went down the steps until we saw Lenin's mummified body. No one uttered a word.

What we had forgotten was that the President's hearing was already not good, and when the Russian protocol officer briefed us the President in all likelihood didn't hear the instructions. We were all quiet, almost admiring the body of the dead Communist leader. It was kind of spooky. And then, without any warning, the President with his booming loud voice said: 'So, how long has he been lying here?' The protocol officer was shocked beyond belief and looked at us for explanation or order, I don't know which. No one responded, out of pure shock, and the President repeated the question to even more chaos. Zenani, his daughter who accompanied us on the visit, then said to him, 'Daddy, you are not allowed to talk,' and he whispered back but loud enough for anyone to hear: 'Oh OK, I'm sorry.'

We also went to watch the world-renowned ballet *Swan Lake* at the Bolshoi. I was very impressed to be able to say that I stayed in the Kremlin, saw Lenin and watched *Swan Lake* at the Bolshoi. The fact that I walked that history with Nelson Mandela added to my delight. And for an Afrikaner this was something quite out of the ordinary, having spent so much time during my childhood praying for the abolishment of communism in these countries. Indeed times had changed.

The ballet was every bit of what I had imagined it would be. The dancing, decor, music, everything was brilliant. I sat right behind the President because he always wanted to know where I was in case he needed something. I touched his shoulder before the show started and told him I was right behind him in case he wanted water or anything.

Russians have a custom that they add 'ina' behind a man's surname to identify the wife of that person. Therefore Yeltsin's wife would be called Yeltsina. Just before the visit, I am told there was a discussion about my name in Maputo. The names that run in the Machel family, like Gracina, Josina and so on, sparked the discussion and apparently the President decided there that my name had to be changed to Zeldina. In Russia, with the occurrence of 'ina' at the end of these surnames, he was reminded of this discussion in Maputo and so he kept calling me Zeldina. We all found it very amusing. Needless to say, the name stuck and he called me Zeldina right up to the end, as every other person now does. I am reminded of him every time.

The President never realized the loudness of his voice and how recognizable it was. Between two of the ballet items he turned his head towards me and in the silence of the moment after the audience had stopped applauding he said, 'Zeldina, you and I should be doing that,' and pointed to the stage and ballerinas. We all burst out laughing and luckily I think only the South Africans and the few people in the audience from other countries but Russia could understand. It was hilarious and for minutes later we all laughed out loud. Luckily our laughter was drowned in the music but he enjoyed his own joke and kept on smiling for a long time.

It is also the only time I saw the President drinking any strong spirits, such as vodka. He was a stern believer that you should do what is possible not to offend the host, so he did exactly what was required of him. At the night of the state banquet he was heavily in conversation with President Yeltsin. President Yeltsin was a dramatic talker and, not knowing what they were discussing, it looked like they were arguing. In between they took a few vodka shots although President Mandela was only sipping his, and then without announcement President Yeltsin jumped up and left the room. He left President Mandela at the table for about fifteen minutes and it made me nervous as I thought they really had had a fight and he had left. He returned later to say that he had a call from President Clinton which he had to take, and apologized during his speech. Back in the Kremlin I told the President about my worries and he laughed at my assumptions that he would have an altercation with President Yeltsin. He did however raise the issue of Lenin's burial with Yeltsin, telling him it was time for Lenin to go to his grave. President Yeltsin was adamant that Lenin should stay in Red Square. President Mandela disagreed with him. But they remained on good terms.

From Russia we went to Hungary. I think the President was excited to end his term in office and therefore the visit was relaxed and enjoyable. Our protocol officer in Hungary told us about twenty times that Budapest, the capital, is actually two separate cities, Buda and Pest, divided by a river. We ended up teasing one another about it, repeatedly asking everybody around us: 'Did you know that Budapest is actually two different cities?' Even the President checked a few times whether we knew it was two different cities and we enjoyed him participating in our teasing. His sense of humour never failed.

From Budapest we went to Pakistan for a two-day state visit and then continued on to Beijing in China. If you thought that you had a problem in Russia with food and the language barrier, China was worse. We were told that two days before our visit all factory activity was stopped to clear the air of pollution. Whether that was really honestly the truth I don't know, but I probably wanted to believe it. Again I noticed in Beijing that everything worked like a machine. Emotions were far off and people were rehearsed in their responses. Some of the delegation went to see the Great Wall of China but I didn't feel that it was wise to leave the President alone for that long, especially in a country where hardly anyone spoke English and he definitely didn't speak or understand a word of Mandarin. Our colleagues returned, exhausted, and I was a little sad that I didn't see the Wall but decided that everything was worth the sacrifice.

Returning to South Africa we were gearing up to take our leave from the Presidency after the elections. Luciano Pavarotti was hosting a concert in Pretoria and the President and Mrs Machel attended the concert. It was very emotional for us all and almost announced in a stately way the beginning of the end of the term. The President was looking forward to his retirement. Little did I know that he was looking forward to doing less of what he had to do and doing more of what he wanted to do.

On 14 May the Presidency hosted a farewell for its entire staff attended by the President. It was a wonderful event and a party for us all. Once the President left the function we danced until late at night, saying our goodbyes. By now we had fostered great friendships and we were celebrating a successful term and great achievements. In any normal office environment you become friends with people, but in a Presidency it is as if you know there is a shelf life to the particular structure's existence and when the sell-by date approaches you become sentimental and emotional, even if it feels to you at the time that the term was dominated by challenges. You don't even necessarily like everyone but you foster bonds with people probably because you are forced into a situation of this highly stressed environment and you learn to co-exist for the benefit of the success of the legacy of that term. We had a fairly small office in comparison to the other Presidencies that followed. We were effective and although we had made our fair share of mistakes, we had done a good job in supporting the President's focus on reconciliation and building national unity.

We were campaigning for the elections day and night and travelling around the country non-stop in the weeks leading up to the vote. I was tired and emotionally depleted from pure exhaustion. The President repeated the same speech, off the cuff, over and over again to such an extent that I could anticipate exactly what he would say next. It is that last stretch when you see the finish line and you decide to give it your everything until you cross that line. He was there; I was about two laps behind him. People would often say: 'If the President can operate at that speed, why are you tired?' What people didn't consider is that the support staff didn't have their own support staff. No one bought the bread in my house, no one did the washing or drove me from point A to point B. You had to invent ways to deal with the ordinary course of life in between while dealing with the rest of the President's life on his behalf. I wouldn't say it was easier on him, and he was more than twice my age, but one underestimates the stress the most mundane things can cause in your life if you continuously work at such speed as we did.

On 19 May, His Royal Highness Crown Prince Abdullah bin Abdulaziz Al Saud from Saudi Arabia arrived in South Africa for a farewell visit. His plane was set to arrive at around 7 p.m. By 11 p.m. I was still at the airport awaiting him. The President asked me to be at the airport to ensure that things went smoothly. We waited and waited and I was irritable by the time the plane touched down. We still had a dinner to attend and I kept phoning the President to update him on the Saudis' arrival time. Even though he was tired he was willing to wait until the Crown Prince arrived and willing to attend a dinner at whatever hour. By midnight the Crown Prince had arrived at the Presidency in Pretoria with his entourage of fifty-plus and the dinner commenced. One of my colleagues, Lizanne van Oudshoorn from Protocol, was on duty too that night. When the President stood up to start his speech at the dinner, I asked Lizanne to stand in for me as I was at breaking point. It was close to 2 a.m. and having heard the President's campaign speech four times earlier that day I realized that I was too tired to listen to it for the fifth time. Regardless of the fact that he must have been tired, he was optimistic about the elections and the future of South Africa, sounding ever so energetic whenever he spoke about the prospects of the new South Africa. The President wasn't fazed about the time and he enjoyed the Crown Prince's visit.

On 2 June 1999 the second democratic elections were held in South Africa. President Mandela went to the polling station close to his house and cast his vote. It was always intriguing to watch. When the President wasn't doing anything impressive or spectacular, there was no audience. When he went about everyday life, few people were interested. But the day he voted, the strangest people showed up wanting to accompany him to the polling station. Few people actually took the time and trouble to take interest in what was challenging for him. It was clear that self-interest was going to become an agenda for many people even way beyond his retirement. After his vote the media asked him: 'Who did you vote for, Mr President?' and he responded: 'For myself.' I thought that was funny although people could have misinterpreted it.

Before the elections President Mandela called me into his office one day. He asked me to sit down and I knew that something serious was to follow. He hardly ever asked me so formally to sit down. But a formal request like this was different and his tone was serious. 'Zeldina, I want you to retire with me.' My response was: 'Well Khulu, I'm a bit young to retire but if you mean you want me to keep working for you, of course I will.' He just laughed. After five years he knew me better than anyone else. He had seen me grow up in a way and thinking back at earlier days he must have laughed when he was by himself about my ignorance and stupidity. But he recognized my tenacity and commitment.

Even though our lives were so different, I realized that there is a chance this person will not abandon me. Nelson Mandela didn't leave me behind. He took me with him. It was obviously one of the greatest, if not the greatest honour of my life, being chosen by Madiba to serve him beyond his retirement.

Every retiring President in South Africa is afforded some rights in retirement. One of these is keeping a full-time secretary on the payroll of the President's office but then using his/her services exclusively. It also included a telephone line, some administrative support such as a fax machine, etc., but that was the basics apart from security and official car transport within South Africa. Days before his retirement we started packing up our personal belongings at our offices in the Union Buildings.

On 11 June the President presented the last set of credentials to incoming ambassadors. I watched him really enjoying it for this last time. I was always surprised at his memory when it came to remembering the names of heads of state.

On 13 June the 'Brother Leader', Colonel Gaddafi of Libya, visited the President to bid farewell. Since the early 1990s the President had been involved in the process related to the court case that dealt with the Lockerbie plane incident in which 270 people were killed. First Mr Mandela asked President George Bush, Snr, in the early 1990s to agree that the trial be held in a neutral country. President Bush agreed to the suggestions from Mr Mandela but the British Prime Minister, John Major, refused. Then when Tony Blair became Prime Minister he put the request to him and they agreed that the case would be heard under Scottish law in The Hague in the Netherlands. A long process followed, during which the President negotiated with Gaddafi to have the two suspects delivered to The Hague, and finally Prince Bandar from Saudi and Prof. Jakes Gerwel succeeded in persuading the Brother Leader to deliver the two suspects for trial.

Later, in 2002, we visited Barlinnie Prison in Scotland where the Libyan Abdelbaset al-Megrahi was serving a minimum twenty-seven-year sentence following that trial. Al-Megrahi was unhappy with his conditions and sent word through Gaddafi that he wanted to speak to Madiba. There was little Gaddafi could do himself, as he was still considered an enemy by the West despite keeping his promise of delivering the suspects of the Lockerbie bombing and compensating the families of the victims who died in the plane crash. Yes, compensation could never bring back a life, but Gaddafi had delivered his promise yet still the West did not suspend all sanctions as they had promised. There was nothing Madiba could do to convince the West to suspend the sanctions. He had great appreciation for Gaddafi acting reliably and was willing to look into al-Megrahi's situation when asked to do so.

As we entered the prison surrounded by Scottish prison officials the mood was sombre. We entered al-Megrahi's cell, which consisted of a living area, a bathroom and kitchen. Comparing that to Madiba's old cell on Robben Island I thought al-Megrahi had something more like a suite. He was obviously touched to receive Madiba and we conversed with him for a long time. He produced evidence that he thought was not taken into consideration in court and he complained that it was very difficult for him to practise his Islamic faith, since he was in solitary confinement and was not able to worship with others. Madiba listened carefully and with sympathy but clearly he was not going to argue for the case to be re-opened. Afterwards, Madiba addressed a huge press conference, during which he pleaded for al-Megrahi to be moved to another prison in a Muslim country. (Al-Megrahi was later moved to Greenock jail out of solitary confinement and later released as he was terminally ill. He passed away in 2012 at the age of sixty in Tripoli.)

Prince Bandar and Prof. Gerwel were both awarded the Order of Good Hope, South Africa's highest honour, for their success in bringing about the trial in The Hague. The President had a close relationship with Gaddafi as a result of these negotiations and Gaddafi had to know that he could trust Madiba before he would co-operate. I also suspected that Madiba was entertained by the fact that the Brother Leader publicly expressed his fearlessness of the West. The West had not supported President Mandela during the time of apartheid, in general maintaining their links with the apartheid regime as a bulwark against communism. It was therefore an emotional day for Gaddafi when he came to bid farewell to President Mandela from his Presidency.

We only saw him on a few occasions after President Mandela's retirement and the last time, during President Zuma's inauguration, I made a point to ask whether he didn't want to pay a courtesy call upon Madiba. I never received a response and Madiba was shocked when he was killed in 2011. No person deserves to die without dignity. I will never condone what he did to his own people but in my view he was always good to us and to Madiba and he earned respect in our eyes for that and always delivering his promises during those negotiations. Madiba was loyal to those in whom he invested friendship and the Brother Leader was one of them. He never omitted to point out the mistakes he thought Gaddafi made, but they maintained mutual respect even while expressing their differences at times. Another of Madiba's great lessons: you can have a vast difference of opinion with someone but that never justifies disrespect.

We travelled to Cape Town for the swearing in of the new President and Parliament and to prepare for the inauguration of President Mbeki in Pretoria on 16 June. Attending the inauguration at the Union Buildings it was the first time that I saw any kind of interaction between Mrs Machel and Mrs Winnie Madikizela Mandela.

Up to that point I had only seen Mrs Mandela at a distance on a few occasions. We had no contact with her of any kind. It was one of those unspoken rules that when you work for the President you don't ask questions about his relationships with his family or his former wives. Apart from the four grandchildren who lived with the President we only occasionally saw Zindzi and Zenani, the two daughters from that marriage. When I saw the look in their eyes when Mrs Mandela and Mrs Machel passed each other in the crowd at the inauguration it scared me. There was no relationship between the two women and I could never imagine them being friendly.

I have learned over the years to have appreciation for Mrs Winnie Mandela. I was angry at her when I learned that she maintained physical distance from Madiba following his release, yet her affair with Dali Mpofu was widely talked about. It must have hurt him. Yet Mrs Machel was the one to bring me around to accepting and appreciating the fact that if it had not been for Mrs Mandela, Madiba may have given up hope over the long years in prison. Apart from the fact that she was mother to two of his children, she represented hope for him and she must have been the person he dreamt about at night; the person he longed to touch and to be with. I grew a sense of understanding for her and also how lonely she must have become without him. It is only once we really experience loneliness ourselves that we can fully comprehend its darkness, and as I matured awareness of these things in life often occupied my mind.

On the day of the inauguration of President Mbeki we woke up as usual and prepared for the ceremony. We attended the ceremony, after which President Mandela returned to his office in the Union Buildings to collect his personal belongings. The office was deserted because it was a public holiday. As I entered the glass doors where I first entered his office five years earlier I quietly started sobbing. He held Mrs Machel's hand as we walked down the passage to his office. I walked a few yards ahead of them and the only sound to announce their arrival was the familiar sound of the security door opening in front of them as they approached and automatically closing behind them. Our offices leading to his were already empty. I left them alone in his office as they went through his drawers and bathroom to clear the limited items he had left in the office. I later took them a small box in which we packed his things and he saw that I was crying. He looked at me and said: 'Zeldina, you are over-reacting.' He said those same words back in 1994 when we first met; he said them under different circumstances and I was crying at that time for exactly the opposite reasons. In 1994 I was crying because of guilt and fear of what lay ahead; now I was crying because it was all over. Little did I know what really lay ahead . . .

PART THREE

Gatekeeper to the Most Famous Man in the World

1999–2008

7

Travel and Conflict

We had made plans to set up office in the President's old house in Houghton. By now he had moved to a new house following his marriage with Mrs Machel in 1998. His old house was a large double-storey house that, despite being his home for over five years, was run down and not well decorated. It was empty though and I knew it would be a good place to set up the office because it was close to his new residence too. I also asked Madiba if I could stay there while I found a place to live in Johannesburg.

At first he wanted me to come and stay on his premises but I turned down the offer, knowing too well that I needed the distance and that it would not be welcomed by all of his family. I arranged for my furniture arriving from Cape Town to be delivered at the old house in Houghton.

I started cleaning the only bedroom upstairs that was liveable – Madiba's old bedroom, which was painted in the ugliest shade of blue one can imagine. I don't think such things ever bothered him. Everything was blue and even though I loved blue it was too blue. It was a modest room, definitely not befitting for a President, and I was happy that Mrs Machel's presence in his life had both enlightened his life but also introduced him to a few more materialistic pleasures, like a bigger room and a dignified space to live in to appreciate the sunlight through your bedroom window, and a room that welcomes you as opposed to depressing you. Still in comparison to the luxuries others with similar positions enjoy, his remained modest.

I called the Ministry of Public Works and asked them to send an official to look at obtaining furniture for Madiba's office, in accordance with government policy. They agreed. They also agreed to speed up the installation of a telephone and fax machine as soon as possible.

In the days to follow I unpacked and settled and started what would effectively be known as our post-Presidential office – the Nelson Mandela Foundation, from where he would continue his public service. Prof. Gerwel drafted an outline of what the office had to focus on and the Foundation's trust deed provided for him to further his ambitions to build schools and clinics, fight the AIDS epidemic, provide a space for dialogue and a physical building to host his writings and memorabilia. Chaos ensued and soon the entire world was looking for President Mandela, trying and pushing to get him to attend to their causes. I didn't know how we were going to pay for them but I had to hire help as I simply couldn't manage by myself. Prof. Gerwel visited regularly and asked one of our former colleagues, Loïs Dippenaar, to help put order in the chaos. One after the other I convinced Lydia Baylis, Maretha Slabbert and Jackie Maggot to join our office temporarily, although the arrangement ended up lasting for many years.

They would sometimes leave me in the afternoon behind my desk when they went home and find me there the next morning. Some nights I didn't sleep and simply read letters and typed responses throughout the night to be faxed the next morning. My argument was, the quicker we were able to respond, the less people were going to call to follow up on requests, so I was trying to bring down the volume of telephone calls so the pressure would be less. Many times I wanted to give up and leave but I never could. On many occasions I wondered what drove a person to make him/her pick up the telephone or a pen to contact Nelson Mandela. It was all just too much and I was at the brim of my frustration levels, more or less something that had become the norm.

I would only go upstairs and shower at around 7 a.m. in the morning before the other staff arrived back at work, and then continued the day without any sleep. After about three days in a row I would crash for an entire day and then start again.

Soon Madiba started coming into the office more regularly, and in the first few days of conducting appointments in his post-Presidential office he reminded visitors who referred to him as 'President' that he was now retired and no longer wanted to be called 'President'. He wanted to be called either Madiba or Mr Mandela.

Since I called him Khulu, there was adjustment for me only in the way I spoke of him and not to him. I now had to learn to speak of Madiba or Mr Mandela and not the President when I spoke of him. He would often ask people when they called him Mr President, 'Where were you when I retired?' so word spread and it eventually stopped. He also didn't want to be awarded titles like Honourable, etc. He was content with Mr Mandela or Madiba and told people on endless occasions: 'Just call me Madiba.' He said a title doesn't change the person that you are, and that was his way of telling us that he didn't have to be given titles – even though by the last count he had been awarded 1,177 tributes, of which 697 were awards of some kind and over 120 were honorary doctorates. When people wanted to address him using the honorary doctorate titles he was fast to explain to them that he didn't study for any of those doctorates and that they were merely honorary titles.

In late 1999 I received a letter from the Presidency promoting me to the post of Assistant Director in the Office of the President. Even though I was still seconded to Madiba, the higher rank could be allocated as a result of the availability of posts within the structures of the Presidency.

It was clear that the Foundation was going to need funding. To run the office we started off by borrowing money with the only surety being the words from Madiba and Prof. Gerwel that 'We will repay it as soon as possible, please don't charge us interest.' Madiba was still an icon to the world, but unlike in other countries former Presidents do not receive funding from the government to allow the person to continue his public life. Yet in our case, the world had the same expectations of him regardless of his official position.

It was clear that Madiba, too, expected things to continue as before. He woke up the morning of his retirement as if nothing had changed. He was as determined as before to bring about change in

South Africa, to reform society until it was free from discrimination of any kind. He called to issue a few instructions and when I dropped the call I panicked, not knowing how I would manage to arrange all the things he had expected of me. He did the same with Professor Gerwel, who jokingly told Madiba that he no longer worked for him. Prof. Gerwel was going to serve as Chair of the board of the Nelson Mandela Foundation and even though I was still employed by the state I had no idea how to make things happen without any infrastructure. Yet, Madiba knew how to drive me beyond my limits. I did not recognize or trust that I had the ability to continue with business as usual despite our entire infrastructure disintegrating overnight. He did. He patiently guided me and I am fortunate to have learned from such a great mentor and teacher.

Even so, in August 1999 Madiba said that he was tired and they needed a holiday. That was a challenge. Where do we go? How do we get there? It suddenly dawned on me that we had lost the luxury of the private plane and that it would cost us over R1 million (today about US$100,000) to travel to the US in a private plane. We didn't have that kind of money and Madiba would never agree to such expenditure on a holiday. He and Mrs Machel had been invited to the Bahamas by Tony O'Reilly, former owner of Heinz and at the time the owner of Independent News and Media, and his wife Chryss to stay at their house in Nassau. They would take care of us once we got there but I had no idea how we would get there. I was panicking.

Madiba couldn't go in a small plane as he needed proper sleep and he needed to be able to stand up straight without having to bend his injured knee, and to be able to use ablution facilities on a plane. He had a problem with his knee as a result of a Robben Island injury and as he aged it got worse. He had difficulty climbing stairs and couldn't manage more than just a few steps at a time.

I called Tokyo Sexwale, one of South Africa's richest businessmen and an old comrade of Madiba's and whom I knew had connections to people with private planes. He put me on to a few people but none of them could help us. I asked all the wealthy people in South Africa with private planes, the Oppenheimers, the

Ruperts and even called up Michael Jackson abroad to ask if we could borrow his plane. None of the planes were available as they were all chartered out or being used by their owners at the time. The only solution in the end was using a commercial scheduled flight. I don't know how we did it, but we managed. As time went by we perfected the art of commercial travelling with Madiba. As long as first class provided a proper flat bed for him to sleep in and the airport had the facilities of a passenger assistance unit that could elevate him to the level of the plane, avoiding the climbing of any steps, we could fly commercially. We just had to keep passengers and crew at bay and avoid him having to sign menus and other items throughout the flight. It was a nightmare at first.

So we set off to the Bahamas on holiday, our first holiday in five years. Madiba, Mrs Machel, Josina Machel (Mrs Machel's daughter), me, security and a doctor. We were all nervous but it all worked out well. We transferred in Atlanta and went on to Nassau. One had to find a way of both accommodating Madiba's needs but also taking facilities at airports and their supporting staff capabilities into account. It was negotiating and compromising all the time. At every airport, disembarking after long flights, people wanted to take photographs with him or ask for autographs. After a sixteen-hour flight an eighty-one-year-old just shouldn't be asked to have photographs taken or sign autographs. He needed space to breathe and to regain strength at every opportunity, and although one didn't want to be nasty to people I would go to great lengths to explain that he was elderly and needed space and shouldn't be bothered with autographs. In most instances people understood although the die-hards always persisted.

After the Bahamas trip we travelled the world trying to raise funds for the newly established Nelson Mandela Foundation. In Germany Madiba met with the Chancellor of the time Gerhard Schröder to ask for support for our Foundation. From Germany we went to Tunis to see President Ben Ali to also ask him for support. He had the most beautiful palace decorated in the finest mosaics.

From Tunis we went to Tripoli to visit the Brother Leader Gaddafi and ask for his support for the Foundation. The leaders from the West turned a blind eye to Madiba's association with Gaddafi. It was always entertaining to see the Brother Leader. One waited for days and days to receive word from him and then suddenly everyone had to jump and move to where he was hiding, sometimes in the desert, always fearing surprise attacks by the West in retaliation of the Lockerbie bombing. On this particular visit he invited us to dinner, and during our audience with him in the afternoon he asked what he could have prepared for us that night. By then I had been with Madiba when he had seen the Brother Leader on a few occasions and your face becomes familiar. He treated me with great respect and made me feel at home.

Earlier in the afternoon Madiba and I had a discussion about camel meat as we drove past camels and, when asked by the Brother Leader what we wanted for dinner, Madiba felt it was appropriate to ask for camel meat. 'Of course,' the Brother Leader responded. (He never wanted to be called President as he felt it was an invention by the Westerners which he refused to accept. To the end, we referred to him as the Brother Leader.) The camel meat tasted exactly like lamb. I was later told that they had to slaughter baby camels as the meat became tough the older the camel grew. I was not going to encourage the slaughter of baby animals so I never wanted to eat camel again. But it was a rare occasion that a head of state would ask Madiba what he wanted for dinner and I quite liked that Gaddafi was so considerate. Conversations were limited to pleasantries and a general view on whatever was happening in the world at the time. They always dwelled back to Lockerbie and the Brother Leader's unhappiness with the West for not delivering on its promises to lift all sanctions. And whenever Madiba travelled to the US, it would be a point of discussion there too.

Back home we were soon in the swing of things and attending to business as usual. We would attend a South African Chamber of

Business and National African Chamber of Commerce dinner the one day, and the next take the Afrikaans Trade Institute to rebuild a school in Qunu. Prof. Gerwel remained our anchor and adviser on everything we agreed to. He remained central to our decision-making process. We were also attending farewell functions, although it wasn't clear where we were going because business was continuing as usual. One such function was the welcoming ceremony hosted by the Qunu community and King Dalindyebo, the King of the Thembus of which Madiba was a clan member. They were hoping that Madiba would return to Qunu in retirement but we realized that even there he would never retire fully, as people would constantly approach him with their problems, considering him as the solver of all their tribulations no matter how mundane – from arguing about someone who stole his neighbour's chicken to serious traditional affairs and differences between the respective clans. Madiba was never overly traditional but he respected the tradition and culture of his clan.

We would welcome visits by groups of children from the organization Reach for a Dream when terminally ill children expressed their last wish as being to meet Madiba, have luncheons and dinners with old friends and comrades, fundraise for schools and clinics and even for the Bushbucks soccer team, the regional team that represented the area where Madiba came from. They weren't doing too well in the soccer league but he nevertheless felt obliged to help them because they were his 'home team'. He would see families of late warders, attend his grandchildren's graduation ceremonies, and in between try and find time to spend with Mrs Machel. He could fly to Botswana to receive an honorary doctorate and back at home that evening have dinner with Helen Suzman, his long-time supporter and friend from the Progressive Federal Party, now sadly departed. The pace was never a consideration to him. He wanted to continue doing as much as possible and squeeze a twenty-six-hour programme into a twenty-four-hour day.

A month later we were on our way abroad again. While we had the full support of a Foreign Affairs department before and the backing of diplomatic services, I now had to deal with negotiations from programmes to VIP rooms at airports to courtesy cars from foreign governments to accommodation needs etc., all by myself, in addition to asking for meetings with presidents, heads of state and people of importance. While at home in Johannesburg I started preparing for the next trip abroad. I also think Madiba just loved travelling, so he accepted invitations for no good enough reason and invented visits because he was determined to fundraise for the Foundation now. He looked for opportunity in everything.

If I ever thought of saying 'I'm sending someone else with you', the suggestion would be met with hostility. Not because of favouritism but only because he trusted that I would know what to do in any situation he would find himself in. I was not scared to tell a minister or a senior official when to stop as I could read his face and the unspoken gestures became easy to read. I constantly had to fend off media requests while abroad and my defence mechanisms were in overdrive. I was playing the role of that actress I'd wanted to become; doing things I could never do for anyone else but the position and the person in question required it.

Madiba called Prof. and told him about his intentions to visit the Middle East. They had discussed this for a while and strategized about the countries to be visited and what agenda to push for. As much as Madiba was our true north, Prof. was Madiba's true north politically and when it came to planning any strategy. Madiba admired Prof.'s intellect and insight apart from the fact that he considered and treated Prof. more like a son.

Our first stop was in Iran. I covered myself out of respect for the Muslim culture and kept my distance as far as possible. We then set off to dinner at the residence of President Khatami. As we entered his residence, a complete palace as one would expect, I fended off some photographers who used flashes while photographing Madiba. It is a known fact worldwide that Madiba's eyes were sensitive as a result of the bright reflection in the quarry where he'd had to dig out limestone on Robben Island for most of the eighteen years of imprisonment on the island. When his eyes were exposed to too much flash light they became red and teary to the extent where he had to wear sunglasses, even indoors and at night. We were all very protective over his eyes and therefore knew to fight off any photographers, with authority. So, of course, I assumed that position even though I was the only woman in sight, fending off the photographers.

President Khatami saw me fighting off the photographers but after Madiba entered his residence I kept to the back of the delegation so as to not offend anyone sensitive to the presence of women and left them to go upstairs alone for dinner. There were no other females present in President Khatami's residence. After about ten minutes at table and our food being served already, I got called by a panic-struck butler to follow him upstairs to where the President and Madiba were seated. I thought Madiba had purely called me as he usually would to introduce me, which he did, but then he said that President Khatami insisted that I sat at their table. I was extremely uncomfortable and didn't know how to behave; it was similar to how I felt being seated next to Queen Noor in 1995. The only difference was we were the only three people in the room this time and I was exposed to the scrutiny of two politicians: a serving and a former president.

President Khatami kept on asking me questions about my upbringing and the Afrikaans culture, almost as if Madiba wasn't even there. I kept on referring questions back to Madiba but Madiba was determined to let me answer and he peacefully enjoyed his meal, just nodding occasionally giving his approval to what I was saying, or then saying, 'Zeldina, what do you think?' To try and stop the enquiry launched at me, I thought of saying, 'Well, I actually just don't think anything,' but that was impossible to conceive. That must have been the least Madiba spoke during any dinner ever.

I remember from our state visit to France in 1995 I was intrigued that presidents could discuss the prices of import and export items, limited to oranges and bananas, and how many Airbuses South Africa was willing to order from France, but here in Iran the entire conversation was limited to the Afrikaans culture. Madiba thoroughly enjoyed the grilling I was getting and only now and then would he come to my rescue with a supportive smile. For years after he would remind people of my importance, of course jokingly, teasing me by reciting this story, telling people that the President of Iran insisted on inviting me to his table, and I would respond by saying that Madiba merely wanted to enjoy his food and therefore put me on the spot that night. Such was the teasing and joking with Madiba; always a story and a moment to remember.

I had to ensure, when drafting programmes for visits like these, that we were seen to do the politically correct thing. We would have to include a wreath-laying ceremony at the memorial site of the late Ayatollah Khomeini. As a youngster I remember a prayer for the people 'behind the iron curtain' and when asked what the iron curtain was, reference was made to the people who lived under the oppression of the Ayatollah Khomeini or the communist regimes. Now I was arranging wreath-laying ceremonies at the Ayatollah's grave. Then we would visit former President, Ayatollah Rafsanjani, as well as His Eminence Ayatollah Ali Khamenei, the Supreme Leader of Iran. As I was the only female at all these events the Supreme Leader noticed me amid a full room of photographers taking pictures of the two eminent people sitting together. The Ayatollah asked out loud: 'Who is that young lady at the back?' Madiba, knowing that I was the only woman in the room, answered excitedly, knowing that he would embarrass me and of course without even looking at me, 'Oh that's Zeldina. My secretary.'

I wanted Madiba to make eye contact with me so I could signal him with my eyes 'don't call me, please'. But he also knew when to ignore me because he knew I would be signalling to please not embarrass me. He avoided eye contact. I felt out of place but took the Ayatollah's instructions to sit next to Madiba, closer, where he could see me. Somehow my presence amused these people and they were intrigued by me, possibly not knowing what to make of a white lady being with the famous black freedom fighter.

I didn't bother about who I considered to be politically right or wrong in any discussion or who seemed progressive in their ideals; I was purely concerned and obsessed with the next five minutes, followed by the next twenty-four hours of Madiba's life, making sure that everything was organized for him in a way that would make life easier for him. Although my general understanding of the world improved I didn't have the space to absorb or understand the intricacies of these countries we visited.

From Iran we went to Damascus in Syria where we met the elderly President Assad. This was only a few years before he passed away. We also met his son who was an impressive young man at the time. The young President Assad clearly also overstayed his welcome and right now he is being challenged by rebels in his own country to force him to step down from the Presidency. Madiba would often say, when referring to people who served in such positions for too long, that 'leaders got drunk with power', and often when a head of state is being challenged like this, I think of those words, whether they apply to his situation or not.

From Syria we flew to Israel, via Jordan. Due to the strains between Syria and Israel we were not allowed to leave Syria and fly straight into Israel. Whenever I shared my frustrations with Madiba about these political difficulties we faced, trying to do the right thing, he would always say to me: 'No Zeldina, you see they just make life interesting', trying to encourage me to bear up. But sadly, in that moment, they were not so interesting to me.

Upon arrival in Israel we were rushed to our cars like sheep through a crush pen by Israeli police. They nearly left me and Charles (the doctor) behind. I was irritated by the way they handled us and this was one of the many times I had to try and justify my position and why the doctor and I had to be close to Madiba in such a way that they didn't think it was only because we simply wanted to be close to him. That was the challenge of travelling without a delegation, just me and the doctor and security. You had to fight your way open on the spot. There was never any back-up plan and your only concern was for Madiba: you thought of yourself and the rest when you were already in the situation. I am not a confrontational person in my private life but in situations like these I became another person, playing the actress I'd wanted to be trying to defend us all.

We stayed at the King David Hotel, and on the first night I ordered meat for Madiba's dinner and salad with cheese for myself from room service. Shortly after I put in the order a butler rang my door-bell. 'Madam,' he told me, 'we wanted to come and explain to you that this is a Kosher hotel and that you cannot have cheese and meat in the same room. You are not allowed.' I really didn't have the cap-acity to argue about food too. I lost the battle and sat with Madiba during dinner and then went to my room to have my cheese salad. The next morning we visited the grave of Yitzhak Rabin, the person who was believed could have negotiated a settlement between Israel and Palestine had it not been for his assassination. From there we visited President Weizman and then Prime Minister Ehud Barak. I liked President Weizman. Prime Minister Barak appeared some-what intolerant of Madiba and I didn't enjoy their interaction.

We walked on the Via Dolorosa in the Old City of Jerusalem. It was touching for me as a Christian when I was told that Jesus carried the cross along this road. They made a huge fuss over Madiba walk-ing the Via Dolorosa and hardly allowed him enough space to comfortably walk on the cobbles. We were all nervous as he could trip on the cobbles with his problematic knee and then injure it badly. He was already unstable on his feet. I touched the ancient cobbles and then asked our guide once again, 'So you mean that Jesus walked on these exact cobbles?' 'No,' he responded. There are apparently around seventeen storeys of building on top of the original road, but this is more or less the road he followed. I was very disappointed.

We then went to the Holocaust museum. One leaves it feeling traumatized and deeply disturbed. As we exited the museum a microphone was pushed in front of Madiba's face and his impres-sions of the museum were asked for, despite me explaining to journalists outside that he was not prepared to answer questions. He never liked to be pushed into a corner and he was irritated by any surprise factors. His response was simple: 'This is a tragedy that happened to the Jewish nation, but one should never lose sight of the fact that this burden is carried by the German people too. The current generation of Germans suffer to rid the stigma they have had to carry as a result of these events for which they themselves cannot be held accountable at this time and age.' These comments were not appreciated by the Israelis. I sensed some hostility and I was uneasy. (When we arrived back home Madiba had received several letters of complaint from Jewish friends from as far as America about these comments.)

We had a meeting the next day with the President and Prime Minister. They discussed politics and Madiba stuck to his guns around a solution to the Middle Eastern conflict. These conditions had to be adhered to by both parties before any settlement could be reached: 1. Israel had to acknowledge Palestine as an independent country. 2. Palestine had to acknowledge Israel within its clearly defined borders. 3. Parties had to identify a mediator that would be trusted by both. Madiba repeated this over and over again but it fell on deaf ears. There was no chemistry between Madiba and Ehud Barak or the Minister of Foreign Affairs, David Levy. President Weizman was older, however, and a bit more lenient and less aggressive in his response to these suggestions.

From Israel we went to Palestine and met with Yassar Arafat, whom we had encounters with on a number of previous occasions. He was very respectful towards Madiba but by now I was getting irritated by people's general feeling of victimization in the region. Everyone was a victim and I decided that that was half of the problem in the region for me. People should start feeling pride and dignity regardless of the past. The Palestinians were as unreasonable in their approach in solving the Middle Eastern conflict as were the Israelis.

While Madiba explained to me that the current conflict was started back in 1967 during the Six Day War (when Israel captured and occupied the Golan Heights, West Bank and Gaza Strip) I could clearly see myself that it had escalated to levels to which we won't see solutions in our generation. To me it visually presented a worse picture than apartheid. Families living 500 metres apart have not been able to visit one another in over thirty years, separated by barbed wire. Wherever there was a blade of green grass it was declared Israeli ground and protected by heavily armed guards. Wherever there was nothing, it was declared Palestinian ground. I found it difficult to understand but, with credit to the Israelis, it was clearly beyond a reasonable fight. The Palestinians lack the leadership to come to a resolve. They tried to compare their situation with that of South Africa but people were generally being extremely unreasonable in their thinking.

Madiba was scheduled to address the Palestinian parliament on the day before our departure. Prof. Gerwel edited the speech back in South Africa and emailed the new version to me. I didn't have time to read it and somehow a virus of some sort crept into the computer program. The last sentence of the speech ended with a mathematical formula. Madiba also didn't read the final edits and as a result he read out the maths at the end of the speech. It was in letters and, although I cannot remember the exact words, it was something like: 'For every two equals four minus seven times eight. I thank you.' We were all puzzled but after his speech the entire Palestinian parliament rose to their feet in resounding applause. The speech was translated simultaneously and either the translator didn't translate the maths formula or translated it into something profound. We were all surprised by the occurrence of this virus but amused by the fact that no one picked up on it. Prof. and I had many laughs about this incident for years to follow. The right thing would have been for us to proofread the speech prior to Madiba delivering it, but that was one of the disadvantages of travelling with a non-existent delegation and working at the pace and pressure we were subjected to.

From the Middle East, we travelled to Washington to meet with President Clinton. He was still in office and it was the first time I entered the White House. President Clinton was his charming self to Madiba, respectful and relaxed. He listened to Madiba's assessment of the Middle East and generally agreed with his suggestions. He was determined to try and help find a solution to the conflict. In our minds President Clinton was the right person to spearhead a peace process there as he had the trust of both parties. Or so we thought.

On the night of our stay in Washington we stayed in the Watergate Hotel. I felt weird as it was the Watergate scandal that saw the end of the Nixon era and I also believed that Monica Lewinsky, the woman who gambled with the future of the Clinton administration, also stayed in the Watergate apartments.

We had dinner with Madiba's old friend Morgan Freeman and the next day we set off to Dallas in Texas with Prince Bandar. The Prince had bought the Dallas Cowboys football team and we attended a real American football game with him. What an experience, but it was a chaotic day to say the least and it felt like every American in the stadium wanted to shake hands with Madiba. The following day Prince Bandar took us to a proper Texan café where we had tacos and tortillas, something Madiba had never eaten before and I am sure if questioned about it afterwards he would not have remembered what it was. It was very strange to him. What we ate and such traditions never appealed to him like they appealed to me. He liked his simple Xhosa home-cooked food. He was more interested in Prince Bandar's company and conversing with him, discussing the world's problems and probably on a few occasions successfully concluding how to bring about world peace.

From there we travelled to Atlanta to do a CNN interview, and from Atlanta we travelled to Houston to address the university. Our schedule was tight but Madiba loved every minute of it. He would never agree on doing something if he didn't feel up to it, and if there was an open space in his diary he had to find a cause to fill it. Security was tight on this visit because of Prince Bandar's involvement and this was probably the closest I ever came to assaulting a bodyguard. As we arrived at the university the car in which the doctor and I were travelling got cut off by security guards. We tried to tell our driver to insist on passing through the same entrance as Madiba's car, but he adhered to the traffic police instructions. As a result, Charles and I had to get out of the car and start making our way to Madiba. It was about a 600-metre walk. While we didn't mind the distance we did mind Madiba disappearing somewhere where we were not able to find him again.

Charles had his heavy medical bags to carry and I had my flaming temper and we walked at a fast pace. As we approached the building we could see that Madiba had already entered with Prince Bandar.

A bald-headed, massive American bodyguard stopped us; we told him that we needed access as we were part of Mr Mandela's delegation. He point blank refused. He didn't give an explanation nor was prepared to listen to an argument; he just said 'no'. Charles kept me calm and said wisely that eventually Madiba would look for us. As if he knew, the next minute Madiba appeared in the door again. He had come outside to look for us – something very unusual for a person of his stature. Ironically, the black man came to look for his two white servants, to rescue us. We could see him standing on the steps and he could see us, but the bodyguard was facing us and refused to turn his back on us to see for himself that Nelson Mandela was standing on the steps of the building calling us.

I was tempted to plant a flat open hand on his bald head when Prince Bandar's bodyguard, Neigfh, came running towards us to 'rescue' us. Due to previous interactions with Prince Bandar we knew Neigfh and he was an extremely kind gentleman. I turned round to the bodyguard and said: 'Are you happy now? Did it take Nelson Mandela to come outside to come and fetch us? You can bloody well hear we don't have an American accent. You can see the doctor has medical equipment . . .' I guess looking back at events today, he was just doing his job and I was being unreasonable, but sometimes people are just not open to persuasion or then even attempting to find out whether there may be any truth to your story.

People would always comment on the unlikely event of Madiba appointing a white fiery Afrikaner as his assistant, and Prof. would say, 'She has a good healthy mind', and Madiba would add, 'with logic and simplicity'.

I was feeling responsible for Madiba's well-being and I got the sense that he knew it, always enquiring where we were and looking out for us. Our presence made him feel secure in a way as he knew we would deflect any surprises or challenges. It was a professional co-dependency. We equally felt insecure not knowing where the other one was.

Because of all our travels together Charles and I had become close friends and, being the same age, we could relate well during our experiences in this world unknown to anyone else. Like many of the other doctors Charles deeply cared for Madiba too but people would jokingly refer to him as my slave. Madiba only once or twice fell ill during all our travels abroad and Charles was therefore on stand-by most of the time, not having much to do himself. We worked well together as a team and I would often ask him to do small things, like help to fetch laundry, or search for a newspaper or check up on a room service order for Madiba, wrapping a gift, finding a printer, etc., and from there his title as my slave was born. We had much teasing about it.

I sometimes didn't have time to unpack myself, or as soon as I sat down to make a telephone call back home there would be a foreign protocol person or hotel staff knocking at my door – President Mandela this and President Mandela that. I was the only point of contact in our delegation, for everything, and Charles sometimes had to man my door to enable me to just finish one thing at a time. The pressure was relentless. It sometimes felt like I was going crazy not being able to deal with the pressure but then people like Charles eased the pressure by helping with the mundane issues. He was the only other semi-permanent fixture to our team. Doctors rotated to travel with us too, but because of our hectic travel schedule not all of them wanted to sacrifice their medical day-to-day practices to accompany us. Our security teams also rotated and it was not often that the same team accompanied us on consecutive trips abroad. And when you spend that much time with someone it starts feeling like family.

We were very tired when we returned to South Africa but had the luxury of Prince Bandar's plane in which we all had proper beds to sleep on. It was always a big spoil to be hosted by him as he spared no expense to ensure that we had the best food and service possible. He was a gracious host, very tolerant of Madiba's age, and he had great respect for Madiba as a person, something which I in turn appreciated and valued.

Returning home, Madiba called a few influential Jewish people, such as Elie Wiesel, in the United States, warning them about the risks they were facing in that prominent American Jewish leaders were clearly agitating for America to take sides with Israel. Hoping then to bring about peace in the region was not going to happen as long as the mediator clearly took sides.

We heard that President Mbeki was not happy with Madiba's visit to the Middle East. Our visit there interfered with the South African government's diplomatic agenda. It is one of those situations where you are doomed if you do and doomed if you don't. Madiba wanted to try to help along the Middle East peace process and was continually asked to lend a hand, but in the end it seemed that sensitivities with the South African government prevailed. Thinking back it was also not the right thing to do for him to jump on a plane and try and resolve the Middle East war. Prof. Gerwel had to intervene, like on so many occasions, to neutralize the situation. It was clear that the external pressures from people were going to cause a lot of conflict for us in South Africa but ultimately Madiba's loyalty to his friends is what caused us to be in such situations.

On 6 November 1999 Nelson Mandela nearly died. Along with his team.

We were in Postmasburg, a small town in the Northern Cape. It was mid-summer and it was extremely hot. Gauteng (where Johannesburg and Pretoria are found) has a summer rainfall and the area is known for its intense thunderstorms in the midsummer afternoons. Despite trying to finish our work on the ground early, we took off later than we would have liked. We were travelling to Waterkloof, the military airforce base in Pretoria, on a King Air, a twin-propeller light aircraft. It was an ongoing battle to try and persuade the government to allow Madiba to use jet aircraft and they were running out of aircraft due to the busy schedules of President Mbeki and his deputy. Madiba was no longer priority but on this particular day a bigger plane could not be used because of the length of the landing strip in Postmasburg.

About thirty minutes before landing back in Pretoria the pilot turned around and called me to the cockpit. He told me that both

Waterkloof and Johannesburg International airports had been closed as a result of thunderstorms and that we might have to go and land elsewhere. I relayed the message to Madiba. He sat calmly, strapped in his seat watching the every move of the pilots. Soon we started hitting turbulence and the atmosphere in the plane was becoming tense. From where I was seated I could both see Madiba's face and hear the pilots' communication. It was growing urgent as the pilot was informing the control tower that we were not able to circle for much longer since we were running out of fuel and that they were being forced to decide where to land. All neighbouring airports were closed. As we dived through the clouds the turbulence was getting worse and at intervals the pilot had to let go of the steering column of the plane completely to allow the plane to be guided by turbulence. It was terrifying.

Madiba had a frown fixed on his forehead and was pouting his lips in dissatisfaction and Wayne Hendricks, one of the bodyguards, made a few jokes to try and ease the tension. At first he was funny but then I started getting angry at him out of panic. Wayne always had a charming and funny way to ease tension with his sense of humour and under the circumstances, even though he failed dismally, it was nice that he tried.

Madiba didn't say a word. One of Madiba's grandsons, who was also on the plane, looked half-sick when we hit an air pocket which threw the plane a few metres down. The contents of my handbag flew across the plane and we were holding on for dear life. The grandson's cellphone flew from the top pocket of his shirt across the plane and Wayne caught it mid-air in the front like bodyguards do. I could hear the pilots panicking but they were determined to try and land the aircraft at Waterkloof. Emergency services were being called on standby at the airport and by now tears were streaming down my face uncontrollably. I was crying reprehensively. Wayne was comforting me, trying to tell me that we were going to be OK but I couldn't see us emerging from this alive. At last we landed. The pilots were perspiring as they brought the plane to a standstill on the ground. Madiba put his hand on my shoulder and said: 'Don't worry Zeldina, we are safe now.' We disembarked, got into our cars and proceeded to Houghton.

I immediately left to go home but as I drove around the block I got a call from Xoliswa, Madiba's long-serving chef at the house, saying that Madiba wanted me to return to have coffee with him. I returned and he called me into the lounge. His grandson was still sitting with him. Madiba made me sit down and he could see I was visibly still in shock. He said: 'Zeldina, today was a terrible experience. But we should forget about it as soon as possible and the best thing for us would be to get on to a plane again as quickly as possible.' He was comparing it to like falling off a bike. The best you can do is to get back on again as soon as possible. He continued: 'I never want to fly in a small aircraft like that again and I never want to travel with any of my grandchildren again.' What he implied was that it was too risky for him to fly in a propeller aircraft and if anything ever happened to him he didn't want to risk his grandchildren's lives as well. From that day we refused for him to travel in propeller aircraft again. It created a lot of trouble for us with the airforce as they did not have a large fleet of jet-engine aircraft and they often had to charter. It contributed to the strained atmosphere between us and the Presidency but it was not something I was willing to compromise on after this experience.

Years later we were also in a helicopter incident. Madiba travelled to a rural area in the Transkei on one of our schools and clinics building visits and on our way there the pilots had expressed their concern over something in the engine overheating. They were convinced though that they would be able to fix it once they landed and they were not overly concerned. They thought they had managed to fix it but we were nervous before our return. We told our security on the ground about our concern, and as soon as we took off again after the event they left by road for the direction of Mthatha, where we were heading. About fifteen minutes into the flight oil sprayed all over the outside of the windows. We could no longer see through the window and you could clearly see it was oil spill, which obviously created a fire hazard. The pilots told us that we had to land and they slowly manoeuvered the Oryx helicopter to the ground.

They landed in a piece of open velt and, since the entire region was rural, there were no houses or people in sight. While we landed I called the security men on their way to the airport to tell them that we had had to do an emergency landing. We didn't land too far from the road and if they approached us they would see us in the velt. They arrived about twenty minutes later, but before they arrived I was concerned about our presence in the region, with the community not knowing why a military helicopter with heavily armed bodyguards outside it had landed in the middle of nowhere. The pilots tried to find the problem but they were unable to fix it. We subsequently got into the cars and drove to Mthatha where our flight back to Johannesburg departed from. Madiba was inclined to think that there may have been deliberate sabotage involved but I managed to convince him otherwise.

Huge parties were being planned around the world for the turning of the millennium and South Africa was bracing itself for the same celebrations. By now tension appeared to be growing between Madiba and President Mbeki. We heard rumours that the President seemed to be of the opinion that Madiba was conducting himself like a head of state. Madiba was doing what he always did – responding to ad hoc requests and trying to please everyone possible. Even though we sometimes disagreed with such decisions, he was the captain of his fate, the master of his soul (as he recited the poem 'Invictus' from his prison years) and he wanted to continue what pleased his soul. It was very difficult to focus on what we had hoped his post-Presidential office and its focus would be. Then there was always the feeling of entitlement from people across the world. They felt entitled to him in a way because some of them supported the struggle against apartheid and they expected him to do certain things, and he would eagerly oblige also feeling the need to repay dues. Secretly I think he also just loved travelling, and having been incarcerated for such a long time I do think that it was normal for him to want to travel and almost make up for lost time. The result of these influences, whatever its purpose was, is what constantly guided his actions and landed him in trouble from time to time.

I was not sure how deep the so-called rift was between Madiba and the President and how much it was imagined in other people's minds. For example, in November 1999 Madiba received a call from President Mbeki asking him to lead negotiations in the war-stricken Burundi. Personally I thought that Madiba couldn't take on more work but he agreed. Because of Madiba's intervention in Zaire (now known as the Democratic Republic of the Congo) during his Presidency, I assumed that President Mbeki thought it would be easier for Madiba to try and broker peace against the backdrop of what happened in the DRC. President Mbeki's agenda was also to try to bring about peace in Africa, as it would have economic advantages for South Africa. I also felt that it was perhaps a way for the government to keep Madiba occupied elsewhere and that giving him such a task would fully occupy him and distract him from being tempted or persuaded to interfere as he had done in the Middle East, or in what was going on at home for that matter.

I felt somewhat for President Mbeki. He was expected to fill the shoes of an icon in history. Yet I also believed that the ANC was responsible for creating this icon, identifying him as the symbol of freedom for the oppressed and it was wrong for ANC people to now feel that Madiba was behaving out of line. Publicly Madiba remained firm, saying that South Africa had never had a better President or Prime Minister in its history than President Mbeki. Sometimes I thought that President Mbeki probably felt that Madiba was patronizing him but Madiba believed in what he was saying, and years later his vision in this regard became apparent. Our country has never been economically as stable as after the Mbeki Presidency, and as a result we were completely shielded from the worldwide economic meltdown of the late 2000s.

There was never any ill intent or deliberateness in anything

Madiba did and therefore no reason in my mind why people would feel that Madiba was upstaging the President. It was these prophets of doom's own insecurities that showed. Whether it was really the President himself or his staff that were responsible for this perception I will never know. Madiba would often ask to speak to the President and was told that the call would be returned and it never happened. I felt people were becoming intolerant of the elderly Madiba. We would ask for appointments and were told the President was too busy. What the ANC should have done was to set out an agenda for Madiba but I understand it was difficult precisely because Madiba had such a strong will and determination to do what pleased his heart.

Alan Pillay, who was the administrative officer in our office during Madiba's Presidency, was one of President Mbeki's private secretaries and unless Alan acted as go-between, communication was extremely difficult between the two. Somehow when Alan helped, things happened and worked out fine without politicking.

It was difficult to manage that publicly though. Madiba was making a concerted effort to make sure that he spoke well of the President. Whenever Madiba and the President were together I had the task to ensure that Madiba showed the necessary respect by following protocol and ensuring that we were not seen to undermine protocol and the President in any way. It was difficult because people and the public would still give Madiba the standing ovation, the loudest welcome, and make a big fuss about him.

The President and Madiba were scheduled to be together on Robben Island for the turn of the millennium. At first a verbal invitation was extended and when we heard that the President would be there, we declined, precisely because we feared that Madiba's presence would put the President in a difficult position. We then received a call from the Presidency confirming that the President wanted Madiba to be there. Madiba refused again. We had to convince him by telling him that all his old comrades would be there, and it would be necessary for him to go to see them as there would be a live broadcast worldwide. He eventually agreed.

It was a beautiful evening on Robben Island and I remember chasing people back into the tent to try and force them to show some respect for the President, and not follow us as we were preparing to leave, deserting the tent to follow us while President Mbeki was still inside. I was becoming increasingly unpopular no matter what I did. While I was trying to be loyal to Madiba, I assumed the duty that he had to appear respectful towards the President, but the public and people made it difficult. I would also have to do it in a way not to make Madiba feel inadequate in any way but that he still got afforded the respect he deserved. Every little action therefore turned into a complex situation of thinking about scenarios and analysing everything that got proposed, and it took a lot of energy and emotional capabilities to please everyone and do the right thing. But then you have to stand firm and do whatever the person who employs you expects of you and take criticism and politics on the chin. I had to learn not to be a coward.

People would often write to Madiba to ask him to intervene in matters that were clearly the jurisdiction of a President. And then when I corrected them and referred them to the President's office I was often blamed for overprotecting Madiba and/or controlling him. I was called his 'minder' and I joked to say yes I don't mind. Yet Madiba himself didn't want to be involved in many things. He wanted to continue raising funds for his charities, to build his schools and clinics, but also to have the freedom to speak out on issues for which he was well known – issues of morality and human rights. People insisted on Madiba's attention and personal intervention and it was a lost battle no matter what one did.

Madiba was well known to be an outstanding fundraiser. He raised millions of dollars for the ANC following the unbanning of the party in the 1990s. Now he was focusing on his charitable causes. The ruler of Dubai had agreed to support his Foundation but due to interference from a South African diplomat in Dubai this particular effort was fruitless. We were only able to speculate as to the reason for the interference and on whose behalf the diplomat acted.

Madiba often boasted about his fundraising abilities. He said as long as it was for a good cause it was easy. Relentless in his approach, and because he never asked for money for himself, it was easy for him to put pressure on someone by arguing the importance of the cause. At first I couldn't figure out how it was so easy for him but after seeing him in action I understood that if you believed in the cause you fundraised for, it comes naturally.

Something which has puzzled me over the years is a story Madiba often repeated and went to great effort to report to President Mbeki and other ANC officials. Madiba was never a great administrator and he genuinely trusted people until the contrary became apparent. It would amaze me how he recited his fundraising efforts and the simplicity with which he considered the process. During his fundraising days for the ANC the moneys would simply be handed from one official to the next and he never mistrusted anyone in the process.

It was an arrangement I thought sounded practical and made sense. Madiba would receive the money, hand it to Tom Nkobi, the Treasurer General of the ANC at the time, to have the moneys deposited. (In our fundraising he refused to receive money personally and would insist that it be deposited or given directly to the Foundation or the Children's Fund, whichever he was trying to help at that stage.) Madiba was removed from society for twenty-seven years and he knew very little about banking or investments. I would then ask Madiba, while he told the story, whether anyone ever kept a record of the money. I was not suspicious of anyone but found it surprising that Madiba himself did not know how much money he really raised.

There was no doubt in his mind that the money reached its final destination, but then he would add that Tom Nkobi later suddenly died of unknown causes. I don't know how this related to the fundraising but it puzzled me and I would lie awake many nights trying to imagine what had happened. Madiba told us how he was sent from pillar to post when he tried to find a reason for Tom's sudden illness and that when he managed to visit him in Durban he was not left alone with him. Madiba said there was an 'awkward fellow' present, the Indian male nurse who was looking after Tom. Tom lived in Johannesburg, yet when he got ill he was sent to Durban, whereas we are supposed to have some of the world's best medical practitioners in Johannesburg.

In recent years, when the South African businessman Schabir Shaik was charged with corruption and fraud I simply noted the coincidence that his company was called Nkobi Holdings. Madiba, however, was concerned about then Deputy President Jacob Zuma's friendship with Schabir Shaik. Call it a sixth sense, I don't know. Part of Shaik's fraud charges were that he wrote off more than US$150,000 of loans made to Jacob Zuma. In South Africa, the donor of money to a private individual is liable to pay tax if annually that amount exceeds about US$10,000. It was argued that these amounts were paid to Jacob Zuma to influence the outcome of tenders around a controversial South African arms contract to supply the government with world-class artillery.

Shaik was found guilty of corruption and in the court proceedings the judge said that a 'corrupt relationship between Jacob Zuma and Schabir Shaik' had been found.

Madiba went to great lengths to try and discuss this with several ANC officials and on more than three or four occasions we were running around after officials trying to find time for Madiba to raise this matter and ask that it be looked into. No one ever got back to him and I was slowly introduced to the hypocrisy of politics. They would sit in front of him, listen to him and sometimes even agree with him, but then as soon as we left the matter disappeared. On tens of hundreds of occasions I heard him saying to crowds and in speeches that people must guard against only doing what serves their best interests but remain loyal to the cause and to their conscience. More and more even today, you see the hypocrisy that he warned against. As if he could see it coming. Some people have lost the passion for the party, the purpose of the cause: representing the people. It has become a selfish, self-righteous war in South African politics where self-interest is the only agenda, and that has become the cancer of corruption.

We visited Arusha in Tanzania for the first time as part of Madiba's negotiations in the Burundi peace process. After Arusha we went to New York. It was my first trip to New York too. We stayed in the Waldorf Astoria Hotel and I remember being impressed by the size of the room, although we were guests of the late US Ambassador to the UN, Richard Holbrooke, and didn't stay in the ordinary part of the hotel. My experience of New York was limited to having a proper Waldorf Salad in the Waldorf hotel and visiting the UN. As we had no protocol or media liaison people around us – it was just me – I became even more adamant not to leave the hotel, in case anything happened or Madiba needed me during my absence.

Madiba was interested in engaging with Ambassador Holbrooke to help us raise funds but also to discuss the issues he touched on during his visit to Israel and Palestine the year before, as well as briefing him about Burundi. During our visit Ambassador Holbrooke hosted a reception in his apartment. It was the first time I met Whoopi Goldberg, whom I was told by Madiba did a lot to oppose apartheid during his incarceration. She made a powerful speech during the well-publicized 'Free Mandela Concert' at Wembley Stadium in England in 1988.

I fondly recall meeting Robert De Niro for the first time too. He brought Grace, his wife, and his lovely sons to meet Madiba. Madiba was completely at ease but one of the boys didn't want anything to do with him. Over the years I've come to the conclusion that Madiba has almost been turned into a fantasy character as a result of media exposure. Children do not know how to react towards him and then usually they don't react the way parents expect them to. It's similar to children's reactions when they are confronted with Santa Claus or someone dressed in a Disney character suit. Robert pulled his son to the side and said: 'You will regret this for the rest of your life . . . now behave.' The little boy of about seven years of age had little understanding of that statement and both Madiba and I were amused by Robert's efforts to get his son to react in a way that would be valuable to him in future. The child just refused to co-operate.

It was impressive to visit the United Nations, a body for which Madiba had great respect. We met with Kofi Annan, the then Secretary-General, and I couldn't help but feel the aura of respect between the two men.

Madiba was scheduled to have an interview with Larry King on CNN. In my negotiations with the producers I asked them countless times to provide us with a set of questions or topics to be discussed as Madiba wanted to be prepared for the interview. They refused and said that Larry never provides such material before an interview. I let it go. Not one of the best interviews Madiba had ever done and it was to Larry's detriment. Madiba closed down and his answers were short and to the point, very unlike him as the warmth of character got lost. He answered the questions he was asked but he didn't really engage. It was clear that the producers were more interested in adding Madiba to Larry's interview CV than getting really good content had he been prepared for the interview. It was a very different experience when Madiba appeared with Oprah. She was warm and friendly and supportive of his work and her team had no problem providing topics beforehand; as a result Madiba responded better.

People always asked very similar questions of Madiba, whether they met him for interviews or extended interactions at functions. They would usually ask him one of a few things and his responses would be standard, sometimes adapted to fit the circumstances during the interview but usually more or less the same: to 'What do you consider the characteristics of a good leader?' he would respond, 'A person who serves his people' and elaborate on that. To 'Do you have no bitterness or regret after spending so much time in prison?' he would respond: 'Regret is the most useless of emotions because you cannot change anything. I made the choices I did because they pleased my soul at the time.' They then frequently asked, 'How would you like to be remembered?' and he would say without hesitation: 'One would leave that to other people to decide how they want to remember you.' I found that funny. He could have said 'a humanitarian', 'a person that served his people', or whatever, but he simply wanted to leave it to others to decide and not be dictating history.

When he passed away in 2013 I noticed how many people had stories to tell about Madiba – some of them so unbelievable and sometimes a bit out of character that made them hard to truly believe for those who knew Madiba well. Yet, at that point I was reminded of his wish that people should be left the freedom to remember him as they wanted and I specifically made a point in an interview, when asked about it, to say that people should be left to do exactly that. Whether their memories were good or bad or even fictional, it really is about what happens in the heart when you hear his name, providing that such stories do not betray his legacy.

We also visited the estate of George Soros, as Madiba asked him for a donation for the Foundation. Sadly nothing happened and we returned to New York empty handed. I heard later that Mr Soros wasn't completely clear on the strategic direction of the Foundation, hence his hesitation to support it financially, which I thought was fair. The Foundation tried to cater for Madiba's changing agenda. First it was schools and clinics and his post-Presidential office, then the latter remained but its focus shifted to AIDS and education, and later dialogue was added too. It was confusing to the public.

We often found ourselves (me, the doctor and security) waiting for Madiba in these palaces, grand hotels and houses we only ever before saw in movies. On the first few occasions you admire other people's success in life and I think then you are envious, but later a house becomes a house and you don't even notice any longer. The grandeur loses its charm. The only concerns I had was that there should be no stairs to where Madiba was supposed to go, as he had difficulty climbing them, and that he should never be left alone where he could be caught in any situation where he felt compromised and we were not close enough for him to call on us when necessary. I usually settled him in at the meeting and then started monitoring the watch. He never wanted to stay longer than thirty or forty minutes anywhere and usually got to the point of his discussion pretty fast. After thirty minutes, if I was not inside the meeting (which I usually tried to avoid to be able to do other things while waiting outside), I would go in to remind him to watch the time. He would then jokingly tell his hosts, 'No, you see, this is my boss and I have to listen to her otherwise I would lose my job', and people would look at me with strange expressions, from 'oh that's funny' to 'oh yes the whites were the apartheid regime so I'm sure they still do that', totally confused with such remarks. I usually laughed at his comments to try and ease the tension one felt in the room as not everyone got his sense of humour immediately. So whether it was funny or not, I forced a laugh to try and show people that it was just a joke. If he was still there twenty minutes after my first announcement, I would then remind him again and he would without fail get up and announce that it was time for him to leave.

He expected to be 'rescued' sometimes as well. In some meetings he would call me to ask 'how much time do we have?' and that would be an indication to me that I should watch the time and not allow things to drag on for too long. Time was therefore always a matter of great contestation between other people and myself. Not to Madiba, but to outsiders who felt he should or could stay longer or that he was being disrespectful. To try and please so many people one needed a thirty-six-hour day and it was simply impossible. He was, however, never someone who would do anything against his will. He was a born leader and the person who wanted to remain in charge even when he made others feel that their input was of vital importance to his decision-making process. He had an excessive need for discipline but then also a very very strong will that bordered on hard-headedness sometimes.

★

On 28 April 2000 we visited Bujumbura in Burundi. It is one of the most beautiful cities in Africa, surrounded by trees and beautiful landscapes. Sadly the roads and infrastructure have been damaged by the civil war and clearly much had to be done to repair not only the infrastructure but also faith by potential foreign investors. It was tense in the area and although the Burundian people were very happy to receive Madiba, one had to be very careful not to be aligned to any one party involved in the negotiations. We travelled right into the war zone where Madiba addressed refugees and gave them the one thing people needed: hope.

On 3 May we paid a one-day visit to London in order to appear in the royal court in London, following Madiba's appointment as a Queen's Counsel by his friend Queen Elizabeth. We really tried to convince him not to travel to London for one day but he insisted. He wanted to honour his warm friendship with the Queen. I think he was one of very few people who called her by her first name and she seemed to be amused by it. I was entertained by these inter-actions. When he was questioned one day by Mrs Machel and told that it was not proper to call the Queen by her first name, he responded: 'But she calls me Nelson.' On one occasion when he saw her he said, 'Oh Elizabeth, you've lost weight!' Not something everybody gets to tell the Queen of England.

We travelled like businessmen who often go to Europe for one day. It was however difficult as Madiba was growing old and the logistics weren't as straightforward or simple as hopping onto a plane for a one-day visit overseas. We could only stay for one day as we were scheduled to attend a farewell dinner for Madiba's close friend Dr Mamphela Ramphele at the University of Cape Town the next evening. She had been appointed to the World Bank and was leaving Cape Town. She was the first medical doctor to attend to his health after he was released from prison and she referred him to some of the best cardiologists in South Africa at the time.

Life also continues to happen even when you are this busy. Madiba's good friend and colleague Dr Ismail Meer passed away and we flew to Durban to go and pay our respects to the Meer family. I noticed that more and more of his friends were passing away and he clearly noticed it too, which must be unsettling for any elderly person. He knew so many people and frequently we found ourselves attending funerals over consecutive weekends. Still it was also something that was expected of him and little consideration was given to what impact it must have on an elderly person to be attending funerals almost weekly.

In May 2000 we travelled to Monaco upon the request of South African billionaire businessman Johann Rupert. Johann provided a private plane to fly Madiba to Monaco where he attended the first ever Laureus Sports Awards. We also met with the now late Prince Rainier and young Prince Albert. It was the first time we met the singer Bono, who was introduced by Naomi Campbell. I had to take time to explain to Madiba who Bono was, that he boycotted South Africa with his music during apartheid and that he was a musical legend to my generation. I was sad to leave Monaco, being a Grand Prix fan, as it was only a day before the qualifying rounds in Monaco. We could hear the Formula 1 cars being tested in the streets and I left feeling disappointed that I came so close to attending a Grand Prix, but I simply couldn't stay.

Then in late 2000 Madiba was invited to visit Australia to attend the 'What Makes a Champion?' conference. He was also scheduled to receive honorary doctorates from the University of Sydney and the University of Technology. Whenever we had to prepare for an honorary doctorate we had to send his measurements in advance for the particular university to prepare his academic robes, including his head measurements. Whenever I would ask to take his measurements he was tolerant but he was eager to get it done sooner than later. He was not the most patient person when it came to fiddling over him. He would agree but urge me to be quick.

By now I had changed so much and I was comfortable around him. He had managed to destroy all my prejudices about black people. I had a deep sense of caring for him like one would care for your own elderly grandparents. Whenever I didn't see him for a day or two, I would kiss him when I saw him again as we greeted. Later it became every day even if I saw him consecutive days. How much I had changed! I started missing him whenever a day passed that we didn't work. He often held onto me when he walked or took my hand when climbing up or down stairs. I could touch his hair without thinking anything of it, trying to push down on disorderly hair whenever the wind or a hat rumpled it. I had come such a long way and felt angry about the prejudices we were brought up with.

Madiba was always well groomed and took great care in making sure that his skin was well moisturized, and I remember how I sometimes had to struggle during his Presidency to get a particular lotion that was not available on the South African market at the time – simple Palmer's Body Lotion that he used while he was imprisoned. I think the company may have stopped manufacturing it in South Africa for a while and we had to ask people in the United States to buy it in bulk and send it to us in South Africa. The same with the eye drops he preferred: Refresh Plus, the blue and white box. He was just so meticulous about certain things.

In Australia he was scheduled to have meetings with Prime Minister John Howard as well as the famous and rich Packer family, concerning a donors' internet portal to raise funds for the Nelson Mandela Children's Fund and Foundation. His meeting with the Prime Minister was merely a courtesy call. The attempt to persuade the Packer family to donate to his charities was one of the efforts that never realized a donation and I don't know why.

The flight to Australia was tiring but the captain of our commercial plane offered Madiba the crew rest room for him to be able to have a flat bed to sleep on. I thought it was very kind and we were extremely grateful.

Arriving in Sydney we settled in, and after adjusting to the time difference we took Madiba to Sydney's famous zoo. We were allowed to feed giraffes, hold baby kangaroos and koala and watched dingos being fed. I am convinced that we would not have had these privileges if we were not in the company of Nelson Mandela. We toured past the Opera House on a boat and went to have lunch at Prime Minister Howard's residence. I liked him. He was really a kind man and without any pretence. They debated the Aborigines' issues and Madiba was under pressure to speak out against the government for their treatment of the Aborigines. Madiba maintained what he had said for a long time – that he would listen to the grievances of people but that he would not interfere in the domestic affairs of another country. While he acknowledged and respected them he refused to be drawn into any controversy. It was shortly before the Sydney Olympics and we visited the South African team in the Olympic village, where Madiba addressed them and wished them well.

From Sydney we went on to Canberra where we were hosted by the Governor-General, the equivalent of a head of state. We stayed in his beautiful guest house where one could see the kangaroos through the window while having breakfast in the dining room. On these occasions and while we shared meals Madiba would recite all the knowledge he had about a particular topic. On kangaroos he gave me a long lesson about their pouches and he freely offered knowledge until I asked a question that he didn't know the answer to. That was usually the end of that particular conversation. He didn't like me asking difficult questions.

We also visited Melbourne and it became clear to me that unless one experiences another country by moving around with the ordinary people, it would always be difficult to figure out why so many South Africans move to Australia to start a new life there. Staying in government guest houses and being hosted by them never gives you a real sense of life in another country.

Back at home the pressure was on the increase. Madiba was more in demand than ever before. He was becoming the saviour of everything and everybody. Whenever people didn't get satisfactory responses from government they would turn to him. He was seen as the person who could intervene in anything and resolve any problems anyone had. People elevated him to a saint-like status and he would remind them: 'A saint is a sinner who keeps on trying.' I loved that saying.

Often people wrote to him from pure frustration when they didn't get solutions from government. We could never interfere with service delivery or matters that could be seen to tread on government territory. We had no desire and we had no time, and sometimes it was really a blessing in disguise to be able to say 'we simply can't'. One had to understand though, that when a person turned to Nelson Mandela it was almost in a last desperate attempt – no matter how frustrated we as administrators became with the endless paperwork involved. Even people writing to him from prison had to be given the dignity and consideration they deserved of a response, even if it was just an acknowledgement of their existence. Something I didn't ever want on my conscience was a person committing suicide or something happening to someone as a result of our ignorance: if we didn't respond to a letter or simply ignored it.

Being a public figure and making that choice to be in public like Madiba, one has an obligation to the public. It drove my colleagues insane that I would insist on acknowledging people's correspondence even if we couldn't help or weren't interested. Floods of letters were being received from people who needed schools, clinics, medicine, financial assistance, scholarships and every kind of help imaginable. Sometimes it was as simple as: 'Dear Mr Mandela, Can you please buy me a bike.' Madiba was, according to the writer of every letter, their only hope, whether it was poverty, education, social issues, disputes, he was still their President and President to the world.

How we agreed upon things came down ultimately to what he essentially felt like doing. He was, however, never able to turn offers down personally as he never wanted to disappoint people, and if someone had to do that, it was me. I often relied on Professor Gerwel to give us guidance and input but things were pretty much left to Madiba himself to decide. But often Madiba would be convinced to do something by someone who saw him at a meeting and talked him into taking another trip. Madiba was equally to blame. He could say no, but secretly I think he just loved travelling. It was bordering on the ridiculous, though. We were all exhausted. No other person of Madiba's age followed such a gruelling travelling schedule loaded with formal engagements as he did. Yet he would never complain about being tired and always look for another opportunity to travel or do more. His duties were never going to come to an end.

Apart from the Burundi peace process and the schools and clinics project (as well as trying to please the entire world), Madiba was also depended upon by leaders from the rural area he came from. So he received a call from the head of the Pondos, King Thandizulu Sigcau, one day. The call was short and to the point: 'I want you to arrange two bursaries for my daughters to study in the United States', and that was the end of the conversation. There were no other words in that conversation and Madiba, the subject, knew what to do. So he arranged the two scholarships through Coca-Cola. His relationship with the Pondo King was strange and I had great difficulty trying to understand and comprehend traditional affairs. Whenever we travelled to Qunu over Christmas, King Thandizulu would appear with a sheep as a present to Madiba for Christmas. This gesture meant a lot to Madiba.

The King's daughters successfully completed their studies in the United States and they really made us all proud. They've become role models in their own right and didn't waste the opportunities they got, but grasped them and worked hard. Sadly the King passed away in 2013 while Madiba was hospitalized and we were unable to reach out to them in time to pay our respects. I nevertheless maintained contact with them.

In 2000 I turned thirty. It was an emotional time for me and I felt as if my youth was over. Silly as one can be at that age. Madiba made fun of me, understandably, and teased me. He would repeatedly ask how old I was supposed to turn in October with a broad smile on his face, and I would respond every time saying thirty!! He would laugh and say, 'Oh no, you are still very young.' He would deliberately pretend to forget just for the sake of teasing me. I didn't feel young and every time he asked I would be upset. He knew that but he loved teasing me, though there was no cruel intent from his side. He would also always ask: 'How many boyfriends do you have now?' And I would come up with any number. Sometimes he would ask when arriving in the office whether I had called all my boyfriends and I would play along and say I couldn't get hold of one or two of them but the rest were all taken care of. My responses in playing along created great laughs on both sides. He had standard questions to all the female staff and teased people in different ways. His humour never failed.

I reflected on matters over the years and decided that even today, in my forties, I am emotionally immature as a result of the stress and pressure of the years. It was a young age for me to have experienced the things I did and absorb the pressures I did. I never had a normal relationship after I started working for Madiba: I was working all the time and when I didn't work I was resting. I never got in touch with mainstream youth apart from my colleagues but I was also never in the same place for long enough to even maintain stable platonic friendships. As a result, I still lack the emotional capability to deal with very ordinary things. But I was becoming good at understanding politics, how the world operated, taking care of Madiba, and perfecting the art of dealing with logistics and arrangements around the most famous person on earth, and that was my only concern at the time. Still I would never exchange the experience and opportunity of working for Nelson Mandela for any other privileges.

Again, we got called by former President P. W. Botha. He seemed insistent on holding Nelson Mandela personally responsible for his grudges and grievances with modern South Africa. Many people who have not accepted the new South Africa do that. Whenever something goes wrong, it is put on Madiba's shoulders. People inherently want a scapegoat or someone to say 'I told you so' to when something doesn't go their way. For whites to have surrendered power they were always going to be over-critical of a black government, and when things no longer pleased them it would be blamed on the fact that blacks were inefficient and unable to run the country as they insisted they could. Some people just love complaining, they make a life of it. There is a difference between really being concerned about service delivery and incompetence and just complaining for the sake of it. It is just part of human nature but the racial issue complicated matters.

One day I received such a call from Mr Botha's residence and was told that the former President wanted to speak to Madiba. I returned the call and connected them. I was never Mr Botha's biggest cheerleader and because he didn't address Madiba in a respectful manner to my liking I was always on the back foot when he called. Whenever someone referred to Madiba as 'Mandela' or 'Nelson' my neck hair raised. Yet Madiba was always overly friendly and courteous to Mr Botha. I was reminded of a well-known statement Madiba made saying that it is easier to change others than it is to change yourself. I had to work on my perceptions about Mr Botha. Madiba truly and honestly didn't hold grudges. He had, as a result, no reason to be anything but friendly with his former enemies.

They spoke briefly, after which Madiba asked me to get the Minister of Police. He told me that Mr Botha had complained about the number of bodyguards he was given while he (Madiba) and former President de Klerk received a full contingent of security personnel, yet they were all former presidents. To me, the older you became the less the threat level against you, and the less you moved in public the less security you needed; I also didn't see how this was Madiba's problem. I nevertheless did as I was told.

We called the Minister and Madiba asked him to look into the matter. Madiba had also promised Mr Botha that I would call him back in a few days and give him a progress report. Two days later Mr Botha called again: '*Juffrou* [Miss], when am I supposed to get a report from Mandela?' Not 'how are you?' or anything, just that. I deliberately over-emphasized titles in my response, saying: '*Mister* Botha, *Mister* Mandela has spoken to the Minister and we are awaiting feedback. I am sure that *Mister* Mandela will respond to you as soon as we have a response from the Minister.' He insisted that I remind Madiba to talk to 'them', implying the government. It was a common occurrence among white South Africans to talk of 'them' and 'us'. 'Us' referred to white South Africans and 'them' or 'they' referred to black people more specifically. The more tolerant I became of certain things such as people's diversity and allowing them to believe what they want without the urge to force my opinion on matters, the more intolerant I was growing to the use of language that demonstrated lack of respect from my own people.

In the old South Africa people used the 'k-word' (*kaffir*) to refer to black people. It is a derogatory term and now considered hate-speech in our new constitution. Strangely, in my immediate surroundings or whenever I was in their presence family and friends who sometimes used the 'k-word' stopped doing so or avoided it whenever I was around. If they did use it I would reprimand them and possibly avoid seeing them again. It is something that became unbearable to me. And not only the use of that word but also people's generalizations and judgements when it came to black people. Those generalizations were baseless and unjustifiable and I often found myself in heated debates with whites about issues around respect. I would point out the same to black people on social media whenever they used derogatory terms towards whites too, but it could easily get out of hand as I, being white, would cause a furore for trying to reprimand black people, which distracted from the initial argument.

I told Mr Botha that Madiba had spoken to the Minister but he ended the call with 'tell him I'm waiting'. Dropping the phone I thought: I don't think so. There was really no need for me to report this to Madiba and agitate him. I knew that he was waiting to hear from the Minister and that the Minister would act on it. Two days later Mr Botha called with the same questions and orders. I told Madiba this time and asked whether he could speak to Mr Botha to calm him down; perhaps he then would stop calling me. Madiba said no. I couldn't believe what I heard and laughed at his response. I thought at first he was joking with me. It was not that he was not willing to help either Mr Botha or myself but he didn't want to talk to him again. End of story. And I knew when Madiba felt like that about something or someone, there was no use in trying to convince him otherwise. He didn't often respond like this, so when he did you knew it was the end of the movie. I don't know whether the matter was resolved but we didn't hear from Mr Botha again. I left the matter at that and really couldn't care about how many security guards he had. It was as if he intended to say to Madiba, 'I started the negotiations around you being freed and the ANC being unbanned and now I don't even have enough security guards.' Mr Botha wanted to hold Madiba responsible too. Well, approach determines attitude.

Increasingly, we were working on peace missions around the world. In March 2001 we travelled to Seoul to talk to the Prime Minister of South Korea about the idea of a Peace Park connecting North and South Korea. The Peace Parks Foundation negotiates and establishes conservation areas that stretch over national borders, creating an area to restore ecological communities. Madiba was the Patron of the Peace Parks Foundation, headed by Prince Bernhard of the Netherlands and Dr Anton Rupert. Prince Bernhard and Dr Rupert had been friends for centuries and together they established the World Wide Fund for Nature Conservation with great success, followed by the Peace Parks Foundation. On our visit to South Korea President Kim Dae-jung was receptive of the idea but clearly expressed his disbelief that North Korea would come to the party. Our requests to meet with the Chairman of the National Defence Commission of North Korea, the supreme position of power held by Kim Jong-il at the time, fell on deaf ears and we never received a response.

The public probably thought that Madiba would be welcomed anywhere in the world. Well, no. North Korea was one such place. No interest whatsoever. We tried to avoid situations where we felt there was a chance of failure but because of Prince Bernhard's and Dr Rupert's involvement in this particular case Madiba wanted to try at least. We sat around in South Korea for a few days, and when we realized that the North Koreans were ignoring us we simply returned home. Strangely, being so far away from home and not attending to official business gave us a bit of a break from the craziness back at home. On this particular visit I was again asked to be in Madiba's room when the masseuse came to his room for treatments. As usual I tried to give that task to one of the security men, until I noticed that the masseuse was blind. Even though I had told Madiba in Afrikaans that she was blind he was alert all the time during the massage as opposed to being relaxed. I feared that at some point he was going to tell her to stop and I just couldn't control myself from laughing out loud. It's not that I didn't have respect for her or her disability but more about Madiba, who appeared so tense in the situation. She was, contrary to what I expected, exceptionally professional. They say if you are born without one of your senses some of the others overdevelop and I got to see that. It was clear that she was an excellent masseuse and had 'healing hands'.

Madiba had this strange habit of keeping his watch on local South African time no matter where in the world we were travelling. We had to wake up at the strangest hours in order for him not to adjust his body clock to time difference too much so that he would not suffer from jet-lag when we returned home. And then, wherever we were in the world, in whatever time zone, we had to call Mrs Machel wherever she was in the morning and in the evening. I remember being in Seoul and not finding Mrs Machel immediately and Madiba insisting on staying awake until we did. It was one of those precious things he insisted on, being a husband. She had to be called in the morning before she had breakfast and in the evening before she went to sleep. 'How are you Mum, how was your day?' he would say. Upon which I would leave the room to give them a few minutes of privacy before resuming our programme or getting on with business. It would also give me the opportunity to then tell Mum what we were up to during the day.

We were then invited for Madiba to receive the German Media Prize in Baden-Baden and to be flown to Germany courtesy of Mercedes-Benz. By now I had appointed an assistant, Marianne Mudziwa, and Maretha was filling the gaps where necessary. They relieved me of much of the admin pressure. The staff in the office were still relying on me for guidance in terms of responses to people who wrote to Madiba. Since we didn't have a protocol or media section, all liaison where it concerned Madiba personally was pretty much left to me. So were the media enquiries. Madiba and Prof. Gerwel were my only guides. I would sometimes call Madiba twenty times a day to ask his advice on things whenever he didn't come to the office. He patiently answered me and told me how to do things, how to respond and where to find answers if he couldn't give them to me, and then always consult Prof. Gerwel.

He would explain his strategy to me, how he thought it best to approach a particular issue he wanted to raise or what his plans were to achieve an end goal in the greatest detail, and I was expected to ensure that we stuck to whatever strategy he decided upon. And when he spoke, you listened. I always made notes of things he said, of crucial keywords. I would often repeat something to him after he had said it but then he would correct me or go into more detail if it was necessary or he suspected that I misunderstood. Semantics subsequently became a passion to me. It is not easy for someone whose first language is not English to speak it fluently and I realized I had to be extremely careful of what and how I said things. Sometimes I got it right, sometimes I didn't, but Madiba was patient and he never pointed out mistakes but would find a subtle way to explain things to me differently. 'No, you see . . .' followed by the explanation. Most of the time though I managed to get it right. I couldn't afford to be a liability to him.

The trip to Baden-Baden was approaching in March 2001 and, having a full travelling schedule ahead, I had to focus my attention on organizing the upcoming trip, liaising to ensure that travel, accommodation, planes, trains and automobiles were all organized to not only befit Nelson Mandela but also to his best comfort. The pressure was increasing and for two nights prior to departure I worked right through the night, preparing for the visit and trying to avoid a situation where I left the office behind with a backlog of correspondence.

As flights from South Africa to Europe leave early evening we departed for Germany on a Thursday evening. I usually sat next to Madiba in the plane if the seat beside him could not be left open to afford him more space or Mrs Machel didn't accompany us, and on this night the Lufthansa flight was full so my seat was next to his. I would usually settle him in once we got on board the plane, making sure he didn't want anything to eat or drink, and then prepared his bed for the night in the best possible way in a first-class cabin after take off. Generally airlines were great in having specific food on board for him and making sure we had enough pillows and blankets for him to be comfortable. After helping him to settle in I strapped myself in my seat for take off and promptly fell fast asleep, only waking up the next morning as we landed. I had slept right through the night and I deserted Madiba. I hadn't even brushed my teeth or washed my face, something I never neglected no matter what.

I was angry at myself and questioned the security staff about his comfort through the night. The crew took care of him together with security and he was fine, but it was inexcusable to me as I failed in my task. I felt guilty for days after.

I noticed when I woke up I was covered with a blanket and had a pillow behind my head. When I asked the security who had covered me they said Madiba did. The poor man. Here I was supposed to take care of him but he was taking care of me instead. Madiba was worried that I was not getting enough sleep and he would complain to Prof. Gerwel often that I was working too hard – however it didn't make Madiba stop calling me or slow down either.

I remember on another occasion on a British Airways flight waking up during the night because of movement around me. Madiba went to the bathroom in the middle of the night, under the watchful eye of security. I lay awake waiting for him to return to his seat to see if he needed anything and when he passed me on his way back to his seat, he stopped and covered my feet with a blanket. These moments touched the most inner part of my heart. I couldn't remember as a child being tucked in by my parents, yet here the man we all had feared in the late 1980s (when we became aware of his existence) was covering my feet, worried about my well-being. Sometimes when I was tired I would silently weep, appreciating how much this man cared for me. It felt like no one else loved me as much as Madiba did. He treated me like I was part of his people, caring for me like you would for your own. And my history made it almost impossible to accept that I deserved any of this care and love.

There was never really any down time and we spent hours together each day. When we travelled without Mrs Machel or one of the daughters he didn't want to be alone during meal times and I would therefore often have to sit with him. I wanted to give him space but he would insist on me returning shortly after I left him anytime.

I enjoyed sitting with him at meals while we travelled, listening to his stories but also hearing his views on so many things. He remained adamant that the biggest challenge that faced 'our people' was education and the rationale behind his belief made perfect sense. I understood all the challenges the government faced, not having been in power before and having to deal with the financial challenges involved in reworking the financial system and replenishing the funds that were used to keep apartheid going. Few people realized that the apartheid regime borrowed money from the state pension funds to support apartheid and now that a new government was in power no one knew where the money would come from to rebuild those pension funds. It was not something that was revealed to the ANC before they came into power and now they had not only to deliver on their promises to the people but also find the funds to replenish pension funds.

I valued these explanations from Madiba. Simple and to the point and in terms I could understand. It changed my way of thinking and soon I would defend the ANC in debates with my friends. I started withdrawing from my more conservative Afrikaans friends as few of them understood the new political reasoning.

Madiba was everybody's hero. Black people hailed him for bringing them freedom, and whites simply because he wore a Springbok shirt to the Rugby World Cup final in 1995. He achieved his goal to unite the country, but it didn't bring relief to the poorest of the poor. While he was acceptable to most white people there were still 'pockets of racism' as he described it. And sadly South Africa is still dismally failing its youth. For example, in 2012 some schools in the impoverished Limpopo Province to the north of the country did not receive textbooks for their pupils from the government for an entire academic year, despite being ordered to by the courts as a result of action taken by a non-governmental organization. They just didn't deliver them to the schools and the books were found in a warehouse. It was precisely during these travels and conversations that I got so much of an understanding about politics, its mechanics and how the ANC operated.

From Baden-Baden we travelled to India, where Madiba received the Gandhi Peace Prize. We also visited Kerala, a province in India. We were taken from Delhi by helicopter to Kerala and although it gave us a picturesque view of India's landscape I was not completely convinced that we were safe aboard the huge helicopter they transported us in. (I would often invent stories in my mind about tragic headlines whenever I didn't feel safe. It was stupid but one cannot help but contemplate these things when you travel that much in so many foreign countries, sometimes facing challenging situations. You can't ever tell your host that you feel unsafe.) It was visibly old and bigger than some planes we had flown in before, yet in the back of my mind I knew that the Indian government wouldn't risk Madiba's life while in their country and that made me feel safer.

The Indian people were hospitable and they adored Madiba. If there is one thing Madiba and I shared a love for it was eating biryani, an Indian dish made from rice, spices, meat, chicken or fish.

Madiba had loved it before he went to prison, enjoying it with his Indian friends. It is one of the things he greatly missed while being imprisoned, not having the food that he enjoyed. And in India we were looking forward to having Indian meals and had biryani or samosas at every possible occasion. I never knew what biryani was until he suggested I try it. After that, I could comprehend his fondness for it.

On a visit to Ireland in April 2001, while being hosted by Tony and Chryss O'Reilly after being invited to address an event for the Independent Newspaper group, news broke about South Africa's cricket captain, Hansie Cronje, being embroiled in match fixing. Being the Chairman of the Independent Newspaper group at the time and a great sports man himself, Dr O'Reilly debated this matter with us. Both Madiba and I were adamant that these were merely allegations and that we were convinced that there was no truth in them, but Dr O'Reilly doubted Hansie's innocence. We called Hansie to wish him strength. In the days to follow Hansie Cronje, who was everybody's hero in South Africa, was disgraced when he admitted to the match fixing.

The following year, on 1 June 2002, I was with Madiba at Shambala, the house built by businessman Douw Steyn on a game farm in the north where Madiba intended to write his memoirs, when I received a call in the early morning from the media, asking for comments on the rumour that Hansie had been killed in a plane crash. I started panicking. I had received a voicemail message from Hansie the week before congratulating me on my birthday, and I still wanted to call him to tell him he was light years away from my real birthday date which is only at the end of October. But I hadn't. We were friends and I couldn't believe what I heard.

A few hours later, confirmation was received. I went to tell Madiba of the news and I was very sad when I broke it to him. Hansie was a kind, gentle human being and yes, he'd made mistakes but at some point we all do. The last time Madiba saw Hansie was a few months before, after Hansie had admitted to match fixing and was banned from the sport for life. He was a broken man. At the time

1. My brother Anton and me.

2. Proof that riding a motorbike is in my
blood: my grandmother Betty la Grange
(on the right) on her motorbike in
the 1940s.

3. My early childhood (early 1970s),
dreaming of becoming an actress.

4. Greeting Madiba at the military airport upon his arrival back from holiday in Saudi Arabia, 1994. To his left, behind him, is Mary Mxadana, his Private Secretary at the time.

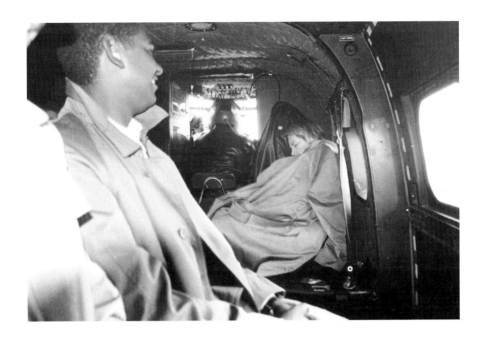

5. Desperate measures: I mastered the
art of sleeping anywhere, here covered
with Madiba's raincoat, on board an
Oryx military helicopter flying off to
a school-building project in rural South
Africa. To the left is Linga Moonsamy,
one of the bodyguards.

6. A silhouette of Madiba on board our
presidential plane, the Falcon 900, 1998/9.

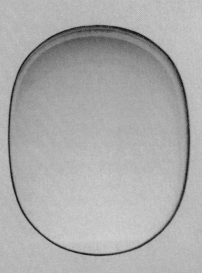

7. I learn to dress up. (1): in my designer *abaya* on the stairs of the government guest house in Riyadh, Saudi Arabia, late 1990s.

8. I learn to dress up. (2): Early 2000s in Iran with one of Madiba's bodyguards, Anton Calitz; 9. Madiba's last state visit abroad as President, standing in the Bolshoi theatre in Moscow with my colleague Priscilla Naidoo, 1999.

10. Assisting Madiba out of a meeting
with his good friend President Bill
Clinton, at the Waldorf Astoria
Hotel, New York, mid 2000s.

11. Meeting Pope John Paul II at the
Vatican during Madiba's state visit.

12. Adjusting Madiba's hearing aids
at an event at the Nelson Mandela
Foundation. 13. Seeing Madiba off outside
the office after his day at work.

14. Christmas in Qunu, with Madiba
and Mum in the early 2000s.

15. During the launch of the 46664
campaign in Cape Town, 2003. Bono and
The Edge visit Madiba at his house in
Cape Town.

16. Keeping Madiba busy in the office
while we wait for the mould of his hand
to set. The cast of his hand was sold at his
ninetieth birthday celebration in London.

17. Photo taken in 2008 while I was busy
explaining to Madiba how a cast would
be made of his hand. The hand that
changed my entire being.

we went to Fancourt, a hotel resort with an adjacent estate, for a few days' rest and Madiba asked Hansie to visit him as Hansie had a house on the estate too. He sat him down and told him: 'Boy, you made a big mistake. Now you have to man-up and face the consequences. It doesn't mean we won't forgive you. You have admitted to your mistake, now move on.' Hansie was just getting back on his feet again when he died on that cold winter's morning. I was also taught that no matter what mistakes a person makes, you yourself cannot expect to be forgiven if you are not willing to forgive. It reminded me of a piece Madiba wrote in prison that was later published in the book *Conversations With Myself.* He wrote: '*Don't* run away from your problems; *face* them! Because *if you don't deal* with them, they will *always* be with you.'

It was a very sad winter's day as I also received a call from my father to inform me that his nephew Ettienne, whom I had been very fond of, had been in a motorbike accident in Cape Town. He was returning DVDs his children had rented and took a quick trip with his motorbike. He hit an oncoming car. A week later Ettienne died in hospital. It was a sad time and I didn't understand why two such young lives had to end so tragically. All my senses were over-reacting and I felt extremely alone that night in that big house. Madiba was never an overly emotional person and it was therefore difficult to lay my sadness out in front of him. He would go quiet and that was his way of dealing with things. I wanted to give vent to my emotions but it sometimes felt reprehensible. I felt very lonely.

Back at home, the normal day of business included time with family and business people. Madiba always had a cause to fundraise for. If it wasn't a young AIDS sufferer, it was a youngster who performed well at school but struggled to find a bursary, or even relief for areas hit by severe floods. Madiba also insisted on staying in touch with ordinary people and so he went to have lunch at the residence of the family that owns and runs a major dry-cleaning business in Johannesburg. They had been handling his dry cleaning for years, and despite the fact that he insisted on paying for it he felt compelled to have a meal with the family who had looked after his clothes with so much care.

To me it is still one of Madiba's greatest virtues: his attention to people that not anyone of his stature would usually pay attention to. He recognized and really respected the small people. No one was treated as a servant.

He also didn't want to be removed from his old colleagues and people of his age group. He would ask to have lunch with the musicians and stars from his generation, like Ken Gampu, Miriam Makeba, Hugh Masekela, Dorothy Masuka and Dolly Rathebe, and after the lunch he would decide to raise 'cars' for the women who struggled financially to make a living with their singing. These women all used their music to convey political messages during the struggle years and Madiba felt that he owed them a gesture that would show appreciation. He felt responsible for everyone around him: his family, his colleagues, his staff and in this case even the people that supported the anti-apartheid movement while he was imprisoned. He found inspiration through their art while being imprisoned and felt a great deal of gratitude towards them. We would then phone all the major car companies in South Africa and convince them to donate cars to these struggle heroes.

A little boy of about eight years of age wrote to Madiba one day, in quite a formal tone, asking for an appointment. His only reason for wanting to meet with Madiba was to discuss matters relating to South Africa. The letter was formal and amused us as he also said that his parents didn't think he stood a chance in being granted an appointment with Nelson Mandela. I showed the letter to Madiba and we agreed to grant him the appointment. He visited Madiba and he was as formal in his interaction with Madiba as he was in his letter. 'No, there was no particular reason for my asking for an appointment with you, Sir; I simply wanted to meet with you.' Madiba was entertained by the young man's honesty about the matter and it gave us great joy to experience such moments that really made him happy to be in contact with ordinary people without any agenda, just wanting to meet him because they were intrigued by him.

Madiba also had the needs of his grandchildren to cater for. Whenever we left for an overseas trip the boys (the three youngest of his eldest son), Ndaba, Mbuso and Andile, would give me a shopping list of the things they wanted their grandfather to bring them like all children do when their parents go abroad. He then sometimes sent me out on the streets of wherever we were to try to find things I had never heard of before myself. Not having my own children it was quite difficult to even distinguish between animated characters, let alone computer games. When Sony introduced PlayStation, we had to call the Japanese Ambassador to ask him to ship a PlayStation to South Africa as the children could simply not wait for it to be released here. One of the very few privileges of the children having Nelson Mandela as their grandfather was that they would always be the first to have the latest games and gadgets, before many of their peers.

During a visit in Cape Town he was again going from pillar to post trying to oblige with expectations, and after recording a TV interview he felt dizzy and nearly fainted. As he was generally always well these spells whenever he wasn't feeling well created great concern. Despite that he continued and only the next day, after visiting an area in the Klein Karoo where a school had to be built, did he agree to visit a doctor when we returned to Cape Town. He was stubborn and insisted on going to the school and not cancel it to see a doctor first. The cardiologist examined him and couldn't find anything alarming. It was pure exhaustion.

Madiba was scheduled to leave for London that night. We protested and begged him not to go, but he insisted. He said he was fine and he didn't want to alarm anyone by cancelling the visit. We left for London and then went on to visit Morocco (where we saw the King and asked for a donation for the Foundation) and then to visit Sharjah, an emirate within the United Arab Emirates and the cultural capital of the UAE. There we found the same diplomat who was involved in our previous visit to Dubai (when we had failed to secure a promised donation from the Ruler). Before we landed I made sure that the Embassy received our message that we wouldn't need any diplomatic support and that diplomats were not required to accompany us during the visit. Yet when we landed that same man was there.

Madiba was beyond angry at him but somehow he left it to me to deal with. By now I could read his facial expressions. He was blunt and unfriendly. The diplomat sat around in Madiba's lounge when we arrived at the hotel. I entered and told Madiba that it was time for him to retire for the day. I told the diplomat that he was free to leave and he announced that he would still stay for a while. He also asked for the programme for the following days. I got irritated and in front of Madiba told him that I had sent a message that while we appreciated he had a responsibility, we would call him if we needed any assistance. Madiba's eyes went big and years later he would still tease me over the matter and warn people that if they didn't listen to me, I would deal with them. I really wasn't that stern but he enjoyed it that I had the courage to set someone straight like that. However, I also think he was only too grateful that I did it rather than him having to do so.

In May Madiba visited a urologist, Dr Gus Gecelter, accompanied by Mrs Machel. He was taken to Parklane Clinic in Johannesburg the following day where some tests were administered, but he didn't say anything and I didn't want to interfere or question him over his private matters. I knew from previous experience that if there was anything to share, he would do so.

In June 2001 the head of Coca-Cola in South Africa invited Madiba to address the Coca-Cola group of Africa on a cruise the company undertook through the Mediterranean. By this time the company had built a school in rural South Africa and helped with other donations for projects whenever he called upon them. Madiba felt obliged to respond. I didn't complain about a trip on a luxury yacht for five days and it also meant we would be away from the pressures in Johannesburg, the endless requests via telephone and faxes being received and considered daily. At least we would have five nights to sleep in one place and on a ship where no one could find us.

When I read some of the guests' names to Madiba, including the world-famous boxer Sugar Ray Leonard, he became excited. He used to box in his youth and still enjoyed the sport and would often quote Muhammad Ali or Sonny Liston. His favourite quote from Ali was 'move like a butterfly, sting like a bee'. I would ask him what he meant and Madiba would explain in great detail how important it was to be light on your feet in the boxing ring, and that Ali's punch stung like a bee. 'Painful,' he would say, pulling a face while he said it to make me understand that it must have been really painful if Ali hit someone. He loved talking about all the boxers, some of them names I had never heard before.

The trip on the cruise was pure bliss. The hospitality outstanding. The captain of the ship told me to 'drink as much champagne as you can, in fact bath in it if you can because you'll never find another ship with so much champagne on board'. We couldn't really drink too much however, as we had to be 'on standby' for Madiba twenty-four hours a day. Madiba was expected to attend two events while on the ship and to make a speech at one of them, encouraging loyalty and dedication from the employees and congratulating them on the company's achievements in Africa while he inspired them to continue having the goodwill of the previously disadvantaged at the top of their agenda.

However, Charles, the travelling doctor, and I decided to join the festivities. When Madiba retired to bed at night we sneaked out to go and join the party on the deck. We couldn't go far because we were stuck on a ship and the security men knew where to find us at all times, so we had a bit of freedom to move around on the vessel. Unlike any of the trips we had been on before. One morning we were the last ones dancing and got back to our respective cabins just in time to prepare to join Madiba for breakfast. Charles had no obligation to be with Madiba during breakfast, but I did. I could hardly keep my eyes open and suffered the entire day. We were cruising and I took Madiba outside to enjoy the view of the beautiful coastline while he sat and read his newspapers, now and then staring across the ocean to the endless horizon. I sat next to him, snoozing on and off from time to time. After five days on the ship Madiba became uneasy and we all started to get 'cabin fever'. It was time to return to the fast-paced life.

We were scheduled to stop over in Barcelona on our way back to South Africa in support of an initiative for the Nelson Mandela Children's Fund called Frock and Roll. This was a concert and fashion show organized by Naomi Campbell and Bono. The rest of U2 were present too, and while performing their hit 'One' Madiba was scheduled to enter. I felt so proud that Nelson Mandela belonged to our country. The crowd first went completely crazy when Bono took the stage and we could hear and see their reaction from the wings until Madiba was prompted to walk on. The crowd erupted with joy to see him. It was not announced that he would be there and he caught the public by surprise. Bono introduced Madiba and it took some minutes for the crowd to quieten down to allow him to speak.

Upon embarking the plane for our departure back to South Africa, Madiba sat down and stared in front of him for a while. He then leaned towards me and said: 'Zeldina, this Bono chap, it seems to me he is quite popular.' I couldn't help but laugh out loud and told Madiba that Bono was one of the world's music heroes and that he had a following that few other musicians could reach for. Madiba seemed interested in this 'Bono chap' and he looked impressed that a young man was so popular among young people. It was the first time he witnessed his following.

8

Working with World Leaders

Although Madiba appeared healthy and strong, he was not. In July 2001 he was diagnosed with prostate cancer. One afternoon after having his lunch at home, he called me to his house and I could hear that there was seriousness in his voice. I had forgotten about the medical tests a few weeks earlier. I rushed over and found him in his usual comfy chair reading papers with his greeting smile as usual. He said: 'Zeldina, sit down.' Which I did. And then he said, 'Now you know we've been for tests the last couple of weeks. I don't want you to be alarmed but we have prostate cancer.' The way he delivered the news made me want to laugh and cry, all at once. By now he knew me so well and knew that I would never say anything disrespecting him, but he also knew my sense of humour. I replied: 'Khulu, oh no. I am so incredibly sorry to hear that but I am sure you are going to have the best treatment possible . . .' He smiled and was appreciative, and then I said, '. . . but I have to tell you *we* cannot have prostate cancer.' He laughed and then explained the treatment to follow. It was so considerate of him to share his condition with me before he went public with it, and it really showed me that he knew how much I cared for him.

He could never speak in singular terms or in the first person. He could never speak of 'me' or 'I'. It was part of the humble man that he was and everything included everyone around him. It was also part of the collectiveness of the ANC which was imprinted upon him while incarcerated. He was determined that the cancer was merely a little stumbling block that *we* would overcome in no time. He instructed me to call a press conference where he and

Dr Mike Plit, his physician, would explain the situation and treatment to follow. He always insisted on being extremely open about his health or any medical condition. The next day he started with radiotherapy which continued daily for six weeks. By the second or third week he was losing strength and I was extremely worried about him. I stopped going to the oncology centre with him and Mrs Machel, as it was hard for me to see. She was there every step of the way and they grounded themselves in Johannesburg to slow down the pace and give him time to recover from the treatment. He was OK but stressed from going to the clinic every day.

People prayed and sent good wishes daily. We were inundated with well wishers and that posed its own challenges. The heading of the daily newspaper in Johannesburg, *The Star*, read on 24 July 2001, MANDELA HAS CANCER. LOW GRADE PROSTATE MALIGNANCY SHOULDN'T SHORTEN LIFE SPAN, and it didn't. I am convinced today that the butterfly effect had a lot to do with his healing. All the prayers and good wishes, the positive thoughts from the public and the complete outpouring of love, in addition to God's grace, of course, is what healed him. Although we didn't travel he insisted that his schedule continue as usual during his six weeks of radiation therapy. He would have appointments in the morning and only go to the clinic early afternoon. After about four weeks we had to simply lighten his work burden as he was becoming tired and worn out, no matter how much he wanted to push forward. He had no particular focus at work and his appointments were really to ensure that he didn't feel isolated while receiving treatment.

Madiba and Mrs Machel needed a holiday after the treatment was completed. The question was, where do we take him? It felt like there was nowhere in South Africa, and in fact nowhere in the world (barring North Korea), where they could have peace and quiet. But we did find a solution. Madiba and Mrs Machel were invited by El-italia, Italy's communication network, to visit Rome and Venice for a holiday the previous year and we decided to accept the offer. They didn't have any expectations from Madiba and Mrs Machel but purely offered time to come and enjoy Italy. It worked out perfectly. Madiba got to see the Coliseum as they managed to close the entire site for a private tour for him. I was grateful for that because by then I realized that he was merely a prisoner in another life again. He couldn't do the ordinary things we take for granted because he attracted too much attention in public. It was logistically impossible for him to move around without crowds following and people wanting to get close to him, take a picture, touch him, talk to him. While he didn't mind attracting crowds it sometimes became too much.

He was not doing the ordinary things of life and the ordinary pleasures were limited for him. He spent so many years almost chained down by the determination of his own cause and working towards a better life for others, I wondered at what point he himself would stop and do something for himself. His was indeed a life of service. He did whatever he could always to the benefit of others. He was, however, happy when Mrs Machel was with him and that, at times, was enough for him. With her in our company we did many things that Madiba would never agree to if we were by ourselves. She managed to convince him to try the local cuisine and do touristy, normal things, such as take a tour through Venice on a boat. It was precious to see him trying his very best to be like a tourist. Our hosts were gracious and very respectful of Madiba's privacy.

Soon afterwards we visited Los Angeles, where Madiba had hoped to raise some funds for the Foundation. Hollywood, it turned out, either wasn't that generous at the time or not prepared for our visit. The only support we did get was from the people who were known to have supported the anti-apartheid struggle. Again I didn't leave the hotel in fear that Madiba might need me and I missed really seeing Los Angeles. But our hotel rooms were beautiful. Sadly, some of the people who made huge promises to Madiba never fulfilled them.

★

On 11 September 2001 I was attending a course in Cape Town. Proceedings took longer than anticipated and when I arrived back at my parents' house, where I was visiting, my dad told me that two planes had flown into the World Trade Center in New York. I watched the report on CNN and immediately called Madiba, as he was not accustomed to watching news during the day and unless he was in the car he no longer listened to the news on the radio over lunch. He was shocked and I took the opportunity to ask him for a message, as I knew the media was going to start calling for comments. (Whenever anything of any significance happened in the world, the media would call us instantaneously, wanting a comment, advice or an opinion from him about something.) And soon they did, and I relayed his words conveying condolences to the American people. We heard through staff that this angered President Mbeki who felt Madiba was too quick in releasing a statement. The Presidency felt the right thing would have been for us to wait until the President had issued a statement.

While I understood their concerns, I felt that Madiba never issued statements or spoke on behalf of the country but as a humanitarian. Why couldn't he express his sadness and sympathy? Again I will never know if it was really President Mbeki's concern or that of his staff.

The benefit of our small team was that we could respond to situations immediately. I was not paid extra to deal with the media all hours of the day or night but it became part of my job to be Madiba's spokesperson in addition to being his personal secretary and managing his office. The advantage was that I had two calls to make to react to anything. First to Madiba to ask what he wanted to say, and secondly to Prof. Gerwel to get his opinion on the matter. We were not tied up in bureaucracy because we were such a small team and it worked well.

Even though the media knew I was a rookie they tolerated me and respected me. But Madiba would jokingly tell them sometimes when they still wanted to pose a question after we had ended a press briefing: 'You'd better listen to her, she is my boss.' At one stage I called a Professor of Communication at one of the local universities. I asked for some guidance in dealing with the media and he spent some time with me giving me rules to follow and protocols to apply. The most important were: don't let the media own you or control the territory you are responsible for. Always make sure your territory is clearly defined in which you control them.

I took these lessons to heart. However, to many people I seemed like a bitch: I have been described as a lioness, a witch and a Rottweiler dog. Being the gatekeeper to the most famous man in the world meant I just had to be tough and brusque sometimes. Few realized the challenges I had in trying to deal with the world's media in addition to the other ordinary tasks I had. However, I befriended many people in the media and we built a common trust. I learned from mistakes others made around me and I tried to steer clear of those pitfalls. The effort and stress that goes into counting every word you say has its price. It's exhausting. But the most important advice anyone ever gave me was, *never lie to the media*. There are literally a million ways to deal with any situation and Madiba was the best teacher in tutoring me to see those ways, but lying was never an option.

We were scheduled to pay a visit to the United States to attend a special session at the United Nations late in September 2001. At first we thought that the meeting would be cancelled as a result of 9/11 but they pressed ahead. Cleaning operations were still under way as we visited Ground Zero. It was very touching and very moving. It was just a few weeks after the actual incident and there was a haze above the area. It was as if I could feel the souls of those thousands of people still drifting in the air. The workers all stopped when they saw Madiba and started applauding him. Only once we stood at Ground Zero did the enormity of the tragedy sink in. Madiba was visibly shocked and disturbed by what he saw. We conversed with Mayor Giuliani for a while and he explained the clean-up operations.

Following our visit to New York, we tried to get in touch with President Bush but he never returned our call. We realized he was facing huge challenges. I called the Situation Room at the White

House and asked to schedule a time for Mr Mandela to speak with the President. One also had to reveal the topic of such a conversation. I explained that we were in the US and Madiba simply wanted to offer his support for the challenges the President was facing. Whether the President simply didn't want to speak to him or whether the person in the Situation Room decided for him, we will never know.

We were still taking part in the negotiations in Arusha in Tanzania on Burundi. Judge Bomani, the administrative head of the negotiating process, then brought some of the rival parties to South Africa where Madiba met with them in Johannesburg to listen to their sides of the conflict. Many of the rebels had never travelled to South Africa before and they were obviously impressed and excited to be in Johannesburg. It was clear that they were nowhere near a peace deal though. The peace negotiations continued for two years. Over the following two years we would travel to Arusha, a town close to the foot of Kilimanjaro in Tanzania where the peace talks were situated. It was necessary for the parties to meet on neutral grounds. Madiba was extremely tough on all parties in the negotiations. Our visits were kept short as facilities in Arusha were limited. He would sit in meetings for hours and hours, negotiating but also forcefully reprimanding all parties. Sometimes Prof. Gerwel and I became nervous and embarrassed as Madiba would be very hard on some people. He was, however, never disrespectful and despite his tenacity and determination the various parties simply didn't give ground.

We visited Bujumbura in Burundi only on a few occasions, but while we were there one could hear the gunshots in the distance of ongoing fighting in the mountains. In the book *Conversations With Myself*, Madiba wrote: 'Leadership falls into 2 categories a) Those who are inconsistent, who[se] actions cannot be predicted, who agree today on a [matter] and repudiate it the following day. b) Those who are consistent, who have a sense of honour, a vision.' It was clear to me that if these leaders were consistent in their pursuit for a peaceful solution in their country, if they consistently showed their commitment to driving the process towards a settlement, he would have had more patience with them as it is a leadership style he could then respect.

Often President Mkapa of Tanzania and Presidents Museveni of Uganda and Moi of Kenya, the neighbouring states, would attend joint meetings with us in Arusha. They all referred to Madiba as 'Mzi' – which I gather means 'great one'. People were friendly and hospitable but it was a process that took way too much of Madiba's energy, and I personally felt he could have made a bigger difference by spending that energy in our own country, assisting the government to fast-track delivery of services to the masses, something which now became critical to the people who voted the ANC into power. But it seemed the Mbeki government didn't want him to help; they saw it as meddling.

After two years of negotiations in Tanzania, Madiba called on former President Clinton, President Chirac of France and others to support the signing of an interim peace agreement by all parties involved in Burundi with President Buyoya as an interim head of state. Personally I didn't think they would sign the deal but Madiba sat night after night, sometimes until three in the morning, talking to the parties involved and convincing them that they couldn't disrespect the President of the United States of America by not signing the deal. He said it would be a very bad reflection on them as leaders and a sign that they were not serious about peace.

Thinking back it was actually funny that he used the title of the President of the United States to convince them in this way. Their reasons for not signing were not reasonable and he had exhausted all other avenues by then, trying to convince them that peace was the only solution. There was a budget for the peace process and each participant received a daily allowance, food and accommodation while in Arusha negotiating. For many rebels who lived and fought their battles from the bush in Burundi it obviously paid to be involved in such peace talks as they could then collect money to support their battles. They therefore dragged out the talks as long as possible and sometimes stayed for two or three weeks while we only went for three days at most. The people in the negotiations, leaders of rival groups, were all highly educated, many of them educated in Europe, and there was no way that they couldn't comprehend the advantages of a peace deal. But like in all similar circumstances they were not necessarily willing to surrender their personal power base for the sake of their country's future. Madiba would remind them continuously that that alone was a sign of a lack of leadership qualities, and even though it sometimes felt as if he rarely stopped short of insulting them, no progress was made.

President Buyoya was an impressive charming intelligent gentleman, apart from the white socks that he wore. On 18 April 2001 some rebels invaded a radio station in Bujumbura and news spread across the globe that it was the start of a coup. Madiba was somewhere and couldn't be reached for several hours. I couldn't get hold of Prof. Gerwel and Judge Bomani's phone was switched off too. Media started calling our office and wanted confirmation about the coup. At first I was sarcastic about it and asked the first caller whether he/she thought I would know about a coup sitting in my office in Johannesburg. I then decided to call President Buyoya as he was the only one I had a number for and who would be able to confirm such a rumour or not. I spoke to him and he was as friendly as always and happy to hear from 'Mzi's' office. 'Oh Miss Zelda, I am happy to hear from you, how is Mzi?' he asked. He explained that it was simply some rebels who'd taken over a radio station and I told him what the international news bulletins were reporting. I urged him to issue a statement to dispel the rumours and from our side we were able to confirm that there was no coup. I clearly remember that I had had plans for that evening to socialize but spent the entire evening fielding media calls. As soon as Madiba became available I briefed him. He laughed at all the unnecessary commotion of which he was completely unaware.

Dr Percy Yutar requested to see Madiba one day. Percy Yutar was the state's lawyer in the trial that sent Madiba to life-long imprisonment. He was in financial difficulty and wanted Madiba to assist him to sell the Rivonia Trial documents. They had seen each other once since that time, while Madiba was President, when he invited Dr Yutar to lunch at the official Presidential residence in Pretoria. He explained that he had tried to convince the government to buy the documents from him, but we refused to help too. I couldn't quite comprehend how he ended up having these documents in his possession but thought he probably owned them because it was the case in which he appeared. Luckily the documents were later bought, by the Oppenheimers and Douw Steyn, and most of them are now in the National Archives.

When Madiba asked to see Yutar for the first time after his release, in the 1990s, I felt sorry for Yutar, knowing that he had to live with himself after all of that but now it somehow disgusted me that this man sent Madiba to life imprisonment, had a wonderful free life himself, and then he still wanted Madiba to help him to sell the exact documents that sent him to prison. Those documents belonged to the government; how did he manage to take them to his personal archive after he retired? It just didn't sit well with me and I decided even before Madiba declined to help with the sale of the documents that I would not be party to that deal on principle.

On 2 November 2001 Douw opened the house on his game reserve in the Limpopo Province called Shambala that he had built for Madiba as a retreat. Shambala is the Tibetan word for 'heaven on earth'. Douw Steyn's generosity didn't stop the time he housed Madiba for six months after he left Soweto in the early 1990s after he'd separated from Mrs Winnie Mandela. On one occasion Douw invited Madiba and Mrs Machel to his farm Shambala in the Waterberg. It was a relaxed luncheon that was planned with just Douw, his wife Carolyn and his staff on the farm. When Madiba and Mrs Machel returned they told me that Douw had offered to build a house on the farm for Madiba and Mrs Machel's use, where they could relax and go to as no one would be able to disturb them there because of the privacy of the farm. Madiba and Mum (as we started calling Mrs Machel, imitating Madiba) knew not to refuse the offer as Douw didn't take lightly to being refused. In no time he built the most beautiful house on the farm, before even completing his own.

In many ways Douw Steyn reminded me of Jay Gatsby. He would always host short-notice, over-the-top lavish parties at one of his residences. Madiba only attended a few of these but he always valued spending time with Douw and was most entertained by the lavish lifestyles of the rich and famous. Douw would tell Madiba about his extravagant deals and it would intrigue Madiba that one person could have so much wealth. After his release Madiba was introduced to Douw by members of the ANC. When Madiba left Soweto in the mid-90s, separating from his wife Mrs Winnie Madikizela Mandela, Douw housed Madiba for six months and it is there that Madiba completed his memoirs, *Long Walk to Freedom*, and regularly met with ANC officials to work on an interim constitution for South Africa. That residence belonging to Douw was later converted to the Saxon hotel.

Finally there was a space where we could hide. Even though Madiba loved people and being with people it was difficult in the city to find time for peace and quiet, time to think. He was confronted by requests in the city from many people he eagerly wanted to please, but if there was a place where people would have difficulty to find him, we could create the space where he could think and perhaps write. Shambala is a good distance from Johannesburg and we all agreed that few people would actually go through the trouble of travelling there to visit Madiba. He would visit this house on a few occasions and instructed us to clear his diary for a few weeks at a time to spend time there.

The launch of the house at Shambala coincided with a visit of the Miss World contestants to South Africa and Douw hosted them on the farm at the same time. Madiba had made a point before to always meet the Miss South Africa winner after she was crowned every year. Then one year he indicated that he wanted to meet a Miss World who was visiting South Africa but at that stage he had not yet met the reigning Miss South Africa. I warned him he couldn't meet Miss World and not Miss South Africa because we'd be in trouble for not paying attention to our own people first, and he agreed to meet the Miss South Africa first. Then he repeated the story of how well I advised him. I would have rather preferred to be known as someone who advised him about preventing a major world war, but he was very impressed about my good advice about Miss World vs Miss South Africa. Friends and associates of Madiba complained that he spent too much time with beauty queens and that it negatively impacted on his image. Just one of the struggles we had to face. He admired beauty and these seemingly frivolous interactions were purely because he enjoyed being in the company of these beautiful women, who of course all adored Nelson Mandela.

Early in November 2001 we visited Brussels where we spoke to Prime Minister Verhofstadt about the settlement being reached in Burundi and how the European Union could support the country – on 1 November we had travelled to Bujumbura for the swearing in ceremony of the new interim government. I felt that the peace deal was somewhat forced but if Madiba hadn't insisted on it they would still be negotiating. He was relieved that it was over. A South African peace-keeping force is present in Burundi to this day.

In December we proceeded to Tripoli to visit the Brother Leader, after which we set off to the US to attend a fundraiser for the Mosaic Foundation, a foundation run by the wife of Prince Bandar. We also visited Maryland as well as delivering a report to the United Nations on Burundi. We then proceeded to Toronto and Ottawa where Madiba was bestowed with Canada's highest honour by Prime Minister Jean Chrétien. We were tired after a very long year and Madiba's age was not on our side. Yet his urgency to make a difference didn't diminish. He wanted to continue to spread the good news of a new South Africa to the world. He wanted to encourage foreigners to maintain confidence in our country and to invest. And in between, he wanted to maintain relationships with his friends.

Before travelling to Tripoli we had again visited Saudi, Oman, Bahrain and Kuwait to fundraise for the Foundation. I liked Oman and Bahrain and the King of Bahrain was very hospitable, as was the Emir of Oman. In Kuwait something strange happened. We've all taken bath soaps or toiletries in our own bathrooms when travelling to luxury hotels. In this particular guest house Madiba's bathroom was stocked with a very expensive brand of soaps, aftershave, body-wash, etc. While we were at an appointment away from the guest house, someone, presumably a bodyguard as they were the only ones who remained behind, decided to help himself to some of these toiletries in Madiba's bathroom. Little did he know that Madiba had taken note of every item in his bathroom before we left. Upon our return he noticed that something was missing and he called all the security detail to stand parade. He also called me and told me to come in as 'witness'. The lawyer in Madiba was holding court. I wanted to hide my face in embarrassment on behalf of the bodyguards.

He questioned them and gave 'the villain' the opportunity to replace the item or else he would report him to the Minister of Police when we returned home, or else he would have all of them fired if the 'villain' didn't come forward. He wanted me to call the Minister there and then from Kuwait to report the case, but I thought it was better that we left it until our return to South Africa (and pretended that I couldn't get hold of the Minister immediately). Madiba was very serious. The next morning the item was replaced and he forgot about it, as he promised he would. He didn't mind you taking the toiletries from your own bathroom, but not from his. And when we left, he didn't want to take any of the items in his bathroom with him; he left it all untouched and unopened. He never wanted to take advantage of our hosts and he expected everyone to behave that way.

On another occasion elsewhere someone nabbed cutlery from our host and when he was caught by his senior I knew I had to deal with the matter with the utmost discretion, as Madiba would not tolerate such things. I decided that we had to deal with it internally rather than call on the 'lawyer' to become the 'prosecutor'. Because teams rotated, people never knew what happened to others while we were on trips abroad and therefore this particular team had no experience with the 'prosecutor'. I insisted in this case that the guy be disciplined within his force structures upon our return home even though we returned the cutlery to its owner before we left. The one thing Madiba was totally intolerant about was dishonesty. Whether it involved a bar of soap or a political agenda.

To me, Madiba was a kind, generous soul but principled and disciplined in every sense of the word. I don't know whether it is as a result of my Calvinist upbringing or my sensitive personality and having grown up in a house where the only violence experienced was that of my father's loud voice, but I get scared whenever someone raises his/her voice. I avoid confrontation of a personal nature and rather become quiet and withdraw myself completely. It is not that I fear confrontation as such, but I get nervous whenever other people raise their voices. It was the same when Madiba raised his voice. He had a loud voice by nature but increasing the pitch just a little made me nervous. It wasn't as if he had raging outbursts and I only heard him raising his voice on a few occasions during the years I worked with him. It was usually only in situations that really angered him, like when someone betrayed him or was dishonest or over a personal matter. I would cringe for the other person's sake and then as soon as the person left, I would try and defuse the tension. Those close to Madiba knew when he got angry. But he would never take out his anger on others then. He would become quiet too and disturbed.

During the latter part of his Presidency, when I often found myself 'manning' the office in Pretoria by myself, I would often call his bodyguard Rory Steyn, whenever he was on duty, to give me an assessment of the President's overall mood before he arrived at the office. The bodyguards would drive the President from his home in Houghton to the office in Pretoria and Rory would be one of the people who would know whether the President was serious, in a humorous mood, or if his mind was elsewhere occupied. Rory's assessments helped me to ease into the day with the President without making inappropriate comments or an overly friendly greeting when he didn't feel up to it.

*

By these accounts of all our travels it sounds as if the Nelson Mandela Foundation raised millions but in fact we didn't. It was clearly easier for Madiba to fundraise for the ANC, a liberation movement, than for a foundation. The Foundation was not well established, or rather, its direction was constantly changing, and I think people hesitated to donate, not knowing whether it was merely a family foundation or a NGO implementing projects.

In early 2002 I ran into someone from the Protocol section at the President's office. I was told by this particular person that paintings and photos in which Madiba appeared had been removed from the display area at the Spier wine estate in the Western Cape, in preparation of a visit there by President Mbeki. I had no reason not to believe this person and it was confirmed when it appeared in the local *Mail* and *Guardian* newspaper a week later. It put validity to my point that it was not necessarily President Mbeki who fostered the particular feelings towards Madiba but that it was aggravated by actions like these from staff. Surely it must have been an embarrassment to President Mbeki to read something like this in the newspapers. It is so petty and there is no way that I could believe that the President would instruct his staff to remove any items that bear relation to Nelson Mandela.

In March 2002 Madiba gave me a task. He wanted me to organize a gala dinner for struggle veterans, similar to what he did during his Presidency when he hosted wives of struggle veterans by inviting them for tea at Mahlamba Ndlopfu. Even though they no longer shared the focus of a liberation struggle he felt it was necessary for them to be honoured and that he was not seen to have forgotten them even though his life had moved on beyond the struggle. Only this time, it had to be around 1,500 guests. We quickly fundraised and set up a task team for the event.

The memories of this event and the difficulties we faced in organizing it will remain with me for the rest of my life. It was worth every effort though when one witnessed how old people's faces lit up when they saw friends and colleagues they hadn't seen in many years, often not knowing if people they were close to in the struggle were still alive. Most of them still lived in poor circumstances without basic services despite their history in the liberation struggle. I somehow also felt angry for them and did what I could to ensure that at least once they were paid tribute to in a festive way.

It was impossible to make everyone happy. Simply, Madiba was never keen on staying anywhere too long. He wanted to keep moving and I think an urgency drove him to do as much as possible before he got too old to move around. He was attending at least five to seven public events per week at the time and every event was the same story. There was no reason for him to sit at an event for two hours to listen to endless speeches. I recall him once bringing a priest's prayer to a rude halt when he asked the Master of Ceremonies to go and stop the priest from continuing to pray. When I asked him about it afterwards he said that he didn't have a problem with praying but that it was not necessary for the priest to try and convert us all with one such long prayer. He was right. The prayer was not limited to blessing or opening the ceremony but was longer than a sermon!

There was a fine line between appearing to be disrespectful and allowing the programme to reach its functionality. In February 2003 Mathatha Tsedu wrote an editorial in the *Sunday Times* criticizing us for not allowing Madiba to remain longer at an opening of a school. Mathatha wrote: 'It was very embarrassing, and many people here say because Mandela's life is run by some white woman, when he attends black events he is always in a hurry. "We understand that when he attends white events he stays longer," an organiser told me.' He continued:

> I know Zelda la Grange, Mandela's personal assistant, and believe she would not snub occasions simply because they were black. The question must be asked whether Mandela's office is managing his diary correctly to ensure that he not only attends fleetingly to issues and events but stays long enough not to be seen to be just passing through.

Easier said than done. Madiba was the one who would look at a draft programme before we attended events and tell me where to insist they cut the programme, and then it was up to me to make sure I got him out of an event, usually about thirty minutes after arrival. Yes it was 'fleetingly passing through', but he wanted to fleetingly pass through irrespective of race, the nature of the event, or where it was.

The reality was that the fact that I was white was never going to be overlooked by many people. Race was still an issue and many people have not come to terms with the fact that that we are all South Africans, irrespective of colour. The damage done by apartheid was underestimated and it manifested in ways that whenever no other excuse could be found for a problem, race was the easiest issue to blame. I had learned from Madiba that two things would destroy the validity of your argument immediately if you used them: race and insults. When your argument is based on principle there is no reason for you to grapple with issues of race or try and insult your opponent. Stick to the principle, and if you can't it means you don't have an argument.

(In 2008 I was awarded one of the ten Women of the Year awards by *City Press* and *Rapport*, two Sunday newspapers in South Africa. Mathatha was the Editor-in-Chief of *City Press* then and I appreciated the gesture regardless of our earlier differences. I'm sure he did not argue for this award personally but it must have passed by his desk and he could have objected to it if he'd wanted.)

There were two things Madiba was completely intolerant of as far as events were concerned: a briefing and a waiting room. He argued if we could be on time, everyone could, and he refused on many occasions to go to waiting or holding rooms. He would enter the events and by his presence force proceedings to start whether people were ready or not.

In April 2002 South Africa had its first space traveller, Mark Shuttleworth. Mark was well known in the country for his invention of an internet banking security software program which he sold for billions abroad. He was South Africa's youngest billionaire and, of course, he got tasked to build a school too. Mark visited us on a few occasions and it was agreed that he would call Madiba on my cellphone once he was in space. It was very exciting. We all watched him flying off into space but on the next day we went on with life, and while his trip dominated the news we had to continue with business as usual.

The agreement was that Mark would call on a particular day and I of course forgot to make a note of it. My cellphone rang and the number was disguised as 'private number'. Usually I don't answer those but I did as Madiba was next door in the office and he heard the phone ringing. On the other end of the line the person said: 'Hello, is that Zelda?' It sounded like a call from America and I was irritated as I hated people disturbing me during the day on my cellphone to tell me about their long proposals or to have lengthy discussions while I was attending to Madiba. I said: 'Yes, can I help you?' The person said: 'I'm calling from the ISS.' I thought: What is the ISS? Again, now slightly irritated, I asked the man how I could help him. He repeated, 'It's Mark from the ISS.' I thought it could be some organization and tried to think quickly so as to not sound stupid. His last attempt was: 'Zelda, it's Mark, I'm calling from space.' Oh my word. The penny dropped and I said: 'Oh *Mark*, how *are* you . . . ? Just hold on for Madiba.'

I rushed into Madiba's office and he too didn't know at first what I was trying to tell him when I said 'It's Mark, Mark Shuttleworth, he's calling from space.' It was funny at the time though and later when Mark returned he came to visit to tell us about his experiences and he enjoyed our story. We were very proud of him.

It was about this time that Madiba announced on one of his visits to Qunu that he wanted trees to be planted on his farm, big full-grown trees to protect the view of his house from the road, the N2 highway that ran past his farm. He tasked me with this and I didn't have a clue where to start searching for someone who could do this. I called my dad and asked him whether he knew who one contacts for something like this and he said that he would make a few calls and get back to me. Comprehending my sense of urgency about everything in life he soon called back and said he would try and help me to find someone. Then a day later he called to say that he managed to get a quote from someone to do the job and he would forward it to us. It was way too expensive and I reported back to him. He said he would try to find a solution. Being a daddy's girl I always expected my dad to find solutions for all my problems. And so he did. He called back to offer to go and do it himself.

I was hesitant and sceptical about this. I asked him to put his proposal in writing and I gave it to Madiba. Madiba was receptive of the idea and asked to speak to my dad. By this time they had already met and Madiba liked my father's unpretentious attitude, and because of Madiba's influence in my life my dad's attitude had changed towards him. I then made it very clear to Madiba that I did not wish to be involved in these dealings at all and that my dad had to report to his lawyer, Ismail Ayob, who was responsible for all payments. Madiba understood my concern that I didn't want to be blamed by anyone for nepotism.

Exactly as I expected my dad put his heart and soul into the project and soon the trees were planted. To the end Madiba always asked after my parents and specifically about my father's well-being. My father didn't charge Madiba for the work he had done, but only for procurement of the trees, groundwork and the labour he had to bring in from elsewhere. Madiba was extremely appreciative. We teased my dad and said: 'You see, times have changed . . . here you are, the old conservative, planting trees in a black man's garden!' and we would all laugh about it. My dad was extremely proud of his job and always asked me to report about the trees whenever I visited Qunu. My parents were so appreciative of the opportunities Madiba had granted me that it changed them and softened their hearts too. Those interactions, Madiba's genuine appreciation and the respect with which he dealt with my father, changed my father for ever.

We returned to New York in February of 2002 to attend the launch of the Tribeca Film Festival established by Jane Rosenthal and Robert

De Niro. Following the attack on the Twin Towers in Lower Manhattan, Wall Street was desperate to rebuild its reputation as a safe environment in the city. We were also invited to a cocktail function in City Hall hosted by the new Mayor, Michael Bloomberg. We loathed going to cocktail parties or stand-up informal events with Madiba. People would just overwhelm him completely and, in addition, it was useless talking to him in such circumstances. His hearing aids would cut out all sound completely once too many people talked around him or the surroundings were too noisy.

We entered the room where about 200 people were gathered. There was no one to meet us and we started making our way through the crowd until we came across some children in the room. Madiba immediately started conversing with them as all chidren attracted him like a magnet. He had to bend down to hear them properly and I was trying my best to repeat what they were saying so that he could respond to them appropriately. While bending down a man approached him from the back and pulled on his shirt to try and draw his attention. I thought: What on earth . . . ? He continued and I turned to him and said, 'Excuse me Sir, but what are you doing pulling on Mr Mandela's shirt? He is busy with the children.' He looked around as if to try and get help from someone and then said to me, 'I want Mr Mandela to greet these people, they are my friends.' My blood rose and I said: 'Well, can you give him a chance to finish with the children please?' He then said, kind of tongue in cheek, 'Do you know me?' and I abruptly responded: 'No I don't, but please just stop doing that.' A third person appeared and whispered in my ear, 'It's Mayor Bloomberg, he is the host of the function.' You could bowl me over with surprise. I apologized but nevertheless told him to please not pull on Mr Mandela's shirt as he was already unstable on his feet, and that he would turn around once he had finished with the kids. The Mayor didn't like me but I had no choice.

As we moved through the room a little later I saw another familiar face, that of British actor Hugh Grant. Everyone in the room wanted their picture taken with Madiba and soon chaos ensured.

Hugh Grant didn't ask to meet Mr Mandela but he smiled and from the look on his face I could gather that he was obviously excited to see him. Hugh moved in right next to Madiba and while still holding his own camera turned it around to take a picture while he was standing next to Madiba. A selfie as we have now named it. I then said, 'Excuse me Mr Grant, I am Mr Mandela's assistant. Can I please help you take a photo?' I had become the ex officio official photographer as I always had to take the pictures people wanted and became an expert on how people's cameras work. I didn't mind if the time and place was right for it. He was grateful. I didn't explain to Madiba who exactly he was.

On 16 February 2003 Mathatha Tsedu wrote another editorial, this time attacking the Treatment Action Campaign for using Madiba's face on a t-shirt. The TAC was in the forefront of pushing government to give the poor access to anti-retroviral AIDS drugs, something that Madiba was supporting and prepared to fight for publicly. At that point South Africa was fast becoming the country with the highest incidence of AIDS in the world. The government did not give people free access to AIDS drugs. Madiba tried to meet with the now late Minister of Health, Dr Manto Tshabalala-Msimang, on several occasions to discuss this issue and he was upset and disgusted that she had paid so little attention to the matter. South Africa was becoming the laughing stock of the world because of its AIDS policy and behind the scenes Madiba was trying to fight the battle on behalf of faceless and nameless people. He didn't mind the TAC using his face and again Mathatha attacked Madiba's office for not conducting itself in the right way by protecting Madiba's image from 'abuse like this', as he put it. I was starting to feel rebellious about many issues, this being one of them. Abuse to me consisted in the fact that people without a voice and platform didn't have access to drugs and were dying by the millions. By not providing treatment the government was denying people their human rights.

We were extremely frustrated by the lack of response from the government on Madiba's calls to meet with them and to discuss the issue of HIV drugs. On one occasion, Minister Msimang only met Madiba for thirty minutes and then she told him that she had to leave as she had an appointment for a dress fitting.

The denialism reached right to the top. President Mbeki said that he had never seen a person with AIDS, yet Madiba helped countless people to get access to AIDS drugs – people who then recovered and led some quality lives. The President also denied that there was a relation between HIV and AIDS. We helped a young lady who was on her last legs when she came to see Madiba to ask for help. She couldn't eat by herself. He had her admitted to hospital and when the drugs she took created side effects another cocktail was prescribed. She was later discharged and today she is happily married with children and leads a normal life. Because of both local public and international pressure, and also pressure from people like President Clinton, government now provides anti-retroviral drugs and South Africa's AIDS incidence rates are lower than before.

On the evening of 5 May 2003 I received a call from someone who told me that Madiba's best friend, Walter Sisulu, had just passed away. They were imprisoned together but had been friends since they were young. I immediately called Kgalema Motlanthe, whom I respected and liked, to ask him to confirm it. Kgalema was the Secretary General of the ANC at the time. He didn't know about it either but another source soon confirmed it. It was already late at night and Madiba was asleep but I knew he would want to know immediately if anything happened to Uncle Walter. Mrs Machel was in her home village in Mozambique and couldn't be reached and so I drove to Madiba's house. I entered and told the household staff why I was there. I knew that this was not the kind of thing that one did over the telephone as this would be a great shock to him. I went up to his bedroom and for the first time I was scared to wake him up. I often woke him when we travelled but this was different.

I first touched the duvet around his feet and said, 'Khulu, Khulu, I need to speak to you, please wake up.' The second time around

I touched the duvet close to his shoulder and he woke up. All he said was 'Yes Zeldina?' as if he expected me to ask him something. I said: 'I'm very sorry to be the one to have to tell you this but Uncle Walter passed away.' He either didn't hear me at first or he was in shock. I repeated myself. With one hand he reached for his hairline on his forehead and exclaimed: 'Good God.' It took him some time to sit up straight. I decided to sit at the foot of his bed for a while to make sure he was OK and repeated that I was very sorry to be the carrier of such bad news and told him what I had heard. I also told him that I thought he would want to know and he responded: 'Yes, yes of course.'

We agreed that he would go to the Sisulu residence very early the next morning and he asked me to wake him in the early hours. It was hard for Madiba too to see the sadness of Aunt Albertina, Uncle Walter's wife. He had known these people his entire life and they were part of him. He had so much respect for Uncle Walter and always commented on his admiration for Uncle Walter's humility and simplicity, and also for his outstanding leadership and always being willing to lead from behind and to push others forward. Silently I thought that was exactly it. Uncle Walter must have pushed Madiba to the front those years they were imprisoned. Madiba often told stories about their interaction and how often they discussed things. It was indeed a sad day for everyone. South Africa lost one of its biggest heroes.

It was becoming time for Madiba to slow down. He simply could not keep up his schedule and continue to respond to every request that was put to him by friends, colleagues and associates. He would divide his time between Johannesburg, Qunu and Maputo and then spend some quiet time at Shambala whenever he wanted to write. The house at Shambala also presented the opportunity for him to entertain high profile visitors who couldn't go to a normal game farm, as Shambala was completely private.

A few prominent artists suggested that Madiba's prison number be used to start an AIDS campaign. It would be called 46664. Madiba had always felt strongly against his face, image or name being commercialized, whether it was for charity or commercial purposes. The artists therefore came up with this idea of using his prison number to help raise funds for the AIDS campaign. They proposed launching the brand at a big concert to be held in Cape Town, all of them of course offering to perform free of charge. While some of the singers were rehearsing in Cape Town the CEO of the Foundation decided that Madiba should speak to the artists to thank them for their tireless dedication in their efforts to support a cause close to his heart.

We were at Shambala at the time. A telephone call was scheduled when the singers would all be together so that Madiba could speak to them. I typed out their names, for instance 'Brian May – Queen' and 'Dave Stewart – Eurythmics', after briefing Madiba. I tried to explain to him who everyone was and gave him the piece of paper in order for him to remember the names. Brian May was first on the line. I stood beside him to point to the piece of paper who he was talking to. When Brian answered he said, 'Hallo Madiba, how are you?' Madiba politely said, 'Hi Brian, I'm well thank you and how are you?' Brian responded to say he was well and that they were excited to be part of this event. Madiba acknowledged and then asked: 'How is the Queen?' He then spoke to Dave Stewart and asked him 'How is the Eurythmics?' He had no idea that these were bands. He'd lost track of technology during his imprisonment and it was hard to explain to him even what a CD was, let alone musicians and bands that were familiar to us – I'd overloaded him with the wrong information. It was precious to watch such innocence but the intention behind it was pure.

Earlier that year Madiba turned eighty-five. I was tasked by the CEO of the Foundation to organize a celebration for Madiba's birthday. I fundraised for the event and over 1,200 guests were invited to the black-tie event. Associates of Madiba from all over the world were invited – supporters, friends, politicians, royalty, etc. I guessed that I would be in the middle of the firing line when people started taking the guest list apart. I invited from gardeners to royalty to ensure that the group was fully representative. I worked day and night and my task was simple: we needed to ensure that Madiba was celebrated *during* his lifetime. When we walked to the elevator on the night of the event for Madiba to depart, close to midnight, Mrs Machel said: 'Well done Zeldina, Madiba was really honoured tonight.' Those words stuck by me despite all the flak I had to endure. People were complaining that Madiba was being 'poppified' – being made a pop star – because many celebrities attended the event, but no one paid attention to the gardeners, drivers and security who attended the event as guests, clearly because they were not considered famous or important enough to receive attention from the media. In addition, when we wanted help from the international community the celebrities were always called upon to give time and effort for free.

Madiba liked parties. He had gone over the guest list several times and approved of every person that was there. Some family members were angry as they were not seated around the main table, yet there were royalty and heads of state present. I subsequently wasn't invited to Madiba's ninetieth birthday at his farm in Qunu, and when Mrs Machel insisted that I be there, I was deliberately seated at a children's table right at the back of the tent. Not that I had hoped to be at the main table but it was a clear sign of some of the family's value of me in their father's life, and an indication of what was to be expected. I never discussed my problems with Madiba because I felt he had enough to worry about. That day, perhaps, I should have spoken to him.

On 7 November Madiba travelled to Shambala where we organized for him to spend the weekend with ex-Robben Islanders and ex-colleagues. A smaller group this time and people who were close to him during the struggle years. It remains one of my best memories, to see them all interacting, enjoying and reminiscing about old times. They all enjoyed visiting Shambala and we made sure they were well treated and spoilt. I loved listening to their stories and teasing one another. These were the men that drove the struggle,

planned sabotage and actions to try and bring the apartheid government to its senses. They'd spent a lifetime in prison and now they
were all elderly men, enjoying their senior years, free at last. It was
a proper reunion and everyone tried to outdo each other's stories.
One of those exceptionally precious occasions.

We had come such a long way in South Africa. Here I was enjoying time with ex-Robben Islanders, while at the time I was growing
up I'd considered it a good thing that they were imprisoned. I
became fond of many of them, such as Ahmed Kathrada, Eddie
Daniels, Mac Maharaj and Andrew Mlangeni. These were the
people we had to thank as they'd kept Madiba's spirit alive in prison.
And I often wondered if they ever lost hope during their time in
prison or whether they ever had imagined that they would be there
that day, on a private game farm, enjoying reminiscing with Madiba.

9

Holidays and Friends

By now we were spending weeks without end at Shambala. Madiba often invited people to come and visit him on the farm and we had to be mindful to not allow Shambala to become just another venue for people to flock to where he would soon feel overwhelmed by visitors. On one such occasion he invited Zwelinzima Vavi and Blade Nzimande, secretary-generals of the Council of South African Trade Unions and of the South African Communist Party respectively. Madiba enjoyed lunch with them after which he asked me to accompany them on a game drive, which I did. Shambala hosts the Big Five game animals and one could easily see four of the Big Five, including lion and elephant in a short game drive. I liked Blade and Zweli as they had always treated me with respect and dignity despite all the whispering about my white presence in Madiba's life. They never considered me as just the hired help. By now the SACP and Cosatu were in a tripartite alliance with the ANC. Zweli and Blade enjoyed the game drive and at one point I turned to them and said, 'You are not allowed to enjoy this, are you?' They laughed and I continued: 'Communists and socialists are not allowed to enjoy capitalism, so if you're enjoying it, just don't show it!'

Towards the end of 2003 Madiba received a visit from Sol Kerzner, the hotel tycoon from South Africa. In the past, people usually knew South Africa for two things: Nelson Mandela and Sun City. Sol built Sun City to much controversy in the mid 1980s, as the property is situated in what was then known as Bophuthatswana, one of South Africa's 'homelands', run by President Mangope. Mangope was perceived to be supportive of the apartheid government in the

1980s. After his release Madiba called Sol and convinced him to show support for rebuilding South Africa, which Sol was happy to help with. Eventually Sol sold his stake in Sun City and started Kerzner International abroad. He told Madiba about their resort in Mauritius and extended an invitation to Madiba for a holiday. We made arrangements for Madiba, Mrs Machel and some of the grandchildren to go.

It was like arriving in Paradise. Sol had booked a private villa for Madiba and Mrs Machel at the One & Only Le Saint Géran Hotel in Mauritius while the rest of us were accommodated in the hotel adjacent to the villa. Of course Sol knew that Madiba and Mum came with an entourage; no President or former President travels without. One also had to be careful not to make people feel, no matter how wealthy they were, that they were being exploited. They offered to pay for me and the doctor, in addition to the grand-children that Madiba chose to accompany us. What I always greatly appreciated about my boss was that he was very aware not to over-play someone's hospitality. So despite them paying for us, we didn't clean out the mini-bar or make international calls on the telephone, but rather dealt with the hospitality with the greatest respect.

I had now been working for Madiba for ten years and I had never seen him enjoying a holiday this much. He had private time with his wife and grandchildren and we all enjoyed meals like a big extended family. For the first time there was no rush. And it was difficult to get used to. Mum had to remind us constantly to relax and that we were on holiday. We watched performances by Mauritian dancers and it is one of the only two occasions that I remember Madiba dan-cing with Mum. He also jokingly insisted that we do the pata pata. 'Pata Pata' is a song by the legendary late South African singer Mir-iam Makeba, co-written by another legend, Dorothy Masuka. The song was released in 1957, before Madiba's imprisonment, and it reached the Billboard Hot 100 in 1967 in the US when Madiba was already imprisoned. The Xhosa song means 'touch-touch' and while singing it you are supposed to show how you 'touch-touch' your dancing partner. One of the bodyguards, Sydney Nkonoane, showed me how to dance the pata pata, much to Madiba's amusement. He was so fond of the song that I could well imagine him dancing to it back in the 1950s.

Security and I would exercise in the mornings while Mum did her walking, have a late breakfast and then swim and be in the sun for the rest of the day around Madiba. He would sit in the shade on the lawn overlooking the sea and wave at tourists walking by 'half naked' as he described them – people in swimming costumes. He enjoyed having us all around all the time. We were so busy back at home that one hardly ever got time to really appreciate the time spent together and here we were looking forward to actually having meals together.

The only connection to home was of course the news clippings. Every morning, before he woke up, I had to ensure that staff at the office in Johannesburg selected news clippings from the papers and faxed them to us. He wasn't interested much in the international publications that one found at a resort of this nature but insisted on news from home. Well, and we couldn't wait for him to finish with the clippings so that we could all catch up on the news too. The suffering staff back at the Foundation offices had to be in the office at all hours to prepare the clippings to be sent to us wherever we were.

After a few days Madiba announced that he wanted to go into the water. We were hesitant as we were not sure whether he would be able to stand in the water. He was having difficulties walking and was using a walking stick. Security took him down the terrace to the water and he sat on a chair in the water allowing the waves to break over his feet. The pure joy on his face touched my heart in a way that is difficult to describe. How could something so ordinary, something we take for granted, bring such pleasure to a human being?

We then discovered that Madiba hadn't swum in the sea for over forty years. The last time he had been in the ocean was when he removed seaweed from the water while on Robben Island, but that was manual labour under the watchful eye of prison guards and in the cold Atlantic Ocean, and at the same time he slipped on the rocks and injured his knee for ever. This was so different. Mum helped him to experience the simple things again, like family meals, sunshine and appreciating the beauty of life in flowers, land-scapes and music – things that just seemed to pass him by after his release.

Madiba was getting tired of his busy schedule and wanted to spend more time at Shambala, writing. He started saying that he wanted to 'retire' and I reminded him that he was retired. We discussed it with Prof. Gerwel and called a press conference to announce he was retiring from retirement. Madiba addressed a press conference on 1 June 2004 where he said: 'Don't call me, I'll call you.' Well, they never stopped calling. The public pressure con-tinued for him to honour their events, to open their projects or intervene in any situation where people felt they had reached a dead-end. Everybody saw themselves as the exception, the one for whom Madiba should step out of retirement. Madiba made every-one feel special and people therefore always felt that they had a special relationship with him. The same people who complained that he was too busy or was seen doing too much of this or that were then the ones for which he sometimes had to make the excep-tion. You sometimes feel like going crazy in that environment. Many of the people who claimed they had special relationships with him did, but it is precisely this that made it difficult for him to retire until the age where he was simply no longer able to do anything physically.

The ANC came calling too. The next election was approaching and the ANC came to announce to Madiba that they were in finan-cial difficulty. Big business was reluctant to be seen to support any one political party and so Madiba roped in former President F. W. de Klerk too. The two former enemies jointly set off on the streets to fundraise for both the New National Party (the former National Party) and the ANC. I had to make appointments for them with the CEOs and together they went cap in hand asking for financial assistance for the parties they had once led. Of course any company enjoyed having both Madiba and Mr de Klerk in their offices and the fundraising attempt was successful.

In March 2004 Charlize Theron became the first South African to be awarded an Oscar at the Academy Awards in Los Angeles, for her role in the movie *Monster*, and soon she was back to visit her country of origin. Madiba was in Maputo but he agreed to return to be in Johannesburg to meet with Ms Theron. The media was in a frenzy. We ordered *koeksisters*, an Afrikaner delicacy that Charlize mentioned she was hoping to eat while in South Africa. Madiba offered her *koeksisters* and although she took one, she never ate it. She announced her intention to start an AIDS charity but I wasn't sure how informed she was of the intricacies of the disease. They appeared in front of the media following their meeting and she told Madiba in the presence of the world media how much she loved him. Women always loved Madiba as he was charming and generous in paying compliments. A real charmer.

It couldn't have been pleasant for Mrs Machel to hear people declaring their undying love to Madiba and him charming them; however, she never complained. I recall an incident in the Presidency at some stage when it became too much and all female staff kissed him whenever they greeted him. Female staff were then asked not to kiss the President in public. It was funny. Everyone just adored Madiba but it was becoming a liability for him to be seen being kissed by women every day wherever he moved.

About a year later we were looking for Charlize to ask her to record a message in support of Madiba's 46664 AIDS awareness campaign. First we struggled to get hold of her and when we eventually did, we were told by her publicist that she was busy filming and unable to record a twenty-second promo. I insisted that she could find five minutes to do this but I was told that it was not possible. We were offended because on the occasion she visited South Africa Madiba flew from another city to meet her in Johannesburg. Only when she heard about it personally did she intervene.

Sometimes staff can cause considerable damage to your reputation and relationships, as we'd learned.

One of the ministers Madiba had appointed in his Cabinet, the Minister of Intelligence, Joe Nhlanhla, had had two strokes and was bedridden. Kgalema Motlanthe, the Secretary General of the ANC at the time, reported to Madiba that Joe was not well. We visited him in hospital and were told that he didn't have the financial means to be taken to a hospice. Madiba mobilized business to start a fund for Joe Nhlanhla and soon he was moved to a high-care centre. I was sad to hear of his death but I was saddened that the responsibility of these things kept coming back to Madiba, as if he was for ever expected to pay down on a refund for what people had done for him in the past. At times, the requests were relentless, and it seemed everybody wanted him to personally bail them out of whatever financial mess they found themselves in.

On 24 March 2004 we set out on another visit to Saudi Arabia. Sometimes it was for fundraising, sometimes just to honour a request from the Saudis. I now had my own *abaya* and was quite comfortable wearing it and moving around in Riyadh. After my previous experience, I knew I had to tone down my frustrations with the Saudis. I grew to enjoy our Saudi trips because I knew exactly what to expect, I knew what to do and not to do and was happy to follow their rules because I no longer had unrealistic expectations. I still had difficulty communicating with some of the officials as they wouldn't take instructions easily from women, but while I was with Madiba they obliged.

We were scheduled to meet with the King and as usual I was told that I was not allowed to accompany Madiba as no women are ever allowed to meet the King. Madiba insisted and, surprisingly, the messenger returned to say that I would indeed be allowed to accompany him. The appointment time arrived and we set off to the King's palace. Upon arrival Madiba did what he usually did whenever he was scared that I would go astray. As soon as he exited from the car he stopped and asked, 'Where is my secretary?' The men would run around looking for the secretary and then rush me to him. I sometimes deliberately remained in the car for a few seconds longer because I knew I would not be able to fight my way through the security on my own and unless Madiba called me I would get stuck. As we entered the palace, surrounded by a mass of people, he took my hand. I was uncomfortable as I knew it was unheard of for me to be there and then, secondly, it was not proper for an unmarried woman to be seen to have any physical contact with a man. But he didn't let go of my hand and he knew the rules very well.

We were escorted to the waiting room where we sat until the King called for Madiba. Again Madiba took my hand and we entered the King's chambers. He greeted the King and left me standing behind him. I wanted to turn around and run, but I didn't. I just felt so uncomfortable. Madiba then turned around and said, 'Your Majesty, this is my secretary and granddaughter, Zelda la Grange.' I knew I was not supposed to make eye contact with the King either and I didn't. I bowed my head and smiled although I knew not to curtsy. Madiba was very intolerant of people being submissive in situations like these. But I was really scared. The only thing that went through my mind was: The King can see I'm not black; I can't be your granddaughter. The King extended his hand to shake my hand and I saw Madiba nodding his head in approval of me sticking my arm out. So I did. The King held my hand and I could feel sweat dripping down my back.

The King was visibly old but he seemed friendly. He was talking to us through a translator and welcomed me. I wanted him to let go of my hand but he didn't. He asked me how I was and Madiba interrupted and told him that just before I left Johannesburg on our way to Saudi I was involved in a smash and grab robbery incident in my car, where thugs stole my handbag from the front seat. I was indeed very upset when we boarded the plane the previous night – my life was in the handbag that was stolen and for the first time I boarded a flight without even so much as a cellphone. However, right there I was more concerned about my defiance of the Saudi culture just being in the same room as the King. Madiba told him that I was still in shock and the King expressed his sympathy. He eventually let go of my hand and we were all seated to have tea with him. The King no longer often received visitors as he was old and ill. Nevertheless we had a brief chat to him before we departed. He was clearly very fond of Madiba and appreciated the courtesy call.

Madiba had also asked to meet with the Crown Prince and in the afternoon we set off to meet him. Clearly he was already ruling Saudi Arabia and he was more serious and pressurized for time. His office and environment were a bit more reformed and we had no trouble with my attendance. We had a few days to spare in Saudi and Madiba had an idea for us to visit Medina and Mecca, the place of pilgrimage where Muslims travel to annually to pay their respects. We had everything arranged when I was told that I was not going to be allowed to travel with Madiba as I was not Muslim. My response to the officials was, 'But Madiba is not Muslim either!' They were stunned. They thought he was Muslim. It never ceased to amaze me about Madiba – that he could associate and relate so well with people that they started believing he was 'one of them'.

We ended up going to neither Medina nor Mecca. From Saudi we were set to visit Tunis and then Iran. In Tunis Madiba was supposed to attend an African Infrastructure Fund board meeting and in Iran he was scheduled to receive the highest honour of that country from President Khatami. In Tunis Madiba was tired and he didn't attend the board meeting but only a short reception. Cyril Ramaphosa accompanied us and he explained that Madiba was tired and unable to attend the board meeting. It was the first time I saw him simply being tired and not wanting to do anything. For me it was a big crisis. I didn't know how we would explain that to people. Luckily Cyril did all the explaining and I didn't have to take the blame. I also called Prof. Gerwel and both he and Cyril spoke with one voice: 'If he doesn't want to do it, he shouldn't. He is entitled to be tired.' Then Madiba announced that he no longer wanted to go to Iran but he wanted to return home. He had never cancelled an international trip before nor had he simply not felt up to travelling.

We informed the Iranian government and they were clearly very disappointed. He wanted to spend time at home with his wife and not to have a life dictated by a schedule. I had expected these signs much sooner than they appeared, but gave him the freedom to decide when enough was eventually enough; however, it still came as a surprise.

When we were back in South Africa, Madiba decided that he had to send a gift to both the King and the Crown Prince of Saudi Arabia to thank them for all their hospitality over the years. He asked me for suggestions. The Saudis are so rich this was a huge challenge. I suggested that we perhaps send them each two springbok and two oryx antelopes. I had done my research and knew they would survive in the Saudi environs. What kind of presents do you give to people who have everything their hearts desire? I learned that they both loved their animals and therefore the antelope would be a welcome gift. Madiba agreed.

We asked the farm manager at Shambala at the time, Dries Krog, to assist us. The animals had to go into quarantine before leaving and it took weeks to organize all the necessary paperwork and export permits. People often asked me over the years what exactly my job entailed. I didn't know where to start but would say, 'I can type, answer telephones, call press conferences and export springbok and oryx to Saudi Arabia.'

Back at home we attended another ANC rally prior to the elections but by now Madiba had lost the appetite to actively campaign. They would have ANC National Executive meetings during which people would voice their unhappiness about his alleged disrespect for the President. These people were never willing to confront Madiba directly and he had to hear of these discussions from other attendees.

South Africa was bidding for the 2010 FIFA World Cup. Madiba was informed about the initiative but we saw our role being minor if anything because it was the role of the head of state to drive these initiatives. In late April 2004 Tokyo Sexwale, former premier of

Gauteng Province and then running a multibillion-rand business empire, visited Madiba in his capacity as one of the members of the bid committee. Tokyo announced that they wanted Madiba to go to Trinidad and Tobago to help in the lobbying. Madiba was tired and he didn't feel like travelling. At first he said no. Tokyo didn't let go and two nights later we were on our way to Trinidad and Tobago. We were unable, as his advisers, to maintain the consistency of implementing his decisions. The public was confused about who held the structure of power around him. I declined to accept that responsibility on many occasions, and as much as I tried to execute his wishes, the decision-making really depended on a lot of external influences as well as decisions by Madiba, Prof. and the CEO of the Foundation. Ultimately Madiba had to decide to do anything, and once he had agreed or been convinced it was difficult to persuade him otherwise; the same would apply to his refusal to do anything. He would just become stubborn.

I insisted that this visit be downscaled and that the programme be minimized. The reason for the visit was to convince members of FIFA who resided in Trinidad and the region to vote for South Africa's bid. We flew in a comfortable plane but Madiba was used to complete silence when he slept. The configuration of the plane was of such a nature that one had to walk past him while he was sleeping to get to the toilets. He didn't sleep well and that worried me. Tokyo tried his best to ensure everybody's comfort but when we landed I looked through the aeroplane window and saw that the government had put out a full guard of honour for Madiba's arrival, when we had asked them not to. It was not practical to expect Madiba to perform any ceremonial duties after such a long flight. When I noticed the guard of honour Tokyo and I had words and I asked him to step in. He himself could see that Madiba was tired so he called Jack Warner, the FIFA member in Trinidad who obviously wielded power in that country, on board the plane to meet us. We were told that the guard of honour was simply a receiving line and that Madiba would be free to depart from the airport immediately.

The entire visit was a battle. Merely two weeks after our visit to

Trinidad we travelled to Zurich where South Africa was awarded the bid to host the 2010 World Cup tournament. I suppose it was worth it. After Zurich we went to Douw Steyn's estate in the countryside in England where we could take a breather for a few days.

I cannot recall what year it was but during one of our visits to London we paid a courtesy call to Prime Minister Tony Blair, as we did on many occasions. I loved going to 10 Downing Street, especially after it featured in the 2003 movie *Love Actually*. When Hugh Grant was dancing as Prime Minister in one of the rooms in Downing Street I smiled, having been in that room myself before. Not dancing though. But on this particular occasion we hurriedly got ready for the appointment at Downing Street. Prime Minister Blair was always warm towards Madiba and we returned to the Dorchester Hotel where we stayed, satisfied with the meeting.

It was autumn and the sun rose later and set earlier. Added to that was the usual cloudiness outside. When I stepped out of the car upon our arrival back at the Dorchester I noticed that I was wearing two different shoes. You idiot, I thought. I was too ashamed of myself to point out my mistake to anyone, but later confided in the doctor with us and we laughed at my stupidity. I always stayed in a particular room in the Dorchester whenever I was there with Madiba, kindly arranged by a South African ex-pat, Nigel Badminton, who had become a close friend due to all our visits there. This room had a small dressing room, but it was more a corner than a room. There was no natural light and I had to rely on artificial light. I was in such a rush when we left, trying to gather everyone and to make sure Madiba was ready to leave, that I didn't notice that I had put on two different shoes. The two pairs I had were more or less the same style with similar heels and therefore I didn't feel the difference when I was walking. The one was black though and the other dark brown. It is to this day probably the most stupendously ignorant thing I've ever done. You try and reverse such an action a thousand times or try to remember if anyone in Downing Street might have noticed.

From London we set off to Spain where Madiba and Mrs Machel attended the wedding of the son of King Juan Carlos and Queen Sofia of Spain. This was nothing short of a fairytale. Mostly royalty from other countries attended and hardly any other politicians were invited to all parts of the celebrations. We would tease Madiba about it and he would remind us that indeed he was born into royalty too. To us it may only be considered Xhosa royalty but still it was royalty and he loved being reminded that he was a prince.

On 24 May 2004 we received a visit by the renowned boxing promoter Don King. He was a controversial character but this was another occasion on which we were told that Madiba had to do it. Of course, being a boxer himself, Madiba didn't object. I was in my office when the receptionist called to say 'King is here'. I'd forgotten for a moment that we were expecting him and responded: 'The King of what?' We all laughed and indeed it was King, the King of boxing. There were many of these moments that lightened the days and kept us sane in a way.

As expected, after a brief rest (and despite his retirement) Madiba decided that he wanted to attend the International AIDS Conference in Thailand. He was hoping to continue the fight even in retirement and to leave a strong message behind. This was shortly before his eighty-sixth birthday. On our way back from Thailand I wrote a piece for the *Sunday Independent*, a message for his birthday. On the Sunday of his birthday the article appeared on the front page reading: 'Khulu, my wish for your 86th birthday is time – Zelda'. I truly wished for him to have time for himself, time with his wife and time to reflect. But as soon as things became too quiet, he would initiate things again. Soon the retirement status changed to 'to allow him to choose to do what he wants' and off we went again. I sensed that it was a struggle within himself between staying at home and being isolated from the world. We came to the conclusion that he would just never stop and as soon as he sent out signs that he was available again, the usual suspects saw their way in to approaching him again.

I felt as though some of the family and their associates

disapproved of my presence in his life. For some it seemed personal and for others it seemed to me as though they were uncomfortable with him depending on a white woman. I felt caught between my duty to Madiba and the perception that I was a public burden to him. If I tried to make myself scarce, he would call me and sometimes become irritated that I wasn't at my post. He was becoming more and more dependent on me for very simple reasons: he was old; he needed someone there when he entered a meeting because he needed to be reminded of what to expect or what was about to happen. His memory wasn't as good as it had been. I felt stressed and he saw it.

Madiba would sit me down and give me a lecture about the fact that I worked for him, that I had to do as he told me and that I shouldn't allow people to distract me. Thinking back now, I should have told a few people back then, when he was still able to defend me, that they had to voice their complaints directly to him, but I never wanted to burden him with my personal battles. I had to face the fact that a young white Afrikaner woman caring for him was always going to be an unlikely and unpopular situation. Yet I was determined to never abandon him for as long as he wanted me. He told me about such disgruntled visitors on a few occasions, explaining how they challenged him for appointing a white Afrikaner woman. The first time he told me, he was cautious about the way in which he conveyed it, but after a few occasions both of us would laugh whenever he repeated it.

Xoliswa, Madiba's long-time chef, and I spoke a lot over the phone, as she was usually working whenever I had to be connected to Madiba on the telephone. We came to the conclusion that everybody wanted our jobs, but few people were prepared to put in the hours and effort.

Back in early 2003 I had noticed Madiba was disturbed about something. He spent days being reserved and withdrawn. Madiba told me that his only surviving son Makgatho had been to the house to tell him that he had AIDS. I was devastated by the news but I assured Madiba that I would do whatever to support him.

When Makgatho was admitted to hospital in December 2004 I went with Madiba to the hospital on the first afternoon. There we found Makgatho already in the High Care Unit. Madiba went inside and insisted that I walk with him. We only saw Makgatho occasionally and he really only became part of Madiba's life in later years. I was fond of him even though my dealings with him were limited. He was always very courteous and respectful in his dealings with me and helpful whenever I asked him to help with something around Madiba or attend an event on his father's behalf. I didn't know why children from his first marriage were absent from Madiba's life at that stage but I did see how Mrs Machel tried to bring the family together. She constantly tried to broker peace between the different parts of the family and insisted that all his children become part of his life. It wasn't easy for her because some of his children felt bitterness towards him. I was an employee and never interfered with the family matters, and never lost sight of the fact that I was an employee.

I was sad to see Makgatho in hospital. He couldn't talk but Madiba spoke to him, and just before we left I bent down and whispered to him: 'Hi Makgatho, this is Zelda. Remember, we love you very much and be strong.' I had seen a person with AIDS recovering before and I was hoping that he would too. Before we left Makgatho's sister Makaziwe entered. I was asking the nurse what Makgatho's temperature was so as to try and give Madiba some kind of comfort or something and Makaziwe told me: 'Leave my brother's medical records alone. It's got nothing to do with you.' I was desperate to tell her I had known for two years that her brother had AIDS and I had never done anything to harm him or talk about his condition. I wasn't about to start; my asking was purely to try and hopefully give Madiba some comfort.

I was on holiday over December in Paternoster, a small coastal town on the west coast of South Africa, when Meme, Madiba's housekeeper, told me that it was better to return as things were turning for the worse. I knew we had to assist with support to the household if that was the case and so I cut my holiday short and returned home. While I was driving home, Makgatho passed away and I never saw him again after that one visit. I was never asked to stay away but you just know when your presence is not wanted. I informed Mrs Machel that I was back at home but I waited two days before I went to Madiba's house to pay my respects. When Mrs Machel asked why I hadn't come before I said that I was mindful of people hurting and mourning and that I didn't want to add to the burden or be an irritation to them. She was irritated with my assumptions but understood how I felt. Makgatho was the father of Mandla, Ndaba, Mbuso and Andile. I hurt for these children as they were part of our everyday life and I felt like I grew up with them. Those years they mostly treated me like a sister and we had a close bond.

I tried to stay away from the family as it mourned but I did try to help with logistics. It was a very sad funeral and my heart broke for Madiba. In African tradition the body is brought back home for a night vigil before the burial the next day. The person 'sleeps' in his/her bedroom for the last night and the next morning a prayer service is held in the foyer or entrance hall of the house where the body is displayed for the last time before the burial commences. Madiba insisted that I be there and take part in saying our last farewells. Mrs Machel was next to Madiba and held his hand in a tight grip throughout the ceremony. I had only once before seen someone who was dead, when my grandmother from my father's side passed away while I was still a child. That memory haunted me for many years. Makgatho looked peaceful though, being back home. It must have been one of the saddest times with Madiba, seeing him burying his son. Mrs Machel held his hand tightly throughout the proceedings.

In the early 2000s Madiba called on Douw Steyn and asked him to think of methods to generate an extra income. Madiba was receiving only a pension as former President but not nearly enough to maintain his residences and the needs of his extended family. I got a sense that he felt responsible for providing for everyone around him – his continuing desire to support people – and whenever someone needed something, they would turn to Madiba. Even during prison years, letters now published in the book *Conversations With Myself* point to the fact that Madiba was always the provider.

At the time Madiba's lawyer was Ismail Ayob, who used to handle all his finances. Madiba never handled any money himself and would simply request any of his lawyers to deal with financial matters on his behalf. Life had evolved while Madiba was imprisoned and he didn't know how to operate the technology around banking in the modern world.

Madiba had the ability to trust people unconditionally. I got to know of Ismail Ayob early in the Presidency and whenever Madiba needed something that cost money, Ismail would be called. Ismail took his responsibilities very seriously. He also dealt with all Madiba's intellectual property and the use of his image. Whenever someone promised Madiba money for whatever project they agreed upon, the money would need to be in the bank first before the door was opened for discussions. Madiba never handled such matters personally and, from my experience, half the time he didn't know what Ismail was negotiating on his behalf, but Ismail was tenacious when it came to dealing with Madiba's financial matters.

Whenever anyone wanted money, Madiba would send them to Ismail. But he would call Ismail first and instruct him how to handle the matter. On many occasions Ismail would question the expenditure intently. That irritated people and in my experience no one ended up having a good relationship with him. And sooner rather than later everybody said: 'Ismail must go.' But he didn't. Madiba was also a very loyal person so despite what others' opinions may have been Madiba was steadfast in his loyalty towards Ismail.

Another of Madiba's lawyers was George Bizos, who had been a lawyer for Madiba for decades, since before his imprisonment; he was even part of the team that represented him at the Rivonia Trial.

He was someone who commanded authority as a result of his legal experience and knowledge. He was also one of the few people who shared a very special friendship with Madiba and someone of whom Madiba was extremely fond.

Douw Steyn came back to Madiba after Madiba's request with an idea to generate some income to support his family. However the idea involved a commercialization of his image to some extent. The proposal was circulated to the lawyers, who were all vehemently opposed to it. It would create enormous difficulty in trying to stop illegitimate commercialization of his image in future, and therefore Douw's idea was declined. His intentions were nevertheless good. We had always been consistent in maintaining Madiba's wishes not to allow his image or name to ever be commercialized, something he tasked the Nelson Mandela Foundation with after his Presidency.

We were offered money over the years for many things but there were a few unwritten rules no one was ever going to compromise on, no matter what amount was put on the table.

There were just certain things Madiba was never willing to compromise on. Jeopardizing his relationship with the Queen was one, association with tobacco and alcohol another, and never selling his time. On one occasion a famous alcohol brand offered us US$2 million. They wanted nothing in return from Madiba, but alcohol and the association with Nelson Mandela as a humanitarian didn't fit and we declined. Once we were offered money from the South African Breweries as a donation and Ismail declined that too.

In Paris we were offered US$5 million from a well-known luxury brand for Madiba to do an advertisement for them. I liked the people but I knew that we could never commercialize his name. And so we never sold Madiba's time either. People wanted to pay to meet him, we declined and sometimes they met him but we refused to take the money nevertheless. To me the rationale was that if you didn't believe in the legacy of Nelson Mandela and only wanted to pay if you could benefit from the human himself, it meant that your intentions were not pure. We have indeed lost millions over the years but we succeeded in avoiding commercial exploitation or association with anything that didn't relate to the legacy of Nelson Mandela. Or at least we tried and mostly succeeded. That doesn't mean we liked people less who produced alcohol or people that made such advances. People are sometimes oblivious and it is in no way a reflection on their integrity. Most celebrities worldwide, and even world leaders, lend their images to advertising or contribute auction items by putting a lunch or dinner or a rare experience with them up for sale. It's a good way of making money, but not for someone with the moral responsibilities of Nelson Mandela.

Here, though, it was for personal benefit, to support some of his extended family, and it was more complicated. Ismail came to Madiba a few days after the proposal from Douw was declined with a counter-proposal. Madiba would create artworks that were reproduced from drawings he was guided to do, sign them all and then they would be sold. As Madiba became older he kept reminding those around him that he had a large family to provide for, which indicated to us that there was urgency to the matter. He fundraised for an education trust as he was adamant that his grandchildren should all be well educated. There was nothing sinister about it; people understood that he'd been imprisoned for a long time and felt that he had to support his family somehow to compensate for his absence.

Ismail's proposal was accepted and soon he entered a deal with businessman Ross Calder on Madiba's behalf and they brought an artist to Madiba's house who helped him to colour in some drawings and do some charcoal sketches. The initiative was based on another project done by world icons who did similar amateur-like art and it ended up being very profitable for them. The first phase was completed and then reproduced and Madiba then started colouring and again those were reproduced. The next phase was for him to sign thousands of these prints. And so I was left with scheduling the signing sessions. Every few days Madiba would sit for an hour or two signing these sketches. Hundreds or perhaps even thousands of them. I don't know. As Madiba fully trusted Ismail I was not present at all these signing sessions. Sometimes they were done at home and sometimes they were done at the office. No one kept a record and there was no reason to question the conviction with which this project was being run. After all, as Madiba was always quick to point out, never question a person's integrity until you have valid reason to do so. Moreover, I found Ismail in Madiba's service back in 1994. I never questioned their relationship or Ismail's authority because they had a history, and as I so often got pointed out to me, I didn't.

In April 2005 an article appeared in the *Noseweek*, an investigative magazine, with the title CIVIL WAR IN MADIBALAND. The author wrote:

> In order to understand the civil war that is breaking out in Mandela-land, it is useful to imagine a medieval monarchy when the King is nearing the end. The family, and factions within the family, are agitating for position in the aftermath. The court is rampant with whispers and plots.

At the centre of this 'civil war' was the issue of who controlled Madiba's future income and, more importantly, the licence that trademarked his name and image. Madiba wanted objective people such as his lawyers Bizos, Bally Chuene and Wim Trengove, not his family, in control of his estate. More so, he was disappointed at Ismail's conduct. Someone planted a seed within Madiba's mind that Ismail should report on progress, and when he started questioning Ismail and asking about the project, in my opinion the relationship started deteriorating. Madiba made a turn-around on his decision about the project. He instructed George Bizos and others to halt the project. Papers were served on Ismail and Calder's company and an order was obtained to stop the sale of the artworks. This caused anger among those who profited from the project and war ensued.

In the latest legal battle in 2013, two of Madiba's daughters – Makaziwe and Zenani – and Ismail served papers on Bally Chuene, arguing that his appointment and those of Advocate George Bizos and Tokyo Sexwale to the trust controlling the proceeds from the artworks were not legitimate. The case was withdrawn in September 2013.

We were often, now, at Shambala. Shambala not only created the perfect setting for him to write but also much needed peace and quiet time. Madiba often said that he missed prison. I was troubled and surprised by this. He then went on to explain that in prison he had time to read and time to think and I comprehended what he meant. He would insist on going to Shambala for weeks at a time as he was eager to complete his memoirs. It was a long and tedious task. He would write every page in longhand, finish about five pages for me to type and once I'd typed them he would make factual corrections. Then, instead of giving me the typed page with his corrections on to execute the corrections, he would insist on rewriting the entire page in longhand. I suggested sitting with him with my laptop to type as he spoke. He refused. He didn't like technology and he wanted to be able to put pen on paper. I even suggested that he simply spoke into a recorder and I could type from there, but to that he also said: 'No, you know, I wouldn't like that.' We also appointed a researcher but Madiba was simply not up to writing.

Extracts from the manuscript are published in *Conversations With Myself* and hopefully soon the unpublished parts will be used in a sequel to *Long Walk to Freedom*, this time dealing with his Presidential years only.

The reality of the matter was that we were slowly but surely putting on the brakes. Even so, in May 2005 Madiba went on his last visit to the United States. Our first stop was in New York. There a fundraiser was organized by the former chairman of Goldman Sachs and Madiba was scheduled to attend a dinner. Mrs Machel couldn't join us in New York and Madiba was grumpy as he was becoming uncomfortable when she was not around. Madiba took his usual nap on the afternoon of the event and when I went to wake him to get ready for the dinner he announced that he was not feeling well. My heart came to a standstill. We called the doctor. The doctor couldn't find any sign of serious illness and it was probably pure exhaustion. We agreed that we would bring the main donors to the room for him to greet but that he didn't have to go to the dinner. We were all nervous at people's reactions when he decided to cancel something.

The sponsors were very understanding though, and I wish all people were so accommodating. The next day Madiba was fighting fit. He got up for his meeting with President Clinton and was happy to see him as usual. It was also a day closer to Mrs Machel joining us and that always cheered him up. Two nights later we went to a dinner hosted by Sol Kerzner and Robert De Niro and organized by Jerry Inzerillo in Tribeca. It was a lovely dinner attended by a lot of good friends but also celebrities from the music and entertainment industry – half of whom I didn't know myself. They swamped his table to greet him and we had to be firm to keep people away from the table; I had to 'instruct' Madiba to focus on eating his food to keep up his stamina. Madiba didn't have the faintest idea who many of the celebrities were. Some of the names and faces he recognized from reading about them in newspapers but most of them were strangers to him. I think this may have been quite a shock to them as he didn't always react when meeting some of them for the first time as their fans usually did. It was entertainment in itself to watch. They were flocking his table. When we walked out one of the gentlemen we stopped to greet was Richard Gere. I looked at Madiba as he was introduced to him and wondered whether he knew how many women across the world would literally do anything to be in his shoes at that moment. He was completely oblivious, but as he introduced me I think he could see that I was dumbstruck.

It reminded me of another occasion when we travelled to Ireland in support of the Special Olympics. As we were about to enter an elevator I saw a man rushing around the corner to try and catch it too. He wasn't aware who was inside. When I looked a second time, it was Pierce Brosnan. I whispered to Madiba, 'The man about to enter the lift is a famous actor. He plays 007 in the James Bond movies.' I should have stopped just after 'famous actor' but was overtaken by surprise myself that he moved without any entourage. And of course as he entered the lift Madiba was still asking, 'He plays who?' I didn't respond and instead said, 'Khulu, you remember the famous actor Pierce Brosnan?' And Madiba said, 'Oh yes, of course, pleased to meet you.' I was relieved when the elevator stopped on our floor and we could get out. Mr Brosnan eloquently greeted us.

A similar incident happened when Brad Pitt visited South Africa in support of the Mineseeker project, an initiative started by Richard Branson to fund the detection and destruction of landmines in previously war-stricken areas. Nelson Mandela's life revolved around politics, not entertainment, and apart from the few movies they were shown in prison he literally didn't have time to visit the cinema and there was nothing relaxed about his life that would allow him to for instance watch a DVD. He ate, slept and lived for politics and his humanitarian efforts. I tried to explain to Madiba who Brad Pitt was but it was difficult. When they finally met the next day Madiba asked (as he usually did) whether Brad had a business card with him. Of course Brad didn't. Madiba asked: 'So what do you do?' I luckily had explained to Brad that he had to understand that Madiba was not aware of developments in Hollywood and the film industry in general. And Brad was every bit gracious in his response and said: 'I try acting for a living.' I added, 'And he is very modest because he is one of the best actors in the world.' Brad didn't make a fuss nor was he surprised or embarrassed in any way. He was a true gentleman.

The night before his visit I got called by a mutual friend who was with the Mineseeker project. He said that Brad wanted me to join them for dinner. At first I declined. I told a colleague of mine and she enquired after my 'sanity' and asked who on earth declines to have dinner with Brad Pitt? Well I do. Although I appreciated the fact that the dinner was meant to give him an overview of South Africa and what to expect when meeting Madiba, I had had enough of dinners and evenings out talking about my boss. As much as I loved Madiba, I didn't want to feel that I had to entertain people with him. I had to reconsider this invitation though, and I was happy I did. Brad was an exceptionally pleasant, humble person and we shared a love for motorbikes; we even discovered that we drove the same motorbike at the time. He wasn't only interested in hearing about Madiba but in really interacting with people who could give him a sense of South Africa and its future.

Our American trip continued after the New York party. This time President George W. Bush did return our call and Madiba went to Washington to meet him. For the first time, we stayed in George-town at the Four Seasons and the hotel used the pseudonym Mr and Mrs Smith for Madiba and Mrs Machel. I thought that was quite ironic. In South Africa the Smith surname is considered a white sur-name; it was shortly after the release of the movie *Mr and Mrs Smith* about a spy duo who fall in love, played by Angelina Jolie and Brad Pitt. There were always these moments that provided much humour to the most stressful situations. Having my sense of humour also helped because I could quietly laugh at things to keep me sane.

While in DC, Madiba addressed the Congressional Black Cau-cus. We couldn't greet any of the attendees as it was a huge group of people and we were mindful of pleasing some and offending others. Back at the hotel after Madiba's address to the Black Caucus, I heard that Barack Obama, who was a senator at the time, hadn't attended the caucus as he didn't agree with their views on a spe-cific issue. There was also a request from Senator Hillary Clinton to see Madiba and due to our relationship with the Clintons over the years, and knowing that it was more a social call than politics or business, we agreed, despite the fact that Madiba was exhausted by now after a busy programme in New York. The long-distance travel was just too much for him this time too. He still had to visit

President Bush and we had to save any reserve energy he had. We also got a message that Senator Obama wanted to have an opportunity to greet Madiba. John Samuel, our CEO at the time, Prof. Gerwel and I unanimously said no to that request. Madiba was just too tired.

We were told by a long-time American friend of Madiba's, Frank Ferrari, that it would be just a handshake and that Senator Obama could be the first black American President in future, and quietly I thought: Ye right. We eventually agreed to the meeting in which they greeted and exchanged pleasantries. He was overly respectful to the elderly Madiba and it also struck me how he paid attention to everyone, from the door man to the 'secretary'. Something very similar to the character of Nelson Mandela. The small people mattered, which speaks of the greatness of any man. Madiba didn't even get out of his chair to greet him as he was simply too tired. I cannot recall who took the picture of Madiba and the Senator but a picture showing Madiba seated was taken with only Senator Obama's silhouette showing as he bent to shake hands with Madiba.

This was the first time we would see President Bush after Madiba had pronounced that America was wrong to invade Iraq and that Prime Minister Tony Blair was merely acting as a Minister of Foreign Affairs for America. Ouch! He also said that President Bush didn't respect the wishes of the UN because Kofi Annan was black. Double ouch!! Madiba had a number of issues to discuss with President Bush and the plan was that they would appear jointly in front of the media following their meeting to show their 'agreement to disagree' to the rest of the world but that they were friendly again after all that had happened. Madiba often said that one should never be scared to hide your differences but that you should always remember that they are differences and that it doesn't determine the rest of any relationship. In the same way he had differences in opinion with Gaddafi but never snubbed him as a result of those differences.

I was worried Madiba was too tired and just too fragile for a meeting of this nature. So I made a note for him with pointers for the discussion. We entered the White House as we had done before and proceeded to the Oval Office. In the waiting room we were met by an intern who tried to make silly small talk with Madiba. My face usually shows my emotions and he quickly got the message. The President was available immediately and the meeting started. I appreciated their punctuality. At first I thought that he was friendly but when Madiba repeated himself the third time I could see that President Bush was getting impatient. Madiba didn't stick to the pointers and dwelled on conversation and then when he returned to the pointers he would repeat something he had already said. I was getting nervous as I could see President Bush had little understanding of the limitations of his old age. Before Madiba could finish, President Bush said, 'Well Mr President' – meaning Madiba – 'it's time for us to go and see the media.' Madiba wouldn't stop as he was not finished. The President interrupted him and repeated his request. I was disturbed.

To me it appeared as if President Bush was more interested in appearing in front of the media than in listening to what Madiba was trying to say. To his credit President Bush agreed to increase aid to Africa, but that didn't change my mind about my experiences that day. I felt disempowered and I felt sorry for Madiba as I couldn't do anything to support him more in those circumstances. But he carried himself with pride, even realizing himself that he was starting to be forgetful and that his mind often wandered. He would often say, 'you know I am almost one hundred years now, I forget things', and my heart would go out to him, sometimes just squeezing his hand or touching his shoulder to try and show him some comfort, that we understood and that we were there to support him even as he became forgetful.

I lived on the West Rand in Johannesburg at the time, about 21 kilometres from Houghton where our office and Madiba's residence was. In normal traffic it took me about forty minutes to get to Houghton or back. In peak-hour traffic it took me about two hours.

It was killing me. In addition Madiba would call me for anything. On a Saturday morning while I was working in the garden Madiba would call and ask: 'Zeldina, are you busy?' Of course I would never say I was busy and would ask, 'How can I help Khulu?' He would then convince me that it was not something he could discuss over the telephone and could I come over to his house. So I cleaned up, dressed up and went to his house in Houghton. When I got there, nine out of ten times he couldn't remember why he had called me.

I tried to get him to write down whatever was on his mind at the time so he could remember when I got there, but he wouldn't do that. Then I tried to convince him to tell one of the household staff what it was about so I could remind him when I got there, but he wouldn't do that either. I had to make another plan. I had to start looking for a new home closer to him. I had bought my first motorbike at the time and my father convinced me to grow up, sell my toys and invest in property. So I bought a house much closer to the office and Madiba's residence.

But really I simply could no longer maintain the pace at which we were working and travelling in addition to taking care of 'Zelda'. The administration was overwhelming and being every day absent from the office, attending events with Madiba, created an administrative backlog for me. Happily the Foundation's CEO approved the appointment of three assistants to help me. They were angels sent from heaven. The extra hands helped and I managed to delegate some of the duties so that I could find head space to strategize about everything around Madiba, from media communication to time management. But nothing ever happened according to plan. Madiba wanted to know from me what was expected of him every second of the day. And yet no matter how much I planned and paid attention to detail it was never flawless. I am told I am a slave driver myself and not an easy person to work with. I am a perfectionist and my expectations from others are sometimes too high. As Madiba got older I became more pedantic about detail around him, but at the same time strangely I grew more patient with others.

And sometimes Madiba was difficult. If I didn't pay him enough attention or didn't attend enough events to his liking, he would find a reason why I should do something myself and not delegate it. And then I would be caught up between the staff, trying to spare their feelings and protecting them from feeling that they were being shunned. I was no longer the shy scared white girl and he was very used to my obsessive-compulsive behaviour and perfectionist ways. They suited him. He would tolerate a lot of tardiness from other people but not from me.

In October 2005 we set off to Kenya for two weeks to spend time with Mrs Machel as she was working on the African Peer Review Mechanism in Nairobi. It was probably the longest two weeks of my life. At home I had a friend packing up my house and in Kenya all I wanted to do was go home. Madiba was talking less but even so he had never been the kind of person who can be unoccupied for long periods of time. He was frustrated too but it was a catch-22 situation. He wanted to be with his wife but he didn't want to be stuck in one place.

We first stayed in a hotel in Nairobi, beautifully surrounded by lush green trees but these blocked the sunlight coming into his room. As Madiba could not freely move around without being overwhelmed by people, we stayed indoors most of the time. After a few days, we decided to move to a golf estate where at least we had some sunlight and he could sit outside. There was, however, little else to do apart from reading the news clippings from home and receiving a few visitors. Across from the room where Madiba stayed was a lake, surrounded by trees and bushes. My imagination runs wild when there is nothing to do and I imagined that the lake looked like Loch Ness. It was quite an eerie and strange lake. I told Madiba that I thought it was Loch Ness and told him about the Scottish myth about the monster in the lake. A few days later I referred to the lake as Loch Ness when Mrs Machel was home for lunch, and she told me to stop as I was scaring Madiba. Me? Scaring Madiba? We laughed.

With the help of my friend I moved home as soon as I got back to South Africa. I then decided that it was time for some normality and since I've always been a dog person, I decided to get two Boston terrier puppies. They were called Winston and Roxy. I had decided much earlier that I would never have dogs with mediocre names. They had to represent famous political figures. Winston looked every bit like Winston Churchill and only needed the cigar to be picture perfect. Roxy was a powder-puff girl and had no resemblance to any political characters. In hindsight I could have called her Christina after Christina Onassis or Madeleine after Madeleine Albright rather than Roxy, but Roxy suited her too. Soon they were my children and since Madiba was no longer eager to travel it was easier for me to give my pets the attention they needed.

Madiba spent even more time in Maputo but gave up on his writing. At home he still wanted to meet with interesting people and after the South African Idols competition he would read about it in the newspaper and announce that he wanted to meet the youngsters, and we would arrange it. Then a policeman got shot eleven times while on duty and miraculously survived. Madiba read about it in the paper and he wanted to see him. Some days he would say that he wanted to meet people and when they arrived he simply wasn't up to interacting with strangers. It became more difficult to predict what he wanted and it was clear that more patience and understanding was what was required from us. It is a natural process, part of ageing. You change your mind more frequently as the years progress and we get older.

From this time, everything started to calm down. Madiba was in Maputo with his wife most of the time and would only come to South Africa when he had important engagements to attend. Mrs Machel had to continue with her work. Being the dynamic person that she is, she had to keep her work going and we spent most of the time at home and subsequently became bored. In my personal opinion, one of the characteristics that Madiba found attractive in Mrs Machel was the fact that she was dynamic and passionate; that she had the determination and commitment to bring about change not only in Mozambique but also across Africa and in effect to change the world. She was ambitious and while he wanted to spend time with her, he never expected her to give up what and who she was. She had a passion for children and improving the lives of her own people in Mozambique. She received the Nansen Medal from the UN in 1995 in recognition of her work with refugee children and she was determined to continue pursuing that agenda, to be a voice for the voiceless, something Madiba appreciated and admired and often boasted about when she was not around.

In January 2006 we set off to Mauritius again at the invitation of Sol Kerzner. This time we made sure that Madiba's schedule was clear and he could stay for ten days as opposed to one week. It was as enjoyable as the first time. As usual, Jerry Inzerillo from Kerzner International made sure that all our needs were taken care of as requested by Sol Kerzner. The same manager, Mauro Governato, was in charge of the property and he left no stone unturned to make sure Madiba had the time of his life. We enjoyed complete privacy and he returned to South Africa rejuvenated and ready for another year.

I met a young Mauritian trainer in the gym, Prakash Ramsurrun, who claimed that he was a trained biokineticist and when he asked about Madiba visiting the gym I told him that Madiba could no longer walk freely without assistance or his walking stick. Prakash challenged me and said that if he could do some stretching exercises with Madiba he guaranteed me that with some resistance training he would be able to walk again. I was usually very irritated when people made suggestions like these. Madiba had medical doctors around him at all times. In my own frustration I thought people underestimated our care for him. Didn't they think that we had looked into things already by the time they approached us? The doctors didn't want to listen to these suggestions, so I had to. And I had to invent the excuses why it wouldn't work or wouldn't happen.

I discussed Prakash's suggestion back at the villa with Madiba and Mum and they agreed that he could come round to show some stretching exercises. The next morning Prakash started with his training. Of course, he had to do the stretching on me first for Madiba to approve of what would happen to him next; I was the guinea pig. Before we knew it Madiba took to the programme and he was co-operating with Prakash. Upon our departure Madiba was walking, unassisted, without his walking stick. He looked radiant and I wrote a note to thank Sol for the hospitality afterwards, stating that his generosity 'added years to Madiba's life' because I really believed it did. We brought Prakash to South Africa to train our masseuse but it needed determination and tenacity to keep Madiba going – not something Madiba was always open to. So a few months later, he was back on the walking stick.

Returning home Madiba spent more time in his lounge, and one day announced that it was time to get rid of some colonial art that was hanging there. Mrs Machel asked me to source African art and I had bought some similar art the previous year for my new house of individual Xhosa women. I went back to the shop and asked for the owner to come and show some African art to Madiba. At first he was happy with a painting depicting three Xhosa women. It was colourful and bright, and then two weeks later he decided that he was not happy with it and said: 'No, you see, this cannot be correct. This painting only shows women, there has to be a man too.' A man had to be added. The painting was returned to the artist, who added a Xhosa man to the image. I realized that Madiba's mind was programmed to be completely representative and balanced in any and every way. It was no longer a conscious decision but part of the fibre of the person and a response that came naturally. There had to be space for everyone and everything had to be perfectly balanced.

When you witness this every day, you become a little like that yourself. Your entire being changes being around someone like Madiba. Indeed as they say, be kind to every person you meet because we don't know their battles. I've learned to appreciate strangers more, to thank a person properly and to try and be respectful, always keeping in mind that the way you approach a person will determine how that person treats you – one of the great lessons from Madiba. Through watching him over the years I've come to realize the truth in the saying 'people will forget what you said, but they will never forget how you made them feel.' And even just greeting someone in a friendly and respectful manner has shown me the truth around this.

President Clinton visited South Africa regularly. In 2007 he agreed to participate in a fundraiser which would benefit the Foundation. This was one of those occasions on which I called on some of the friends of ours to support a fundraiser like this. And they did. President Clinton donated some memorabilia to be auctioned and so did the Foundation. We raised a whopping R18 million (US$1.7 million) in one night only, with less than a hundred people in attendance. Unprecedented in South Africa. The money was added to the endowment fund for the Foundation to ensure its sustainability.

Sadly, to date the Nelson Mandela Foundation is the only one of the three Mandela charities that has not been able to reach its endowment. We often had to share proceeds with the other charities whose area of focus, children and scholarships, are things that easily attract goodwill. I was never paid an extra salary for fundraising. It was never part of my job description to arrange events or fundraisers, but it was what I expected of myself. I so believed in the necessity for us to preserve Madiba's legacy, for people and generations to come to be able to learn from the man, even after he was gone, that I wanted to leave no stone unturned to make sure everything was a success. Yet it is sad that I then got asked by some of his family: 'Why does a secretary get to do this and that . . . ?' I am unable to answer them and guess the best answer is, because no one else did it. I remain eternally grateful to people who answered my calls, who supported when I asked them, and for the friendships and relationships built over the years.

During a visit of President Clinton to the Foundation the day before the fundraiser he made a very moving speech in which he said about Madiba:

> I regret very much, more than I can say, but I was never in a position like Robert Kennedy to speak out against or do anything to help my friend [Madiba] when he was suffering all those long years. But he did live, and I believe God ordained it for a reason, and now in the grace and beauty of his later years, he doesn't even have to say any-thing for us to know that you look better, you feel better and you live better if you think our common humanity is more important than our interesting differences.

It was moving and touching in every possible way and to me one of the best speeches President Clinton had ever made in our presence.

We also started to befriend Gordon Brown and his staff. We knew him as a British politician but he was very passionate about Africa as Chancellor in the UK and worked hard at pushing governments as best he could to meet the Millennium Development Goals. He was preparing to take over from Prime Minister Tony Blair, who was suffering politically as a result of the UK's involvement in Iraq. Gor-don was a very humble person and Madiba was fond of him. The ANC was an ally of the British Labour Party but not as long as it supported violence or war. Gordon had ideals to withdraw from Iraq, but in the same way President Obama inherited a very complicated situation from President Bush, Gordon inherited equal challenges from Tony Blair. Tony was charming and I was close to his office staff too, but it was as if the private and public persona didn't marry: in private talks I liked him and his ideas but politically when in public he pronounced decisions that contradicted that person. Gordon epito-mized a generous giant to me. He also visited Mozambique where he launched an education project with Madiba and Mrs Machel.

A few years later, Shaun Johnson, the Chief Executive of the Mandela Rhodes Foundation, wanted Madiba to meet with David Cameron on one of our visits to London. He was the leader of the opposition Tory Party in Britain at the time. Shaun also said that David could be the next Prime Minister. This time I knew not to say out loud even though I thought: Ye right, as if in my lifetime a Conservative will become the Prime Minister in Britain again – similar to my reaction when I was told that Barack Obama could become the first black President in the United States. But both did, and so I'm glad we agreed to meet with David Cameron at the time too.

Still, Madiba sent conflicting messages to us all about his 'retired' status. One example was the launch of the Elders, a global group of leaders and opinion makers who jointly speak out on matters relating to peace and human rights. The idea had come about in the early 2000s during a lunch at entrepreneur Richard Branson's home in London. The musician Peter Gabriel and Richard Branson suggested the idea, an organization of elderly statespeople to give guidance in terms of the world's ongoing struggle to find justice and peace. Although a brilliant initiative Madiba was already too old and tired to participate in something like this actively but he was adamant that he wanted to support it. It was agreed from the start that he would launch it and then resign immediately as a result of his retirement. In principle he gave his consent that the initiative be launched with his support, taking in mind that the formation of the entity would provide much-needed advice on issues globally from an independent group of influential and respected people.

The more things changed, the more they stayed the same. At times Madiba would be at home for a few days and then announce that he wanted to go to a shop to buy a pen. I would then offer to go and buy the pen as I knew exactly which pens he preferred writing with – normal Bic plastic ballpoint pens. When I offered to go and buy the pen, he would resist and say that I would buy the wrong pen, and I would know that he simply wanted to be among people and it was the perfect excuse to have to go to a shopping mall. It was the security men's and my worst nightmare. We had great difficulty trying to get him in and out of shopping malls and one couldn't trick him by taking him to a stationery shop with an entrance from the street. It had to be a shopping mall. He would return with his simple pens.

On one occasion he went to Sandton City, a big shopping mall on the outskirts of Johannesburg. He was determined to buy a pen and the security detail took him to the Montblanc store, somehow not knowing that a Bic pen would have been totally adequate. I wasn't with him at the time. He selected the pen and when he was about to pay he realized that he didn't have any money on him and that none of the security had the amount, even if they added up all the cash they had together, to pay for the pen. Of course not. The police in South Africa are some of the lowest paid people in our country, yet they are expected to 'protect and serve'.

Nevertheless, Madiba never really carried money with him and only occasionally he would ask for cash from whomever, but then he would forget when he had given it out to grandchildren and as a result his wallet was always empty. The only permanent fixture in his wallet was a business card of Mrs Machel inside. It was sweet. I then got a frantic call from the security saying that Madiba said I should please pay for the pen. I asked to speak to the shop owner to make arrangements but the gentleman then said he would call me back later and send me an invoice.

Montblanc belongs to the Rupert family. They have been friends with Madiba for many years, first the father, Dr Anton Rupert, and later the son, Johann Rupert, who now runs the dynasty of some of the most successful luxury brands in the world, such as Cartier, Montblanc, Van Cleef & Arpels, etc. There was no way Madiba would have remembered or known that Montblanc belongs to the Ruperts and it was an honest intention by the security to find him a good pen when they took him there, thinking that he would have the money on him to pay for it. Of course Johann was not going to allow Madiba to pay for the pen and the word came back that the pen was a present. Madiba didn't want to accept it but eventually he had no choice and Johann won the battle. Until he got ill Madiba wore the pen in his pocket, referring to it as a Presidential Pen. It was a fountain pen that regularly had to be refilled with ink and it usually didn't have ink in so we tried to avoid using the pen purely because it would start a process of finding ink and refilling it, and then it would not write immediately and so whatever had to be signed was usually a mess.

Madiba had very few personal things that he was religiously holy about. His two pens, his wristwatch, his empty wallet, his ivory walking stick and the holder for his reading glasses, as well as his hearing aids. The most important, of course, was his wedding ring which he wore without fail whether he was indoors or outdoors, working or resting. These items had to be neatly placed beside his bed every night and they were the first items he looked for when he woke up. Whenever we flew overseas in commercial planes, he would give his wallet to me to keep until we arrived. He thought it was safer with me than with him. Yet I was usually just a few seats away from him, not any safer or unsafer than he was. And then it was always empty. On one occasion the household packed something in his suitcase as opposed to his hand luggage and he insisted on having it with him during the flight. It took some convincing for the captain of the aircraft to allow me and security to go down into the hold to look for our luggage to search for the item, as he would not rest without it. He was meticulous about certain things and these were some of them.

The other thing that was considered holy was his newspapers. One was not allowed to read his papers before he got to read them. He didn't like newspapers that had been opened. You had to remove the advertisement brochures inside without opening the papers. He would point-blank refuse to take a newspaper that had been opened before. And no matter what one did, you could never offer to refold them when he had finished reading them. He insisted on doing it himself, whether the Queen or the Lord was waiting for him. He took his time in folding newspapers and knee blankets with the greatest precision. I came to the conclusion that these were the proof of a person living in isolation for twenty-seven years and there was no reason or need for us to try and change that. Clearly he had time to be as meticulous but then it becomes so entrenched that it becomes part of one's daily life. I often removed his shoes for him and then helped him to put his feet on a footrest. And woe betide me if the shoes were not put neatly next to him where he could see them. Don't think you could hide them under a chair or put them down loosely. You would soon be called back and asked to correct them. It was part of the disciplined person he was. 'Zeldina, just come and correct this,' he would say, calling me back to put down the shoes where he could see them, precisely next to each other facing the same direction.

On many occasions Madiba would announce that he wanted to go to a bookshop. He had more books than many libraries owned and I would then try my luck by asking what he was looking for, as I could go and buy it for him to avoid us being overwhelmed in public. He would then either say he wanted to go and look for a specific book, and I knew not to ask for the title, or he would be completely honest and say he just wanted to go and look at books. But he meant he wanted to see people too. Soon the bookstore would be in complete disarray. People didn't know why they originally wanted to come to the bookstore themselves, while I was trying to get him to focus on titles and sections in the store so we could leave as soon as possible. People overwhelmed him completely and we often feared that people would eventually kill him out of kindness.

He would sometimes page through a book and if the print was too small, even though the book was interesting, he would leave it behind. On more than one occasion did we ask Naspers, one of the biggest publishing holding companies in South Africa, to reprint a book for him in a bigger font. They were only too happy to oblige. And of course Madiba always left with a few books he got for free, but he usually insisted on paying and being treated like a normal paying customer or he would threaten the managers to never return if he was not allowed to pay. Other people would just accept anything for free, wherever they could get it from. Not Nelson Mandela. He insisted on paying and only occasionally accepted freebies. Sometimes he would buy one book and sometimes we would leave with boxes of books. Many of them I'm sure never got read to a second page.

He loved South African authors and biographies. One of his favourite books was a poetry book by an Afrikaans poet, C. Louis Leipoldt (1880–1947). He subsequently visited Leipoldt's grave in the Western Cape in 1999 as he always loved his writings. And on some occasions he bought a book by Antjie Krog, the famous South African writer who wrote *Country of My Skull*, and I tried to reassure him he already had two copies at home, which I knew he did, but he insisted and it was pointless arguing. He even got angry at me once when I said we already had the book, so we bought the fourth or fifth copy at the time.

He would also announce sometimes that he needed a dictionary. After we bought a few dictionaries on different occasions I realized that one of the most stupid things I could do was to tell him that we had already bought a dictionary, just a few weeks ago. The dictionary was only an excuse to go to a bookstore and I think I may have bought twenty big print Oxford dictionaries with him. Even in foreign countries he would sometimes announce that he needed a dictionary, and we would set off to find the closest bookstore to our hotel, buy the dictionary and bring it home without a page being turned in it ever. He just couldn't say 'I want to be among people' or 'I want to see the city'. I think he thought it would appear vain if he did that so he'd rather settle for using a bookstore or needing a pen as a good excuse. It is one of the disadvantages of being such a famous person. He could never do things we just take for granted but only once that freedom is removed from you do you know what it is to appreciate it.

Strangely the Afrikaans section in bookstores always attracted him. He refers to his love for the writings of the Afrikaans writer Langenhoven in *Conversations With Myself*:

> Well, firstly he wrote very simply. And secondly, he was a very humorous writer, and of course part of his writing was to free the Afrikaner from the desire to imitate the English. His idea was to instil national pride amongst the Afrikaners and so I liked him very much.

I clung on to these words, trying to instil pride among the young Afrikaners for who and what they are. It was important to him that one remains an individual and embrace your history and ancestry and I often recited these words when I found myself in conversations with young Afrikaners.

We also went to a bookshop in Pretoria once, in the area close to the University of Pretoria right in the middle of the student area. We were on our way from his grandson's graduation ceremony when the convoy came to a complete standstill. I jumped out of my car (as I usually drove along in my own car) to ask the security why they were stopping. The answer was simple. We are going into the bookstore. We paged through a few books and then he stopped at the shelf where material on foreign languages was displayed. You could buy tapes and books to help you to learn a different language at the time. And so we bought the set to learn Portuguese. As Madiba spent a lot of time in Mozambique he wanted to learn the language and he wanted to understand what Portuguese was spoken whenever he was in Maputo. He made me promise not to tell Mrs Machel that he was going to try and learn Portuguese as he wanted to surprise her by learning her language, a very romantic gesture. I don't think the packet ever got opened and I don't know what happened to the DIY kit but we only managed 'morning', 'thank you' and 'please' in Portuguese.

On 14 November 2006 Madiba was heading to the Saxon Hotel where he was meeting Morgan Freeman for lunch. We drove in the convoy as usual and I drove my car at the back following the convoy, as I usually did. We were late. I always had a battle to get people away from Madiba in order for him not to be late for anything as I knew how much importance he paid to punctuality. This was one of those events and we were nervously trying to get out of the traffic to still have him arrive in time for lunch. It was blue lights and sirens everywhere trying to get through the stationary traffic.

At a traffic intersection where we had to turn right (keeping in mind that we drive on the left side of the road in South Africa) we were entering a crossing at the traffic light and the police closed the intersection as usual by blocking off traffic with one of their vehicles to allow the main car and back up to smoothly enter and exit the crossing, even though the traffic light may be red for oncoming traffic. So they did exactly that and we started entering the crossing. A gentleman in a sports car came speeding down the road with earphones in his ears and obviously did not hear the sirens or notice what was happening in front of him. He drove full speed right into the security car that was blocking the intersection. Everything seemed to happen in slow motion. I could see the X5 BMW lifting into the air from the impact. The convoy stopped for a few seconds and it was really the first time I saw the Presidential Protection Unit in full operation. They were exceptionally good.

The security guards in the car that was hit by the sports car got out, grabbed their firearms and bundled into other cars, including mine, for us to get Madiba away from the scene as quickly as possible. We left the damaged car and two of the bodyguards behind and proceeded straight to the hotel. Madiba was looking in another direction at the time of the accident and he didn't hear the impact as his car is heavily armoured and therefore soundproof to some extent. The security dropped Madiba at the hotel and then rushed back to help their colleagues. I called a friend whose office was right across from the scene of the accident. She sent some of her staff outside to help our guys. Madiba had lunch with Morgan as if nothing happened. Lori, Morgan's business partner, who was with him, said we all looked visibly shocked when we arrived except for Madiba. This was reasonably typical of life with Madiba. Very little affected him because wherever he was layers and layers of protection absorbed the pressure of everyday life around him.

It was the year that the movie *Last King of Scotland* appeared on the movie circuit and, running out of ideas how to keep him occupied without him having to work, I asked Madiba whether he wanted to go and see the movie as it related to history he knew so well. Nu Metro booked out the entire cinema for Madiba and arranged a private screening at a time convenient to him, helping us of course to get into a back entrance to the cinema. When someone offered him popcorn he said: 'No I've had enough of that in my life, it is now the turn of the young people like them [pointing at me and security] to have that.' I doubt Madiba was ever introduced to popcorn, but since he had never 'snacked' in his life he was not eager to do so now. He thoroughly enjoyed the movie and when I told him that Forest Whitaker, who played Idi Amin in the movie, was visiting South Africa, he was eager to meet him. On two other occasions he also went to the movies, once to see *Fahrenheit 9/11* – the Michael Moore movie – and once to see *The Queen*. During the screening of the latter he turned to me a few times and whispered when he saw Helen Mirren on the screen: 'By the way, that is the Queen, right?' It was precious to see someone like Madiba enjoying a movie, something he was not used to but something we take for granted.

I remember when South African film director Gavin Hood won an Oscar for the film *Tsotsi* featuring South African actors Terry Pheto and Presley Chweneyagae. The three came to visit Madiba at his residence in Cape Town after returning from Los Angeles and we were extremely proud of them. This was only the second time South Africans had won an Oscar (following Charlize Theron) and it dominated the news for days. Madiba was so excited about holding an Oscar that he jokingly asked them whether they would not consider giving it to him. There was complete confusion on Gavin Hood's face. Of course you would even give your Oscar to Nelson Mandela. Or not.

Early in 2007 Prince Albert of Monaco offered to host a fundraiser for the Foundation together with his own Foundation later in the year in Monaco, providing that Madiba attended. Madiba was tired of travelling and only wanted to stay home and spend time with Mrs Machel. However when royalty invited him, he was more eager to agree. Occasionally he would suggest we travel somewhere but then he would forget and we knew that he wasn't too keen or else he would remember. I was tasked by Achmat Dangor, our CEO at the time, to work with a colleague and the Royal office in Monaco on the event.

I would travel to Monaco every month. We had meetings with the office of Prince Albert but it soon became clear that they had, like any administration, their own power struggles. It was one of the most difficult tasks to negotiate.

I contacted every person I knew with a little money to their name to sell tables to them for the event. I emailed people I'd met over the years to tell them about the auction items that would go on sale and that we hoped they would support us, and they did. At the end most of Madiba's friends from over the years showed up. It took me nine months of intense communication with people worldwide to persuade them to support the initiative and to travel to Monaco at their own expense to come and support an auction. It was a successful fundraiser. It all paid off and I was proud of what we had achieved. The Foundation raised a considerable amount of money, building a much-needed endowment to ensure its sustainability into the future yet still not enough to feel secure.

I fell ill during one of my visits to Monaco and ended up being admitted to hospital for X-rays. I thought I had pneumonia. Apart from the fact that no one could understand a word of English, which made a simple procedure like examining a patient almost impossible, the hospital was not great. As soon as I could stand up straight, I took a plane to London where two of my ex-colleagues, a doctor and bodyguard, lived and I had to rely on them for help. The irony was that here I was, thinking that I was dying and the only people to help me were ex-colleagues. There was no other support structure in my life than those who worked with me, and I realized how isolated I had become from life in general.

Before travelling to Monaco Madiba and Mrs Machel stopped in London to unveil a statue of Madiba at Parliament Square. In between organizing Monaco I also had to regularly meet with Wendy Woods, wife of the late Donald Woods, both anti-apartheid activists, with regards to arrangements around the unveiling. Wendy was heading the organizing committee together with Richard

Attenborough. I adored him and loved meeting with him. It was a historical event and one of the few occasions Madiba could be convinced to unveil a statue of himself. He was never in favour of things being named after him, statues being erected and him being honoured everywhere. He constantly reminded us that there were other struggle heroes too who had to be recognized and honoured. And then if he agreed to a statue like this one, he would not be in favour of unveiling it himself out of fear that he may appear conceited.

We had a close relationship with the Browns and their staff and it was always pleasant to visit them. Even though Gordon Brown would be present at the unveiling of the statue a few days later it was appropriate for us to pay a courtesy call to him before meeting him at the unveiling ceremony. On 28 August 2008, before entering 10 Downing Street I briefed Madiba about the press awaiting our arrival and that we had agreed with the Prime Minister's office that there would be a short photo opportunity with the media when the PM met Madiba and Mrs Machel. Madiba was becoming very forgetful and even admitted so himself, in public. He needed constant reminders of what was expected of him and minute-by-minute warnings of what he had to do next. But then there were always these moments of complete clarity when he would surprise us all with his sharp sense of humour, totally aware of what he was doing and getting up to.

I had told him that he would not be expected to answer any questions from the press upon his arrival in Downing Street but he could simply say that he was happy to be there and to meet with Gordon Brown. When we entered the two exchanged pleasantries and Madiba turned to the media and jokingly said: 'My wife and I are proud and happy to be here because as you know, this was one of our rulers, but we overthrew them. We are on equal basis now.' Everybody started laughing. Everybody except me that is. I was shocked and didn't know how the media would perceive such a statement. Madiba had a very good sense of humour and this was his way of emphasizing that we had moved away from colonialism.

We tried to be careful not to allow situations to occur where he could feel overwhelmed and it increased the stress and tension. I no longer felt worried whenever I had to deliver his speech to the podium. My insecurities now revolved around him. Was he going to be OK? Could he handle the pressure? But every time he walked onto a stage and stood behind a podium, the old Madiba was back and he was as strong as ever. It was hard for us younger people to witness the ageing process, and also not always knowing how to deal with it. You had to adapt and adjust things all the time, thinking, planning, providing for every possible scenario just to make sure that he would be OK and that every possible eventuality could be catered for. Over the years making simple appointments for others with him changed from 'Yes for sure it's confirmed' to 'Let's confirm closer to the time' to 'It's difficult to predict any day right now' to 'It's simply no longer possible'. It had its own metamorphoses and ageing timeline to it.

After the successful fundraiser in Monaco we also went to Paris. President Sarkozy came to the airport to meet us, and Madiba was touched by his kind gesture and repeated for years to follow that it was extremely courteous of a serving head of state to come all the way to the airport to meet a former President. It was the first time we had visited the Ritz Hotel since the death of Princess Diana. Being who I am, I secretly asked the manager to show me the route she'd walked and recite the exact events and steps from that night. I was not trying to investigate the matter but trying to comprehend what that night must have been like.

I was aware that many of those I loved were growing older. Madiba turned eighty-nine in 2007. I made sure we never forgot other people's birthdays, or when someone was ill we would send flowers and sometimes just enquire about their well-being without wanting something from them. It was my simplistic way of investing in relationships and to me it didn't make sense (and it was rude) only to call on people whenever you wanted something from them. I recently read: 'Life takes a little time and a lot of relationship' and that captures it all.

I think people often wondered what I was busy with at the Foundation as it was difficult to measure outcome apart from specific
fundraising initiatives I was tasked with. I was maintaining relationships. I attended luncheons, breakfasts and had more coffee than was
good for any human being to show our appreciation and interest in
people genuinely, whether they gave us money or not. Sometimes I
felt overwhelmed by people, not being a people person generally
speaking. But I showed interest nevertheless and it was always genuine and with the best intention. I made sure they all got Christmas
cards or good wishes for Ramadan or Jewish festivities. As Madiba got
older he could no longer do these personally and then the Foundation
could no longer afford to print thousands of cards. I nevertheless tried
to maintain these small gestures. After all, Madiba taught me the
most important thing any person can give you is his/her time. He
wrote in a letter to his daughter Zindzi, dated 1 March 1981, while he
was imprisoned and published in *Conversations With Myself*:

> Often as I walk up and down the tiny cell, or as I lie on my bed, the mind
> wanders far and wide, recalling this episode and that mistake. Among
> these is the thought whether in my best days outside prison I showed
> sufficient appreciation for the love and kindness of many of those who
> befriended and even helped me when I was poor and struggling.

What I read from it was that it was of vital importance to him to be
courteous and grateful at all times, as we never know whether we
will have the opportunity to thank people or pay respect whenever
they have been good to you.

It was also my father's seventieth birthday that year and my
mother's seventieth the following year. We decided to all go on a
family holiday and my brother, his partner and I decided to share
my parents' costs. They hadn't been to Mauritius since the late 1970s
and we'd hardly had time for a family holiday so we set off to Sugar
Beach resort in Mauritius. While on holiday my brother's partner,
Rick, received a call from his parents who were looking after all our
dogs. I think there were about ten dogs on their smallholding outside Pretoria. I remember him taking the call and getting up from

the table. He returned and I went to fetch food from the buffet. Upon returning things were sombre at the table and I asked after my dogs and they said everything was fine. My brother is a strange person though. He seemed irritable with me and I could sense something was wrong. On the night we got home I rushed off to the smallholding to fetch the dogs. As I parked my car, I realized my dad was already there, having rushed from the airport to arrive at the smallholding before I could. He walked towards me, took my hand and said: 'Zelda, Roxy is dead.' My baby. My poor baby was dead. She was in season when we left and the bitches were all kept in a small area where a fight broke out and the rest of the dogs formed a pack and killed the weakest.

It was one of the saddest days of my life. I regretted every minute I didn't spend with her and I wanted to blame my work for not spending enough time with her. How could I have children if I couldn't even find the time to spend with dogs? This was my child or the closest thing to a child I ever had and I felt that I had failed her.

I had to sit for a long time and decide that these are choices I had made in life. There is no one to blame but myself but I cannot use the word 'blame' when there had been so many privileges and opportunities. I cried and mourned and didn't go to work for three days over the death of Roxy. It was five days before 46664 was hosting a concert in Johannesburg. I couldn't pull myself together and it was the worst thing that had happened to me until then. It took me at least a year to get over her death and to this day she has her proud place in my house.

Roxy had had a litter the year before and I'd sold off her puppies (and two had died while very small). They all got names, proper politicians' names, before they left me, including Indira, named after Indira Gandhi, the third Prime Minister of India who was assassinated in 1984. However, in the April after Roxy died the people who'd bought Indira called me up to say that they would have to put her down as she was not adapting well and they were worried about their child. They wanted to tell me if I found another home for her they would be willing to give her to another owner but otherwise they would put her down. I had her delivered to my house the same day and apart from her father Winston, she is now the love of my life. Having Boston terriers is therapeutic for me. They have seen me through the most difficult times. They are the ones I miss when I travel and they are the ones that I think of when at work during the day. I like to joke and say that at least I don't have to pay school fees for my 'children', so their school fees can be spent on my motorbike riding!

The Biggest Fundraiser of My Life

Madiba was turning ninety and I was thirty-eight. I never had imagined that he would turn ninety or that I would still be with him at the age of thirty-eight. Yet it felt like time passed so quickly. I was starting to realize and comprehend the full value of my privileges and experiences. And, more than ever, I was willing to contribute whatever it took to ensure that his ninetieth was the biggest fundraiser in our organization's history in his honour.

Madiba was no longer keen to leave the country to go on holiday. Like every year in January, the house in Houghton had to be closed for a few weeks to enable the staff to go on leave. The staff would also serve Madiba in Qunu, which meant that going to Qunu was not an option. Mrs Machel asked me to look at a few other options and I contacted a good friend, Jabu Mabuza, who is the Chairman of Tsogo Sun in South Africa to ask for advice. We decided on Noetzie where a few old castles are built on the shore, not easily accessible for the public. The castles are surrounded by the Knysna forest and Madiba loved sitting outside looking at the forest. Long after that holiday he would ask me sometimes: 'By the way, Zeldina, you took us to the Knysna forest, right?' 'Yes Khulu,' I would say, although he didn't mean that I really took them but rather that I made the arrangements.

Early in the year we received a call from a former Minister of Foreign Affairs during the apartheid years, Mr Pik Botha, indicating that Professor Stephen Hawking was scheduled to visit South Africa and that he wanted to meet Madiba. Mr Botha had contact with Prof. Hawking through a university in South Africa he was involved with. In the year 2000 Mr Botha had left the old National Party and joined the ANC, much to the public's amusement. Madiba of course welcomed such a move in favour of the ANC, whatever the motives may have been. At first we said no to the meeting and then we were talked into reversing that decision, as was the case on so many occasions.

We agreed with Mr Botha about a protocol for the meeting. Madiba was no longer able to deal with any surprises in meetings. He was becoming old fast and he needed clear direction and guidance. Mr Botha was accompanied by Professor Block, a gentleman from the University of Johannesburg who was famous for physics and his distribution of pieces of 'moon rock', a piece of which he'd given to Madiba years before.

It was amazing to experience Prof. Hawking but it took some concentration to get a ninety-year-old who knew very little about technology to communicate with the Professor, as he was talking through a computer. Mr Botha, not knowing the circumstances of Madiba's difficulty in communicating, kept interfering, and at some point I felt my face going red as I told him: 'Mr Botha, please stop. We cannot all try to tell Madiba how to do this. Let him figure this out himself as I have explained to him.' It was often the problem with people. They either thought Madiba was completely unintelligent or different people in the room thought they had to tell him how to do something, because of his age, which didn't help the situation at all. Madiba's hearing aids would soon cut out all the voices in the room trying to tell him what to do and he would appear confused.

When you tried to tell people not to interfere they took it personally or thought you were being territorial, yet they themselves had no experience dealing with a ninety-year-old trying to conduct a professional life. The meeting with Prof. Hawking was therefore not a great conversation, and to crown it all, despite agreeing that they would not throw any surprises at Madiba during the meeting, books and messages appeared that Prof. Block and Mr Botha wanted Madiba to sign, personalize and inscribe. I was furious. It was clear that they had no respect for the protocol they had signed and agreed to prior to the meeting.

Surprises threw Madiba, and he would then look at one with helplessness in his eyes and one would be left to explain or argue with visitors. By now Madiba knew me well enough and I didn't pretend to be anyone I am not. We instituted some protocols. We also had had enough of people approaching us with a particular request and then, once they sat in front of him, presenting a totally different agenda. People knew he found it hard to say 'no' to them. Soon, when the protocols became known to people, some tried to argue that it was like the behaviour of the Gestapo. What do you do? We insisted as we were left with no options. People kept on pushing their luck.

It was also in June 2008 that we learned of the sudden illness of John Reinders, the Chief of Protocol during Madiba's Presidency. Madiba liked John a lot and was grateful for his service. John was already in a coma in a hospital in Bloemfontein by the time we visited him. An outcry followed in our inner circle about Madiba travelling to Bloemfontein to see a white man in hospital. It is not something anyone would ever dare to confront Madiba with personally but I wasn't spared the backlash. I never managed to send people to him to lay such complaints but simply absorbed them and walked away. By now I had the skin of a baby rhino and even though it hurt to think that Madiba was to be deprived of visiting people he liked, it was now becoming like water off a duck's back to me.

I made a point of responding to newspaper articles that dealt with race issues to remind people of what Madiba so often repeated, that if we continued to judge people by the colour of their skin, chances are that we have a long way to go building the rainbow nation we all dreamt of. And he was right. I was getting sick of being labelled according to the colour of my skin too. I'm a South African and that is all that mattered.

46664, headed by Tim Massey, was organizing a massive ninetieth-birthday concert in London's Hyde Park in July. Again we relied on friends and relationships and started preparing them to budget for a ninetieth celebration fundraiser. Tim and I proposed a fundraising dinner to be held together with the concert.

Although it was often tiresome and tedious to arrange an event for Madiba in a foreign country I made sure that a South African element was always present, even when it came to the detail of the food served. The guest list was another problem. Everyone and his mother wanted to be there but we only had limited space.

Tables were sold in tiers and we filled up a massive marquee that was erected in Hyde Park. People always wanted to be invited to these dinners but they didn't always want to pay. You just get to live with it. Some people will never see the common sense that the more free seats you give away, the less your chances of fundraising, and having a hundred free guests as opposed to twenty free guests increases your overheads and the fundraising becomes less successful. Some people, having done little to nothing to fundraise or support any of Madiba's work, always wanted to be on the free-seat list. And at some point you just have to put your foot down because your professional reputation is on the line and the success or failure of the fundraiser will come back to haunt you.

Together with a friend who I knew from her time in the White House, Sara Latham, and the Nelson Mandela Children's Fund in the UK we put together a guest list to ensure that it would be a profitable event. The event was sold out and we included some of Madiba's friends, family and fellow struggle veterans to ensure representation. In the days leading to his arrival London was buzzing and I couldn't believe that Madiba's birthday was around the corner and in London there was so much excitement, even among ordinary people.

It was while preparing the logistics for the trip that we got caught in the middle of another power battle. President Mbeki was still

President in South Africa and politically it was an uncertain time for many. In 2005 President Mbeki and the ANC 'released' Deputy President Jacob Zuma from all his duties, following a ruling by the Durban High Court which found a corrupt relationship between Schabir Shaik and Jacob Zuma. In 2006 a family friend of Zuma's laid a rape charge against him, while Zuma argued that they had consensual sex. Zuma was cleared of the charge at the end of the trial and it was widely speculated that the Mbeki administration was waging a political war to prevent Zuma from ousting Mbeki at the four-yearly ANC national conference in 2007. Indeed, in December 2007 President Mbeki was unseated by Jacob Zuma, who was elected ANC President.

The leadership struggle manifested itself on all levels of society. You were either a Mbeki or a Zuma person. As much as the nation was united following Madiba's Presidency there were clear divisions deeply rooted in every level of society. Once Zuma was the President of the ANC the ANC also 'recalled' President Mbeki as President of South Africa in a very humiliating way, arguing that he no longer served the interests of the party and its people. The Deputy President at the time, Kgalema Motlanthe, was appointed President until the next national elections, when Jacob Zuma was elected the country's President.

The Nelson Mandela Foundation was non-political. And Madiba himself had detached himself from politics. With his retirement he stopped going to ANC meetings and announced that although he was never going to part with the ANC and that he would always remain a loyal member, the running of the party was up to the younger generation. However, people willingly perceived us to be anti-Mbeki and therefore Zuma loyalists. It was in the middle of this power struggle, preparing for Madiba's visit to London, that we informed the South African High Commission in London about our intention to visit.

Three days before our arrival for Madiba's ninetieth-birthday celebrations in London I received a call from the South African High

Commission logistics office, indicating that they would not extend the usual courtesy of allowing Madiba to move through the VIP room at Heathrow domestic arrivals and they would not pay the few hundred pounds it cost. I exploded: 'What? Are you serious? For the past nine years you allowed him, organized, paid for the use of the VIP room because he is a former head of state of South Africa and now you expect him to what? Walk through the terminal building like a normal passenger?' I even wrote an email sarcastically pointing out that had it not been for Nelson Mandela many of us wouldn't have jobs. I was bordering on being ridiculous but I was beyond anger.

I declared my 'fight' to our CEO and Chairman as I was willing to do whatever it took to stand by my principles. I have never burdened Madiba with my problems or challenges, and in this particular case I also thought that it would hurt and upset him to learn about this matter. It cost a few hundred pounds to pay for the VIP lounge. I was in principle not going to allow the Foundation to pay for it. This sudden change of decision that a former head of state of South Africa was no longer allowed the courtesy of the support of the foreign mission to move through a VIP room had to be changed at Cabinet level as far as I was concerned. It was not a decision to be taken by an office bearer. They simply didn't give in and told me because it was not an official visit tasked by the South African government they couldn't pay. Yet they had paid on many other occasions when there was nothing official to the visit.

People assumed that Madiba was aligned with Jacob Zuma in the ANC's power struggle and therefore did things that would be seen to carry the approval of President Mbeki. Mr Mbeki would never have been so petty himself to decide to withdraw a privilege like this to a former President, and it was evident that this incident was a manifestation of that divide among South Africans, of either being a Mbeki person or a Zuma person. (I eventually called Prime Minister Gordon Brown's office and asked them to arrange for the use of the lounge from their side, which they did.)

★

The event was a massive success. We raised over R105 million (around £7.5 million at the current exchange rate) clean profit and to date it was the most successful fundraiser of any of the Mandela charities. The money was split between the Nelson Mandela Children's Fund, the Mandela Rhodes Foundation and the Nelson Mandela Foundation to further their respective mandates. My favourite auction item was a cast replica of Madiba's hand bought by Sol Kerzner for £2.9 million, making Sol the biggest donor of any of the Mandela charities at that point.

Madiba was almost intrigued by other people's wealth and fame. Yet that was never the consideration with which he dealt with people. He just found it fascinating that someone could be as rich as a Bill Gates or Sol Kerzner. He would often boast about the wealth of his friends in South Africa – Patrice Motsepe, Tokyo Sexwale, Douw Steyn, the Ruperts and the Oppenheimers to name but a few. They were all good to him and whenever he called on them to support his charities, build a school or clinic or support a cause he was arguing for they willingly did so. Yet it was critical to him that even when he didn't call upon them, they were always treated with the utmost respect and courtesy. He wrote in a letter to Zenani Mandela, quoted in the book *Conversations With Myself*, 'But the habit of attending to small things and of appreciating small courtesies is one of the important marks of a good person.' And so we never forgot a birthday or an anniversary and we made sure he spent time with people even when there was nothing to be asked of them, as these were part of the 'small things'. To honour Madiba, you have to honour his relationships with people.

Madiba insisted on staying longer than expected at the fundraising event and when he eventually went to bed I escorted him back to the hotel to enable Mrs Machel to remain at the event a little longer, so it didn't appear that they both deserted the main table at once. Afterwards I returned to the event, which certainly was one of the highlights of my career. I didn't want accolades or awards but I so desperately wanted Madiba to feel honoured and celebrated in a proper way while he could still enjoy it, and that night I felt we had achieved that. Driving back to the event from the hotel my heart was filled with pride and joy that he was able to witness just how much people revered him. Famous people and celebrity friends of Madiba all helped us to attract big donors and they were the people who travelled at their own cost, gave their time at no expense to honour Madiba and help us draw attention to his causes. Yes, they also benefited from the association, but one hand washes the other.

The concert the next evening was an equal success although the travelling was taking its toll on Madiba. He was tired. The usual scramble ensued for people to go up to Madiba and greet him. I watched from a distance as I could see there was going to be a fight about who got to greet him and who not. I felt incredibly sorry for him as I felt he really wanted to just enjoy the music and performances by South African, African and international artists, all performing for his birthday. I remember us watching a performance of a South African band named Mafikizolo in Tromsø, Norway, and how he enjoyed seeing them playing for him on an international stage. After all, this time it was his birthday.

Before Madiba went on stage I was approached by a tiny woman whom I didn't immediately recognize as Emma Bunton, the former Spice Girl singer. Emma was one of the celebrities making announcements or statements during the concert. Emma told one of the stage directors that she insisted on giving Madiba her present personally, either before or when he walked on stage. It was a huge box. I couldn't imagine that she would herself accept a huge box with a present inside from someone and carry it around all night. In addition I was also still p-ed off with the Spice Girls after I had learned that they had boasted about stealing toilet paper from Madiba's official residence while they visited him when he was President. So I had a preconceived opinion about her already. I didn't allow her to hand him the gift as he needed his hands to be free at all times.

As she walked on stage I could clearly see that she was upset and I told our security to keep a close eye on her as she was forcing her way to Madiba while many other, African artists were being pushed to the back. She may be a perfectly innocent lady, but in those circumstances you straighten your spine and tell off even celebrities if necessary. Part of my duty was to be proactive and to try and ensure that situations got resolved before they actually happened. I knew that Madiba would want the African artists present to take a prominent role around him while on stage and I wanted to make sure that he didn't get upset if the contrary happened. As Madiba walked onto the stage the crowd erupted. Some people cried and the noise was deafening. I was overwhelmed with excitement and joy for him.

Pressure was mounting on Madiba from the media and the public to speak out on the gross neglect of human rights in Zimbabwe under President Mugabe. We had been withstanding pressure from around the world for Madiba to make some kind of pronouncement because of the previous incidents where he was criticized for working independently from government because they felt his actions could interfere with diplomatic process. However, at the end his simple line was: 'Nearer to home we have seen the outbreak of violence against fellow Africans in our own country and the tragic failure of leadership in our neighbouring Zimbabwe.' And saying less meant more and not saying certain things meant saying others. The press around the world grabbed this and it headlined the news for a couple of days.

The following day Madiba also met with some old colleagues of his, all people who were in the Rivonia Trial with him back in the 1960s. It was more than forty years since the trial that sent Madiba to life imprisonment and he had not seen some of them since that time. He could vividly remember all of them and enjoyed spending time with them. Here they were having tea in the Dorchester Hotel in London while they last saw each other as prisoners in cells awaiting trial over forty years ago. Back at home the Foundation also arranged a private celebration for him with his former political colleagues from the Rivonia Trial and fellow ex-prisoners who were still alive and lived in South Africa. It was moving to watch these people interacting and I wished that I could have talked with some of them for hours, asking so many questions. The conversations were dominated by 'Have you seen so-and-so again?' 'Whatever happened to so-and-so?'

His ninetieth-birthday celebrations in London were the perfect ending to his international appearances. Twenty years earlier his seventieth birthday was celebrated at Wembley Stadium in England, viewed by more than 600 million people worldwide. The concert was named 'Free Mandela' and two years later he was a free man. Even though these celebrations were smaller it was a befitting way to end our travels, him being present where they celebrated his life. After that, we never went abroad again. He was becoming too old to travel.

Madiba sometimes called me from home to say that he was about to take the elevator down to the ground floor in his house. He was scared of being stuck in the elevator and I needed to call him in ten minutes to make sure that he was not stuck. At the time I thought it was funny but I now become sad when I think of it. Being there and answering those calls made me love the man even more, perhaps the fact that he depended upon me, yet it is exactly that admiration and love that caused so much animosity.

These calls also reminded me how much he had aged. Just a few years before, if he was stuck in an elevator he would be the person making everyone feel safe. Years earlier it had happened in Kampala with the Deputy President of Uganda. Of course, in addition to the people that needed to accompany him, everyone would try and fit into an elevator with Madiba. It made me very claustrophobic so I took the stairs. And as the devil may have it, he was stuck that day. For twenty minutes we stood outside on the ground floor waiting for technicians to come to their rescue. Emerging from the elevator eventually the Deputy President was in a panic and somewhat embarrassed, but Madiba had kept everyone entertained with his humour.

Mrs Machel taught me that I was to be true to myself and to always remember that the only thing that matters is my relationship with Madiba, that I cannot be held accountable for other people's relationships with him, and when I do something I must listen to my inner voice because it will always tell me what is right and wrong. If I was concerned about something or something troubled me, there was probably a reason for my feelings and I should go with what made me feel safest. Mrs Machel and I have not had an easy relationship over the years. I have been very sensitive to the fact that a young woman spent all this time with her husband, a white woman told them when to get up and when to relax, and it couldn't have been easy to have people around you all the time. But despite that she is the one person who shows appreciation and respect and affords me dignity. I salute her ten thousand times for keeping her cool and teaching me the things she did.

Around his ninetieth birthday we also made sure Madiba enjoyed meals with many of his old colleagues and comrades, staff and friends in smaller groups. He also received a set of stamps from the national post office printed as a limited series commemorating his birthday. The stamps featured two of my favourite pictures of Madiba.

He had lunch with his former ANC ladies, Barbara Masekela, Jessie Duarte and Frene Ginwala, then with the artists from his generation – Dorothy Masuka, Miriam Makeba, Abigail Kubeka and Thandi Klaasen – and he attended an ANC rally in his honour on 2 August, during which attendees all enjoyed celebrating with him. The government also wanted to host a concert for the people but due to only last minute advertising the concert wasn't well attended. The June 16 Foundation was also allowed to hand over a statue to Madiba (16 June being Youth Day in South Africa, commemorating the start of the Soweto uprising in 1976). It was a beautiful statue of Hector Pieterson and I felt touched when Madiba received it. One of the board members made some remarks towards me about how grateful they were that I had taken care of Madiba, and I deeply appreciated this coming from an organization like theirs, established to remind the public about events that led to that fateful day in 1976. We had come a long way in this country. I was an Afrikaner and here they were thanking me.

It was around the same time when Madiba had the dream one night that I had resigned to take another job, and very seriously told me the next morning in the office that he dreamt that I'd deserted him. Me? Zelda la Grange? I reassured him that I would never, ever do that. I overcame my insecurities and was determined to serve him until the day one of us passed away.

PART FOUR

What Next?

2009–2013

Staying Until the End

It was January again and the house in Houghton needed to be closed to enable the staff to go on holiday. We had no idea of where to take Madiba. It was difficult to take him to a hotel and we either had to find a big-enough room where he could be indoors all day or a private place where he could move outdoors without being in public. Challenging! And so the idea came up of taking him to Sun City. It is merely a thirty-minute flight from Johannesburg and he wasn't keen on going too far.

First I received a call from one of his daughters complaining, 'How can you take Madiba there?' As if the decision had been mine. I referred it to Mrs Machel. Only once his daughter understood that the Presidential suite was being offered to him free of charge, and that the three-room suite was big enough for him not to feel isolated in and that he could sit outside out of the public eye, did she settle.

In Sun City on one of the mornings Mrs Machel and I had agreed to go walking for exercise. My cellphone rang at 7 a.m. and I thought she was going to postpone our exercise. I thought it was strange that she didn't call my hotel room, but as I answered my cellphone I smiled as I was preparing for her to say that she would sleep in. She didn't. She just said: 'Zelda come quickly, bring the doctor.' I ran down the corridor as fast as I could. I knocked on the doctor's door and yelled at him 'Harold come quickly.' He was dressed and without me explaining anything he grabbed his bag and we ran off to the suite grabbing one of our bodyguards too almost in mid-flight. Madiba had slipped and fallen on the bathroom floor and hit his head against something. It wasn't serious but a head wound bleeds excessively. We helped and the doctor immediately did all tests needed, cleaned the wound and reported to Dr Plit, the physician in Johannesburg. When Madiba was finally on the bed with the doctor treating him, he saw me moving in and out of his room and his face lit up and he said, 'Oh Zeldina, you are here.' If ever I had thought to leave, that was the day I decided to stay until the end.

Unconsciously my body went into shock. I have never had such a big fright in my entire life and my shoulder and neck went into spasm. It took me three weeks of treatment of every kind possible to get rid of it – massages, acupuncture, medication, nothing helped. Mrs Machel was in trouble too. The family was furious and wanted to blame her for taking Madiba to Sun City and for his falling. He could have slipped anywhere and that is just the way it was. Old people fall. Period.

Madiba was no longer talkative every day; he was becoming more reserved. Whenever he was at the office – occasions that became few and far between – he would sit quietly by himself, thinking and only really converse on days that he felt strong and talkative. I always had to make sure that someone sat with him, whether he just read papers or wanted to be quiet in his chair. He did love interacting with all the colleagues at the Foundation and whenever new staff joined I made a point of introducing them. I also made sure every-one greeted him whenever he visited the office so that he could feel a sense of belonging. He had standard jokes for some of the staff. To Maretha, when she was pregnant with her first child, he would repeatedly ask, 'How many babies are you expecting?' because she is of small frame and carried large during her pregnancy. To Vimla, Mrs Machel's assistant, he would say, 'You appear to have grown taller,' because Vimla is short.

On a few occasions he would catch me by surprise when he said: 'Oh Zeldina, we have been together for a long time, haven't we?' And I would smile at his peculiar choice of words. What he meant was that we had been working together for a long time. If you work for someone for that long, you no longer need a detailed explanation for everything they say and you are familiar with intent. I would respond: 'Yes, Khulu, we have. We've now worked together for fifteen or sixteen years', and my answer would be met by a surprised 'Gee whiz'. I never asked why he was so surprised about the years we'd worked together, if he had expected me to leave earlier or whether he was surprised that time had gone by so fast.

Over the years we had built a close relationship with Morgan Freeman and his business partner Lori McCreary. We occasionally saw them during trips when we were abroad or whenever they visited South Africa. In Monaco they attended our fundraising event and told us that Clint Eastwood had agreed to direct the movie they were planning to make about the 1995 Rugby World Cup in South Africa. It was to be called *Invictus*, named after the poem Madiba recited in prison, which ends 'I am the master of my fate: / I am the captain of my soul'. Teams of people from Hollywood visited South Africa in preparation of the film and I would often meet with them to direct them to people who could assist or help with logistics. They also asked if I would be willing to assist them in Morgan's interpretation of Madiba's character. I read the script and agreed to help. I wanted as much as them for the movie to be a success even though I did not play a prominent role in Madiba's office in 1995.

After asking for help from the Presidency at the Union Buildings the pre-production team was allowed to do a site inspection. The Foundation also supported them with research and I gave them legitimate examples of letterheads and access cards and drew plans of the layout of the office. I knew they would get it right, but I didn't realize that when Hollywood recreates, they do it perfectly. When I walked onto the set on the first day, I walked into a replica of Madiba's first house in Houghton. I was finding my way through the crew and stood behind a half-open door until they could give me the green light to enter the set. Then, unannounced, I heard Madiba in the room next door. My instinctive thought: What is he doing here? and then I realized that it was Morgan doing a scene of Madiba sitting in the lounge of his house. It was scary to hear as he sounded *exactly* like Madiba. Over the years we all commented that the older Morgan grew the more he started looking like Madiba.

I only stayed for the day on the set and helped with small things that I picked up around the house or in Morgan's interpretation of 'Madiba's role' that could be improved. Morgan was the perfect Madiba and for someone who knows Madiba fairly well it was the closest to him that we've seen portrayed in a movie. The only thing I could really help Morgan with was some small mannerisms which he quickly picked up. He was crossing his legs too often or using his hands too expressively.

It was exciting but soon the day was over and I had to return to Johannesburg. I could only take a day's leave but soon when more scenes around Madiba or bodyguards were being shot, I took more leave and joined the crew, trying to assist them and pointing out whenever I thought something could be done differently to make it even more authentic.

During Madiba's ninetieth-birthday celebrations we had asked people, friends, ordinary people to send messages of congratulations to Madiba which we would put in a book for him to keep, together with the pictures to remind him of the celebrations in Hyde Park. One such note was a letter from Bono. He wrote: 'Happy Birthday Madiba. I am working to make July 18th a public holiday in every country that acknowledges that the struggle of Nelson Mandela is not over until every individual who yearns for freedom has the chance to grasp it. I believe your birthday should be an occasion around the globe to honour those who still struggle.' Tim Massey and I looked at the note and smiled. There was much more to this than what met the eye. How do we achieve this? We toyed a bit with the idea, and after consulting Fink Haysom, Madiba's legal adviser during his Presidency who now worked at the United Nations, the Foundation and 46664 decided to ask the South African Ambassador to the UN to put forward a proposal to the UN to declare 18 July International Nelson Mandela Day.

The UN unanimously accepted the proposal and the resolution

was passed. Our Ambassador to the UN, Baso Sangqu, was outstanding in lobbying with his fellow ambassadors to gain their
support. We were extremely proud when we were told that the
resolution had been accepted and although 18 July was not to be a
public holiday, it was declared a day of service for people to make a
difference worldwide in their own environments. Even though
Bono refused to take credit for the idea I often remind him that his
sometimes crazy ideas make the world a better place and this was
the perfect example.

We held another 46664 fundraiser in New York to raise money for
the Foundation, but it was difficult. We were trying to raise money
during a world economic recession and it was our first attempt at
fundraising without Madiba being present. People were not keen to
be seen to be ostentatious during a financial crisis, not even for charity, and again most people who attended were the people who we
always relied on. The fundraiser wasn't a big success but we had
prepared ourselves for that. The good part about it was that a boyfriend at the time accompanied me for the first time abroad, at our
own expense of course. For the first time in sixteen years I had
someone to turn to at night when the work was finished.

The loneliest part of my job over the years had been the nights
alone in hotels across the world. I had had the odd boyfriend, relationship or fling over the years but no one really understood my
environment. There was also the constant thought and occurrence
of people befriending me for the wrong reasons, whether it was to
get a book signed, to benefit from my contacts or to meet interesting people. After a few disappointments I started behaving like a
modern version of a recluse. Hence I was always alone. There was
no one to call and no one to say goodnight to, so you tend to turn
to your job and become even more focused and almost emotionally
reliant on what the job offers you to compensate for that loneliness.
I think at some point it became less complicating to share my life
with someone. I didn't have to find excuses to work or be so dedicated, and although the freedom allowed me to grow as a person,

I had missed the sharing and caring from a soulmate. This time it was different.

For year end the plan was that Madiba would spend a few days in Shambala for him and Mrs Machel to rest, and to give the staff at the Houghton house the opportunity to take leave. It was becoming clear towards the end of our stay in Shambala that Madiba was getting older much faster than we anticipated and his strength was deteriorating.

Madiba no longer moved easily by himself. Something was bothering him. Near the end of the trip he awoke one morning in a bad mood. He refused to eat and wanted to leave the farm immediately. 'Mum,' he said to Mrs Machel, 'we have a crisis.' Mum and I questioned him about the crisis but he wouldn't tell us what it was. And then he would start again: 'Mum, can you not see the crisis?' Madiba insisted he leave immediately. He usually flew to Shambala by military helicopter. The drive to Johannesburg was too far for him. It was the holidays and finding pilots to act on such short notice was difficult. Douw Steyn, the owner of Shambala, was on the farm too and Mum asked him to help find a helicopter.

In the meantime some of the security called Makaziwe, Madiba's eldest daughter, in Johannesburg to report that Madiba insisted on leaving immediately. Makaziwe called Mum and instructed her: 'Release my father now . . . release my father.' I could hear it all on the phone standing next to Mrs Machel. I cringed. We were trying to ascertain what the crisis was that Madiba was referring to. We were also waiting for Douw to help organize a helicopter. The next minute the security pulled up in their convoy, loaded Madiba in the car and started driving him back to Johannesburg. Panic struck. Never before had the security abandoned or left Mrs Machel behind. Madiba was not registering clearly what was happening. Mrs Machel, a former First Lady of South Africa and the wife of Madiba, was left stranded at Shambala without any security or transport. Between Josina (her daughter) and me we had to figure out how to get her home.

In the meantime Douw had managed to organize a helicopter and he was chasing the convoy from mid-air. Not knowing how the South African Police Force operated, he instructed the helicopter to land on the highway – not realizing that the helicopter would probably be shot at by the bodyguards. The farm manager, Tinus Nel, sped behind the convoy trying to catch it to communicate Douw's plans to them and only when the convoy stopped at the KFC drive-through in a nearby town, to apparently buy KFC for Madiba for lunch, did he manage to catch them. The helicopter was diverted and Douw was asked to fly to Johannesburg to meet Madiba there.

When Madiba left Shambala he was furious, but none of us understood what the furore was about. All he repeated was that there was a crisis. Little did we know that Madiba had had a vision of the years that lay ahead for him. That of ill-health and suffering. He knew his body was changing but he was unable to tell us what he felt.

I had been angry on many occasions over the previous sixteen years but at some point laughter at the irony takes over from anger. Some of us had spent those many previous years looking out for Madiba, caring for him, making sure that he ate the right food at the right time, that he was treated with dignity and that things happened according to his wishes, and then suddenly the situation changes, and you are on the outside looking in. I had never imagined that anyone would take Madiba to a drive-through KFC, but suddenly that was happening.

He arrived home while we were still trying to pack up in Shambala and rush Mrs Machel to Johannesburg. Shortly after Madiba's arrival, Douw arrived at the Houghton house too and then Makaziwe arrived. Madiba was deeply disturbed, and still not able to verbalize his frustration. But he chased everyone except Douw out of the house. 'Get out!' he said. 'Get out!' and they left. Madiba said he didn't want anyone interfering with his business.

At times like these when Madiba got angry I honestly feared for his health. He got so angry that I sometimes thought he was close to having a stroke. A day or so passed and Madiba calmed down again, and they soon left for Qunu where they had planned to spend Christmas.

Early in 2010 we were approached by the organizers of the *Top Gear* show in South Africa and asked whether the Foundation would consider partnering with them and in turn they would then make us the beneficiaries of their fundraiser. The request went, like all requests, past our committee, consisting of the CEO, Chairman and some senior staff members, and finally we asked Madiba whether he would be interested in meeting them. Upon running down their credentials he agreed. The organizers, contrary to what was subsequently reported in the media, asked whether Jeremy Clarkson and his team could pay a courtesy call to Madiba. Seeing that *Top Gear* is the most viewed TV show on earth we agreed, under condition that the Foundation would be featured somehow as it provided a platform to introduce the Centre of Memory's work, hoping to secure Madiba's legacy into the future, to the world. All parties agreed. On the night of the fundraiser around 800,000 rand was raised and we were happy. Despite promises of Clarkson and James May attending the event, they were nowhere to be seen. I had hoped to meet them to get a sense of them as they were paying their courtesy call to Madiba the following day. Personally I had always been a fan of *Top Gear*.

On the same day as the fundraiser, Neil Armstrong, the first man to walk on the moon, in 1969, visited Madiba. Madiba was imprisoned in 1969 but he remembered the prison warders telling them about it as they had no access to newspapers or a radio at the time, and of course no television. As opposed to many other meetings at the time, Madiba found it very curious and captivating to engage with Mr Armstrong. Mr Armstrong had been a recluse most of his life and we didn't know much about him. I was inquisitive about the reality of his life after such an extraordinary experience and he was eager to share his experiences with us. I was fascinated and almost in awe of him and asked him the strangest questions once Madiba ran out of questions himself.

Madiba found it most intriguing. Neil Armstrong was a gentle soul and one could sense in his character that he had a different understanding of life having gone through such an experience. He was also elderly, and it was easy for Madiba to relate to him. This has to be one of my top ten moments with Madiba, seeing the two of them conversing as elderly men, exchanging their most awkward life experiences.

I knew that Jeremy Clarkson was humorous but I thought he had tact. As he walked into Madiba's office the next day he asked Madiba if he had ever had a lap dance. I thought it completely inappropriate for him to ask something like that to an elderly statesman and Madiba looked at me as if he expected me to answer. I turned to Madiba and said: 'You don't have to answer that, Khulu.' I looked at Jeremy and I was on guard. He could see that I thought it was a stupid question to put to a ninety-one-year-old.

They took their seats and I reminded Madiba who they were, obviously explaining that they had the most popular show on TV and recited the number of viewers worldwide and elaborated a bit. He listened and took note and entertained what they said. They handed him their books and he paged through them. He didn't feel like conversation and appeared a bit withdrawn.

The first problem, which I was not aware of at the time, was that Clarkson thought Madiba had asked to see them and Madiba thought they had asked to see him. Jeremy then asked Madiba whether he often came to the office and Madiba said no, it was his first day in the office for the year. Yet I knew that it was reported in the papers that he had met Eddie Izzard and Armstrong the previous day. I corrected him as I usually did and said: 'No Khulu, remember you were here yesterday. You met Neil Armstrong, remember he was so interesting as he told us about his trip to the moon.' Madiba responded and said: 'Oh yes that's correct, now I remember.' Looking at Clarkson and May he had little else to say to them and jokingly asked, 'Have you ever been to the moon?' He was trying to crack a joke and if Jeremy could make jokes out of line, surely Madiba could make a joke too?

Yet later, Clarkson wrote an article in which he very inappropriately said that Madiba mistook him for Neil Armstrong, which was definitely not the case. He may not have known who Clarkson was, but he definitely didn't confuse him for someone else. Theirs was an underestimation of Madiba's intelligence because he was old. In my view, there was no respect.

Added to that, the organizers met with us a few days later and told us that the close to 800,000 rand we thought was raised during the fundraiser, and which was reported to have been raised for the Nelson Mandela Foundation, was not entirely all ours. They still had to offset the costs of the dinner and event and then we would be left with about half the money. I was furious. In terms of governance it created difficulties for us. It subsequently all appeared in the *Mail* and *Guardian* newspapers in South Africa and I came across as an utter bitch towards the organizers, but I didn't mind a bit. I was just sick and tired of, as it seemed to me, people taking advantage of Madiba and us and people pussy-footing around issues rather than saying it straight. The Foundation did accept the money but we had to follow up with each of the buyers separately. It created hassle and was far away from what we believed the arrangement to be. Coupled with what I felt was utter disrespect for the Foundation, it was a difficult pill to swallow. People later asked how we could have allowed Clarkson to meet with Madiba, but we followed due process and the matter was discussed with all Madiba's advisers and at the time, like in many other cases, what was presented on paper – and more specifically the opportunity to showcase the work of the Foundation to an international audience – appeared advantageous. It was not all about the money but about the promise of giving much needed exposure to the work of trying to preserve Nelson Mandela's legacy. And so you learn . . .

In 2010 South Africa hosted the FIFA World Cup. Madiba was only visiting the office occasionally. He was starting to show signs of his age. We were not surprised but the public was. He was more forgetful and sometimes he didn't feel like seeing people or getting up.

Other days he would not want to be isolated and he would ask to see people. Most days he wanted to spend time at home resting. Soon we were overwhelmed by artists, visitors, tourists and every head of state present in South Africa for the World Cup all wanting to pay a courtesy call on Madiba. It was impossible for him to grant all these appointments and we decided to close his diary in fear that he may be too exhausted by the time of the opening ceremony, which he was meant to attend.

And then there was FIFA. We joked that we felt invaded by this world body and I decided that FIFA was not a worldwide football organization but a country by itself. But they were particularly accommodating as far as the planning around Madiba's attendance at the opening ceremony. Generally people in South Africa felt that the World Cup cost the country too much money as we had to invest a lot on the infrastructure to deal with the number of visitors. The majority of people in South Africa still lived in poverty even though it was sixteen years since the ANC took power. Delivery of basic services was slow due to the frequent and diverse challenges faced by a developing country, and even while we were promised good returns on social responsibility projects from FIFA for hosting the World Cup soccer there was little proof of that at the time, or since.

I thought I enjoyed a generally good relationship with FIFA officials, regardless of friction sometimes over them wanting to overburden Madiba. I attended many meetings in preparation of the opening ceremony where all involved parties would be present. Afterwards I would put Madiba's needs to the executive and they changed and adapted plans to work for him. Of course they were desperate to have him appear and 'endorse' the opening of the tournament but I also wanted to believe that they honestly cared enough to really accommodate all his needs. I was extremely open to Danny Jordaan, who was the CEO of the Local Organizing Committee in South Africa, and FIFA executives about the need to avoid exploiting Madiba and about the difficulties involved in him attending a function like this in the middle of winter.

All presidents and deputy presidents in South Africa have a team of medical staff that move with them. This privilege was also extended to Madiba whenever we travelled abroad, even past his retirement from public office. As his age progressed the team became more prominent, and by the time he was ninety-two they accompanied us even to all local events. After one of the briefing meetings to prepare for the opening ceremony Jérôme Valcke, the CEO of FIFA, called me aside and told me that he had received a call from the Surgeon General, responsible for Madiba's health care. However, it wasn't the Surgeon General that had called but General Dabula, the Surgeon General's second-in-command and the person overseeing the medical care of all the former presidents. Until that point we mostly saw General Dabula whenever an important visitor came around to see Madiba.

Jérôme told me that he had received instructions from General Dabula that he (Dabula) was the only one to decide anything about Madiba's movements. His decision was that upon arrival Madiba would go to SAFA House, the office building close to the stadium which housed the South African Football Association. Madiba would be taken to a holding room in Chairman Irvin Khoza's office, and then when the time came for him to go onto the field he would be taken to a golf cart and driven about a kilometre to the entrance of the stadium.

To me, it just didn't make sense in practical terms. Why would you drive an elderly person – in mid-winter – that far in an open golf cart? It was two days before the opening match that Jérôme received these instructions. I could see that he was puzzled. I had been working with them for years prior to the World Cup and now he received a call from someone he had never spoken to or seen before just two days before it began. Luckily, the Head of the Presidential Protection Unit, Brigadier Dladla, was also present during the meeting that had just adjourned. I called him and asked Jérôme to repeat the story, which he did. Brigadier Dladla would have none of it. Security had always decided on the means of transport and Madiba's movements, in accordance to the programme we developed.

I was stunned by this interference and the odd logic of their choices. Luckily, the matter was put to rest after Brigadier Dladla called General Dabula. But it was evident that there was a battle over authority. The medical staff under General Dabula felt, now, that they were the ultimate authority, while the security staff under Brigadier Dladla viewed themselves equally. Madiba's office had a long working relationship with his security teams and a respect and deep sense of understanding for our respective fields of expertise. It felt as though there was an attempt to undermine the authority of the Foundation and Madiba's office: the older he became and the less able to express his own wishes, the more people were going to move in and get him to do what they wanted him to do, serving their interests rather than his, although they might have seen these as the interests of the country. I was caught in the middle and I found it hard.

Sadly on the evening of the opening concert of the FIFA World Cup, prior to the day of the official opening of the tournament, Madiba's beloved great-granddaughter Zenani was tragically killed in a car accident. I woke up the next morning to a message from the Presidency asking whether the rumours were true. I checked and indeed it was the case. I was numbed with shock. Zenani was the sweetest, most loving child imaginable.

Hearing of Zenani Jnr's death I immediately assumed that Madiba would not be able to attend the opening ceremony. Yet I was receiving confusing reports. Mrs Machel had left the house to go and support the family and I couldn't reach her immediately. When she called she said that the family had met and decided Madiba should not go. Barely thirty minutes later I received a call from the household telling me that Madiba was definitely going. When I asked how this had come about I was told that some of the staff at the house went to convince Madiba to make a short appearance. I called again to check who was at the house and it seemed that between the medical staff and security they had convinced Madiba that the world was waiting to see him. Indeed the world was and they were playing the guilt card, but they were looking for a way to go to the opening ceremony themselves and by convincing Madiba to go, they would get in clearly at the expense of him and his family during such a challenging time for them. I was spitting fire. I reported this to Mrs Machel again and when she arrived home she resolved the issue. Until minutes before the opening ceremony people were trying to change plans to get Madiba to go.

It was becoming clear that the struggle for authority over what Madiba got to do and what he didn't was going to be a tough battle. Madiba didn't go but appropriately attended a vigil with the family. The battle for authority was exhausting. The medical staff clearly had the desire to assert their authority in Madiba's life. Those who have served Madiba for years were steadily being sidelined. Little did I know what lay ahead. At the time I felt for Madiba. I imagined him feeling like an antelope hit by a vehicle, confused, being pushed around by people and no longer being able to have a clear sense of reason himself.

Despite this sad day for us all, the country exploded with excitement as the first match kicked off at Soccer City. Again South Africa was a united nation. Sport brought us all together and after a successful opening match people dispelled fears of failure. There were tourists everywhere and business was blooming. Flags of each country hung everywhere and people draped their cars and houses with the flag of the country they supported.

Zenani's funeral was the week after the opening game. Two weeks later, while I attended a match with the Clintons, my grandmother also sadly passed away. I had two sad funerals during the World Cup and it left me with mixed emotions; I found it difficult to be swept away by the national celebrations. Mrs Machel and Josina attended my grandmother's funeral in Pretoria. My family was extremely touched and grateful. Never ever had I expected that they would take the time and make the effort to drive that far to support me or my family. She was the last of my grandparents and regardless of the fact that I felt a bit bitter about her putting my mother through the trauma of having to go into an orphanage, I was nevertheless very, very sad about her passing. My wonderful mother didn't have grudges and was very close to my grandmother. She was with Grandma right to the end.

Mrs Machel comes through at the most surprising times and she has a motherly instinct to know when one needs her support. It made me think about support for her. Madiba was getting older and it was becoming difficult for her too, to see her husband ageing. She is not a machine and she needs support as well. She has been there for me at times when I was heartbroken about boyfriends that left me, or when life was simply getting too much. More so than any other person.

Madiba's entire being was based on respect. Respect for your friends, respect for the enemy, for those poorer than you, those worse dressed and those less educated, and even those who harmed you or those who made mistakes. But also for those more powerful, those wealthier and smarter than you. There was not one day that I felt that Madiba disrespected me because I was a lesser person than him, knew less, earned less, knew so little about life and sometimes, yes, well, was so stupid. Not one day. Not *one* occasion. Mrs Machel is the one person who made Madiba truly happy and just for that she deserved respect if there was ever any doubt that she earned or demanded it. She deserved it.

In May I decided that I had to do something for Mandela Day. After toying with an idea with a colleague, Sello Hatang, I decided to organize a ride with a group of motorbike riders. The idea would be for a representative group to ride between Johannesburg and Cape Town (approximately 1,400 km) to advocate for Mandela Day. Along the way we would stop at charity projects where we could offer sixty-seven minutes to support the charity. Mandela Day is an ethos we can all subscribe to in honour of Madiba. It is a day of service and Madiba, having spent sixty-seven years fighting social injustice, asks only sixty-seven minutes of your time. The idea was also to demonstrate to people that if we all do just that, we can change the world for the better.

Between the pressures of the World Cup I was also looking after business people who visited South Africa for the tournament as well as organizing the bike trip. I had started a business the year before specifically catering for VIPs' logistical needs whenever they travelled to South Africa. My role at the office was slowly diminishing and I had to keep busy, which made me decide to start the business. During the World Cup I took on a few such high profile clients and my time and energy was thinly spread amongst all my responsibilities.

The day after the tournament ended, our bike trip departed from the Foundation in the cold of mid-winter. It was enjoyable and a great success, and seeing that Morgan Freeman and his business associate Lori McCreary were in South Africa for the World Cup, they too accompanied us on the biker trip. The trip was successful and we got coverage for Mandela Day countrywide, and on international networks worldwide. And, most importantly, we touched thousands of lives. It is something I hoped to continue into the future. The entire group felt good at the end of the ride. We felt like we really made a difference to people's lives.

On the Thursday before the final of the tournament, Madiba indicated that he definitely wanted to attend the closing match or at least make an appearance, as he'd been unable to attend the opening match due to the death of Zenani Jnr. I informed all parties about his wishes. We had to put all mechanisms in place again for an appearance.

On the Sunday of the closing match we finally had all arrangements in place for Madiba to go onto the pitch at the closing ceremony to at least wave to the crowd. He was excited but it was winter and we knew to make his appearance as short as possible. Upon our arrival at the stadium, General Dabula and the entire Defence Force top brass were there waiting for Madiba. I couldn't see why as they were all line managers and were not going to deal with any situation, if anything happened, themselves. While the security team had prepared a particular golf cart for Madiba the medical team had prepared another. The power struggle started. General Dabula insisted that he accompany Madiba on the golf cart to take the 50-metre drive onto the pitch. The security didn't agree but kept quiet. That arrangement would also mean that there wouldn't be space on the golf cart for Mrs Machel. I wouldn't hear of this and a huge altercation broke out. All the staff were young and fit enough to walk next to the golf cart, if there was any need for them to. In any event, if anything ever happened to a VIP in public you would not deal with the matter there but would rather take him/her to a safe place. Why would Mrs Machel's seat need to be compromised for medical staff? They would have to shoot me to give in on that one. There was just no common sense in this proposal at all. By the time Madiba arrived it had still not been resolved.

The security and I insisted and I could sense the resentment from General Dabula. He wanted to have a final say but we would not make Madiba's life practically difficult to give in to his ways. As Madiba's name was announced the golf cart drove onto the pitch. Of course the cart was surrounded by security and a horde of medical staff. Even the top brass of the Defence Force medical fraternity. I stayed in the tunnel and witnessed the circus from a distance. The noise the crowd made became deafening when they noticed Madiba. He smiled and waved. He had his furry Russian hat on and was dressed in his favourite warm coat, scarf and gloves. Mum sat next to him and they both waved at the crowd. Madiba was happy. It was a befitting ending to his career in public. It was indeed the last time he ever appeared formally at a public event.

Towards the end of 2010 Madiba returned to Shambala to allow his household staff time off. Since Madiba no longer travelled and seldom went anywhere the staff at home were working round the clock. They were stretched to their limits and seriously needed a break. From Shambala they went to Qunu for family Christmas and I spent Christmas with my family.

When I arrived in Cape Town in late December 2010 to be with Madiba and Mum over New Year, I was deeply concerned when I saw Madiba again. He had lost weight since I saw him two weeks before and he was extremely uncomfortable and edgy. When I left for the holiday he had great difficulty walking. I did, as usual, express concern about my boss to the medical staff and they just said to me, 'Madiba is fine.' It was clearly none of my business how my boss was doing.

Mrs Machel was concerned too but it was becoming clear that medical staff were now acting on instructions from certain Mandela family members and that introduced different priorities to those Mrs Machel felt were important for her husband. Sky News later reported that Madiba had bedsores. The Cape Town medics who acted independently were concerned and stressed.

Rodney, a paramedic in Cape Town, and I decided to go and do some shopping to buy medical equipment to make him more comfortable. The nurses and medical staff who accompanied him from Pretoria seemed uninterested in his condition and discomfort. The secretary, so often blamed for inefficiency, was now in cahoots with the Cape Town medics to investigate every possible way to attend to Madiba's medical needs. The mere fact that I am not in a mental institution right now remains a wonder to me. Situations like these made me feel like I was going insane.

My first question was, if his care was in the hands of the government, why didn't they provide these basics? Surely when a person becomes elderly his needs change and it was common sense that one had to continuously adapt the situation to make him as comfortable as possible. I once read in Madiba's *Conversations With Myself* what he had said during a conversation with editor Richard Stengel: 'I moved in circles where common sense and practical experience were important, and where high academic qualifications were not necessarily decisive.' And yes, indeed, I have come to precisely that realization. There were certain instances where the common sense my dad had taught me became more decisive than my lack of degrees and academic qualification.

As days progressed things were deteriorating fast. The situation was reported to those in charge of Madiba's care in Pretoria, General Dabula and Surgeon General Ramlakan. It was clear that Madiba needed a specialist to examine his knee.

In the meantime we realized that Madiba would not be able to return to Johannesburg on 11 January as was originally planned. He had great difficulty walking and we acquired a wheelchair to move him. It would not fit into the current elevator in the Johannesburg residence and it was necessary to replace the elevator with a larger model. That meant that the company installing it would have to enlarge the shaft for the bigger machine. Meme Kgagare, Madiba's Household Manager, and I contacted the company responsible for the installation of the original elevator and made arrangements for them to start work as soon as possible. Meme would keep us posted every day on the progress made in rebuilding the shaft. This would take time and we therefore needed to remain in Cape Town a little longer than expected. By then we were looking at a week's extension of our stay in Cape Town. The odd visitor came to see Madiba but as for the rest of the time an uncomfortable silence descended on the house.

On Wednesday, 13 January 2011, a specialist in orthopaedic surgery at 2 Military Hospital was ordered to come and examine Madiba. He entered the living room while Prof. Gerwel and I were with Madiba. He examined Madiba's knee and Madiba protested from the pain. The doctor requested the medics to take Madiba to the bedroom for a proper examination. He looked shocked when he appeared from the room. He said to us that he would be in touch but that he was concerned that there may be underlying problems that could be the cause of the deterioration we witnessed in Madiba in the past few weeks.

Mrs Machel was in Mozambique on this particular day as she had to prepare her family for her son paying *labola* (paying the price to marry a woman in African tradition). Mrs Machel's family hardly ever depended on her for time and attention but these were among the few occasions that her own children needed her presence in Mozambique. By now, General Dabula was in Cape Town too. The doctor briefed him and expressed his shock over the general care of Mr Mandela as a patient. He appealed to us to admit Madiba to the local Military Hospital in Cape Town – immediately. I indicated that Mrs Machel would return that night and that it was not a decision I could take, and that we would have to wait for her unless they insisted that it was an emergency.

General Dabula said he was more concerned that Madiba was homesick. He suggested that we fly in one of the housekeepers from Johannesburg. I told him that household affairs and the way staff work rosters were determined were not medical matters nor my business, and that in my opinion Madiba had been homesick for almost two years. Anyone who spent enough time with Madiba knew that if he was in Johannesburg, he wanted to be in Qunu, if he was in Qunu he wanted to be in Johannesburg. If he was in Cape Town he wanted to be in Qunu or Johannesburg. It is just the way old people are. I advised that we leave household affairs to Mrs Machel and that he focus on the medical issues. I felt he was upset with me but I saw his actions as another symptom of disregard for Mrs Machel. There was always politics at the house, like there is in any working environment.

Mrs Machel arrived back late on the 14th but I had texted her to say that General Dabula and the specialist who had examined Madiba wanted to see her the next morning, and she agreed to meet at 11.00. By then I had learned that General Dabula had decided not to include the specialist who had examined Madiba but rather to bring in a third doctor, a physician by training. She had not seen Madiba before, yet she was asked to brief Mrs Machel despite never having examined the patient they were discussing.

After our gym session on Friday morning I walked Mrs Machel to her car. I told her that the specialist who had examined Madiba suspected some underlying problem which resulted in Madiba's rapid deterioration, and that they were going to suggest that Madiba be admitted to hospital that afternoon. I was increasingly becoming worried about her too. The constant stress of dealing with family politics put a strain on her and I feared that if she was caught by such a shock announcement that her husband had to be hospitalized she might end up having a stroke. We couldn't live without her being Mum and being there for Madiba. The doctors arrived at the house at 10.30, and after the discussion preparations were made and Madiba was taken to 2 Military Hospital to be admitted for a series of tests. More and more tests were done, including X-rays and scans.

I had often been told by some of the Mandela family members to stay out of Madiba's personal life, but I was extremely frustrated, as any layman could see that things were not being dealt with in the best possible way, and the constant need for the medical team to consider the internal family politics above the interest of the patient was clear. The doctors were also pertinently instructed by some of the Mandelas not to discuss any medical issues around Madiba with me. It was clear that me pointing out certain things was starting to irritate them.

Things went generally well in hospital but Madiba was uneasy as he had never liked hospitals. He didn't want to be there and he protested. On Saturday morning at about 6 a.m. I received a call from Madiba's long-serving loyal bodyguard and driver, Mike Maponya, who had been Madiba's driver since his release from prison. My heart came to a standstill. Mike didn't often call me and it was too early to receive an unimportant call from him. You expect the worst. Madiba wanted me to come to the hospital immediately. I still had to get dressed and make myself presentable and as a result I only arrived a little later. Madiba was furious at me. 'Zeldina, you, you of all people deserted me and left me here.' He had not spent a night in hospital in years and he detested it. Mike tried to diffuse the situation by telling Madiba that Mum was about to arrive at the hospital herself, as she was. I explained that the people were there to take care of him and to examine him to make sure he was OK but he wouldn't take any of it. Luckily Mrs Machel arrived soon and that calmed him down. It was difficult to see him as uneasy as that and I disappeared from the room as soon as I could find an opportunity. I couldn't bear seeing him not being well and so frustrated. The doctors were busy with him all the time and had several closed door discussions. I was relieved because I knew they were now paying full attention to him and he was in specialists' hands, which is all I really cared for.

General Dabula was nowhere to be seen and the GP on duty with Madiba was off sick with tonsillitis. It was of great concern to me that two of the key role players concerned with Madiba's health were absent. Mrs Machel informed Madiba's three daughters of their father's hospitalization and I informed Prof. Gerwel. I told Prof. that I was not alerting anyone at the Foundation as it was critical that we kept this under tight wraps or else we would be overwhelmed at the hospital by media and the public.

The Minister of Defence at the time, Lindiwe Sisulu, paid a visit to Madiba on Saturday night at hospital. She is the daughter of Madiba's late friends Walter and Albertina Sisulu and also a cousin of Makaziwe Mandela. In South Africa, the Ministry of Defence is responsible for the healthcare of heads of state and former heads of state. I wasn't there but Mrs Machel was and the Minister was also concerned about Madiba's well-being. Late on Saturday night rumours started doing the rounds in the media that Madiba had passed away. The government wanted to issue a statement to say that Madiba was admitted to the military hospital in Cape Town for tests, but I advised against disclosing his whereabouts to give him privacy. They wanted to stop rumours from running that he had passed on.

In the meantime the Foundation contacted me to ask whether there was any substance to the rumours of Madiba's passing. I said: 'Madiba is alive, but please speak to Prof. for any other info.' I didn't want to be the one to give out information as I knew what could happen and I was often blamed for leaks to the media. We had already suspected that our phones were being monitored as confidential discussions somehow appeared to leak for inexplicable reasons. In instances like these it is better for senior officials to discuss the process. A statement was subsequently issued that read that Madiba was on holiday with his wife and there was no substance to the rumours that he had passed on. I advised the Presidency that such a statement had been issued and they decided not to issue their statement.

On Sunday Madiba was discharged after all the specialists saw him for the last examination. We arrived home around 1 p.m. to find the GP who had been off work because of tonsillitis at Madiba's house in Cape Town. I wondered to myself, couldn't she have gone to the hospital that morning to receive discharge instructions from the specialists if she was now well enough to come to Madiba's house? But if she was sick, surely it was not the best thing to be around Madiba? Aren't old people – especially in a vulnerable state of health – more susceptible to infections?

On Monday and Tuesday Madiba was showing progress. The medication was obviously starting to work. On Thursday morning I was eager to hear from the Doctor on duty how Madiba was but I was told by medical and security staff that the Doctor was not at work. When I asked where she was I was told that she had gone shopping. For me, this was too to much. How could shopping be a priority three days after Nelson Mandela had been discharged from hospital if you are the doctor? I was stepping way out of line to think that I could question the doctor for not being at work and soon I was reported to the family.

Mrs Machel left for the traditional wedding of her son, Malenga, in Maputo. She was told Madiba was OK and it was safe for her to leave, although we agreed that we would be in constant contact with one another to update her on progress.

On Saturday Madiba's daughter Zenani was scheduled to arrive in Cape Town; Mrs Machel had asked her to come and be with her father while she attended the wedding in Mozambique. She arrived at the house around 10 a.m. and her father was not out of bed yet.

The specialists were going to see Madiba at 11.00. Zenani, Shirley the housekeeper and I ended up chatting in the kitchen and lost track of the time. Sometime after 11.00 I enquired about the specialists and was told that they could not come to the house by themselves but were awaiting orders, like in any military bureaucracy, to be fetched from the hospital and brought to the house. When I called them and asked whether they couldn't drive themselves, I was told they were not allowed. I thought to myself: What if there was an emergency? Do we wait for Pretoria to issue orders for specialists in Cape Town to be fetched from the hospital because they are not allowed to drive there themselves?

I was stressed and beyond anxious about Madiba's health and went to see Prof. Gerwel at his office in Cape Town to tell him that the situation was turning for the worse and that we needed intervention. Because of all the politics within the medical team and family there was no way that anyone could make all parties agree to something. Prof. was my point of call on anything and everything. Madiba hardly ever took decisions without consulting or soundboarding it to Prof. Prof. was Madiba's point of balance in a way. He knew exactly how to find mutually acceptable ground between what Madiba wanted to be done and what had to be done. I was one of the few people who could always get hold of Prof. irrespective of the time of day or night. He was engaged on many fronts but he knew that we depended on him with our lives. He also knew that whenever an emergency occurred he would be my first port of call. He offered to speak to the Minister of Defence, and they arranged to meet on Monday after Mrs Machel had returned from Maputo.

On Sunday when Mrs Machel returned, Madiba's situation had deteriorated further. Madiba didn't want to lose sight of any of us and insisted that someone stay with him all the time. He was pale and weak. He was seriously ill. I was prepared to say goodbye but not without giving this fight my last shot to ensure that everything in our power was done to guarantee that he was in the best possible hands.

On Monday morning one of the specialists was dismissed because of disagreements over the best course of action with Madiba's care. Another specialist was flown from 1 Military Hospital in Pretoria to join the team. He examined Madiba and had some serious concerns. There was no way that we could fly home with Madiba in his current state. He advised that Madiba be taken to 2 Military Hospital again for a chest X-ray. I suspected that Madiba had pneumonia. Most deaths among old people are the result of septicaemia or pneumonia. In the meantime Mrs Machel, Minister Sisulu and Prof. Gerwel met and Mrs Machel provided details of the past weeks. Prof. Gerwel was as concerned as she and I about Madiba's health and care. Mrs Machel felt hopeless and undermined. Because I'd raised concerns and because the specialists were also all white, I felt that it also became a racial issue. There was no way out unless Prof., Mrs Machel and the Minister intervened.

The Minister explored the possibility of replacing the entire team, but Mrs Machel felt that they would (figuratively speaking) crucify her if she dared interfere with appointees endorsed by the family. It was clear to us all that, no matter who appointed who, Nelson Mandela was supposed to get expert attention and medical support. The Minister offered to put together an international team of specialists but Mrs Machel also guarded against something that could be seen as a vote of no confidence in our own medical practitioners in South Africa. She was right. We have some of the best medical specialists in the world.

By Tuesday the specialist from 1 Military Hospital had informed us that we would be going home on Wednesday. An ambulance plane was ordered from Pretoria to collect Madiba, equipped with emergency medical facilities to transport him home. I was informed by Maretha, my colleague who now dealt with logistics, that the plane could only accommodate four or five passengers due to the extra equipment on board, but that a second plane was chartered to transport the extra medical and security staff back to Pretoria.

On Tuesday morning I was sitting at the breakfast table with Mrs Machel and Ndaba, Madiba's grandson, who had arrived the previous day to look after his grandfather, when I briefed them both about the space in the plane so we could determine who got home on which plane. Ndaba said that he insisted that he be on the plane with Madiba as a family member had to be with him. Mrs Machel said that they would sort out spaces once they got to the plane in the morning, but that the doctors should get priority. I felt deeply hurt for her because what Ndaba was saying was that she was not family. It's not the big things that hurt me, but these mundane things. And then of course how it would have hurt Madiba if he'd heard how his wife was being treated. I had already made plans to fly commercially as I knew too well not to get in the way. Mrs Machel asked whether I didn't want to reconsider and fly with the back-up plane but I declined, saying that it was better that there was extra space for whoever wanted it and I needn't get in the way too.

I sat with Madiba at some point with my legs crossed and he touched my leg almost to feel whether I was really there. Tears shot to my eyes and I had to get up to not show him how upset I was. He was no longer conversing and one could see he was terribly weak. I didn't know why he was not hospitalized but was told that we were flying to Johannesburg the following day where there would be a full team of medical specialists that could attend to him.

On Wednesday morning I arrived early at the house. Madiba was at the breakfast table and being attended to. I had coffee and something to eat and then decided to make my way to the airport for my flight back home. I greeted, starting with Mrs Machel, and after greeting Madiba I quickly turned around and walked out so that no one could see that I was crying. I thought I had said my final goodbyes. He was coughing non-stop.

I was anxious at the airport and called the security to tell me once Madiba's plane was in the air. The decision and agreement with the doctors was that Madiba would be taken home once he arrived in Pretoria, upon which Dr Mike Plit, Madiba's private physician for over twenty years, would come and examine him. Madiba literally trusted Dr Plit with his life. Whenever Madiba didn't want to eat, a loss of appetite that occurs with age, we would tell him that Dr Plit insisted that he ate three meals a day. And Dr Plit did. He would then oblige. The thought of Dr Plit being in Johannesburg, waiting to care for him, was therefore a consolation if there could be any in such circumstances.

My plane was delayed and Madiba's took off before I could board my commercial flight. I was tired and emotional and kept my sunglasses on, like a proper wannabe celebrity, to disguise my red-wept eyes. Rumours about his health had quietened down in the public and media and I didn't want to fuel any speculation if anyone I knew came across me with my red eyes.

I had completely withdrawn from my friends and didn't want to see anyone. I didn't want them to sense how upset I was because they would figure out things themselves. They knew too well that my entire world revolved around Madiba and seeing him like that couldn't compare with the worst heartbreak I had ever suffered. I didn't respond to texts and/or calls from friends and just withheld myself from society completely. I was lonely too, as I couldn't share my stress and pain with anyone. I reported to Prof. Gerwel every day and kept him informed but apart from that I couldn't speak to anyone. No one told me but I knew what was best for me and the situation, and that was to withdraw completely.

Usually I find it very easy to sleep on planes or in anything that moves. I had mastered the art of a power nap. However on the flight back to Johannesburg I couldn't close an eye. I was wide awake and aware of everything that happened around me, even though I was exhausted. Upon landing in Johannesburg I didn't switch my phone on at first. I jumped on the Gautrain to make my way to Sandton where my brother would fetch me and take me home. I was anxious to not speak to anyone on the phone in public as I expected to hear the worst.

The first call I received once I arrived in Sandton was from our CEO Achmat. He asked whether I knew where Madiba was and I said that I hoped he was home already as they had left Cape Town before me. He then said they had received calls that Madiba had been taken to Milpark Hospital, a private hospital on the outskirts of Johannesburg. I called the security and they told me that they were arriving at Milpark. I called Achmat back and confirmed what the security had told me. By the time we spoke, a statement had already been issued by the foundation in consultation with the family stating that Madiba had been taken to Milpark for routine tests. I reported this to Prof. Gerwel and raised my concern over the statement being issued. I worried about referring to routine tests.

I went home and was glad to see my dogs and to be with my brother and my long-serving colleague and rock Maretha. I left a little later to go to the hospital. When I arrived doctors were busy with Madiba and I could only see him through a sliding door. I waved at him and he waved back and somehow I knew that he was OK, even though he still looked very weak. He had pneumonia, or respiratory infection as they described it, in addition to the bedsores and inflammation in his knee. All these combined were toxic to his body.

Another two days passed with on and off visits at the hospital. By the second day we discovered a secret route in and out of the hospital so that the media couldn't use me as a 'barometer', as the family put it, for Madiba's well-being. The media started watching my every move, and I appeared in the newspaper with Josina laughing over something stupid between us and it was interpreted that 'Madiba was fine' because we laughed. By Friday afternoon he was going to be discharged and he was already showing improvement. In the meantime I was supporting the housekeeping staff to get the house ready for Madiba to return. A huge press conference followed at the hospital, during which time Madiba was taken home. The security cleverly created this decoy and by the time the media thought Madiba was about to leave, he was safely at home already.

On the Saturday after his discharge a story was being prepared for the Sunday papers that there was tension between the Foundation and family and that government had to intervene, and that was, according to speculation, the reason why no one issued a statement following Madiba's hospitalization after the first statement by the Foundation. That was not the case. There had always been tension between Madiba's staff and certain factions of the family but it was not worsened by the situation. Nor would it be correct to say 'the family', implying the entire family.

As Madiba became weaker over the years, certain family members saw the opportunity to tell his Foundation and staff what they thought we had to do and how we had to do it. If Madiba was strong enough he wouldn't allow it. He guided his staff and guarded us against many things over the years and his weakness presented an opportunity for some family members to step in and start controlling matters to their advantage.

Soon Madiba was much better, but it was taking time for him to recover completely. During his prolonged illness we were running into problems paying accounts and keeping the households running. As no one held signatory over any of Madiba's accounts, an alternative arrangement had to be made. A family feud ensued while trying to make arrangements.

The fight over who controlled Madiba's money continued and got messier as time progressed.

Over the years the bank had always called me to verify transactions on Madiba's account. Because he was a high-profile person and they couldn't speak to him directly, they called me whenever there was a deposit, withdrawal or transfer being made to merely verify the movement in his account and that it was really him requesting the activity. The bank required, with the new power of attorney which now placed Mrs Machel and two of the Mandela daughters in control, a letter to be signed from Madiba that they could still call me to verify such transactions. I prepared all the documents and delivered them to Mrs Machel before I left for New York, where I was scheduled to travel to speak to the Clinton Foundation about another fundraiser for the Nelson Mandela Foundation, and to Tribeca about a joint venture on Mandela Day. I had never been a signatory on any of Madiba's accounts but was merely responsible for the administration, Mrs Machel didn't want to take control. I hated these calls from the bank to verify any movement in his account as it was just an irritation. The Foundation appointed a bookkeeper years ago to isolate me from having any powers over any of his moneys. I preferred it that way. Perhaps we subconsciously knew what awaited us all.

While I was in New York Makaziwe came to the office early on the Monday morning looking for me. She couldn't find me and asked Achmat where I was. He told her that I was in New York and she asked who had given me permission to travel. Achmat as CEO said he had and that I was there on official business for the Foundation. She then asked why it was necessary for a secretary to travel to New York and I don't know what he responded. She questioned why a secretary had to verify transactions when they, the Mandelas, signed documents on Madiba's account. I have learned to know that sometimes it's better to not raise your opinion about something, as the situation speaks for itself.

By now Mrs Machel had lost all her privacy in her own house. One appreciated that Madiba needed round-the-clock medical care but her privacy was just never a consideration. Imagine living in your own house where you couldn't walk from your bedroom to your kitchen with a dressing gown on. Where you can never leave your room without being properly dressed as there are always strangers in your house. Never letting your guard down, and eyes and ears to every move you make.

Another of the great lessons that I learned from both Madiba and Prof. Gerwel is that you sometimes have to allow things to happen and simply be a spectator. Bitterness will make you sick. During his imprisonment they were forced to work in the limestone quarry. Chipping away for no reason. Bitterness is the same. You reduce your own character with such a mindless exercise of cultivating bitterness. You have to allow for things to play out the way they are intended to. Not every situation can be changed by us.

I often during my career wanted to respond to things immediately, but over time and with age I have learned that you must just allow things to take their course. Watching Madiba over the years hiding his disbelief in people, he in a way sometimes, in my opinion, allowed them to create their own fortune or misfortune. Patience is everything.

12

Saying Goodbye

A few months after his first long hospitalization, it was decided to move Madiba to Qunu. He often asked about people he grew up with or deceased family members. Qunu is a remote area in the Eastern Cape and since it is the place where Madiba got sick the previous December, we met the instruction with scepticism. At home in Johannesburg he was close to medical attention, close friends popped in from time to time and some family occasionally visited. One could call on people like Ahmed Kathrada and George Bizos to pop in to visit him but in Qunu that would be difficult. We didn't know what to expect in Qunu. The family insisted and there was no way that Mrs Machel could object. Madiba was emotionally stable wherever she was, whether that was in Qunu or Johannesburg.

I started travelling to Qunu weekly, through the support of the Nelson Mandela Foundation, or every second week at least. Madiba stopped being talkative but he wanted company. Hardly anyone visited him and Mrs Machel was the only one apart from the medical staff and household staff that he had around him. Qunu is remote and it was difficult to travel there. One had to set an entire day aside to travel there and back and it would mean getting up at 3 a.m. and arriving back home at 8 p.m. if you only went for the day. It was probably not easy for everyone to travel there but Qunu became quiet and isolated.

It was announced at the Foundation that the organization was about to restructure to focus more on its core work. I understood and supported the fact that the Foundation had to become a Centre of

Memory, similar to a Presidential Library, to preserve his legacy. Madiba supported the setting up of a Centre of Memory, and the conversion of the Foundation in to a non-governmental organization specializing in memory and dialogue work. He launched the project in 2004, and during the years thereafter made donations of private papers, gifts and awards to the Nelson Mandela Foundation for the Centre's permanent archival collections. However I didn't agree that Madiba's office had to be closed. While Madiba was alive people wanted to remain connected with him even though it was not personally possible for him to reciprocate. His friends and associates, people who all had relationships with him, wanted to feel acknowledged. By closing Madiba's office that would become impossible. But it was expected that we should close his office and transfer relationships to people who did not have the institutional memory our office had. It was envisaged that his friends would be treated as part of the process which I felt would lack acknowledging their respective individual relationships.

Prof. Gerwel and Mrs Machel protested and said that Madiba deserved to have an office and a Personal Assistant to the day he died. Prof. Gerwel, who was Chairman of the Foundation, said that Madiba handpicked me and that he would refuse to sign off on me being made completely redundant when Madiba made that choice when he was in a position to choose the people around him. Madiba's office was closed and we were all made redundant, although I was reinstated on a part-time basis. But I was undermined and sidelined to such an extent that my position really became a ceremonial job. Both Maretha and Thoko, the other two staff members, with equally long service histories with Madiba, were told to go. I had luckily never been in it for the money, and I had been rewarded in ways money can never buy, and decided that I would remain committed to Madiba and Mrs Machel even if I was not paid anything. Loyalty and dedication can't be bought or paid to go away. I had also made a promise to myself and to him that I would never desert him until indeed the last day.

★

By the start of 2012 Madiba was permanently living in Qunu. I would travel there every week for a day or two to spend time with him. On 28 February 2012 I worked my last day as a full-time employee for Nelson Mandela. I didn't expect the next day to be any different but it was. I suddenly felt empty and without purpose. I know Madiba wouldn't have allowed it, but he was no longer making decisions or able to voice his wishes. In fact, he seemed to be slowly distancing himself from us. He was visibly old, needed permanent care and was no longer the jovial man we knew.

I was informed by the Foundation's CEO that my rank had to be changed from Executive Personal Assistant to Personal Assistant. In eighteen years I had gone from Typist to Assistant Private Secretary to Private Secretary to Manager and Spokesperson for his office and now finally back to Personal Assistant. It was actually laughable that love, care, loyalty and trust could take you on that roller-coaster ride.

I never had any aspirations to become anything other than whatever served his best interests, and I was not fazed by these latest attempts to marginalize me. You see, if Nelson Mandela believes in you, handpicks you and defends you until he is no longer able to do so, despite even criticism from the party that moulded him, little else should distract you in life. I never used these events to defend myself but allowed things to happen as they were probably supposed to happen. I never referred to the fact that I was chosen as I thought that it could be interpreted that I am conceited, but I always believed that there would come a time when I had to defend myself and on that day I would rationally think differently about things.

It is, I believe, one of the least attractive characteristics of us Afrikaners: we are brought up believing that we deserve nothing, we are nothing and we can accomplish nothing. Well, those who have achieved did so sterlingly and managed to raise themselves beyond these mental limitations. I really had to work hard at accepting the fact that I was chosen by Madiba to be anything. The upside is that you never ponder about these things and that probably prevents you from becoming absorbed with self-importance. I am the first to admit that I am nothing, was nothing, without Madiba gracing and blessing my life.

The poison within the family was leaking out everywhere. Many of his family had never wanted me around, and they were now getting their chance. But I still refused to abandon him. They didn't want me to fly down to Qunu every week to see him and I heard them asking our CEO 'What does she do there?' Even if I had to find a sponsor to fly me to Qunu every week for me to see him, I was willing to look for that. It was just Mrs Machel, household and medical staff there. He was lonely. President Zuma passed through from time to time and so did a few very close friends who went through the trouble to make the tedious trip to Qunu, but more and more he became isolated from the rest of the world. Whenever someone important visited, there would, however, be a sudden influx of interested parties. And from time to time we called on people like Ahmed Kathrada and other old friends to visit for the day, and one could see how they lifted his spirit whenever they came around.

Madiba always appeared very happy to see me. There was very little conversation but whenever Mrs Machel was around he enjoyed watching us converse and exchanging stories. He needed life around him. He needed people to touch him, care for him and create a sense of normality around him, so that he would not feel left behind. Some days the totality of our conversation would be: 'Oh Zeldina, you are here. How are your parents?' and I would tease him and say, 'Are you not going to ask how I am, Khulu?' and his shoulders would shrug with laughter. He would drowse off and wake up only to reach out to your hand. He did so with most visitors.

It was decided that the house in Qunu needed refurbishment and Madiba returned to Johannesburg for a while. Weeks quickly passed and it was easier to visit him more often. On a particular Friday afternoon Mrs Machel and I spoke about the son of Queen Beatrix of the Netherlands who had been seriously injured after a skiing accident. Mrs Machel tried to reach the Dutch royal family to convey our support. We had been close to them and therefore felt personally affected by the news.

That Friday night I went to bed thinking of the family in suffering. I sometimes put my phone on silent when I go to bed and the next morning I slept in for a little while. When I woke and picked up my phone I noticed that something was wrong. I had seven missed calls and sixteen messages. We were no longer working and there was no reason for the amount of communication in normal circumstances. The first message I opened was from Robyn Curnow, a journalist friend: 'Madiba is in hospital.' I responded: 'What, are you serious, how do you know?' She then told me it had been all over the news. I traced things back and discovered that indeed he was in hospital. I knew nothing. No one had told me. I contacted Josina and she confirmed it. She didn't know any details either. I then texted Mrs Machel to ask whether they were OK. I told her not to give me any detail of where or when but simply to tell me whether they were OK, as I didn't want to be blamed if it leaked. She gave me a brief overview about what was happening.

I don't know of any person alive who has been treated with the amount of disrespect that people have shown towards Mrs Machel. Politics within the family about his funeral took place for years before his death. In April 2005 the first article about funeral arrangements and a special committee dealing with such eventualities appeared in the *Noseweek* magazine. Mrs Machel and some of the children had refused to be party to arrangements about Madiba's funeral. He was still in fairly good health and it was unthinkable to be planning someone's funeral while the person was still happily alive, still being cared for by his wife. It is only much later in 2013 when the Minister of Defence Nosiviwe Nqakula empathetically reeled Mrs Machel in that she was consulted about certain arrangements and briefed about what had been planned. I do know that Mrs Machel had to put up a fight to get my name added to the funeral list. I made a promise to *him* though. I was going to be there right to the end, even if it meant I had to stand at a fence outside his farm in Qunu when they laid him to rest. Unbeknown to me, that would be close to the truth.

It is true what Madiba referred to sometimes . . . to test a man's character, give him power. Once people have power they will always reveal themselves.

Every time Madiba was admitted to hospital we held our breath. I knew by now that I had to seclude myself when he was hospitalized. I became a hermit at such times, not speaking to anyone, not answering my phone or even having conversations with my parents. I would not speak to anyone but Prof. Gerwel, Mrs Machel and Josina. They understood that if I was ever seen to break trust or leak information, I would simply be refused access to Madiba for the rest of my life because then the family would have reason to get rid of me. I was not going to give them that pleasure and I kept my distance and relied on updates from Mrs Machel. I was also becoming worried about her. She had a huge burden to deal with. The family was as divided as ever while she was worried sick about her husband's wellbeing.

At work pressure finally subsided from the public and apart from a few people who could not comprehend that Madiba would ever stop being actively involved, correspondence and requests became less. There was always that one request or proposal that someone thought had to be the exception to the rule and people would find reasons beyond logic why Nelson Mandela was the only one to support their ventures, or at least lend his association to endorse their efforts. I had realized over the years that if you continuously do negative things in your job, like saying no to people, it inevitably has a very negative impact on your psyche. You tend to become cynical by nature and it takes constant effort to pull yourself back from that negativity. With fewer requests and the negativity that came with them it was easier to find balance in life. I was opening myself to the next phase of my life.

People often ask me whether I don't regret not getting married or having children. It would be selfish and extremely ungrateful to use 'regret' when describing my life. I gained so much being with Madiba but I suppose I gave him my youth, and perhaps I gave him my future too. But I will never blame him for it – ultimately, I made that choice. Was it sacrifice? Or not? I don't feel burdened or sad that I might have lost oppportunities. I gained so much. I gained myself. I am completely content with the life that I have.

My part-time status and compromised income meant that I had to generate a salary and find something to challenge me again. I still had limited responsibility to Madiba and was adamant that I was not going to take another full-time job unless I was financially forced to do so. I was determined that I wanted to remain available to Madiba and Mrs Machel whenever they needed me, and I needed to make myself useful, but it was impossible and illogical to think that you could find another part-time job and be available to some-one else when there was a need for it.

It is the weirdest experience though. From being on a constant adrenalin rush for about eighteen years to a complete shutdown of that adrenalin overnight is not a joke. One needs to find purpose. It was hard. Certain factions within the family still wanted me out. On the first day of the 'rest of my life', 1 March 2012, I had a tattoo engraved around my left pulse to be reminded what I had discovered about myself along this journey. 'Pursue your passion.' As long as I did that, I knew I would be happy for the rest of my life. My passion is to serve and I find fulfilment when I serve people. I had the words tattooed in French because I also wanted to remind myself for the rest of my life about what Madiba had said: 'Find your roots', and since my family is of French descent I wanted the words in French.

The first few months of my new life were difficult. I still went to the office from time to time to do some administration and then went to see Madiba occasionally. It was announced that he would return to Qunu once they had renovated the house there. So soon I was back in my routine of travelling to Qunu weekly or every second week. Sometimes Madiba was talkative, sometimes he wasn't. Sometimes Mrs Machel and I would debate for the entire day about whatever was happening in the world and South Africa, the politics in the ANC, and world events like the Arab Spring and developments in other African countries, and occasionally Madiba would just smile at us with approval of the liveliness around him. We would sit in the lounge and converse, with Madiba suddenly pointing out to me that my handbag was on the floor and that I needed to pick it up. He was always there and totally aware of things happening around him. Sometimes I would call Prof. for Madiba just to say hello to him over the telephone. It always lit up Madiba's face whenever he heard Prof.'s voice. 'Oh Jakes,' he would say. 'I am happy to speak to you.' While sitting with him Madiba often drifted off into a nap in his favourite chair but then would suddenly wake up to check that we were still there. And once one thinks your privileges come to an end, there's sometimes even more. I had the most precious and valuable times there with them then.

Whenever Mum wasn't there, he would repeatedly ask: 'Where is Mum? When is she returning?' and then you had to recite the day of the week and exactly when she would be back. Mrs Machel and I would sometimes pass each other in mid-air – she would be off to Johannesburg for the day and I would visit Qunu – and by the end of the day it felt like Madiba asked one about two hundred times: 'Where is Mum?' He was totally reliant on her presence and unsettled whenever she was not around.

People were busy and hardly anyone visited. It was really a schlep to get there, in addition to the fact that Madiba didn't feel like seeing people every day so it was not always easy to invite even his closest friends for social visits. We stopped scheduling visits by people who weren't very familiar to him, but of course later realized that whenever we were not there occasionally some of the family would take advantage of our absence and take strangers to see Madiba. The Foundation then had to defend Madiba again when photos or reports of such visits appeared in the media. People would say: 'But if so and so got to see him, why can't I?' and the battles would start all over again, with us trying to diplomatically tell them that we didn't approve of the visits as we had been instructed that visitors would not be allowed any longer. On some occasions the Foundation declined a particular request for him to endorse or sign something, or even see certain people, and then would learn afterwards that the request had been agreed by someone in the family and they had allowed whatever to happen when Mrs Machel or I wasn't there. Some people started to take advantage of this when they realized that he no longer had the ability to argue or stand by his principles. Business people would call us to ask about strange requests they'd received from Madiba personally.

Madiba no longer really talked a lot so it was awkward to take people to him who didn't know him. There would be uncomfortable silences during visits.

By now I had moved from the neighbourhood I had so loved in Johannesburg because I could simply not afford to live there any longer. I was now staying on the outskirts of Johannesburg, which made travelling to and from the city a daily challenge. I wasn't bound to office hours but I had to watch my finances. I also started missing the friends and closeness I shared with people from my neighbourhood and I had to stop myself getting depressed. I felt neglected by the Foundation and removed from my friends and I realized that I had not built a steady support structure for myself over the years. Generally people were also getting on with their lives and I really had to struggle to find my feet again and pull myself together. I also lacked the courage to share my fears with many of my friends, probably also because I knew people perceived me to be a strong person and I had to keep up appearances. I also missed politics and having inside information about everything that happened in our country.

Prof. Gerwel hadn't seen or spent time with Madiba in many months and we decided that we had to make a special trip for him to go and visit Madiba. In August 2012 Prof. and I agreed on a date and I met him in East London, from where I drove him the 260 km to Qunu to see Madiba. We had a very special day and both Madiba and Prof. enjoyed seeing each other. They had a few good laughs and when I left to take Prof. back to East London that afternoon it crossed my mind that this was really an exceptionally enjoyable day for Madiba.

I loved Prof. but I think Madiba loved him even more. Mrs Machel also hardly ever saw Prof. and enjoyed spending time with him. We left agreeing that Prof. would start writing about Madiba's Presidency. Prof. and I drove back to East London and laughed about the years in the Presidency, the many things that had happened, the stressful times, and we both agreed that if we had known what lay ahead we would probably have made different choices when we were not so emotionally attached to Madiba. The three hours back to East London took us on a journey through memories of eighteen years, and when we said our goodbyes at the airport I knew Prof. was happy and pleased about the day he had spent with Madiba. He sent a text message later that evening when he got home, thanking me that I'd insisted he made time in his busy schedule to be with Madiba. He was engaged on so many fronts, served on countless boards and was involved in so many things but I was happy that I forced him to take a day out to travel so far to see Madiba.

When a few months later I received the news that Prof. had died, I was sleeping in my bed in the Holiday Inn in Umtata, about 40 km away from Qunu. When Madiba was told by Mum of Prof.'s passing the sadness and sense of loss was visible in his eyes and he went completely quiet for hours. It is difficult to tell how a person of that age will react to such news and Mrs Machel had to ensure that her timing was impeccable so as to soften the blow of such a shock. She was scheduled to travel to Johannesburg for the day but subsequently cancelled her travels to be with Madiba, uncertain how he would digest such shock and sadness.

It is difficult to try and put value to Prof. Gerwel's role in the previous eighteen years of our lives. Take whatever you believe anyone could mean to you and multiply it by 100. That's more or less it. Prof. had a way of dealing with things in the most unconventional ways. When we all tended to grapple with a particular issue he would be the one to come up with the most balanced solution that would make everyone feel that they were winners, even though they were actually compromising in a way, as Koos Bekker, the CEO of Naspers, put it at his funeral. He was definitely not a push-over and people easily respected him. He would watch things silently from a distance and then make one pronouncement to steer the issue in a totally new direction and thereby assist you to come up with your own solutions. He listened to every word I ever said to him, no matter how mundane or how much complaining I did, and if I was wrong he was the one person to honestly and openly but respectfully point it out to me.

During Madiba's Presidency Prof. used to travel with us a lot and he was very involved in our everyday lives. After retirement from government that involvement diminished but Prof. was always just a phone call away. I could call him from anywhere in the world to ask his advice on any matter. And he would be my first point of contact whether it was a major incident or something really stupid or funny that happened. We gossiped and joked, but then when it came to serious matters he was a leading father-figure to me. He loved his Afrikaans and we would have very open, honest conversations and, in joking, then sometimes use very expressive Afrikaans sayings that made us both laugh. He was a person who related to anyone in any situation and he role-played perfectly. He could guide a conversation with a foreign head of state and the next minute address the most junior office staff and make them feel like their interaction was more enjoyable than that of the more important people.

On the day of Prof.'s memorial, Chief Justice Arthur Chaskalson also passed away. He was appointed by Madiba as the head of the Constitutional Court in South Africa, the most senior judicial position in the country. Minutes before we entered the memorial, I received a message from the Judge's son to tell me his dad had died. One of our favourite ministers, Trevor Manuel, was presiding as programme director during Prof.'s memorial and I told him about the Judge's passing. So before proceedings started we also observed a minute of silence for Judge Chaskalson. Two key figures in our lives that passed on in one week. It was too much to bear. I was heartbroken: the one person I expected to be by our side right to the end was Prof. I was also angry, in a way, that he wouldn't be there the day we buried Madiba. But such is life. Whenever Madiba spoke about mortality or people started discussing his, I realized that any of us could go before him. And Prof. leaving us was proof of it.

A few months before, the security personnel with Madiba, Mrs Machel and some household staff noticed that two new people had joined the medical team looking after Madiba. Mum, security, some of the household staff and I wondered if they could possibly be intelligence agents. The permanent medical team looking after Madiba didn't know them either. I sent a message to President Zuma's office to ask whether they were aware of this arrangement. I received a response that they would look into the matter and get back to me. I heard nothing. So I sent another message, this time adding 'this situation could potentially cause a huge embarrassment to government as this is clearly infringing on Madiba and his family's privacy and dignity.'

I immediately received a response that the matter was reported to the Minister of Intelligence and that I could expect a response from him soon. And so I did. Minister Siyabonga Cwele called me minutes later to enquire about the situation and again about an hour later informing me that the staff did not belong to National Intelligence but that he would still discuss the matter with the Surgeon General to assess whether the military approved of such placement. I repeated to the Minister what I said in the text to the Presidency. I never heard from the Minister again, but three weeks later these two characters disappeared and then reappeared a few weeks later despite our enquiry. We could never figure out their mission. I was disgusted at how I understood state resources were being used and there is little else that angered me as much. Influences were at play that allowed people to abuse state resources for their own benefit. We had a terrible problem with corruption within government – probably the biggest threat to our democracy – and this was a clear example of a corrupt government that allows this kind of interference in their business.

Kgalema Motlanthe was our Deputy President at the time. His relationship with Madiba dated back many years in the ANC. Madiba was very fond of Kgalema and he hadn't seen him for some time. A visit was arranged to Qunu on Friday, 7 December. On Thursday I was made aware of Kgalema's intention to visit. I was happy to hear that but had no intention myself to get onto another plane that week. Then suddenly Kgalema's office called to say that the visit was cancelled from our side. Meme, the housekeeper, told me that Madiba was not having a good day but in order to control wild speculation she had asked the Deputy President's office to cancel the visit from their side. But now the Deputy President wanted to know from me what the reason was for cancelling the visit. The ANC's national conference was planned to start in a week from that day. We all had our suspicions whether there was any political interference about the cancellation of his visit. I called back to say that it was really just that Madiba was not having a good day. It was an awkward situation. Yet, by now, we were used to Madiba just not feeling up to seeing people on some days and he would prefer to stay in bed. We really assumed it was one of those days.

On Saturday, 8 December I was in a radio studio when Achmat Dangor called. By now I had agreed to co-present a Saturday lifestyle show on a local radio station. I couldn't take the call and called him back as soon as the show ended. He said that there was speculation about Madiba's health and that the Sunday papers were trying to put a reason to the cancellation of Kgalema's visit. I called Meme and she assured me again that Madiba was fine. I could actually hear him talk in the background while on the phone to her and I called Achmat back to tell him that. The phone didn't stop ringing.

Two hours later it was on the news. Madiba had been admitted to hospital in Pretoria for a routine medical check-up. And again my response was 'What?' I sent Mrs Machel a text: 'Mum are you OK? I hear Madiba is in hospital.' She didn't read or respond to the message at first. We suspected that our phones and conversations were being monitored. In South Africa, if you pose a threat to the stability of the country, or you plan an act of terrorism, your phone could be tapped. We did neither of these but we wondered if government officials including medics were under instructions from some of the family to report Mrs Machel's every move to them. I later got a call from Meme explaining that they had been told by the medical team not to tell anyone what was happening, but indeed that Madiba had been taken to Pretoria to a hospital. I didn't understand this. Why did they have to rush him so secretively to Pretoria?

Again we started holding our breath. This was just unbelievable. I am not superstitious at all but couldn't help thinking that Prof. may have gone first to prepare for Madiba, and my own thoughts scared me. Soon Mrs Machel told me what was going on and I could hear that she was under tremendous pressure. She was stressed, worried and concerned. It was clear that I had to wait for the storm to pass before I could try to go and see him. Eventually Josina and I went off to see him a few days later. I was anxious and didn't want to make the same mistake as I'd done with Prof. – by the time I managed to visit Prof. in hospital in Cape Town before he passed away he was already unconscious and I didn't want a repeat of that. Madiba recognized me and briefly interacted with me and that calmed me down. I just needed him to say 'Oh Zeldina' and I would be fine. I relied, like everyone in the world, on him being well. We spent some time with Mum and then we left.

The public were anxious about events as the government failed to issue regular statements to update them on his progress. By now we had been told that the government would handle all communication around his well-being and I had no desire or wish to interfere with that task. I knew too well how difficult it was to deal with things around Madiba – something very few people wanted to ever give me credit for – and now it was their turn and I was happy about that while I dealt with my own emotions.

I was deeply troubled about Madiba's illness and as with any ninety-four-year-old his condition changed every day. One day it was good, the next day it was not so good. I soon packed my things and left to go to my parents for the holiday. I couldn't take it any more and I was unable to visit him.

While on holiday Mrs Machel sent me a message one day to say that Madiba was doing better and that he had started calling one of the white nurses 'Zeldina', and that she thought he missed me. There was nothing I could do. As much as I wanted to be there, I also had to be with my parents for Christmas. I could no longer see Madiba regularly or just pop in, and I silently hoped that he didn't think I really neglected him. My parents were also getting old and I was starting to realize that they too were not going to be around for ever. I had neglected them for years as a result of my job, more than seven years not spending Christmas with them while I was organizing children's Christmas parties in Qunu; it was time to correct that and spend time with them.

When I arrived back from visiting my parents at the coast over Christmas Madiba was discharged from hospital and settling in back at home. I resumed my, now limited, duties at the Foundation and tried to keep busy as much as possible. Some days I really got depressed, staying in bed the entire day. It was not healthy. As much as I wanted to see Madiba I was mindful also that certain staff members in the household texted or called Makaziwe to report to her whenever I was in the house to visit him. I was waiting for them to tell me that I wasn't welcome.

It was time for the first screening of the documentary *Miracle Rising*, in London. It was a powerful story of South Africa's transition between 1990 and 1994. Although questions were asked of the interviewees about Madiba's role in the transitional period, the focus was very much on Cyril Ramaphosa and Roelf Meyer, who led the negotiations for a peaceful settlement between the ANC and the National Party at the Convention for a Democratic South Africa (Codesa). The production company flew me to London for the screening at end January as part of the production team. I hadn't travelled in a while and was excited to leave the country. The screening was well received and I was proud to have been involved when I saw the final product. I enjoyed seeing people I had lost contact with or no longer regularly had dealings with since we stopped travelling. I wasn't overly impressed with all the celebrities who were interviewed in the documentary but understood that for it to appeal to the broader public the celebs were the selling factor. I liked contributing to history in this way as I could comprehend the difficulties we faced at the time. The documentary was also aired in South Africa and was well received.

On 14 February 2013, the Paralympic athlete Oscar Pistorius shot and killed his model-girlfriend Reeva Steenkamp when he allegedly mistook her for an intruder. The country went into a complete state of shock. One of our heroes had fallen, and with him our hope, and everything the new South Africa embodied, the miracle, somehow stumbled. I don't know why it mattered so much, but we all felt a sense of loss that Valentine's Day. People, especially South Africans, always wanted a hero. Madiba was every man's hero and so was Oscar for overcoming his disability and putting South Africa on the map. People idolized him. Madiba always warned against people idolizing others, including him, too much. He knew too well that one could easily fall. We'd put Oscar on a pedestal so high that the fall was greater than we could have anticipated.

In *Conversations With Myself*, Madiba wrote in a letter to Winnie Mandela on 9 December 1979:

> We are told that a saint is a sinner who keeps on trying to be clean. One may be a villain for ¾ of his life and be canonized because he lived a holy life for the remaining ¼ of that life. In real life we deal, not with gods, but with ordinary humans like ourselves: men and women who are full of contradictions, who are stable and fickle, strong and weak, famous and infamous, people in whose bloodstream the muckworm battles daily with potent pesticides.

He believed that there was good and bad in every human being and made me change my thinking about people whenever something like this happened. I realized again how much Madiba had changed my thinking and perceptions about things we consider straightforward.

On 9 March 2013 Madiba was back in hospital. I was told by Mrs Machel that it wasn't serious but for a simple medical procedure. Again it was a reminder of just how vulnerable he was. Every time he got admitted to hospital, I was reminded that my time with him was becoming limited.

On 22 March after his discharge I tried to visit Madiba three times. The first time I arrived at his house, Makaziwe was there. She had made it clear in a previous discussion about me that I was not welcome to see her father. I no longer had work to do there. I was adamant that she was not to determine that and decided that I would try and avoid her but that I would not stay away just because it pleased her. Mum had to defend me once again, arguing that she was willing to defend Madiba's decisions whether they liked it or not, and that she was going to see that his wishes were fulfilled until the day he passed on. She told them that my presence from time to time provided him with emotional stability and when I heard that she said that I quietly thought: Yes, *my* emotional stability too, selfish as it may seem. I couldn't help but feel that one gets chewed and then spat out when people no longer see a use for you. I know too well how Madiba would feel about that, but it is not my place to try and judge how or what he may have felt at this stage. I was torn between fighting and leaving things to play out, and the latter seems to be the lesson I'll take with me.

The second time, at around 3 p.m., when I wanted to visit again, Makaziwe was still there. By now Mrs Machel had left for her office. I decided to return home and agreed with Mrs Machel to return at 6 p.m. I hadn't seen Madiba in two weeks and planned to spend time with my family for the days to follow and was therefore eager to see Madiba before I left. At 6 p.m. when I went back to the house Makaziwe had gone. Mrs Machel was seeing someone when I arrived and because I also had business to discuss with her, I agreed to wait until she had finished.

It seemed to me that, as usual, the household staff that sided with Makaziwe texted or called her to tell her that I was there. Soon she arrived again. Mysteriously the staff disappeared as I was waiting in the kitchen. Makaziwe entered and closed the door behind her. She said: 'Oh I've been wanting to talk to you about something for some time. There are rumours going around that you are working on a documentary film with the History Channel entitled "Mandela: The Last Years". I wanted to say to you that since you are one of the people Tata trusted most, it would be highly unethical of you to do something like that.'

What surprised me was that she admitted for the first time in her life that I had any role to play in her father's life. She had probably heard about the *Miracle Rising* documentary, which did not focus on Madiba at all, and confused the two issues but I was not bothered to correct her. My commitment was to her father and my trust relationship is with him. I am committed to protecting his dignity and integrity and that of his wife but my commitment does not go beyond that. People may then argue, why am I talking about it now? But I feel this is different. I am not infringing his dignity. This is not an account of his medical state or how illness and suffering affected him. There are many things that I will never talk or write about. My relationship was with Madiba. Not with the family or anyone else.

As the conversation was heating up Mrs Machel called for me. Saved by the bell, I thought, or I may have said things I would later regret. I briefly saw her and left without seeing Madiba as Makaziwe had gone upstairs to be with her father and I knew she would chase me out. I was deeply disappointed about not seeing him but angry enough to realize that it would not be the best time for me to persist trying to do so. The next week I returned and managed to see him. His face lit up when he saw me and he exclaimed: 'Oh Zeldina, you are here.' 'Yes Khulu I am, how are you?' He just gave me a thumbs-up and then said: 'How are your parents?' I was so incredibly touched. He no longer spoke much and this was again the extent of our entire conversation that day, but he had it in him to ask about my parents. How inexplicably had this man changed my life, my thinking and, most importantly, my heart! I sat with him for a while holding his hand and when he dozed off I left.

A few days later news broke of Zenani and Makaziwe challenging the appointment of Madiba's long-time friend George Bizos, his lawyer Bally Chuene and Comrade Minister Tokyo Sexwale to a trust that managed the sale of artworks from the 'hands and art' project. Madiba appointed these trustees to oversee matters on his behalf. This was going to be an ugly fight. I was deeply disturbed by the news and thought (or was under the impression) that the matter had been resolved a few months before. As these private matters never concerned me I didn't bother enquiring about them often. Insults and counter-allegations followed in the media, each party feeding information to their own sources and lashing out in the most disrespectful way towards one of Madiba's oldest friends, Advocate Bizos. What effectively happened was that Zenani and Makaziwe were challenging their father's decisions. They knew very well that he was no longer able to defend himself or his decisions and it was the time for them to challenge these as they knew no one could rely on Madiba's evidence any longer.

I was not going to enter into their private business now but agreed with the trustees' lawyer that if and when called upon I would support their defence. My resolution was easy. If Madiba wanted to appoint any of his children in charge of his affairs, he would have done so when he was able to. And I was willing to defend his decisions with the facts at hand. The same applied to appointing staff and people in charge of his charities, and his lawyers could vouch for that.

Later it emerged in the lawyer's defending affidavit that indeed Zenani Dlamini and Makaziwe Mandela were acting against their father's wishes. The lawyer produced proof of minutes from meetings that we all remembered too well when Madiba made his wishes very clear. The case was then withdrawn.

I had to remind myself that this was not my battle to fight. I had to focus on ensuring that Mrs Machel had the support she needed and that I gave Madiba the occasional hug and smile and held his hand. I often found Zoleka, one of Madiba's grandchildren, with him whenever I visited during this time. She was the mother of Zenani Jnr, who was killed in the car accident in 2010 just prior to the FIFA World Cup opening. Zoleka wasn't threatened by my presence and was comfortable with me sitting with her grandfather. She had really made an effort to spend time with him almost every day and I could see that he enjoyed it.

On 27 March 2013 Madiba was admitted to hospital again. He had pneumonia again. A few days before I had visited him in the house and recall one of the housekeepers having a terrible flu while I was there. As I left I shook my head in disbelief. And here he was back in hospital with pneumonia. At that age he was much more susceptible to germs. Yet in his own household people were working even though they were sick. If they were sick, why where they still there? One just has to know when to give up. Not because you want to, but because you have to.

And once again the world held its breath. These were the most difficult times I had ever experienced. I've grown to realize that it is good that one never knows what lies ahead because you would easily give up at an early stage. Whatever I had thought were the worst experiences, these were, by far, the most stressful times of anxiety and uncertainty. I was desperate to go to the hospital but realized that I had to stay away as long as Makaziwe was there. I wanted to spare Madiba an altercation and I was simply willing to take the lead from Mrs Machel and Josina as to when I could visit. On the day that they agreed, Josina drove me in. We noticed the media camping outside the hospital and were fearful that they caught us both on camera. Like in 2011, if we were to appear in the media together I was afraid that I would experience what I felt to be outrage from some of the family. When we left, we agreed that I would hide on the back seat to avoid anyone seeing me. As much as we were tense and stressed about Madiba, we had some relief laughing about my lying down on the seat. I felt like I was a Cold War spy being driven from East Berlin to West Berlin. Madiba stayed in hospital for eleven nights and was then moved back to Johannesburg.

Once he recovered satisfactorily, Mrs Machel and I planned to have some of his old colleagues and friends visit occasionally. Weeks before, the ANC executive asked to pay a visit to Madiba. On the day I contacted them to come for the visit, they had some crisis to attend to and asked to postpone. I responded telling them to please tell us when they were ready as we would encourage them to visit. But then Madiba fell ill again and some weeks passed without either party following up on the matter.

By early 2013 Dr Mamphela Ramphele announced that she was establishing a new political party with the aim of contesting the general elections to be held in 2014. The only sizeable opposition to the ruling ANC party is the Democratic Alliance, a party largely still seen as dominated by white people even though they are much more liberal than the old National Party. Dr Ramphele is a well-respected academic in South Africa, a former activist against apartheid and a leading businesswoman. She is also a trustee of the Nelson Mandela Foundation since its inception. Her announcement was welcomed by a lot of people, but the party, Agang, seemed to lose momentum fast. Dr Ramphele was the first person to advise Madiba on health matters after his release in 1990. She introduced him to the cardiologist who treated him for many years until the Defence Force medical team took over his care from private specialists. Dr Ramphele was therefore an old friend to Madiba and a good friend to Mrs Machel. She paid a visit to Mrs Machel on a particular day when Madiba was well enough to sit downstairs in his lounge. She saw him and was disturbed about his deterioration as she hadn't seen him in a very long time. Her visit was brief but she then mistakenly announced in a radio interview that she had seen him.

A week before, the Democratic Alliance had launched its election campaign entitled 'Know your DA'. Part of the campaign was to inform the public of the DA's policy and in doing so they used a picture of their founder, the late Mrs Helen Suzman, where she walked with Madiba, him embracing her. This made the ANC nervous and they lashed out at the DA for using an image of Madiba in their election campaign. The DA's campaign as well as Dr Ramphele's visit made the ANC unnecessarily nervous. No one had ever contested the fact that Madiba was part and parcel of the ANC and that it was a lifelong commitment, yet these interactions made the ANC somehow feel challenged over their 'ownership' of Madiba.

The Reverend Jesse Jackson was in South Africa to receive a national award from President Zuma for his contribution to the liberation struggle of South Africa. Rev. Jackson wanted to see Madiba and someone from the Presidency contacted me, telling me that the President wanted him to ask me about a possible visit to Madiba. Madiba was really not well enough to receive visitors and especially not people he was not very familiar with. I explained to the gentleman from the Presidency that a visit was not possible and he responded that he understood and would convey the sentiments to the President and Rev. Jackson.

One of the people who was on our list to visit Madiba as soon as he was well enough was Deputy President Kgalema Motlanthe, who had been trying and asking to see Madiba for months. He had contested the Presidency of the ANC at their national conference in December 2012 and had lost. He was sidelined by the party and it was clear that his challenge to President Zuma was not well received by all. Madiba was very fond of Kgalema and Mrs Machel and I discussed a possible visit. On the Friday night I contacted Kgalema's assistant to say that we would try something the following week, providing that Madiba was well enough. I told him not to repeat our conversation to anyone.

Since my contract had been changed by the Foundation and I only worked part time for them, there were certain days I didn't go to Johannesburg, when I didn't have work to do on that particular day or when I decided to work from home. On that Monday I was busy with something else and on my motorbike for most of the day. I didn't follow what was happening on Twitter and was pretty much off line most of the day.

While I was away, the ANC had come calling. What was strange was that they had insisted the visit be filmed – as a sort of 'proof of life' that Madiba was 'well'. The ploy backfired – Madiba did not look well or happy with the visit.

Upon returning to Johannesburg in the evening I checked Twitter and noticed total outrage from the public over video material about Madiba that appeared on the news that night. I didn't know anything. I found it on YouTube and was disgusted by what I saw. Madiba was clearly not happy. There was total chaos in his lounge and because it was a visit by the President and senior members of the ANC, flash photography was allowed – something that every South African knew was prohibited because of the sensitivity of Madiba's eyes. In the footage Madiba appeared withdrawn because he was overwhelmed. It was clear to me from what I witnessed that there was no control. Even the medical staff responsible for his health, General Dabula and Surgeon General Ramlakan, were themselves taking photos rather than protecting Madiba's eyes and looking out for his well-being. I was disturbed. Was this what it all had come to? It was like a zoo and Madiba was the caged animal that the tourists all fawned over. He looked helpless. Mrs Machel was attending meetings at the Foundation, literally two minutes from the house, and she was not even informed of the visit.

They didn't tell me about the visit at the house, probably because they knew that I would not tolerate such drama. People detested me for keeping order and telling them what to do around Madiba and it was clear why. If I wasn't there, this is what they did. A war broke out on Twitter and journalists asked where I was. I had to literally sit on my hands to stop myself from replying. The next day when I arrived at the Foundation the then CEO, Achmat Dangor, commented with disgust over the footage, and I said: 'Well this is what they all wanted, isn't it?' Isn't this why people argued so fiercely that Madiba no longer needed a secretary? If I had still been there, I wouldn't have allowed him to go in front of the media looking so weak and vulnerable. I wasn't the only one who was upset. The public and family were outraged with the ANC.

In the weeks to follow it got easier for me to see Madiba. The family eased their 'watch' over him and I could visit him more freely. I never knew on any day if that was going to be the last time I ever saw him.

★

On 8 June 2013 he was back in hospital and the Presidency announced that his condition was serious but stable. It was a recurring lung infection. We were filled with anxiety. We realized that it was on a knife's edge this time. Two days after his admittance I sneaked back into the hospital early one morning on the back seat of Josina's car. He was clearly very sick and weak but opened his eyes and managed a smile.

It was only then that I was told about events of the night of his admission. Someone, either medical or security personnel, decided to take him to hospital in an unmarked military medical vehicle to avoid suspicion from the public. My first question: 'Who in the public is watching him at 3 a.m. in the morning?' Halfway to the hospital in Pretoria the unmarked vehicle broke down. Forty minutes later help arrived. At first I thought this was a joke. How can Nelson Mandela, gravely sick, be stuck along a highway in the middle of winter for forty minutes at three in the morning? How is this possible? It was good that I had not been told earlier. I think it would have pushed me over the edge. I had been disabled in every possible way. Disarmed. I had no influence or power to question these matters any longer. And I felt I had neglected Madiba and Mrs Machel. My heart bled for them. How scared Madiba must have been! How scared Mrs Machel must have been, helpless, stressed! When I saw her she was clearly traumatized. How do things come to this? How does this happen to Nelson Mandela, the world's most revered person alive? And the fact that he was still alive was clearly only a miracle.

Soon the media set up camp outside the hospital. Journalists were flying in from all over the world. Millions of dollars were spent on outside broadcast vans as people around the world watched with bated breath. However, inside, the fighter was slowly making his way back. Some people in public argued that it was time for us to 'let him go'. 'Stop praying for his recovery,' some said. What they had missed was that the hard-headed freedom fighter was going to decide for himself when enough was eventually enough. I worked twelve-plus hours per day responding to people from across the world and at home who wanted answers and confirmation of what the President had said – he was critical but stable. I simply confirmed exactly what the President had said and was vague in my responses but people were anxious. Josina and I had long conversations and we anchored one another. I was mindful that, if one didn't help to ease the anxiety, the anxiety would soon rub off on the family and eventually Madiba would feel it too.

During one of her visits to the hospital, Madiba's daughter Zindzi asked Josina whether I had been there. Zindzi explained by saying that she thought I should be given the opportunity to visit her father, upon which Josina said I had been there a few days before. Zindzi replied: 'Then I can rest.' I was very touched when I heard that. Someone other than the Machels was looking out for me and I was grateful. The day after my visit security at the hospital had been tightened. Josina and I laughed when I told her I had thought that the extra security was probably because I'd sneaked in on the back seat of her car. I then told her I had convinced myself that not everything was about me. Amid the anxiety these unbelievable things at least made us laugh. It was later reported in the news that the tightened security was to keep journalists out. I was happy it wasn't about me.

The last time I saw Madiba alive was on 11 July 2013, the night before I departed on my annual Bikers for Mandela Day ride across the country, doing my bit for Mandela Day. I entered the hospital with Malenga Machel, Mrs Machel's son. We used a back entrance so we would not be spotted by the media. Madiba was still very sick. I gave Malenga a chance to spend some time with Madiba and his mother alone, and they then called me in. Madiba could still open his eyes and show emotion but then drifted off quickly. I was shivering standing next to his bed, shocked to see him in the state that he was in. I couldn't see his hands. I wanted to touch his hand but I couldn't find it. I was helpless, numb. Mrs Machel told him I was there but his eyes remained closed. She then nodded at me that it was OK to start speaking to him.

I knew I had to sound cheerful and not sad and said, 'Hello,

Khulu. It's Zeldina. I am here to see you . . .' and there it was. He opened his eyes, followed by the biggest brightest smile and he looked at me and fixed his eyes upon me. 'How are you Khulu? You look well,' although he didn't. 'I miss you, Khulu,' I said and he kept on smiling. Mum and Malenga were making fun of me, joking that Madiba had not afforded others that smile but to me he did. Then he drifted off again and closed his eyes. I stood there for a few minutes and Mum and Malenga went to the side of the room and Mum said I could talk to him if I wanted to. I said what needed to be said, again. I composed myself and told him that I was leaving on my bike trip the following day, reminded him about his comment about my bike trip the first year back in 2010, when he'd said: 'Why did you do that?' and I responded: 'For you, Khulu.' I was on my way for him again. I was very sad that night to leave but the smile was all I needed to keep me going. I didn't expect that to be the last time I saw him.

Upon my return to Johannesburg after the bike trip I tried to go on a few occasions. But every time I asked Mum there was something that prevented me from going. I went back twice, seeing Mum on other business, but I couldn't see him.

On 15 June an article had appeared on the front page of the *Saturday Star*, repeated in the Afrikaans Sunday paper *Rapport* the following day. Shaun van Heerden, a trusted bodyguard and friend for more than ten years, had snapped. He had been suspended for a second time following allegations from the Surgeon General that he had leaked information to the media about Madiba's whereabouts when he was hospitalized. In the article he referred to the incident at the Soccer World Cup in 2010 and the Defence Force medical staff ruling our world with an iron fist. I felt very sorry for Shaun. He was the one that helped me to see Madiba whenever I was at the house and Mrs Machel wasn't there to get me through the red tape being placed by the family to keep me out. I didn't know how I would cope without Shaun.

A few days later the story about the ambulance that broke down as Madiba was transported to hospital made world headlines after it leaked to the media. Newspapers described Mrs Machel as being 'frantic' during these events. The next day Makaziwe entered the hospital calling Mrs Machel 'Ms Frantic'. Mum was hurt and emotionally brutalized and Josina and I constantly tried to keep her strong by supporting her. Josina often went to support her mother whenever I couldn't. I missed Prof. He would have been there for us, he would have guided us, and his death left a void that is so difficult to explain.

In the week prior to Madiba's hospitalization I'd received word from a good friend who worked at the South African Breweries that they'd managed to track down our old family housekeeper, Jogabeth. She had been on my mind for years and on occasion I'd tried to find her but then abandoned the search when I hit a brick wall. But her husband was on a pension from the SAB and, just by my providing his name and a bit about his location back in the 1980s, they'd managed to find them for me. I immediately texted my mother and brother and we all called Jogabeth and Esau one night. We were overwhelmed with happiness to be reconnected. We planned to have a get-together but then Madiba fell ill and we had to postpone. My heart was filled with joy and my eyes filled with tears when Jogabeth said: 'All these years I have seen you on TV and thought "my Zellie has grown up" but how was I going to contact her again?' I was touched by her feeling of belonging. I hope to meet her soon, to reconnect and to see if there is anything I can do for them to help them in their old age. There was a time she gave up her life for me. It is time to return the favour.

And Madiba never ceased to amaze us. Even through the extended period of his illness he gave us and the world the time to prepare for a life without him. It took its toll on everyone. People were emotionally depleted. I would often dream about him at night. Sometimes good dreams and sometimes nightmares. I woke up every morning and realized with a shock that he was still ill. I would nervously reach for my cellphone to check if there had been any news or messages about him during the night. I was constantly worrying about him. During brief moments one continued with life as normal but then reality jerked me back to this state of limbo we were all in. I started feeling useless and worthless. My job was no longer a full-time occupation and time was treating me like a ship in the perfect storm at sea. Emotional ups and downs every day, frustrated and hurt by my inability to see him or to reach out to him. My dreams became vivid and in the morning I had to convince myself that it was only a dream. They occurred more frequently as I prepared myself to take the final step away from him.

What worried me most and kept me awake was whether during this prolonged illness there was ever a moment when he was conscious enough to think: Why hasn't Zeldina been here? I cringe when I think about the fact that it may have crossed his mind that in the end I had perhaps left him as I promised I would never do. Did he think that I had neglected or abandoned him? And now, nineteen years later, I was longing to put my white hand on his dark skin; to touch the skin I was brought up to believe was not as good as mine. Yet it was that dark skin that gave my life significance. My entire being at the age of forty-three yearned to touch that hand once more, to feel the ripples around his knuckles, to see his smile lighting up the room when I say: 'Don't worry Khulu, I did not desert you.'

13

Tot weersiens Khulu!

There is a scene in the movie *Long Walk to Freedom* where the character of Nelson Mandela slowly walks up a hill in Qunu. His back is towards the camera, as he walks away. The light is gentle, his familiar gait meandering up a gentle slope. I knew it wasn't him. It was Idris Elba, a British actor, but the image was so powerful, so evocative, so gutwretching that I burst into tears in the cinema. The tears came and came, over and over and in a way I have never experienced before. They just pumped from my eyes uncontrollably and streamed down my cheeks. It didn't help that I tried to stop it. That night when I first saw *Long Walk to Freedom* at its premiere in South Africa I also cried myself to sleep, something I had never done in forty-three years. It was like a pre-mourning. I knew Madiba had almost gone. That he was in pain. But this re-enactment of his life pierced through all that and reminded me about him so much.

Madiba never got to see the movie. It was released in November 2013 when he was near the end. It was a story he had given his blessing to almost two decades earlier. The producer, Anant Singh, bought the rights to Madiba's life story and it had taken twenty years for it to come to the big screen, just in time for us to be reminded of his story.

Besides reminding us of Madiba's sacrifices, the movie also reminded me of a younger, fitter Nelson Mandela. His body was so broken, so damaged and deteriorated now but in the movie he was strong, robust, vibrant. He loved to dance, not that shuffle of his later years when his knees had given out, but the jazzy bop of the 1950s. Madiba used to tell us how he went dancing in Sophiatown and through the movie I could now visualize such stories. We would often sit during lunch or dinner on foreign travels, often just the two of us, and he would eagerly offer the details of his early life and he had the perfect audience in me. I had never had a problem allowing my imagination to run with a story and I would question him about his looks, his posture, his dress code, whether he charmed girls and what the dancing was like. He was amused by my directness and I often asked: 'Did women just fall over their feet to dance with you?' and he would laugh in a somewhat shy way and boast with a 'Yes of course!', upon which I would burst out laughing.

I had stopped seeing Madiba a few months before. Mrs Machel called me to the house one day to have tea, after Madiba had been discharged, although he was still considered critical but stable. She said that she knew how much I loved Madiba and that she didn't think it was advisable for me to see his deterioration knowing how I felt about him. At first I had suspected that the family told her to tell me that I was no longer able to see him, but after thinking about it I was happy that it happened. I didn't want to see him in a power-less state. I didn't want to lose control over my emotions in his presence. It was only after his death that I learned that indeed I had been banned from seeing him.

I was constantly battling in my mind, trying to understand why he didn't let go and whether he was able to let go himself. It haunts you. It eats you daily, piece by piece, not knowing and not under-standing what was happening to him.

At times I wondered, like many South Africans, whether he was being kept alive artificially. But Mrs Machel and Josina told me there was a still a spark there, that he occasionally held someone's hand or managed to open his eyes. But by November even that didn't happen. He was slipping away, despite an overwhelming effort by the doctors to keep him alive.

His doctors thought it was amazing that he had such strength even when he was so weak. I often wondered – was he now becom-ing afraid of dying? He was often flippant about death, saying things like 'when you're gone your body is dead'. People raised the issues around his ancestors not having called upon him yet and I wondered whether he was aware of these issues. He was respectful of tradition but not overly obsessed with it.

As the days passed, I was permanently on standby, anxious, waiting for an update on his health. You start living in a permanent state of limbo. I communicated with Mrs Machel and Josina by text and messaging because we were worried. Sometimes I met them trying to resume duties as normal and I would not often ask too many questions but just 'Is he OK?', 'Mum, do you think he is free of pain?' or 'Mum, do you think he is aware of what is happening?' I was also trying to be one less person asking after him and, rather, showing my support to him, through supporting her. He had after all told me the first day I met her in Paris back in 1996 that I had to look after her and not lose sight of her at any given point. I was still doing just that.

And then the message that I knew was inevitable. On 3 December Mum and Josina told me that Madiba's condition was deteriorating. This seemed like the beginning of the end.

I saw Josina on Thursday, 5 December at the Foundation. She looked exhausted.

Early evening on Thursday, 5 December Josina phoned me with instructions from Mrs Machel. I had to inform some of Madiba's closest friends that things were turning for the worse. It was so hard. So brutally frank. It took me hours to get hold of everyone on my list. They included people like Archbishop Emeritus Desmond Tutu, Ahmed Kathrada, Thabo Mbeki, George Bizos and others close to Madiba but who were outside government structures and who would not normally be informed in such instances. I was strong when I started making the calls but their reaction, a mixture of pain, shock and disbelief destroyed the strong spirit with which I started off. After each call I composed myself and repeated Madiba's quote: 'It always seems impossible until it is done', and I would call the next person.

Later in the evening two helicopters flew dangerously low over my house. As I lived halfway between Pretoria, the base where military helicopters were stationed, and Johannesburg, where Madiba's house was, the helicopters had to fly over the area where I lived. Was the military preparing for the worst? Or had it happened? If it was the military it meant that it had happened. There were two issues to consider: firstly they probably became involved at that point from a protocol point of view, and secondly I thought that they perhaps feared the much speculated *uhuru* or 'night of the long knives' when, it was said, blacks would kill whites the night after Madiba died. It was only the extremists that participated in this kind of talk and I knew by now that South Africa was stronger and more capable as a nation of dealing with what we all feared, black and white: Madiba's death.

And then it was done. I just knew he was gone. I didn't have to ask. I was numb for a few minutes and then I jumped up from my chair at the kitchen table thinking it would stop me from becoming hysterical. I went outside and sat quietly alone in the hot summer night just thinking, praying and trying to internalize what had just happened. I was alone at home and my first instinct was that I had to pray, light candles and then get to bed as soon as possible. I knew what lay ahead. My phone started going crazy. I didn't answer anyone and rumours were running. About two hours later I started receiving messages from as far away as Los Angeles: 'Is Madiba OK?' I knew that if I answered one message then it would spread like a velt fire. I also did not want to lie.

My phone didn't stop ringing and I decided to put it on silent, took two sleeping pills and went to bed. I knew that the President had to make an official announcement but I had no idea when that would be done. I told the CEO of the Nelson Mandela Foundation, Sello Hatang, that I needed to meet him at the office at 6 a.m. the following morning. He agreed and off I went to bed.

I sent a message to my brother and his partner Rick, asking them to collect my dogs early the next morning. I said: 'Please don't ask any questions, just fetch Winston and Indira as early as possible.' They would need to be cared for and I knew I would not be at home much over the next couple of days.

On 6 December 2013 I awoke just after 4 a.m. I had twenty-eight missed calls and literally hundreds of emails, texts and messages already. I showered and when I went downstairs to have coffee I sat reading through some of the messages. The world had woken me to my worst nightmare. Madiba was gone. The President made the announcement during the midnight hours and to this day I have not seen the footage of the announcement.

I called my parents before 6 a.m. They had both heard already. They sleep with the radio on in their room and when the usual music on the radio was interrupted by an announcement by the President my dad woke my mom to tell her. My dad, the man who warned me about the terrorist's release back in 1990, wept like a child for Madiba and spent the entire night watching events unfold on TV. When I heard the sadness of their voices over the telephone I broke down for the first time.

I rushed to the office and found some of my colleagues there already. Everybody was emotional but we composed ourselves, like soldiers moving into total operational mode, knowing that we had to get work done right away in preparation for the next few days. Condolence books had to be bought, statements prepared and we needed to create the space for the public to mourn Madiba's passing too. The staff were brilliant and under the leadership of Sello they had created such a space in no time. I also called one of my friends, Minèe, to our office and asked her to supervise my phones and start responding to people. I needed help to contain the activity on my phones. The media started hunting me for comment or a response of some sort and Minèe had to keep the pressure at bay while I tried to figure out what to do next. To try and cage in the media pressure I decided to issue a statement. As I sat in front of my computer words and tears started flowing at the same time.

The Nelson Mandela Foundation agreed to issue my statement. I wrote:

> I often battled with the relentless pressure. But then I looked at him who carried himself with such grace and energy. I never left. I never could. Nelson Mandela did not demand loyalty, but he inspired profound and unwavering loyalty from everybody whose life he touched. And now, as we grieve the departure of Madiba, I am

slowly coming to terms with the fact that I will never see him again. But heroes never die. As sad as it makes me that I will never walk into a room again and see his generous infectious smile or hear him say 'Oh Zeldina, you are here', I have come to terms with the fact that Madiba's legacy is not dependent on his presence. His legacy will not only live on in everything that has been named after him, the books, the images, the movies. It will live on in how we feel when we hear his name, the respect and love, the unity he inspired in us as a country but particularly how we relate to one another . . . I will cherish every smile, the pleasant but also the difficult times and especially my barefoot moments . . . *Tot weersiens Khulu* [until we meet again grandpa]!! Will love you every day for the rest of my life.

The reality of it all hit home as I typed the last sentence. I was saying goodbye. Was this really happening? I had never, ever imagined that I would be sitting at my desk typing these words and it felt as if I was saying goodbye from another stratosphere. Minee was receiving calls and responding to messages on my behalf. People reached out to me from a personal perspective because it was known to them in particular how much he meant to me, but then others also called because I was their link to Madiba. They didn't know how or where to express the sadness over their loss. I first had to figure out what needed to be done before I could start thinking about my own feelings.

For some time I had worked with Mrs Machel and Josina to compile lists for this eventuality. They included people who had served Madiba, people who had been with him during the Rivonia and Treason Trial, friends, the heads and trustees of all his charities, supporters and those we always called upon when Madiba needed something – not only for his charities but also sometimes to get a job for one of his grandchildren or to help a child with something specifically. The lists had been updated several times but the last one was updated in June 2013 when Madiba was hospitalized. The lists were then submitted to Makaziwe and Ndileka Mandela, Madiba's eldest grandchild. They were the only two family members involved in funeral arrangements and they had been planning the funeral for the past eight years.

The state originally had a plan to have the funeral at the Union Buildings, the centre of power in South Africa and the place where all other state funerals were held in history. Although Madiba wanted to be buried in Qunu he didn't specify that he wanted a state funeral in Qunu. He was a simple man with modest needs, somehow underestimating his importance to the world.

This funeral was going to be about maintaining power over the Mandela legacy and roles within the Mandela family.

I felt gratitude to those who remembered me and the small role I had played in Madiba's life. Archbishop Desmond Tutu mentioned me during a very moving sermon he gave at St George's Cathedral in Cape Town. But as a humble reminder of how we are all forgettable, replaceable, he forgot my surname and called me Zelda van Graan repeatedly. He was becoming old too. Fragile and upset at the passing of the man he respected. Amid the sadness people were texting and tweeting me saying that if they were me, they would just change their surname now to Van Graan. It was funny but I couldn't laugh at the time.

I was also incredibly touched by Defence Minister Nqakula's statement about me, thanking me for my years of service. She said that she didn't ever think I had time to have a boyfriend and although I didn't want people to talk about it she was right, and it was the first time someone said it in public. There was a time I couldn't be with a man for twenty minutes without Madiba calling on me to do something. I never got angry. He was my number one. When I occasionally had a fling or a dysfunctional relationship I could never give it my full commitment. My job was everything and I didn't mind it. It was my choice. Her thanking me made me even more emotional. I had never expected to be thanked by anyone. Madiba thanked me. That was enough to me and my blessings having been chosen to serve him were beyond any expectations I had from life. But for someone from the ANC to thank me really ripped my heart apart. I didn't care for Madiba just because I cared for him. I knew millions of others cared for him too and I tried to serve his interests best to ensure that those relationships with others could be honoured.

My Twitter and Facebook accounts, text and emails were suddennly flooded with people thanking me. It was all too overwhelming and simply too many to answer. I am a person for detail and a left-brain thinker and at first I thought I would thank each and every one personally, but as time passed my cellphone constantly froze on me as a result of traffic and I simply didn't get the time to do what I wanted. What made it worse was that the people pouring out their gratitude to me had all suffered the same loss. They all had their own emotions to deal with yet they thought of me. I was deeply touched.

We now had to figure out how the people on those Madiba 'friends lists' got accredited. Sello, the now-CEO of the NMF tried from his side to get info too, while staff worked around the clock putting out fires of disorganization from people who wanted confirmation of arrangements. Sello as CEO couldn't get any detail and neither could his staff. People were calling asking for details about the memorial service to be held at the FNB Stadium in Soweto on Tuesday, 10 December. I couldn't answer anyone as I didn't have information and it was not forthcoming. In addition to the Madiba 'friends list', as we called it, the Machel family was suddenly told that they would only be allowed five accreditations and Mrs Machel would count as the first. So she plus four other Machels would be allowed accreditation at her own husband's funeral. It is so ridiculous that you actually couldn't help but laugh out loud at this.

In the few days to follow before the memorial many of us hardly slept, trying to make sense of arrangements and trying to get information. To say it was chaotic would be an understatement. A combination of bad planning and state secrecy, it seemed surprisingly badly managed for an event that had been inevitable. I had travelled with Madiba across the world, attending functions where there were sometimes hundreds of heads of state present. Arrangements at such big events were always a little haphazard yet I had never experienced such chaos. No one person could give you all relevant information and plans were changed every few minutes. Even those in charge didn't know the answers to anything, it seemed.

On Sunday night, after much fighting and crossfire of words between myself, the government's protocol people and the family, we were saved by a senior ANC official. She came to our rescue when she managed to get the accreditations for the Machel family and delivered them to the Saxon Hotel where Josina and I were meeting.

It was becoming farcical. If we could barely get Nelson Mandela's widow and her children accredited to attend his memorial service, it was becoming downright impossible to get anyone else officially accredited.

In the meantime the advance teams for President Obama and President Clinton had arrived and were trying to get details from everyone – me included. Tempers were flaring as everyone felt the pressure and frustration of the disorganization. I repeatedly asked why they had been planning for eight years and now no one could give us any answers. We appeared unprofessional and caught off guard. We received assurance that we would get the Madiba 'friends lists' accreditation the next day.

Early Monday morning we started calling around. By 2 p.m. one of our friends, Basetsana Khumalo, went to the ANC head office to collect accreditation for the 'friends lists', but then we realized that only half the people on the list had been accredited. The memorial was the next day. There was no way people from abroad would take the risk to fly to South Africa for the memorial or funeral if they did not know for sure whether they would be accredited. No invitations were sent and Madiba's friends were expected to go to the stadium on a first-come-first-served basis to get access and then be seated with the crowds of public people attending the memorial. That included people like Archbishop Tutu.

In the midst of all of this, just when it seemed things couldn't get worse, I remembered an appointment I had scheduled the previous week. Root canal. The pain in my tooth was shadowed by the pain of my heartbreak. A friend, Marli, collected me and took me to the dental surgeon. I couldn't manage to drive and answer the stream of phone calls and queries at the same time. Marli answered my phone during the root canal procedure and then asked me questions while I was lying open mouthed in the surgeon's chair, close to being strapped down by the dentist as illustrated in cartoons. I would write the response to Marli on a piece of paper, nearly illegibly, but she managed to give directions for the hour and a half I was in the chair. The surgeon soon realized that he was not going to complete the job and asked me to return the following week for the rest of the work. He realized I was under pressure and he was exceptionally patient. He managed to stop the pain and off we went.

With a mouth full of cotton wool and enough painkillers to numb my brain as well as my mouth (I did ask him to inject me with more than the allowed quantity of local anaesthetics to try and calm my nerves as well, although he declined), I tried to convey to people that I still didn't have any information. I tried to remain optimistic. But as soon as I managed to answer everyone, the first person on the list would start asking for an update again. I was bordering on a nervous breakdown and couldn't bear the pressure.

At times Josina, Basetsana and I all yelled at one another, then we cried hysterically and then we would pick up the pieces and try to find order again. We knew our outbursts were safe with one another no matter what the nature. George Cohen, the manager at the Saxon Hotel who had become a good friend, as well as the owners, the Steyn family, insisted that I stay at the hotel during the funeral time. George wanted to support me and tried to do so in every possible way. I lived some distance out of Johannesburg and by offering for me to stay in the city he already alleviated some pressure.

As some of Madiba's friends also stayed at the Saxon Hotel it made it easier, not having to communicate with them all in different venues but from within the hotel. Whenever I got one piece of information, no matter how mundane, I would share it with George and he would disseminate it to the friends who were staying in the hotel and even beyond to those he had contact with. The staff at the Foundation were busy with their own arrangements at the office to create a public space for mourning and George and the hotel staff helped me to take calls, they sent drivers around to try and help us get information, and in addition George force-fed me. On more than one occasion he found me sobbing, a mixture of pain and frustration, and he would calm me and help think of ways to find solutions. To me Madiba's friends all felt they were important in his life and their requests for information or detail were legitimate and my inability to help anyone seemed unprofessional and uncaring.

On Monday night the Minister of Defence called to say I had to travel to the Union Buildings in Pretoria to sort out the accreditation of the 'friends lists'. She suggested this to be the only solution at such a late hour. By now I had texted and called every possible person I thought could help us. By 7 p.m. on Monday night, we didn't even know yet what time the proceedings were to start the next day.

It wasn't just us. The media were also unable to plan. The government was working on a 'need to know' basis – slowly giving out information tidbit by tidbit.

In the meantime Madiba was being embalmed at 1 Military Hospital in Pretoria. From my friend Robyn Curnow, who had been briefed by the family for years, I learned that he was being 'escorted' to the afterlife by the elders of the Thembu tribe. They would talk to him, explaining the process of what was going on day by day. Madiba detested red tape and bureaucracy and I couldn't but wonder what his response would be if he had been told about our frustration.

My friend who took me to the dental surgeon drove me to the Union Buildings, accompanied by Sara Latham, the advance for President Clinton and an old friend too. She was sent to South Africa by the Clintons personally to also support me in whatever way possible. Half way to the Union Buildings Basetsana called us to say that they were not printing accreditations at the Union Buildings and that we had to return to Johannesburg, so we did. We were told that we would receive the remaining accreditations by 10 p.m. At 10.30 I called again and Josina and I were told that we would receive word by 1 a.m. Tuesday morning. At 1 a.m. we were told 3 a.m. So, we didn't go to sleep; 3 a.m. arrived and 3 a.m. passed without any word. We were still waiting. By 5 a.m. we started calling around. People like the business tycoon Johann Rupert had flown from Cape Town to attend the memorial, but his accreditation too was not delivered. At 6 a.m. I delivered two accreditation cards at the gate of his house, cards with names on that weren't known to him or his wife. There was no other way I could help him. Johann got on his plane and returned to Cape Town.

Johann was one of the people Madiba always called upon whenever he needed financial help for a project. Madiba's relationship with the family dated back to negotiations in the early 1990s after Madiba's release, yet here this man could not go to Madiba's memorial despite the fact that Madiba considered him as one of his sons.

In addition, none of the Nelson Mandela charities, their respective CEOs or trustees had been accredited. Their names all appeared on the list that was submitted on several occasions over the previous two years. Long-serving staff members who played critical roles in Madiba's life were omitted from accreditation.

At 8 a.m., after sleeping for only forty-five minutes, I arrived at our offices from where the Machel family was going to depart. I profusely apologized to Prof. Ndebele, the Chairman of our Foundation, and to Sello our CEO and I was deeply disappointed, hurt and embarrassed that they had not been catered for. Had my name not been submitted by Mrs Machel as part of her family list, I would not have been accredited. It seemed like chunks of Madiba's past were being whitewashed or ignored. The people he personally appointed, the legacy institutions he established were being marginalized in an act of pettiness.

Advocate George Bizos, one of Madiba's oldest friends and the lawyer whose relationship with Madiba dated back to the Rivonia

Trial, arrived at the office too, as his name was submitted as family too. I helped him onto the bus and asked Lori, my friend from Los Angeles and Morgan Freeman's business partner, to remain with him at all times. Arriving at the stadium it was chaos. It rained continuously and an unrelenting storm passed over Johannesburg. Some people said this was lucky and that the gods were welcoming Madiba. He would have thought that was nonsense. The rain further complicated an already difficult and chaotic situation. Someone recently said that Madiba didn't like too much of a fuss being made over him and that the rain was probably his way of ensuring that not too much of a fuss was being made.

We were sent from pillar to post between suites. Up and down we walked with the elderly Advocate Bizos. At one point I tried to assist Archbishop Tutu, Kofi Annan and the Elders as they were manhandled by police at one of the doors to a suite. It felt so disrespectful to me.

When Bono, Sol Kerzner, Charlize Theron and Douw Steyn's wife and children arrived they were also blocked access to any of the suites. A protocol officer literally chased them away and directed them to 'any open suite' along a long corridor. I escorted them and simply took them to the closest empty suite, where there was no catering and only orange plastic chairs to sit on. At least they had privacy there. What made it worse was that the suite was situated behind a screen to the back of the stage where they could hardly see anything. I told them that I would return to fetch them once I had made arrangements for them to enter somewhere more dignified but that they needed to stay in the suite for now as I did not want them to be manhandled by police or protocol people. The only words that repeated in my mind were: 'to honour Madiba, you have to honour his relationships'. If it was the last thing I would do for him, I would try to honour the relationships he had nurtured.

After fighting, more crying, yelling and losing my temper, Jessie Duarte, the Deputy Chair of the ANC, came to my rescue. I had told her what had happened and she entered the argument with the protocol officials and police at the door to the Ministerial suite to allow Madiba's friends access to a decent suite. She shared my frustration and thought it was unacceptable that people were treated with such disdain. She allocated a protocol person and one of our friends went off to fetch them.

Madiba detested events where endless speeches were made. He detested people singing his praises for hours and hours. He argued that once someone has said something good about you, it was enough. It was hardly the celebration of his life we had hoped for. It was not a public holiday and the 90,000-capacity stadium was not even half-full. It was embarrassing. People had to take time off from work to attend the memorial, and being right before the Christmas holidays many probably simply could not take leave to attend the memorial service.

Josina and Malenga Machel, Mrs Machel's two children and Madiba's two stepchildren, had not been catered for either. They were with us, and the rest of the Machel family, in the Ministerial suite. Halfway through the programme someone came to announce to them that there was provision for them on the field with the rest of the family, but we stopped them from humiliating themselves and walking onto the field as an 'afterthought'. Madiba had spent more time with these two young people than with many of his own blood. They made him smile, yet they were treated with what struck me as the utmost disrespect.

President Clinton called me to the Presidential suite because he, Secretary Hillary and Chelsea wanted to greet me. JD, the President's PA, fetched me and when I saw them I nearly collapsed. It was like seeing your parents and family. I have spent many hours with them over the past nineteen years and they had appreciation for how much I loved Madiba and I knew how much he loved them. They shared the pain we were all feeling. They really deeply loved him, over and above professional admiration. Seeing them made me realize that the loss was theirs too. It was irrelevant how much time you spent with Madiba. Your relationship with him depended on how you felt about him in your heart, and the Clintons understood that.

President Obama had what we described as a Martin Luther King moment and delivered a speech that will go down in history as one of his best. Too many speeches were made though, and it was not the celebration of Madiba's life we had hoped for. It took hours and hours for the speeches to be completed, with very little singing and dancing or musical items – something Madiba would have preferred. It just exposed how badly some people really knew Madiba that they could get it so wrong.

Very embarrassingly, President Zuma was booed by his own compatriots every time his name was mentioned or his face appeared on one of the big screens in the stadium. I was not in the least surprised. It was the same disrespect towards the President that Jacob Zuma had not condemned during his rape trial some years before, when ill-disciplined ANC youth started burning t-shirts emblazoned with the face of the then President Thabo Mbeki, that now manifested itself in a different time and in a different form. It was like a relationship in which abuse occurs. Once you allow it to happen you can never go back over the line that was crossed. It was allowed back then, so why would it not be allowed now? I was embarrassed not only for President Zuma but for South Africa as a whole.

On Tuesday night after the memorial we went to the Houghton house to see Mrs Machel, and President Clinton and his family departed South Africa soon after that. Sol Kerzner, one of the people who always brought a smile to Madiba's face, also left, and the astute businessman had a sadness in his eyes too. Even if Sol or the Clintons hadn't called, I sometimes in the last years told Madiba that they had, and it always brought about a smile whenever I saw that Madiba's mood needed a lift. They visited as often as they could and whenever their business brought them to South Africa, and President Clinton, without fail, always made sure that he combined his other visits to Africa with a visit to South Africa over Madiba's birthday period.

Before I went to sleep I tried to make arrangements for Bono, Naomi Campbell and the Steyn family to go and pay their respects at the Union Buildings the next morning, where Madiba was lying in state. Madiba liked Bono as he used his profile as a celebrity to support good causes. In turn we could always call on Bono to perform at concerts and events to benefit Madiba's charities, without charging an appearance fee or travel expenses. Naomi was the first celebrity to support the Nelson Mandela Children's Fund publicly, and she got christened the first of Madiba's honorary granddaughters. And after Madiba left his Soweto house on his separation from Winnie Madikizela Mandela, the Steyn family housed Madiba for six months and he completed the writing of *Long Walk to Freedom* in their house and where the interim constitution was prepared by the ANC. They entertained Madiba's friends and comrades and provided a space for him to spend time with his son Makgatho's children. These people all deserved their rightful place in Madiba's life and now they had not been catered for to pay their last respects at the Union Buildings while Madiba was lying in state.

Bridgette Radebe, the wife of our Minister of Justice Jeff Radebe, offered to come round to the Saxon Hotel to help us get to the Union Buildings the next morning. Roads were all cordoned off and unless your car was accredited you were expected to go and stand in a queue for hours to take public transport to the Union Buildings. At 6 a.m. on Wednesday morning Bridgette called to say that Jeff would be there at 8 a.m. I waited until 7 a.m. and then asked George, the manager at the Saxon, to wake Naomi, Bono and the Steyns. At 8 a.m. Bridgette called to say that Jeff had been called to another ceremony and that he would not be able to help us. Panic struck again. How was I supposed to get these people to the Union Buildings? Surely the government couldn't expect these VIPs to go and stand in a queue for five or six hours with the public to pay their last respects to Madiba?

I felt impotent. I had always been able to fix things, to open doors, but one by one they were closing. It didn't help to contemplate how this would have angered Madiba. You simply square up and deal with it and find another way around.

While I was having a telephone conversation at the Saxon,

former President F. W. de Klerk, who was also staying at the hotel, overheard me. Mr de Klerk was the President in 1990 when Madiba was released from prison. Madiba liked him and spoke of him with great respect and I shared that respect. After I finished the call he said: 'Zelda, speak to Norman, my security, and see if you can work out something with him to help you.' And at 9.15 we all left in convoy with former President de Klerk and his wife Elita. The irony in this was just too much for me. Here the man who represented apartheid to so many was, in a way, rescuing Madiba once again. It was just too much to handle and it is something I so badly wanted to tell Madiba about. It wouldn't have surprised him though that Mr de Klerk came to our rescue. He truly believed that despite their political differences from time to time, Mr de Klerk was a reasonable and good human being.

Arriving at the Presidential guest house, the celebrities were allowed in but I was shut out together with the Steyns. When Minister Jeff Radebe and wife Bridgette arrived they had to escort me inside and I had to figure out a plan to get the Steyns inside. Eventually we managed to get all our guests transported to the Union Buildings where Madiba was lying in state.

As we walked down the steps of the Union Buildings a calmness came over me. I had to be ready to say goodbye to Madiba. I had to get the words right in my head. I didn't plan to say anything out loud but he would hear me. He always knew what I thought before I could even say it. And when I sometimes told him something or raised something with him he would say, 'You know, Zeldina, it's strange that you mention it, I was just thinking about that now.' It won't be different this time, I decided.

A few steps from the coffin I realized that it was going to be too difficult. I hadn't seen him in a few months. I had already started missing him. Naomi was walking behind me and she then froze. She was scared and again tears streamed from my eyes. I was hysterical and as much as I wanted to help her, I couldn't help myself. I was holding on to Bridgette Radebe's hand but she then let me go and took Naomi's hand. I wanted her to help Naomi too. The next moment Olivia Machel, Samora Machel's daughter and Mrs Machel's stepdaughter, took my left hand and Bono took my right hand with his wife Ali on the other side and it was our turn to approach the coffin.

I was as composed as I could be until my eyes met those of Mandla Mandela, Madiba's grandson, standing guard next to his grandfather's coffin. My heart shattered. A physical pain I cannot describe to anyone but I am sure has been felt by many people. I so badly wanted to walk to Mandla to give him a hug but I couldn't. Mandla was like my little brother.

Bono and Olivia led me to the coffin and there was Madiba. Lifeless. Dead. Cold. Khulu was gone. The first thing I noticed was the scar on the side of his neck where they obviously inserted a tube. Probably a tube from the many that had given him life the last six months. Now there was nothing, nothing left but the scar. The hole was closed but when you work with someone for so long you eventually even know each other's scars. I knew every little mark on his face and this one in his neck was new. Then I noticed that he was a dark grey colour and next I noticed that his chest was completely flat. As flat as the top of a table. It upset me to see him like that but I knew that I only had a minute to say goodbye. Bono took charge and said a prayer, and although it was beautiful I couldn't breathe and suppress my gasping. He thanked God for blessing us with Madiba and asked Him to be with Madiba and with us while we put sense to life after Madiba. Bono led us away and I felt like turning around and running back. I still wanted to say, something. We always have something more to say, don't we? But life has taught me that we will often more regret the things we didn't say than the things we said and I had made sure in the last few years that I told Madiba how much I loved him and appreciated him. I never wanted to regret not saying it, and walking away I knew that it was the one thing he knew about me as he was lying there.

Bono and Olivia held my hands and I cannot remember climbing the stairs up the Union Buildings, probably doing so for the last time. On the journey back to the Presidential guest house, no one said a word. By now I had stopped trying to control my tears, they were just cascading from my eyes. I felt like I couldn't breathe and I wanted to be alone, by myself, but I had others to think about.

Back at the Saxon we had lunch and I was very sad to let Bono and his wife Ali go. I have also become close to their staff over the years and they have become close friends. They have all become somewhat of a spiritual pillar and Bono is a bit of a preacher man. He has a very deep understanding of life and throughout Madiba's prolonged illness he often sent messages of encouragement, never asking for anything or for information but sending a string of beautiful words. I remembered the saying 'we're all just here walking each other home', and it calmed me a little; I was exhausted from the tension and emotions of the day. In a way I also felt that Madiba's friends were all a special breed of people. He attracted a certain kind of person and I know it would have pleased him that they were there looking out for me. 'That's good, Zeldina,' he would say.

The ad hoc lack of planning continued and I had to make a decision on how to survive the next few days. There had been brief moments of breaking down but there hadn't been time to sit and think, to internalize the reality of Madiba's passing. I did not have time to think about myself or fully come to terms with the event. Also, not having seen Madiba for a couple of months made it almost unbelievable to think he was really gone. I'd got used to the fact that he was home, and waking up every morning with the first thought crossing my mind that he was critically ill. You never knew how any day would end but you never expect the end either.

My challenge now was to get Alfre Woodard, Oprah, Gayle King, Stedman Graham, Forest Whitaker and Richard Branson accredited for the funeral in Qunu. It was planned at Madiba's home village for Sunday 15 December 2013. They had all travelled from the US to be there but I was not sure whether we would succeed in getting them accredited. They were below the status of heads of state yet they were above a ministerial level. There was no level catering for their needs.

They had to be treated like the public, with the rest of the masses. I would not have any of that. The bizarre and unnecessary difficulties of an event that had been planned for eight years continued.

Arriving at Madiba's house to deliver something to Mrs Machel I was told by the uniformed police on duty that I could not enter the premises as my accreditation to the house had expired. It was not a person I had seen before and she refused me access. However, next to her one of Madiba's bodyguards was seated. He didn't try to help and kept quiet. I went into the guard house and tried to call the kitchen staff to ask them to verify that I was expected at the house. I couldn't get through on the phone. I asked the bodyguard how long he had worked for Madiba and he responded eight years. I told him that I was called to the house by Mum and asked whether he did not think his behaviour by not helping me to get in was unacceptable. He responded by saying he was not on duty and simply keeping the lady in uniform company. My last response to him was: 'How do you think Madiba would react if he heard you now? Having served him, you should know. I don't have to answer for you. You really ought to be proud of yourself.' I called Mum on her cellphone, of course again in tears, and she sent her bodyguards to come and collect me at the gate.

Arriving in the house I was told that I needed photo accreditation. I went to the room in the back of the garden where accreditation was done by state protocol officials and told them that Mrs Machel, as she had, had asked me to come for accreditation. They refused to accredit me and said my name was not on the list and that Makaziwe and Ndileka were the only ones that could give permission for me to be accredited. I left and went to Mrs Machel again to tell her that I was leaving and would not be staying for the prayer service she'd invited me to. I was disgusted that it was left to the mourning widow to intervene to get us accredited. She instructed Makaziwe's husband, Isaac, to accompany me to the room again to try to get me accredited. Despite him telling them that he was Makaziwe's husband and then saying that it was a 'special request from Mrs Machel' they refused. It was only after a long argument that they agreed. I thought it somewhat strange that Isaac put this to them as a special request from Mrs Machel.

I went to greet Mrs Machel and left. She wanted me to stay for the prayer service but I was too upset. I assured her that I would be around if she needed any assistance. She still relied on me for some of the administrative issues that I had performed while Madiba was alive: paying accounts or making transfers as instructed by them. I think the irony of it all intensified my own emotional feelings. The family was fast to call me to ask whether a transfer to them had been made, but felt that I wasn't good enough to be treated like a human being or afforded just the courtesy of a basic greeting when they passed me, let alone accredited with just a little dignity.

I still had the Oprah/Branson/Whitaker obstacle of accreditation to overcome and left the house.

The next few hours were spent on doing exactly that. I emailed everyone, called, sent text messages to people to ask them to accommodate Madiba's friends, and the same state protocol people told even the Director General of the Presidency that they did not take instructions from him. It appeared that some sections of government were at loggerheads with other members of government. I felt that it was nothing about honouring Madiba or giving him the dignity he deserved but all about asserting power and settling scores. But on the other hand, no one really knew who was in charge. One couldn't help but wonder whether it was just eight years of bad planning, wasting money on foreign travel to consult with other countries about events of this magnitude, or whether it was a deliberate attempt to exclude from Madiba's funeral people who were not aligned with the right people. Surely if you have eight years to plan, you get it right. It was distasteful to listen to and it deeply pained me that people who loved Madiba dearly were to be treated like that. They insisted that Oprah and others came to the accreditation room at the Houghton house to be accredited. I communicated this to everyone.

Sadly I heard that the accreditation was only done after Oprah,

Forest, Gayle and others had had to pose for countless photos with the protocol people. It was revolting. I could not imagine that Madiba would have agreed to this type of treatment of his friends. I would never, ever, have subjected Madiba to this kind of treatment, yet here his friends were expected to pose for photos with fans in order to smooth their way through accreditation. In nineteen years of serving Madiba I had never, not once, asked any of his guests for photos with them. I had never asked Madiba to take a photo with me. Photos were taken in the course of working with him or he would sometimes ask me to join him when a picture with guests was taken and only on a few occasions some of his friends asked that I be included in a photo. But that was precisely one of the reasons why I lasted with him for so long. I never allowed familiarity or opportunity for photographs to distract from how he wanted me to behave. At one point he asked whether it was the case that I didn't want to have my photograph taken with him and I laughed it off and had to assure him that was not the case. This behaviour by them now was totally unacceptable to me.

I eventually arrived in the Eastern Cape on the Friday, together with Josina, some of her family and friends, via the private plane organized by Faizal and Malaika Motlekar. When we landed in Umtata I noticed how lush and green the hills were. It had been raining heavily and still continued to rain, which is something that would have really pleased Madiba and I so wish he could have seen it. He was happy when the soils of his soul were adequately watered and became fertile for grazing and farming. In an interview with Robyn Curnow from CNN, one of his grandsons told the story of how he and Madiba were sitting in the living room of his Qunu house and Madiba urged Mbuso, his young grandson, to go and run naked in the rain. Madiba said that's what he used to do when he was young. He loved life unconditionally despite what life handed him time and time again. Just imagine eighty years ago – a young Nelson Mandela frolicking in these same hills. Naked, unencumbered by the past and unknowing about his future. Perhaps the rain was a fitting way for him to come home.

Driving from the airport I was reminded how I made him smile whenever we were in Qunu and I greeted him by his circumcision name: 'Ahhh Dalibhunga!' The Afrikaans girl was greeting him in his Xhosa name; he was entertained by that and it usually brought about the biggest smile on his face.

We passed a few cattle and I reminisced about his adoration for his cattle. We used to drive on his farm, going out to see the cows and bulls and secretly I think he would have loved to have been a big cattle farmer. He often told me that a man's wealth in their tradition was measured by the number of cattle he had. He had between thirty and sixty cattle at any given point and I would respond: 'Oh Khulu so you are very rich!' and he would laugh.

His easy accessibility, his natural affinity with people was what I remembered. My main role during my years with him was to be his protector – the shield – the person who had to protect him from being smothered with love by others. His openness seemed at odds with the closed nature of the funeral arrangements. It confused me, it saddened me and it even embarrassed me.

The world's media had descended on Qunu. I was reminded how fond Madiba was of journalists and seeing them made me think that he would really be impressed to see so many of them in Qunu and how boastful he would be about his little village to them. He used to call them often, whenever a journalist wrote an article about him that was critical in nature. He would invite them to a meal and at first they assumed they were in trouble for being critical of him. But they soon learned after arrival at his house for a meal that he merely wanted to engage with them to get an understanding of their criticism. The journalists would often leave not having changed their minds, but Madiba didn't attempt to change their minds. He would have an informed opinion after having engaged with them, and even though he occasionally changed an opinion by offering correct information, they never parted feeling hostile. Seeing so many familiar faces in Qunu made me think of many such occasions and how he courted them with his charm. He loved sharing information with the media and appreciated the fact that they had a job to do.

This set-up was so different – the media being kept away and information withheld as a show of where power resided.

On Sunday we woke up at 4 a.m. to get ready for the funeral. I tried
to manoeuvre a plan to get George Bizos to the house so that he
didn't have to get into a bus. He is old and struggles to walk. He is
frail. Ironically again, one of Madiba's ex-bodyguards, Piet Erwee,
helped us to get him there, fighting us through the roadblocks and
police checkpoints, without any accreditation himself but paying
his last dues to Madiba. Piet was employed by Rory Steyn, his
ex-police commander and one of Madiba's close confidant bodyguards from his Presidential days. Rory now has a very successful
security company and his story is another of how you become
successful as long as you serve your passion in life.

Arriving in Qunu it was only proper that George Bizos would go
to the house and greet the family. We entered through the kitchen
door as they locked the front door and refused us access. Makaziwe's daughter was standing on the inside shouting that the door
would not be opened for anyone no matter who. I led Advocate
Bizos and his son through the kitchen door at the back and through
the dining room. Makaziwe passed and barely greeted us. As Madiba
became more frail it was clear that they didn't approve of his choices.
Not in staff and not in friends. And such was George Bizos. Makaziwe had challenged his appointment as trustee to one of Madiba's
trusts earlier in the year and a public mud-slinging followed in which
Makaziwe's daughter insulted and belittled Advocate Bizos. None
of us were welcomed in the house.

We greeted her in a civilized manner and she walked into the
kitchen. In the kitchen I could see her making a determined turn
around and she stormed back into the dining room. 'Zelda we don't
want you people here. Now that Uncle George is here, he can stay
but we don't want you people here.' I responded by saying: 'I am
happy to oblige Makaziwe if someone could just give us direction
of what to do with people like Uncle George.' She repeated her
instructions: 'We don't want you people in the house.' Isaac was

watching and I turned around and left. Uncle George and his son walked past her and went into the lounge where others gathered.

Shortly after us Tokyo Sexwale, an ex-colleague of Madiba's from Robben Island who had served in Madiba's government, arrived and he was also shown the door. Tokyo's appointment by Madiba as trustee on the same trust that George Bizos served was also questioned by Makaziwe; he too was aligned with the wrong side of the family. These people were appointed by Madiba to serve on his trusts for a very good reason. When he became ill and unable to speak for himself the family started challenging his decisions and it was clear that once he was gone, they were going to do that on all fronts. It was also clear that if you were friends or aligned with anyone outside Makaziwe or Ndileka's camp you were not welcome in the house. I was not the only one to be chased out.

I found it difficult and emotionally challenging to reconcile his last years and what we had experienced for sixteen-odd years with what was happening now. To say it was in complete contrast would be putting it mildly.

Qunu is a valley-like community sunk between the majestic mountains in the Eastern Cape. Madiba's farm itself is small but in comparison to that of his neighbours quite lavish. Although the house he and Mrs Machel built in the early 2000s is in stark contrast to the living standards of the surrounding area it is modest in comparison to those of people of similar or close stature. The huge dome erected for his funeral first shocked me. It wasn't just a big tent but a dome, probably the size of a small aircraft hanger. I heard that the dome had been stored away for years to have it ready when the 'life event' occurred. It had been bought from Germany, I learned, and thought that it was probably only Madiba's funeral that could get away with something like that being bought from Europe; the unions would have argued that it could have been a perfect job-creation opportunity to have it made in South Africa. Many years ago we had bought t-shirts in bulk from the East for one of Madiba's campaigns and got a good lashing from the media and public for not supporting the South African textile industry. I guess the funeral was different. From the house to the dome was probably a good 1.5 km. The road that connected the house to the dome was a simple gravel road. To take either the front road or the back road towards the dome one got a pretty good sense of the size of the property and you saw the cows Madiba was so proud of.

I started making my way up to the dome where the funeral was to take place and simply kept Madiba in my thoughts and heart. He would not have approved of the fact that I had been asked to leave the house. He would not have approved of the ostentatiousness of this huge dome on his farm. A few years ago when he was able to take decisions and voice them himself he insisted I be in the house with them for the final ceremony when Makgatho passed away. Now I was being excluded because he could no longer insist on my presence. On occasion Madiba chased people out of the house, as recently as in December 2009 and regardless that I joined in trying to convince him to be more lenient to them; his voice had been silenced.

In these trying times, I had to remember some of Madiba's greatest lessons . . . my relationship was with him and no one can ever remove that from me. People die, relationships don't die and my relationship with Madiba will never die.

Arriving at the dome – where more people were gathering, shepherded in buses from Umtata, almost an hour's drive away – I heard that Oprah's bus had not been allowed onto the premises. We had had great difficulty obtaining landing rights for her plane in Umtata as only heads of state's planes were allowed to land there. It was understandable – until I heard that exceptions had been made already for other planes to land there too. The bus she took from the Umtata airport was not accredited to enter the farm and she was offloaded at the main house. She had to walk up to the dome on the dusty roads, past the cows. Rory, Madiba's ex-bodyguard, managed to get a minister's car to transport her and her delegation the rest of the way to the dome. She had visited Qunu twice before and the last time she joined us and hosted a Christmas children's party for more than 25,000 children in the village and surrounding area. Madiba had also asked her to build a school once, as part of his school-building project, and she established the Oprah Winfrey Academy close to Johannesburg. One of a kind in private schools in South Africa. Madiba had great appreciation for her and her support for underprivileged children in South Africa. He was also entertained by her wealth and repeatedly told people about her generosity to buy all the attendees at her show cars. He would end the sentence with: 'can you imagine that?'

While Oprah, Stedman, Forest and Gayle were making their way to the dome, I tried to find seats for Advocate Bizos, Richard Branson and others. Whenever someone arrived at the door that I knew I ushered them to an area where Bridgette Radebe and her brother Patrice kept open seats for Madiba's friends.

Mum was still in the main house, getting ready to accompany Madiba up to the dome and his final resting place. I could see on footage the day before that she was brutally exhausted. They were preparing Madiba for his final journey up the hill on his beloved farm in Qunu.

Once I had managed to seat all the guests I felt responsible for I couldn't find a seat myself, unless I was prepared to go and sit among the military people who were part of the proceedings. I was too ashamed because I was so emotional so I left and found a spot on the grass outside to sit close to Robyn Curnow, my friend who was reporting for CNN from inside the premises. From there I could hear the proceedings on a SABC speaker and see visuals on a close-by screen attached to the back of a satellite truck. The hearse arrived – with Madiba's coffin on the back of a gun carriage, draped in the South African flag. There was more irony. I was outside and even though I felt shut out, there were very few people left outside and it strangely provided another almost personal opportunity to say goodbye. When the military procession moved past, I couldn't breathe from the sobbing. At first I saw Mandla in the front of the military vehicle, still guarding his grandfather, and after Madiba passed Mum's car followed and I could see her through the window. I so badly wanted to hold her to give her comfort, but also for her to hold me. Madiba was afforded full military honours for his funeral, which meant that all or any cere-mony and protocol from the military applied to his burial.

A furore about Archbishop Desmond Tutu's attendance at the funeral played off in the media 48 hours before the event. He was shunned as no proper arrangements were communicated to him. When he arrived at the dome with Trevor Manuel I could see his own pain and sadness. I hugged him for as long as time allowed. I wanted to console him but I also wanted consolation from him. Madiba was so fond of him.

A stranger, a black man, saw me shivering from pain and walked up to me, put his arms around me and said 'Zelda don't worry *sisi* [sister], it will get better.' I felt like collapsing in his arms but I knew that I had to compose myself and thanked him with a hug. Weeks after I tried to recall this man's face, tried to remember who it was and whether I could trace him again. I wanted to thank him again for doing that. It wasn't just a hug and trying to console me. He genuinely cared. It touched my inner core when strangers, black people reached out to me in this way. How far we had come!

The service started and the stage was beautifully decorated with ninety-five big candles, one for each of Madiba's years. I should have been able to just pay my respects and pray. But I was worried about admin again – and particularly about how we would get Oprah and her delegation back to the house. Rich and famous and people I've never seen or heard of in nineteen years were given accreditation to the burial site. Only 400 of the 4,000 guests were accredited to go to the burial site. I was shown what the accreditation cards looked like but I was not given one.

Ahmed Kathrada, Madiba's long-time friend from prison, delivered the most moving speech during the ceremony. He paid tribute to Madiba and said Madiba had joined the ANC A-team in heaven. He was so emotional and it was sad to see him like that. Kathy, as we fondly refer to him, had been friends with Madiba since before his imprisonment. They spent eighteen years together on Robben Island in addition to the time in Pollsmoor after being moved from the island.

Soon the ceremony was over – speech after speech. Some of the speakers were touching while others wanted to make sure they basked for the last time in Madiba's bright light. The only thing that really reminded me of Madiba was the song sung by children. 'Roli-hlahla Mandela' is a song written to Madiba, and Mrs Machel asked Mbongeni Ngema, a prominent South African artist, to record the song with children the week prior to the funeral. Madiba's infectious smile was vivid in my mind when I heard it. I could so well imagine his liveliness at the sound of these voices. But that was all gone now. This and the 95 candles in the dome depicting Madiba's life were the only requests from Madiba's widow that were adhered to.

While waiting for the proceedings to come to an end I read the obituary in great detail. None of the Mandela legacy institutions that Madiba personally created were mentioned in any obituary, tribute or vote of thanks. As if they never existed.

People started making their way to the burial site. People walked past me, many of Madiba's friends and of course all the family. Some of Madiba's friends asked whether I was not going to the site and I told them that I had not been accredited. Some of Madiba's friends wanted me to put up a fight to get access. I knew that I had said my goodbyes. My relationship with Madiba was not defined by whether I stood next to his grave or not. It was way, way more than that. Rory Steyn, who was looking after Oprah during the funeral, joined me and Robyn outside. Robyn, Rory and I, three white South Africans whose lives had been changed by Madiba's leadership and personal love, stood together and watched the proceedings on the screen. My relationship with Madiba was not about being at his side at key moments in his life. It was defined in the ordinary moments I spent with him. Rory, Robyn and I held each other and knew this was a moment in history where we were on the frontlines. Saying goodbye in person to a great man in our respective ways, our Khulu, our Tata and our Madiba.

We were standing watching the proceedings on the screen and when the twenty-one-gun salutes were fired it sounded like a barrage of tears into the sky. And the fly-past, helicopters with South

African flags flying in unison, low over the hills of Qunu, followed by the fighter jets. The sound of those machines shuddered through my body. It finally sank in. It was over. I burst into loud tears, sobbing on Robyn's shoulder while Rory was holding both of us, consoling us while we shivered from pain. The tears cascaded down my face again. Robyn was not on air at the time and she was just being my friend, but unknown to both of us, her microphone was still connected live. My gasping sobs were heard on CNN across the world as pictures of his last journey were aired. Robyn says the studio in Atlanta shouted in her earpiece, 'The microphone is hot!' She knew my tearful breakdown had been broadcast to millions of people. I didn't. At the same time she felt the dilemma of letting me go. She knew she couldn't let go of me and held on even tighter, consoling me. A few minutes later she stepped back to the camera and described the scene around her and mentioned the powerful sense of departure and sadness, her eyes clearly red from crying with us. She described how I, Madiba's longtime assistant, had burst into tears, explaining to all those listening who had been the person crying. It was only two weeks later that she told me what had happened and what she had reported. I didn't feel betrayed. I needed my two friends Rory and Robyn to hold my heart together from falling apart. I felt I wanted to share my pain with the world and unknown to me I had, but at the same time I have never felt so lonely. I was haunted by loss and the emptiness made me convulse.

They were still busy at the gravesite when I started making my way back to Madiba's house. I had to get home. First to the hotel and then I was determined to get back to Johannesburg as fast as possible. I couldn't take any more and I needed to be home, alone with my dogs. I'd walked halfway down to the house when one of Madiba's bodyguards, Sam, gave me lift in a golf cart. I cannot imagine what I looked like but as we drove past familiar faces, people who had served Madiba in different capacities noticed me on the back of the cart, stopped the cart and had a few words. I felt like a bag of washed out clothes. I had no energy left in my body and I no longer controlled any of my emotions. Old ANC colleagues of Madiba's who were all sidelined or withheld from going to the burial site stopped me to chat. I was tempted to go into the house to have a last look at the empty yellow chair in Madiba's lounge but I was rushing to find transport and decided that today was not a good day to expose myself to more sorrow. I knew I would be back soon.

By the time I left, I had managed to arrange transport for Oprah and her delegation from the dome back to the house where they would find their bus. Richard Branson was sorted and I left transport behind for Advocate Bizos. There was nothing else I could fix. I had made sure everyone was OK and it was time to let go. I left for the hotel and got into bed with my funeral clothes still on. I was depleted in every possible way. I slept for two hours and when I woke I learned that my dearest colleague, Yase, had managed to change my flight to enable me to return to Johannesburg the same night. He just grasped that I wanted silence and solitude and pulled out all stops to change my flight. And so I drove the 260 km in rain to East London where I got the plane back to Johannesburg. I got home after 1 a.m. and it took me some time to fall asleep.

The next few days were spent on paying accounts. The funeral was merely ten days before Christmas and suppliers had to pay staff before the holidays.

I had the rest of my root canal work done, attended Douw Steyn's sixty-first birthday dinner, which was somewhat of a sombre affair as he was also ill at the time, and had some other physical problems attended to that manifested themselves as a result of all the stress of the previous week. In June I thought I had sustained an injury during a gym session at around the same time Madiba was hospitalized. I constantly had a pain in my hip and sometimes it crossed over down into my knee. No matter how I stretched or how many painkillers I took, I couldn't get rid of the pain. On 19 December I woke up in the morning thinking that I had become paralysed. Both my legs were numb. I could feel the same pain in my hip as before but my upper legs were both numb. I called a physio friend back from holiday to help me as I was desperate. After much treatment she managed to get rid of all the spasms I had been walking around with since June. As was the case over the years, whenever Madiba suffered physical distress, the stress and worry that caused me also manifested itself physically in my body.

Finally on Friday, 20 December I made my way back to Umtata. I wanted to go and say my last goodbye and pay my respects at Madiba's gravesite. In the days prior to this trip I had wondered much about the meaning of life, about mortality, and even though we did not discuss it much, as he considered it a very personal matter, what Madiba really believed about life and death. We tried to shelter Mrs Machel from as much as possible over the preceding two weeks but she knew I hadn't been there when he was buried. I was not the only one who wasn't allowed at the burial. Meme, the housekeeper, and Betty, one of the household assistants, had also been pulled out of a row and were prevented from going to the grave, or even being in the foyer of Madiba's house when the casket Arrived from Johannesburg, yet they too had been loyally serving him for years.

The hills of Qunu were back to the slow pace of life. The dome had been removed and sprinklers watered the newly planted grass where the dome was previously erected. The cows and goats were roaming freely as before, unaffected by the change in life. I went straight to the farm to greet Mrs Machel. This would be the first time I had seen her since the Thursday before the burial.

I wanted to know specifics from her about his burial. Did he go in one of his favourite shirts? She said he didn't. It wasn't one of his favourites. He went with some of his personal items, some of the few things that were so dear to him. I asked about his walking stick. An ivory stick he got from Douw Steyn made from the tusks of a bull elephant that had died on Douw's farm Shambala, where Douw had built a house for Madiba to use to write the sequel of *Long Walk to Freedom*. Sadly but not surprisingly I was told that the stick had not been found. I took time with Mum talking about the stick, tracking its journey to the house in Qunu and then to Houghton where we last saw it. Neither of us had the energy or the emotional strength to start looking for the stick and I put her mind to rest that the stick will eventually one day surface, and hopefully one of us will still be alive. Or someone will read this and discover it perhaps. It is clearly marked 'To Madiba, from Douw Steyn' and one of its kind. A solid white ivory walking stick. Madiba should have left with it.

Driving back after 10 p.m. from Qunu to Umtata that night, the most beautiful moon rose over the hills of Umtata. The brightest orange moon I had ever seen. It dawned upon me that here this white Afrikaner girl was driving from Qunu to Umtata all by herself. Madiba would have insisted that security accompany me, being concerned for my safety. Thinking about that made me smile. But I kept my eye on the moon and realized that he had removed all fear from me. I had finally grown up. Almost twenty years ago I wouldn't have dreamt of driving this road by myself at night. But the Transkei, as it was formerly known, gets under your skin. The place becomes part of you. I was fearful of so much twenty years ago – of life, of black people, of this black man and the future of South Africa – and now I was no longer persuaded or influenced by mainstream thinking or fears. I was my own person. Madiba had given me peace and freedom too. He had freed me from the shackles of my own fears. He not only liberated the black man but the white man too. I felt light, free and thankful that my teacher was Nelson Mandela. As much as I grieved for him, I had gained so much and I spoke to him in the car on my way back to Umtata, keeping my eye on the bright moon.

We ended up going to the grave on Sunday morning. We were scheduled to leave around midday. Shortly after 8 a.m. Mum, Josina, Meme, Betty and a few other workers, security and I drove up to the burial site. We had ordered fresh flowers the previous day and we started cleaning the graves of Madiba and his three children. We were quiet and the mood was solemn. The tombstones all had the family crest on them, that which had become familiar to me through its appearance on the House of Mandela wines. We removed the old flowers, bunches of white flowers that had been laid on his coffin and placed around the tombstone, orchids and roses. Now scattered in the wind and damaged by the sun. We replaced the flowers with fresh ones, after which Mum called us together and she asked Meme to pray. Meme said a beautiful prayer and I was shuddering as we were holding hands during it. Meme prayed in Sotho as well, during which my thoughts went off to Afrikaans prayers and my mind wandered, trying to send a message to Madiba. I thanked him again and told him like so many other times how much I appreciated him but that, most importantly, he should remember that I love him.

Shortly after noon it was wheels up from the Umtata airport. It was the longest fifty-five-minute flight from Umtata to Johannesburg of our lives. It was all over. Final. And the next chapter would be harder. I knew that a battle was brewing over the will and Madiba's estate and control over his legacy. It was like they say, a sign of the times. I knew that it was also time for me to start moving away. My duty was done. The last days and months reminded me of the story of Tolstoy. Ironically there were a lot of similarities to the life of that great Russian writer whose work Madiba also loved so much. How crowds gathered before his death, but also the contest for control over his legacy and his estate.

I was seated closest to the door in the small aircraft, facing the back of the plane. It was much better and more convenient than a commercial plane but we all felt somehow exposed, naked, as there was nowhere to hide our emotions. I could feel Mum's pain as I watched her breaking down in tears when our plane slowly made its way through the thick clouds. And eventually we all just broke down, crying in our seats. Me, Mum, Josina, Celina – Mrs Machel's sister-in-law – Betty and Cordier the bodyguard. No one spoke during the flight.

Mum is normally so stoic, so strong. But breaking through the clouds, flying away from him, leaving him alone we all shared a sense of abandoning him, deserting him. The only thing we never wanted him to feel and the one thing I promised him I would never do. But what do we do now? He is home and heroes never die. He will be present in those beautiful hills for ever and I now know he will be even more powerful in death than he was in life.

His image, his legacy must be protected.

I don't know what I will do for the rest of my life. His prolonged illness had forced me to grow up. It has taught me some of the most valuable lessons of life and showed me what not to expect of people. Madiba did not only unify a country once again even through his illness and in death, but he taught us more than we ever bargained for. I will allow life to take its course with me and I now know that I will always be at the place where I am supposed to be at any given point in time. I have no plans other than annually honouring him through Bikers for Mandela Day. Maybe I will find another job and perhaps I will find a man to spend time with, one who knows and will respect that a piece of my heart has already been taken . . . given to an old black man who was once my people's enemy and is now lying, like an ancient King, deep in the soil of South Africa's golden hills of Qunu.

We will see him in every sunset and every sunrise. We must keep looking for him. He will look after us if we remember his lessons.

And slowly we climbed above the clouds, reaching the sunshine and the warm light of the African sun shining through the windows of the plane, eventually heating up our faces and drying away the tears. Whatever happens now, I know we did our best.

Tot weersiens Khulu! Until we meet again.

To be continued . . .

Acknowledgements

I need a separate book to thank all the people who have contributed to or played a role in my life over the last forty-three years. I may forget many names here and in that case I apologize in advance. In a very strange way, even the people who I felt hurt by played a role in shaping me. Every person that crossed my path blessed me irrespective of the role they played in my life.

I pay tribute to people who have suffered and sacrificed paving the way for me to have the freedoms that I now enjoy in this beautiful country of ours.

'I am because you are.' I thank my parents Des and Yvonne la Grange. I love you more than you will ever comprehend. I don't show it often and indeed I am strange being, but I hope you know how much I appreciate your unconditional love and support. You laid the foundation for discipline, principle, the morals and values I cling to today. Commitment, loyalty and determination I inherited from you. I know what it is to love because of you. To my brother Anton and his partner Rick Venter, my second brother, thank you for always being there, and if no one else could be trusted, you stood firm. Thank you for the encouragement, unwavering support and taking care of me. You are my rock.

To the rest of my family, the La Grange's and Strydoms thank you.

To Maretha Slabbert, my long-serving and -suffering colleague, thank you for sticking it out with me. We shared the best times but also the worst. I will love you for ever.

To my long-time friend Jennifer Preller, for your support and motherhood. I remain grateful to have a friend care for me the way you do. Thank you for pushing me beyond what I thought were my limits and for constantly adjusting my attitude and making me strong.

The godparents to my dogs, Johrne and Alet van Huyssteen, I cannot imagine life without you. You lived in my house at one stage more than I did. Thanks for being there at the drop of a hat to care for my house, my dogs and for me and sometimes picking up the pieces. I cannot wait for us to sit on the porch of the old age home together.

To the friend that kept my mind sane and clear Dr Ralf Brummerhof. Thank you for being there to count on, day or night, and even the knee jerk exercises.

To Robyn Curnow and Kim Norgaard and their children Freya and Hella, thank you for an instant family and an enormously privileged and trusted friendship we share.

To Douw and Carolyn Steyn, thank you for loving me and caring the way you do.

For guidance, protection and invaluable wisdom, thank you my pact: Minee Hendricks, Marli Hoffman, Ann-Lee Murray, Lori McCreary, Anele Mdoda, Sara Latham, Dianne Broodryk.

To some very special friends, some associates and a special breed of people thank you for blessing my life in one way or another with your kindness, support or even just consideration: Constant and Hane Visser, Rian van Heerden, Gareth Cliff, Doug Band, Jon Davidson, Justin Cooper, Matt McKenna, Marius van Vuuren, Ian Douglas, Lucy Matthew, Catriona Garde, Rory Steyn, Elaine Saloner, Roddy Quinn, Kim Mari, Basetsana Khumalo, Johanna Mukoki, Rebs Mogoba, Mashadi Motlana, De Villiers Pienaar, Wayne Hendricks, Henk Opperman, Adriaan and Cecile Basson, George Ludeke, Waldimar Pelser, Pauli Massyn, George Cohen, Jonathan Butt, Matthew and Tracy Barnes, Dan Ntsala, Dot Field, Greg Coetzee, Rob and Amanda Flemming, Libby Moore, Jovita Machel, Patricia Machel, Lisa Halliday, Cora Forsmann, Tracy Davenport, Silvia Viljoen, Attie van Wyk, Artem and Sayora

Gregorian, Huma Abedin, Sonja and Coetzee Zietsman, Hannah Richert, Deon Broodryk, Driki van Zyl, Hein and Helmien Bezuidenhout, Deon and Yzelle Stone, Angie Khumalo, Gretchen de Smit, Tinus and Chelyn Nel, Annie Laughton, Adrian Brink, Beverly Loxton, Jean Oelwang, Pieter de Waal and Janice Ferrante, Darren Scott, Donne Nicoll, John Carlin, Thato and Thabiso Sikwane, Niel and Andrea Viljoen, TJ, Louis, Tanya and Liz Steyn, Arpad Busson, Rina Broomberg, Ami Desai, Bryan and Jenine Habana, John and Roxy Smith, Schalk and Michelle Burger, Ryk Neethling, Tim and Clare Massey, Jerry and Prudence Inzerillo, Marilyn Karstaedt, Barbara Hogan, Jabu Mabuza, Graham Wood, Alan Knott-Craig, Mthobi Tyamzashe, Norman Adami, Don and Liz Gips, Rob and Lawri Brozin, Kevin Wilson, Dan Moyana, Karlheinz Koegel, Andrew Mlangeni, Olivia Machel, Frank Guistra, Susan Kriegler, Jogabeth and Esau Shilaluke, Oprah, Gayle King, Richard Friedland, HRH King Willem Alexander and HRH Queen Maxima, Former President Thabo and Mrs Zanele Mbeki, Former President F W de Klerk and Elita de Klerk, Deputy President Kgalema Motlanthe, Judge Themba Sangoni, Khanyi Dhlomo, Unathi Msengane, Shiela Sisulu, Faizal and Malaika Motlekar, Jonathan and Jennifer Oppenheimer, Nicky Oppenheimer, Gavin Koppel, Tommy Erasmus, Bongi Mkhabela, Charles Priebatch, the Kunene brothers, Cyril Ramaphosa, David Rockefeller, Leon Vermaak, Benny Gool, Roger Friedman, Mac Maharaj, Archbishop Thabo Mokgoba, Anant and Vaneshree Singh, Bishop Malusi Mpulwana, Robyn Farrell, Dr Mike Plit, Prince Bandar, Jolene Chait, Alfre Woodard, Roderick Spencer, Yusuf Surtee, Sharon Stone, Arki Busson, Charlize Theron, Advocate Thuli Madonsela, Zwelinzima Vavi, Nigel Badminton, Mauro Governato, Ben King, Whitey Basson, Wendy Luhabe, Bernard Krige, Vincent Maphai, Koos Bekker, Fred Phaswana, Ton Vosloo, Chris Liebenberg, Jeff and Bridgette Radebe, Roshann Paris, Joel Johnson, Amy Weinblum, Esmare Weideman, Denese Palm, Ayanda Dlodlo, Minister Nosiviwe Nqakula, Mayor David Dinkins, Forest and Keisha Whitaker, Prof. Jonathan

Jansen, Zindzi Mandela, Zoleka Mandela, Chief Zwelivelile Mandela, Chief Ngangomhlaba Matanzima, Bantu Holomisa, Patekile Holomisa, Zolani Mkiva, Phoebe Gerwel, Jessie Gerwel, Joseph Kruger. Zondwa Mandela, Mbuso Mandela, Andile Mandela, Zinhle Mandela, Luvuyo Mandela and Nandi Mandela.

To Archbishop Desmond Tutu, Ahmed Kathrada, President Clinton, Secretary Hillary Clinton, Chelsea Clinton, Bono, Ali, Sol and Andrea Kerzner, Naomi Campbell, Richard Branson, Peter Gabriel, Morgan Freeman, Peggy Dulany and their respective staff thank you for the love and support. My life had been blessed beyond measure having had the privilege to know you.

To Johann and Gaynor Rupert, thank you for loving and caring.

Frederick and Natasha Mostert, thank you for believing in me, inspiring me and the many many hours of legal consultation, support, guidance but also a privileged friendship.

Jeremy Gauntlett, thank you for your expert advice, support and consultation.

Bally Chuene, Michael Katz and Wim Trengove, Uncle George Bizos and family thank you for your support over the years and always making time and effort with me.

To Sacha and Christa Held, for allowing me to work on the book at their house in Mauritius, thank you.

To all my colleagues from the Presidency and the Nelson Mandela Foundation, some of whom I have lost contact with, thank you for your patience and tolerance. Special thanks to those I have worked closely with or over long periods of time: Lois Dippenaar, Virginia Engel, Alan Pillay, Vimla Naidoo, Elize Wessels, Morris Chabalala, Meshack Mochele, Joel Netshitenzhe, Tony Trew, Fink Haysom, Fanie Pretorius, William Smith, Gerrit Wissing, Marieta van Rensburg, Hayley Lyners, Pam Barron, Shaun Johnson, Heather Henriques, Lydia Baylis, Jackie Maggot, Meme Kgagare, Betty Dima, Xoliswa Ndoyiya, Gloria Nocanda, Yase Godlo, John Samuel, Achmat Dangor, Marianne Mudziwa, Denise Pillay, Shereen

Petersen, Buyi Sishuba, Thoko Mavuso, Gloria Jafta, Maeline Engelbrecht, Ruth Rensburg, Lee Davies, Tania Arrison, Elaine McKay, Marie Vos, Dudu Buthelezi, Jo Ditabo, Makano Morojelo, Merlyn van Voore, Mothomang Diaho, Ethel Arendze, Sandy Pillay, Ella Govender, Shirley Naidoo and anyone else I may have forgotten.

Thank you Prof Njabulo Ndebele, Chairman of the Nelson Mandela Foundation and the CEO of the Nelson Mandela Foundation, Sello Hatang, for your leadership and wisdom.

Special thanks to Verne Harris from the Centre of Memory at the Nelson Mandela Foundation for helping with factual correctness of this book and for your cameraderie.

All members of the Presidential Protection Unit and the South African Airforce who I worked closely with and that served with diligence, thank you.

The passionate and professional medical staff from the SANDF and private hospitals that cared for Madiba and Mum, thank you.

The staff of the 1st for Women Insurance Trust and Beeld Children's fund.

In memorium: My grandparents on both sides of the family, thank you. Special people who have passed on: Chief Justice Arthur Chaskalson, Oom Beyers Naude, Sean Chabalala, Mary Mxadana, John Reinders, Parks Mankahlana, Eric Molobi, Aggrey Klaaste, Dullah Omar, Marinus Daling, Miriam Makeba, Steve Tshwete, Uncle Raymond Mhlaba, Kader Asmal, Aunt Adelaide Tambo, Uncle Walter and Aunt Albertina Sisulu, Makgatho Mandela, Zenani Mandela Jnr.

Thank you my Prof., Jakes Gerwel. I still miss you every day. You enriched my life both professionally and personally in ways beyond comprehension and I am the most fortunate and blessed to have worked so closely with you. I will pay tribute to you with deep appreciation for the role you played in Madiba, Mum and my life, for the rest of my days.

Acknowledgements

My expert agent Jonny Geller, Kirsten Foster, Anna Davis and the team at Curtis Brown, thank you.

Helen Conford, Penelope Vogler, Richard Duguid, Rebecca Lee, Casiana Ionita and the team at Penguin, with deep appreciation for your enthusiasm and support. Also to Stephen Johnson, Frederik de Jager, Ellen van Schalkwyk and all at Penguin South Africa. And to Clare Ferraro, Wendy Wolf and all at Penguin US.

To all my friends in the media, too many to mention, thank you for your patience and understanding and even for our differences in opinion some times. Thank you for showing me how to grow a back bone.

To everyone who took my call when you no longer had to . . . THANK YOU!

To the unfamiliar face of the black man who comforted me at Madiba's funeral. If I don't get to thank you in person, this is it.

To everyone who spared me a smile, a hug or a word of encouragement over 19 years, I salute you with gratitude.

To Mrs Graça Machel, my second Mum and her children, Josina, Malenga and Samora, thank you for accepting me as your family and for caring for me like I am your own. I love you with the same unconditional love that Madiba taught us. I will remain forever indepted to you with love, care and appreciation and I will keep my promise to Madiba, but also willfully so, to care for you for as long as I live.

Lastly, but most importantly, thank you Khulu!

Picture Credits

Grateful acknowledgment is given to the following for permission to reproduce copyrighted material.

Every effort has been made to contact copyright holders. The author and publisher would be glad to amend in future editions any errors or omissions brought to their attention. Unless otherwise indicated, photos are courtesy of the author.

Inset image 4 © *Sunday Times* South Africa
Inset image 5 © Christiaan Kotze / Foto24
Inset image 10 © The Clinton Foundation
Inset image 12 © Reuters / Siphiwe Sibeko
Inset image 13 © Halden Krog
Inset image 15 © Anton Corbijn
Inset image 16 © Alet van Huyssteen and the Nelson Mandela Foundation
Inset image 17 © Alet van Huyssteen and the Nelson Mandela Foundation *Sunday Times*

Text Sources

5. Travelling with a President
Hansard, 12 February 1997, debate after the President's State of the
  Nation.

7. Travel and Conflict
William Ernest Henley, 'Invictus', *Book of Verses*, D. Nutt, London,
  1888; deliberate misquote.
Nelson Mandela, *Conversations with Myself*, Macmillan, London,
2010.

8. Working with World Leaders
Nelson Mandela, *Conversations with Myself*, Macmillan, London, 2010.
Mathatha Tsedu, editorial for the *Sunday Times*, February 2003.

9. Holidays and Friends
"Civil War in Madibaland", *Noseweek*, 1st April 2005.
Nelson Mandela, *Conversations with Myself*, Macmillan, London, 2010.
Bill Clinton, speech at a fundraiser for Nelson Mandela Foundation,
  July 2007.

10. The Biggest Fundraiser of My Life
Nelson Mandela, *Conversations with Myself*, Macmillan, London, 2010.

11. Staying Until the End
Nelson Mandela, *Conversations with Myself*, Macmillan, London, 2010.
William Ernest Henley, 'Invictus', *Book of Verses*, D. Nutt, London,
  1888.

12. Saying Goodbye
Nelson Mandela, *Conversations with Myself*, Macmillan, London, 2010.